JOSEPH PRINCE

Destined To Reign

DEVOTIONAL

Daily reflections for effortless success,
wholeness and victorious living

Harrison House
Tulsa, Oklahoma

12 11 10 09 08   10 9 8 7 6 5 4 3 2 1

Destined To Reign Devotional
Daily reflections for effortless success, wholeness and victorious living

ISBN 13: 978-1-57794-943-5
ISBN 10: 1-57794-943-9
Copyright © 2008 by Joseph Prince
22 Media Pte. Ltd.
3 Temasek Boulevard
Suntec City Mall, #06-001
Singapore 038983

Published by Harrison House, Inc.
P.O. Box 35035
Tulsa, Oklahoma 74153
www.harrisonhouse.com

Printed in the United States of America.

Foreword

Since the launch of my book, *Destined To Reign*, I have received an overwhelming number of praise reports from people all over the world. It still amazes me that so many take the time to pen their thoughts and share with me how they have been liberated from the truths shared in my book. I am deeply grateful and humbled to have been able to be part of their lives in such an intimate way, and for having the opportunity to point them to the lone figure on the cross — my Savior, Jesus!

My friend, I believe that God wants us to reign in life every single day! Reigning in life should be a continuous thing, and it comes by receiving a fresh revelation of God's love and grace every single day. Therefore, with this desire to help precious believers who have been impacted by God's grace to continue to walk in His undeserved favor in a practical way, I have put together this series of daily devotionals.

In this fast-paced age of computers, cell phones, PDAs, the Internet and television, if we are not careful, we can fall into what I call the "Martha syndrome" — becoming too busy to sit at the feet of Jesus and to simply draw from Him. Whether it is answering hundreds of emails or text messages, doing household chores, sending the kids to school or even serving in various ministries in church, we can get so caught up in "legitimate busyness" that we don't do the one thing that Jesus said is needful — to sit at His feet and receive from Him.

Do you remember Martha? With hair out of place and hands tired from much serving, she cried out to Jesus in frustration, "Lord, do You not care that my sister has left me to serve alone?" Now, observe Jesus' loving reply: "Martha, Martha, you are worried and troubled about many things. But one thing is needful, and Mary has chosen that good part, which will not be taken away from her." (Luke 10:40–42 KJV.)

My friend, are you troubled and worried about many things today?

Do you really believe that only ONE THING is **needful**?

To help you be a Mary and not a Martha, *Destined To Reign Devotional* has been purposefully designed to allow you to spend just five to 10 minutes a day reading God's Word. Each devotional is designed to edify and encourage you, inspire faith and, most of all, remind you of how much you are loved by your heavenly Father. Each devotional is also built around one key thought, which you can take away with you and meditate on as you go about your activities for the day. A wide range of topics is covered, from righteousness, forgiveness and God's love to healing, finances, faith, relationships and ministry.

I am a firm believer in the importance of practicing the presence of Jesus wherever we are and in whatever we are doing. As we commune with God and listen to His Word, we allow His grace to unfold and work in our lives. So come, be like Mary. Sit at the Lord's feet and hear what He has to say to you.

My friend, time spent with God is never wasted time! As you devote some time each day to commune with the Lord in spite of your hectic schedule or the challenges that you are facing, I believe that God will take care of the rest. As you simply allow His word of grace and righteousness to speak to you, you will find faith springing up in your heart, peace guarding your mind, wisdom for the day and a confident expectation of good things happening to you.

Beloved, this devotional is all about receiving, receiving, receiving! As you receive an abundance of God's grace and His words of life, the overflow will cause you to live a life that glorifies Him. You will do the right thing at the right time and enjoy good success! So come and feed. Drink of the never-ending well of life and reign in life every day!

You Matter to God!

John 10:3
³... he calls his own sheep by name...

Do you sometimes feel like you are just a face in a crowd or a number in a system? You are identified by your social security number. Even when you see the doctor, you are called by your queue number. If you feel depersonalized and dehumanized, that is exactly how the devil wants you to feel — that you do not matter much to anyone, especially to God.

But you **do** matter to God! He calls you by name. He knows exactly what you are going through and where you are hurting. He sees you and cares for you, just as He cared for the people when He first walked on earth.

My friend, He will do for you what He did for the woman in Samaria. There was a shorter route from Judea to Galilee, but the Bible says that "He **needed** to go through Samaria." (John 4:4.) In other words, Jesus deliberately took a longer route, so that He could stop by Samaria to speak to the woman who had been searching for something in her life to satisfy her.

This woman had had five husbands and the man she was living with was not her husband. Clearly, things had not been going right in her life. She was probably looking for answers and fulfillment, and must have felt ashamed about her failed marriages and current lifestyle.

Yet, in spite of all this, she mattered to Jesus! He **needed** to go to her to minister to her. And indeed, after she met Jesus, the perfect Man, she was transformed. She was no longer ashamed, and went into the city to tell the people about Him. (John 4:28–29.)

Beloved, Jesus came a long way from heaven for you. You certainly matter to Him. He came to give you life and life more abundantly. (John 10:10.) You are not just a face in a crowd or a number. No, He knows you by name and has a personal love for you. And in spite of the mess which you might be in, He wants to meet your every need and make your life beautiful!

Thought for the Day
**You do matter to God! He knows what you are going
through and wants to meet your every need.**

If It Matters to You, It Matters to God

Luke 12:6–7
⁶"Are not five sparrows sold for two copper coins? And not one of them is
forgotten before God. ⁷But the very hairs of your head are all numbered.
Do not fear therefore; you are of more value than many sparrows."

Many Christians make the mistake of thinking that God is too busy taking care of the "big things" to be interested in the little problems they are facing. Are you one of them? It may be your child's bed-wetting habit, a quarrel with a friend or the small pimple on your face. No matter how trivial it sounds, if it troubles you, then God wants to take care of it!

God wants to take care of every area of your life, even the smallest detail. He loves you so much that He knows the number of hairs you have on your head. And if your loving heavenly Father knows and is interested in the small details of your life, then you don't have to overcome any problem on your own.

When my daughter Jessica turned three, my wife, Wendy, and I decided to take her to Disneyland. Knowing that it was her first encounter with Disneyland and that she could be frightened by unexpected shocks, I decided to watch one of the theatre productions which I had planned to take her to, before I took her to see it.

As I sat through the production, my mind was on Jessica all the time. I was thinking, *Is this too frightening for her? Will she like the mechanical singing bear? Is the place too dark for her?* I decided to take her to the show only after I had seen it myself and was sure that she would enjoy it.

My friend, your heavenly Father cares for you in the same way as He lays out His plans for you. You are on His heart all the time as He carefully considers and makes plans for every aspect of your life, both big and small. And the very thought of you puts a smile on His face because He knows that the plans He has for you are plans to bless you. (Jeremiah 29:11.)

So no matter what problems you are facing right now, you can rest in His love for you. There is no problem that is too insignificant for Him to handle. He is not just God Almighty, He is also your heavenly Father who loves you!

Thought for the Day
God wants to take care of every area of your life, even the smallest detail.

God Remembers Your Sins No More

Hebrews 10:17
¹⁷… "Their sins and their lawless deeds I will remember no more."

I don't know about you, but I would say that Hebrews 10:17 is good news. God sees all our sins — past, present and future — and says, "Your sins I remember no more!" The words "no more" are a strong double negative in the original Greek text. In other words, God is saying, "Your sins I will **by no means ever** remember!"

Has God lowered His standards? No, He is still perfectly holy. He **did** remember all our sins — 2,000 years ago at the cross. Every sin which we have committed or will commit has been punished to the full in the body of Jesus Christ at the cross. That is why today, God remembers our sins no more. We should, therefore, not be sin-conscious.

Each time we fall into sin, God wants us to remember the cross and say, "Lord Jesus, You were sentenced for this sin I committed. You bore the judgment, so God will not judge me for this sin. You were condemned for this sin, so God will not condemn me for it."

If you don't look to the cross, you will become sin-conscious and you will walk around with a certain expectation of judgment. And that expectation of judgment will give the devil a chance to get you thinking that God has something against you because of your sin.

You must come to the place where you know and believe that all your sins are forgiven, that there is no sin that will ever disqualify you from God's blessings, that there is no sin that will ever send you to hell, because you are forgiven and saved eternally.

Hebrews 10:12,14 says, "But this Man [Jesus], after He had offered one sacrifice for sins forever, sat down at the right hand of God… For by one offering He hath perfected for ever them."

You and I are perfected forever because of Jesus' perfect work on the cross. We are perfected by God's full acceptance and perfect delight in His Son's work that has so glorified His holiness. Beloved, hear God say to you, "I will be merciful. Your sins and lawless deeds I will remember no more."

Thought for the Day
***Every sin which we have committed or will commit has been
punished to the full in the body of Jesus Christ at the cross.***

Jesus' Blood Keeps on Cleansing You

1 John 1:7
⁷But if we walk in the light as He is in the light, we have fellowship with one another, and the blood of Jesus Christ His Son cleanses us from all sin.

During the day, the devil may whisper in your head, "You cannot go into God's presence because you have not been reading your Bible and serving in church." Or he will tell you that it is because of the sin which you have just committed.

The devil will always make you feel that you are not qualified or clean enough to go near God. But the truth is, regardless of how you feel and what you have done, the blood of Jesus Christ cleanses us from all sin.

In the original Greek text, the tense for the word "cleanses" denotes a present continuous action. This means that once you are a believer, the blood of Jesus Christ keeps on cleansing you from every sin!

So you can rest knowing that you are always forgiven in this continuous "wash cycle" of Jesus' blood. Because you are continually cleansed, you are always in the light. Of course, you will fail here and there, but you are still in the light because the blood is continuously washing you!

The Bible says that we overcome the devil, the accuser of our brethren, by the blood of the Lamb. (Revelation 12:10-11.) If you have sinned, remind yourself that Jesus' blood keeps on cleansing you from every sin — 24 hours a day, seven days a week — and move on with God! The devil cannot defeat you when your faith is in the blood that cleanses you continuously.

Some Christians are guilt-ridden because their consciousness of their sins condemns them. Although Jesus' blood continuously cleanses them, they would rather hold on to their past mistakes and feel bad about them, thinking that they are being humble and holy when they do this. But this is nothing more than self-righteousness.

My friend, the eternal blood of Jesus Christ offers you **eternal** redemption and **everlasting** righteousness. Accept the payment of His blood as the final, perfect and only sacrifice you will ever need!

Thought for the Day
You can rest knowing that you are always forgiven in the continuous wash cycle of Jesus' blood.

Righteousness Is Not Right Doing but Right Being

Romans 4:5
⁵But to him who does not work but believes on Him who justifies the ungodly, his faith is accounted for righteousness.

What do you think righteousness is about? Something you **do** or something you **are**? Right **doing** or right **being**?

The Bible tells us that after Jesus' sacrifice at the cross, God imputes righteousness not to those who strive to obey the law (Galatians 2:16), but to anyone who believes in His Son. Because Christ took our sins and gave us His righteousness (2 Corinthians 5:21), the moment we believe in Him, God treats us as righteous apart from our works or obedience. (Romans 4:5-8.) This is new covenant righteousness — a righteousness that comes by faith and not works.

You are not righteous because of how morally upright you are. You are not righteous because you exercise self-control. You are not righteous because you read 10 chapters of the Bible daily. You are not righteous because you feel righteous. But you are the very righteousness of God in Christ solely because the sacrifice of Jesus made you so. When you believe this, your faith is accounted for righteousness.

And this is what God wants you to use your faith for. If you are righteous by your deeds, you don't need faith. You also don't need faith to know that you are sinful. But you need faith to believe and declare that you are the righteousness of God in Christ, in the midst of your struggles with temptation and sin.

For example, when you feel lousy because you have just shouted at your spouse, God wants you to exercise your faith to see yourself as still righteous in the midst of that failure. This living revelation that you are still righteous will give you the strength to love your spouse and reconcile things.

The devil may remind you of your foul temper and question your integrity: "How dare you call yourself righteous when you just did that!" Just ignore his lies and boldly declare, "I am not righteous because of what I have done or not done. I am righteous only because of the blood and finished work of Jesus at the cross!"

Thought for the Day
You are the very righteousness of God in Christ solely because the sacrifice of Jesus made you so.

You Have First-Class Righteousness

2 Corinthians 5:21
²¹For He made Him who knew no sin to be sin for us,
that we might become the righteousness of God in Him.

Some Christians believe that they have to work at becoming more righteous. And they kick themselves when they do wrong. They don't realize that by doing these things, they are not seeking God's righteousness, but are trying to establish their **own** righteousness by their law-keeping and right conduct.

Righteousness is not about right conduct. It is a gift from God to us through Jesus. And since it is a gift, we cannot earn it by our law-keeping and right conduct. We can only receive it!

How do we receive this gift? We receive it through the cross. God made Jesus "who knew no sin to be sin for us, that we might become the righteousness of God in Him." So today, we are the righteousness of God in Christ. We are as righteous as Jesus is!

But some of us think that in the body of Christ, there are different classes of righteousness, like the seating classes in an airplane. They think that some of us have economy-class righteousness, others have business-class righteousness and a select few have first-class righteousness.

That is nonsense! When God gave us Jesus, He became our righteousness. So we have **His** righteousness. This means that we are 100 percent righteous in God's eyes! We cannot have anything but first-class righteousness!

You might say, "Pastor Prince, I don't understand. How can I be righteous when I have done wrong?" Think about this: Jesus, who knew no sin, became sin for us. Jesus knew no sin, did no sin and in Him was no sin. But at the cross, He received our sin and became sin for us.

Likewise, we, who were sinners, knew no righteousness, did no righteousness and in us was no righteousness. But at the cross, we received His righteousness and became the righteousness of God in Christ Jesus.

At the cross, the divine exchange took place. Jesus took our place so that we might take His place. He did not deserve to be made sin, but He was made sin in our place. We did not deserve to be made righteous, but we were made righteous because we received His righteousness. What good news! What amazing grace!

Thought for the Day
We have first-class righteousness, which we received as a gift through Jesus.

The Gospel Saves in Every Situation

Romans 1:16
¹⁶For I am not ashamed of the gospel of Christ, for it is the
power of God to salvation for everyone who believes....

Each time you hear the gospel of Christ, you are hearing God's good news for you. And the Bible tells us that the gospel of Christ — the good news that God wants all men to hear — is the very **power** of God for your salvation, not just from hell, but also from illnesses, financial lack, harm, a failing marriage — every aspect of your life that needs saving!

You may say, "Pastor Prince, I've heard the gospel of Christ, but it seems like I am one of those whom the power of God has missed." My friend, when you hear the gospel of Christ, do you really believe it? You cannot just understand it in your mind. You must **know** and **believe** the good news in your heart, and then you will see that it **is** the power of God for your salvation.

But what is the good news that God wants you to know in your heart, which will release the power and salvation of God into your situation?

"For in it [the good news] the righteousness of God is revealed from faith to faith..." (v. 17) The good news is that you are the righteousness of God in Christ, which you receive from faith to faith.

This means that this righteousness comes because you have faith in His blood, not your good behavior, to make you righteous. It is from faith to faith, not faith to works, or works to works.

The good news is not preached to show you what is wrong with you. It is preached to show you what is right with you because of Jesus' work at Calvary, in spite of what is wrong with you!

There is nothing left for you to do to earn God's blessings for your life. You only need to hear and believe the all-encompassing saving power of the gospel of Christ to heal you of diseases, preserve you from danger, prosper your finances and bring well-being to your family.

The world may say that the good news is too good to be true. But for those of us who are the righteousness of God in Christ, the good news is so good because it is indeed true!

Thought for the Day
Hearing and believing the good news will release
the power of God into your situation.

Choose Not to Worry

Matthew 6:27
²⁷Which of you by worrying can add one cubit to his stature?

Many Christians are familiar with Jesus' rhetorical question, "Which of you by worrying can add one cubit to his stature?" But not many of us actually let it get into our hearts and allow the love of God to free us from our habit of worrying.

The truth is, no amount of worrying can lengthen your life or add anything to your physical person. Instead, worrying robs you of sleep, health and many good years. In fact, it is only when you are worry-free that God's anointing flows freely in you, strengthening, healing, restoring and adding to you.

A church member, after undergoing a mammogram, found that she had lumps in her breast. Upon receiving the doctor's report, she wrote this down on the report: "Jesus is my healer. I receive my healing. I am healed. I rest in God completely."

She was due back at the clinic later the same day for a biopsy to see if the lumps were malignant. Her sister-in-law, who was having lunch with her that day, witnessed her cheerful and worry-free attitude while she ate her lunch.

Back at the clinic, this precious sister sat among other ladies who were also there for their biopsies. They looked very worried, so she started sharing Jesus with them and prayed for some of them. When her turn came and she had an ultrasound scan done, the doctor was puzzled — her scan showed no evidence of any lumps!

The doctor went back to consult her colleague who had first discovered the lumps. Stunned, both doctors conducted their own investigations. They returned to her only to say, "It's a miracle!"

My friend, when you worry, you are actually believing that the devil has the power to make inroads into your life that God cannot protect you from. But when you refuse to worry, you are putting your faith in God. You have more confidence in His love and power working for you than in the devil's ability to harm you! When you refuse to worry, but choose to rest in the finished work of Christ, you will see the manifestation of your blessing. You will see your miracle!

Thought for the Day
When you refuse to worry, but choose to rest in the finished work of Christ,
you will see the manifestation of your blessing.

Guaranteed by Covenant

Genesis 15:8–9
⁸And he said, "Lord God, how shall I know that I will inherit it?" ⁹So He said
to him, "Bring Me a three-year-old heifer, a three-year-old female goat,
a three-year-old ram, a turtledove, and a young pigeon."

Are you discouraged because a breakthrough that you have been praying for has yet to manifest? Maybe it has been days or even weeks and you are asking, "How will I know that I will get it?" Abraham faced the same situation and asked God the same question. And God answered, "Bring Me a three-year-old heifer, a three-year-old female goat, a three-year-old ram, a turtledove, and a young pigeon." What a strange answer!

But if you read on (vv. 10-21), you will realize that God took Abraham's question very seriously, and went on to show him just how serious He was about being his provider, protector and prosperity-giver. God was so serious that He was willing to bind Himself to a **covenant**.

What is a covenant? It is like a contract. Yet, it is more than a contract. A contract is binding only for a period of time, like five years or seven years, or until certain terms are fulfilled. But a covenant is perpetual. It is permanent. The only way out is through death. That is why marriage is a covenant, not a contract. It is permanent — "Till death do us part."

In Bible times, when you cut a covenant with someone, you brought an animal, usually a ram or goat, and killed it by cutting it in two. Next, you faced your covenant partner and walked toward each other between the two pieces of the animal, passing each other in the center.

What all this meant was that both parties were obligated to protect and provide for each other. Whatever belonged to you was your partner's and whatever belonged to your partner was yours. Of course, the one who benefited was the lesser or poorer party.

Today, God is in covenant with us. We are the lesser, poorer party. We have nothing to offer God. But God, the richest and most powerful being in the universe, has everything to offer us!

My friend, God has bound Himself to a covenant, an iron-clad guarantee of His blessings and provision in your life, and it is all for your benefit. The breakthrough you are waiting for is guaranteed by covenant!

Thought for the Day
God has bound Himself to a covenant, an iron-clad guarantee of
His blessings and provision in your life.

A Sleeping Partner Who Benefits

Genesis 15:12
¹²Now when the sun was going down, a deep sleep fell upon Abram....

In business, sleeping or silent partners don't work but still take home huge profits. They are like the wife of the boxing champion. He gets badly beaten up to win the prize money. But when he gets home, his wife takes it from him and says, "Thank you very much, darling!"

Do you know that in your covenant with God, you are like the boxer's wife or the sleeping partner?

When Abraham asked God how he would know for sure that he would inherit the land that God had promised him, God made a covenant with him. (vv. 8-21.) But instead of cutting the covenant with Abraham by walking in between the animal pieces with him, God put Abraham into a deep sleep and cut the covenant with Jesus instead.

Jesus, the light of the world, appeared as the pillar of fire and cut the covenant with God the Father who appeared as the pillar of cloud. In other words, Jesus took Abraham's place. He was perfect Man representing Abraham when He cut the covenant with His Father.

By substituting Abraham with Jesus, God was being gracious because if Abraham had done it, he would also have been responsible for keeping the covenant. And Abraham, being a mere man, would fail. But God the Son can never fail! Abraham's blessings were therefore guaranteed because they did not depend on his performance but **Jesus'** performance. Abraham was literally a sleeping partner, a beneficiary of the covenant.

Today, God has also made a covenant with you, called the new covenant. And like Abraham, you are a sleeping partner because the new covenant was also cut between God the Father and God the Son at Calvary. You are simply a beneficiary of the new covenant. You enjoy all its benefits without having to work at keeping it. Jesus, your representative, has already fulfilled all the conditions on your behalf. And because His obedience is perfect and His work is perfectly finished, the covenant blessings for you are guaranteed!

My friend, there is nothing left for you to do, but everything for you to believe. Don't try to work for your covenant blessings. Rest in the Son's finished work and receive them by faith!

Thought for the Day
Your covenant blessings are guaranteed because Jesus, your representative,
has already fulfilled all the conditions on your behalf.

Believing Is Receiving

Mark 5:28–29
²⁸For she said, "If only I may touch His clothes, I shall be made well."
²⁹Immediately the fountain of her blood was dried up,
and she felt in her body that she was healed of the affliction.

You have heard people of the world say, "I will believe it only when I see it." Generally, that is the way the world thinks. But God's ways are not like the ways of the world. The world says, "If I can't feel it or see it, I cannot believe the miracle is here." God says, "If you believe it before you feel it or see it, you will see your miracle."

Believing first before seeing the evidence of what we are believing for is called *faith*. Faith is like a spark and Jesus is the dynamite powder.

In the story of the healing of the woman with the issue of blood, there were many people who touched Jesus (v. 31), but nothing happened to them. They didn't touch Him in faith. But when the woman who had been bleeding for 12 years came to Him and touched Him in faith, He felt power leave His body (v. 30), and it sparked off an explosion of healing in the woman's body!

Hearing about how good, kind and loving Jesus was fired her faith to believe that He could and would heal her. So convinced was she (even when the condition in her body was still evident) that she said, "If only I may touch His clothes, I shall be made well." Did she experience her healing first before she believed? No, she believed first in Jesus' goodness and power, acted in faith and only then felt the healing in her body.

In the same way, God wants you to believe in His goodness and love toward you. He wants you to know how willing He is to act on your behalf to bless you, and how, with Christ, He will freely give you every good thing. (Romans 8:32.)

He wants you to declare by faith that all is and shall be well with you, and to expect to see just that. And then, no matter how long you have had the problem, no matter how bad the experts say it is, an explosion of healing and restoration will take place, and you will receive what you are believing for!

Thought for the Day
Believe in God's goodness and love toward you, and you will
receive what you are believing for.

When You See God's Grace, He Sees Your Faith

Ephesians 2:8
⁸For by grace you have been saved through faith,
and that not of yourselves; it is the gift of God.

Many a time, people ask me, "Pastor Prince, I know that God's promises are true, but how can I be sure that His promises will come true in my life?"

My friend, if you want God's promises to be sure in your life, you cannot depend on yourself. If you depend on yourself — your obedience, goodness, service and even faith — you will not be able to receive God's promises. But when you depend on God's grace — His unmerited, unearned, undeserved favor toward you — that is when His promises become sure in your life.

This was true of the woman with the issue of blood. (Matthew 9:20–22.) She didn't go around saying, "I must have faith… I hope that I have enough faith… I will have faith… I will not lose faith." No, she was only conscious of the grace of Jesus — how He always healed the sick, how powerful He was in raising the dead and how willing He was to use that power for her healing.

She just saw His grace abounding toward her, so much so that she said, "If only I may touch His garment, I shall be made well." And when she came behind Jesus and touched the very hem of His garment, she was healed. At that same moment, Jesus stopped, turned around and said to her, "Be of good cheer, daughter; your faith has made you well."

When the woman saw His grace, God saw her faith! And so it was by grace, through faith, that God's promise became sure in her life.

God wants you to see His grace. And when you see His grace, He sees your faith. God says, "For by grace are you saved through faith." The Greek word for "saved," *sozo*, doesn't just mean to save from hell, but also to heal, preserve and make whole. So it is by grace that you are made whole, kept healthy, preserved and prospered. It is by grace through faith that God's promises become sure in your life.

My friend, don't worry if you feel that you lack faith. Begin to see God's grace in your situation and He will see that as faith. And because He sees your faith, you will receive the breakthrough you need!

Thought for the Day
When you see God's grace, He sees your faith, and you will receive your breakthrough.

God's Word Is Out to Prosper You

Isaiah 55:11
*¹¹ So shall My word be that goes forth from My mouth; it shall not
return to Me void, but it shall accomplish what I please,
and it shall prosper in the thing for which I sent it.*

In the early church, whenever the Word of God was preached, there were miracles of salvation, healings, and other signs and wonders. The demon-possessed were set free. The paralyzed jumped up and walked. People received their loved ones back from the dead.

I remember saying in one of our church services that there was an anointing for couples, who were told that they could not conceive in the natural, to receive the children they had been believing God for. As the word went forth, many couples received their miracle in that service.

One of the ladies who received was serving that day as an usher. She and her husband had been believing God for a child for a few years. A few months after that service, she realized that she was pregnant — with twins! God's anointing is always greater than our asking.

I believe with all of my heart that we are truly coming to the place where as the Word of God goes forth, it produces the very effect that the Word promises. So if the Word on healing goes forth, know that healing is already exploding in your body. Your miracle has already happened.

Very often, as you are reading the Word on your own or listening to anointed preaching of the Word, you will feel God's peace and joy, and feel faith springing up in your heart. As the Word goes forth and you find that you are strengthened to receive your miracle, that is the time to say, "Lord, I receive my healing right now." That is the time to say, "I receive Your restoration for my marriage." That is the time to say, "I receive Your breakthrough for my finances."

You don't have to wait until a church leader or friend prays for you. Every time your faith is strengthened as you hear the Word, release it through your mouth to receive your miracle, for God's Word is out to prosper you!

Thought for the Day
As the Word of God goes forth, it produces the very effect that the Word promises.

Jesus Has Borne Your Diseases

Isaiah 53:4
⁴Surely He has borne our griefs and carried our sorrows....

Imagine the dreadful disease leprosy eating a man alive. The poor leper in Matthew 8:2 could stand his suffering no longer, so he came out into the open to look for Jesus. He needed to know if Jesus was willing to heal him. When he saw Jesus, he fell at His feet and said, "Lord, if You are willing, You can make me clean." (Matthew 8:2.) The Son of God looked at the outcast with love in His eyes, reached out His hand, touched him and said, "I am willing; be cleansed." (v. 3.)

Perhaps you are suffering from some disease and wondering if God is willing to heal you. You are not sure if He is willing because just as you have seen people get healed, you have also seen people not get healed. My friend, don't look to people's experiences. Look to the cross! As surely as Jesus bore away your sins, He also bore away your diseases!

I want to give you a solid foundation today for believing this truth. In Isaiah 53, the chapter on our Lord's crucifixion, it says in verse 4: "Surely He has borne our griefs and carried our sorrows." Now, let's learn a little Hebrew. The words "griefs" and "sorrows" here mean "sicknesses" and "pains" in the original Hebrew text. So Isaiah was referring to physical healing.

Once, I asked a Jewish friend to read this verse in his Hebrew Bible and tell me what it means. He told me that his Bible says clearly that Jesus has borne our sicknesses and carried our pains.

If that is not enough, look at Matthew 8:16–17: "... they brought to Him many who were demon-possessed. And He cast out the spirits with a word, and healed all who were sick, that it might be fulfilled which was spoken by Isaiah the prophet, saying: 'He Himself took our infirmities and bore our sicknesses.'" Matthew quotes Isaiah 53:4, saying that Jesus took our "infirmities" and bore our "sicknesses." The context here refers to physical healing.

My friend, if you will just believe this truth, your days of sickness will be over. You will walk in greater health because the One who has surely borne your sicknesses and carried your pains says to you, "I am willing, be cleansed!"

Thought for the Day
As surely as Jesus bore away your sins, He also bore away your diseases!

God Gives You Undeserved Preferential Treatment

Romans 1:7
⁷… Grace to you and peace from God our Father and the Lord Jesus Christ.

When you fly first class in an airplane, the cabin crew gives you first-class treatment. They ask if everything is okay with you. They ask you what magazines you want to read. They give you a blanket if you are cold. They give you the best kinds of food. They give you preferential treatment compared to those traveling in economy class.

The grace of God is defined as "undeserved, unearned and unmerited favor." And one of the definitions for favor is "preferential treatment"! Today, God wants you to know that you have His favor on you. He wants you to know that He gives you preferential treatment which you do not deserve. And He wants you to depend on and take full advantage of it in your life.

God also wants you to know that His favor in your life can be increased. You can experience more of His favor from day to day. How? The Bible tells us in 2 Peter 1:2 that God's grace (or favor) is multiplied to us "in the knowledge of God and of Jesus our Lord." The more you behold Jesus and His love for you, the more you believe and confess that God's favor is on you, the more you will see His favor work for you.

So if you are a doctor, you will find patients favoring you and you will have more patients than you can handle. If you are a businessman, you will find people just wanting to do business with you because they like you and feel good about you. Then, you will have more business than you can handle and you will need to plan for expansion!

When the favor of God shines on your church, you will find its premises too small for the people who queue up week after week to attend the services! So when people wonder and ask, "What is happening here?" you can tell them, "It is the favor of God multiplied all over us!" And it is all undeserved, unearned and unmerited!

Thought for the Day
**The more you behold Jesus and His love for you,
the more you will see His favor work for you.**

Be Numbered Among the Undevourable

1 Peter 5:8
*⁸Be sober, be vigilant; because your adversary the devil walks about
like a roaring lion, seeking whom he may devour.*

The devil cannot just walk right up to you and rob you of your health, peace or family. He cannot just come into your life to enforce disease and destruction.

If the devil can do that, then he does not have to walk about "seeking whom he may devour." He only has to walk straight up to anyone he wants to devour and devour him! But since the Bible says that he goes about seeking whom he may devour, the truth then is that there are people whom he cannot devour.

You see, the devil goes about like a roaring lion trying to stir up fear in people with his roars. But the people who are not devourable are those who refuse to be intimidated by his roars because they know that the true Lion of Judah, Jesus Christ (Revelation 5:5), has already come and rendered powerless him who had the power of death. (Hebrews 2:14, NASB.) They know that the devil cannot just do anything to them because the Lion of Judah resides in them, and that He is greater than the devil who is in the world. (1 John 4:4.)

My friend, the Lion of Judah is in you. He has given you rights, privileges, authority and power. He redeemed you with His blood. Therefore, everything about you and your life is redeemed by His blood. So if you are fearful about losing your job, cover your job with the blood of Jesus. If you are worried about your children's safety in these days of terrorist attacks, plead the blood of Jesus over them. If you have received a bad report from the doctor, speak the blood over yourself.

Whatever you have covered with the blood of Jesus, God declares, "Protected! Redeemed!" And the devil flees when he sees the blood. And when he flees, he takes with him sicknesses, diseases, pains, sufferings, destruction and loss.

Once the devil knows that you know who you are in Christ and what you have in Him, his days of intimidating you are over, and you are numbered among the undevourable!

Thought for the Day
Everything about you and your life is redeemed by Jesus' blood.

You Are Already Blessed

Joshua 24:13
¹³"I have given you a land for which you did not labor,
and cities which you did not build, and you dwell in them;
you eat of the vineyards and olive groves which you did not plant."

God is more eager to prosper you than you are willing to be prospered! In fact, He is so keen for you to enjoy His prosperity that in His mind, giving you a multiplication of wealth and assets is a settled matter.

God has already promised: "I **have given** you a land for which you did not labor, and cities which you did not build, and you dwell in them; you eat of the vineyards and olive groves which you did not plant."

He did not say, "I may give," which means that it may or may not happen, but He said, "I have given," which means that it has already happened. It is only a matter of time before your revelation of what you have through the work of Christ brings forth the prosperity He has already blessed you with.

During a church service, a couple started believing God for a new home which they did not have the money for. After the service, they went shopping at a nearby supermarket. The purchases they made qualified them for a lucky draw. Weeks later, their lucky draw coupon was picked from among thousands of other entries. The couple won the top prize — a new condominium unit!

My friend, expect prosperity in your life because you are already rich in Christ. Jesus took your place of poverty at the cross — "For you know the grace of our Lord Jesus Christ, that though He was rich, yet for your sakes He became poor, that you through His poverty might become rich." (2 Corinthians 8:9) In Him, you are poor no more.

So stop looking at the lack in your natural resources. Look to the cross and say, "Yes, Christ has made me rich. It is a matter of time before I will see His prosperity in my life!"

Thought for the Day
Look to the cross and say, "Yes, Christ has made me rich."

Be Christ-Conscious

Ephesians 1:7
⁷In Him we have redemption through His blood, the forgiveness of sins,
according to the riches of His grace.

Have you ever woken up in the morning and said, "Today, I will not sin." And as you leave your house, you say, "I must be careful not to fall into sin today. I don't want to sin. I will not sin!" My friend, when you do this, you are no longer Christ-conscious but sin-conscious, even though you have not sinned yet.

Men, have you ever caught yourself thinking, "I don't want to look at any woman in case I lust"? You are being sin-conscious when you think like that. And sooner or later, you will lust in your heart. You may not sin outwardly, but you will sin inwardly.

Have you also tried confessing every sin? I have! As a teenager, when a bad thought came, I would quickly say, "I'm sorry, Lord. Forgive me for this thought in Jesus' name." Then, another thought would come and I would quickly say, "Forgive me, Lord, for that thought in Jesus' name." Then, if I happened to doubt His forgiveness, I would confess my unbelief and ask for forgiveness: "Forgive me, Lord, for doubting You." Before I knew it, I was oppressed in my mind and so sin-conscious instead of Christ-conscious!

My friend, when you fall into sin, God wants you to be Christ-conscious. This means that when you have missed it, God wants you to be conscious that in Christ, you have forgiveness of sins through His blood. God wants you to be conscious that Christ was wounded and bruised for your sins, and that the chastisement for your peace was upon Him. (Isaiah 53:5.)

When you are Christ-conscious, you will have peace with God through our Lord Jesus Christ. (Romans 5:1.) You will know that you are the righteousness of God in Christ because He who knew no sin was made sin for you. (2 Corinthians 5:21.) He took your sin and now you have His righteousness.

So when you fall, don't be conscious of your failure and feel bad or condemned. Instead, be conscious of who you are in Christ, pick yourself up, dust yourself off and continue your walk with God!

Thought for the Day
When you fall, be conscious of who you are in Christ, pick yourself up,
dust yourself off and continue your walk with God!

Jesus Understands Your Struggles

Hebrews 4:15
15 For we do not have a High Priest who cannot sympathize with our weaknesses, but was in all points tempted as we are, yet without sin.

Imagine meeting the new politician who is to represent your district or neighborhood only to discover that he is not familiar with your neighborhood's needs and problems. You will wonder, "Can this guy really represent us? Does he know anything about our living conditions? Is he familiar with the various challenges that families here are facing? Can he help me get my child into one of the schools here?" I am sure that you would prefer someone who truly understands your challenges to represent you!

In the same way, I am so glad that right now at the Father's right hand, we have someone who came as a Man to redeem us, and who fully understands what man goes through. When Jesus walked on earth, He went through every human emotion so that He could identify with us in all points. Jesus is God, but He is in the Father's presence as a Man, representing us.

My friend, you may feel that no one understands your struggles. Listen, while this may be true of man, it is not true of Jesus. He knows exactly what you are going through and He can sympathize with your weaknesses because He was "in all points tempted as we are, yet without sin."

None of us have been tempted in all points. But God allowed Jesus to be tempted in all points so that He can understand and identify with the struggles of every single person on this earth. He can be touched by our humanity — our weaknesses, tears, disappointments, griefs... all points!

There is no trial, difficulty, challenge or temptation that you face that Jesus cannot identify with. My friend, the moment you go through it, right there and then, He feels it too. That is the kind of representative you have in Jesus! That is the love of God so that you will draw near to His throne of grace (not judgment) to find mercy and grace in time of need! (Hebrews 4:15–16.)

Thought for the Day
There is no trial, difficulty, challenge or temptation that you face that Jesus cannot identify with.

The Answer for a Guilty Conscience

Hebrews 9:14
¹⁴How much more shall the blood of Christ, who through the eternal Spirit offered Himself without spot to God, cleanse your conscience from dead works to serve the living God?

Have you heard the voice of your conscience saying things like, "You deserve hell for the sins you committed against your spouse three years ago" or "Why are you surprised that your child is not talking to you? You were never around when he needed you"?

You know, there are people who feel depressed all the time because of a sense of guilt, and they "pay" for their sins in terms of illnesses. In fact, doctors are discovering that many psychosomatic sicknesses are caused by guilt and condemnation because the conscience is saying, "You have done wrong. You must be punished. How can your sin not be punished?"

That is why you must have an answer that will satisfy your conscience. When your conscience says, "You have sinned. You must be punished for this sin or else God is not a just God," you say, "Yes, I have sinned. But this sin and every other sin that I have committed were punished to the maximum in the body of Jesus Christ! So there remains no more punishment for me today, for how much more shall the blood of Christ, who through the eternal Spirit offered Himself without spot to God, cleanse my conscience!"

My friend, the only way to bring peace to your conscience is to look to the cross. The cross of Jesus is the only answer that will satisfy your conscience.

So the next time your conscience condemns you because of sin, don't try to silence it with your good works. Look to the cross and say, "Father, thank You for Jesus and the cross. Jesus was totally condemned on my behalf for this sin, so there is now absolutely no condemnation left for me." Then, your conscience will look at the cross and say, "Ahhhh... peace." My friend, Jesus' finished work at the cross truly sets you free!

Thought for the Day
The cross of Jesus is the only answer that will satisfy your conscience.

God Is Not on a Sin Hunt

1 Thessalonians 5:9
⁹For God did not appoint us to wrath, but to obtain
salvation through our Lord Jesus Christ.

When you think of Sodom and Gomorrah, what comes to your mind? God's wrath and fiery judgment? The truth is that God was not all out to judge the people of Sodom and Gomorrah. He was not on a sin hunt. He was, in fact, on a righteousness hunt!

This is evident because if God was on a sin hunt, He would not have allowed anyone to stop Him. But we know that He let Abraham in on what He was about to do and even allowed Abraham to entreat Him.

Abraham asked God if He would destroy Sodom if He could find 50 righteous people there. God's reply was, "If I find in Sodom fifty righteous within the city, then I will spare all the place for their sakes" (Genesis 18:26). Abraham then asked God if He would destroy the city if there were only 45... 40... 30... or 10 righteous. And each time, God's reply was that He would spare the place for the sake of the righteous.

Abraham stopped at 10. If he had gone down to just one righteous man, I believe God's reply would have been the same because He was on a righteousness hunt.

Now, if God was not all out to destroy then, how much more today, when God has already judged our sins in the body of His Son? At the cross, Jesus exhausted all of God's fiery judgments until there was no more fire of God's wrath left for us!

Today, God is not judging us for our sins because He has found the righteousness of the one Man — Christ Jesus. So do not let anyone tell you that God judges you for your sins and punishes you with cancer, car accidents, business failures or brokenness. God would be unjust if He punished the same sins twice — in Jesus' body and then in yours.

Beloved, God is not out to judge you but bless you today, not because you deserve it, but because Jesus was judged and punished in your place!

Thought for the Day
God would be unjust if He punished the same sins
twice — in Jesus' body and then in yours.

Let Your Heart Be Established by Grace

Hebrews 13:9
⁹... it is good that the heart be established by grace....

God does not want your heart full of worries and fears, tossed and turned by every challenge that comes your way. He wants your heart at rest and established by His grace toward you.

But when you think that the breakthroughs to your challenges depend on your ability to obey God, then your heart will not be at rest. It will be full of worries and anxieties. Why? Because you can never obey God perfectly.

But when you depend on God's grace, that is, His undeserved, unmerited favor, the opposite happens — your heart becomes established. When you know that the only thing that qualifies you to receive God's blessings is faith in the finished work of Christ, your heart becomes established. Then, you will walk without the fear of your troubles swallowing you up. You will walk with full assurance that His blessings will be manifested in your life.

My friend, God wants your heart established, knowing that His righteousness, healing, protection and prosperity are yours — all paid for by Jesus' finished work at the cross. God's blessings are sure in your life because they are not dependent on your ability to keep His laws, but Jesus' perfect obedience.

You see, under the old covenant, you receive God's blessings only if you keep all His laws. (Deuteronomy 28:1–2.) If you sin and fail to keep even one law, you will be disqualified from receiving His blessings. But today, under the new covenant, your sins no longer disqualify you because God Himself has said, "For I will be merciful to their unrighteousness, and their sins and their lawless deeds I will remember no more." (Hebrews 8:12.)

So let your heart be established by God's grace. Because of His grace, you have full access to His blessings. You no longer have to worry about whether you are good enough. You can stand firm on the promises made in His Word and enjoy His blessings today because Jesus has paid the price. Your part is only to believe and receive!

Thought for the Day
God's blessings are sure in your life because of Jesus' perfect obedience.

The Battle Is the Lord's

2 Chronicles 20:15
15... *Do not be afraid nor dismayed because of this great multitude,
for the battle is not yours, but God's.*

When faced with a problem or challenge, we tend to ask ourselves, "What am **I** going to do?" And well-meaning family members and friends will come along and ask, "What are **you** going to do?"

Jehoshaphat faced a multitude of enemies. But instead of focusing on what he would do, he prayed, "O our God, will You not judge them? For we have no power against this great multitude that is coming against us; nor do we know what to do, but our eyes are upon You." (v. 12.)

When we turn our eyes to God, we will hear Him say, "Do not be afraid nor dismayed because of this great multitude, for the battle is not yours, but God's... You will not need to fight in this battle. Position yourselves, stand still and see the salvation of the Lord..." (vv. 15, 17).

But standing still is the last thing we want to do when the enemy is coming against us. It is also the most difficult thing to do because we feel that we cannot just stand around and do nothing — we must try to save the situation. But God wants us to stand still and see Jesus, our salvation, fight for us.

So what do you do the next time you are faced with a battle and don't know what to do? Jehoshaphat sent his singers to the front of the army to proclaim, "Praise the Lord, for His mercy endures forever" (v. 21). Some people will wonder, "Does that mean that I just sing and don't do anything else when I have a problem?" No, that is not what I am saying.

Do what the situation requires, but don't worry and don't trust in what you do. Like Jehoshaphat, rest and trust in God's mercy that endures forever. When you do that, He will turn your battlefield into the Valley of Berachah. Berachah means "blessings." The children of Israel gave the battlefield this name because it took them three days to gather all the spoils of war! God turned their situation into a great blessing! (vv. 25–26.)

Do you have a battle to fight? Stand still and see the salvation of the Lord!

Thought for the Day
God wants us to stand still and see Jesus, our salvation, fight for us.

Don't Look to Your Faith, Look to Jesus

Hebrews 12:2
²Looking unto Jesus, the author and finisher of our faith....

If you are sick, you must know that you are already healed because of the finished work of Christ. Don't ask, "Do I have enough faith to be healed? Do I have the right kind of faith to be healed? What if I am lacking in faith?" You are focusing on yourself and your faith, instead of Christ and His finished work.

You should be asking, "Did Jesus take away this sickness? If He did, then He must have done a perfect work." In other words, fix your eyes on Jesus and His perfect work.

A.B. Simpson, who lived in the 19th century, wrote an article entitled *Himself*. In it, he mentioned his exhausted nervous system, and broken-down heart which could have proved fatal any time. So he sought the Lord for healing. God showed him Matthew 8:17, which says that Jesus "Himself took our infirmities and bore our sicknesses."

A.B. Simpson said that though he believed that Jesus had borne away his sicknesses, he saw many hindrances which stood between him and his healing. And they all boiled down to one thing — his preoccupation with his faith! He had believed that if only he had the "right" kind of faith, he would receive his healing instantly.

He eventually came to the realization that he had to remove that last hindrance — his focus on his faith — and just rest in the finished work of Christ. That revelation marked his complete recovery from his sicknesses.

When you ask yourself, "Do I have enough faith?" you have already put faith as a hindrance between you and Jesus' finished work. The more you focus on your faith, the more faith slips away. But if you focus on the finished work of Christ and see God's grace toward you, God sees that as faith! Without realizing it, faith is there in your heart to believe that you will not die of what Christ Himself has already borne away completely for you, and you will see your miracle manifest!

Thought for the Day
Fix your eyes on Jesus and His perfect work.

Jesus Took Your Place So That You Can Take His

Matthew 27:46
⁴⁶And about the ninth hour Jesus cried out with a loud voice, saying, "Eli, Eli, lama sabachthani?" that is, "My God, My God, why have You forsaken Me?"

Do you know that it was at the cross that Jesus addressed His Father as "God" for the first time? He had always addressed His Father as "Father." But at Calvary's tree, He addressed His Father as "God."

Jesus lost that Father-Son relationship when He was representing you and carrying your sins at the cross so that today, you can call God "Abba! Father!" (Romans 8:15.) and have a loving father-son relationship with God forever. Jesus was forsaken by God and His world became very dark on that lonely hill so that in your darkest hour, God will always say to you, "I will never leave you nor forsake you!" (Hebrews 13:5.)

At the time when Jesus needed God most, God turned His back on Him. God had to turn His back on His Son because His eyes are too holy to behold all the sin that was in His Son's body. And because God turned His back on Jesus, He will never turn His back on you. Instead, you will see God's face of favor shining on you all the time!

Jesus also took your place of no protection at the cross. For the first time, He gave up divine protection so that you can have it every day of your life! And because He became sin, He took your curse at the cross so that today, as you take His gift of righteousness, you receive only blessings from God.

Jesus received the full brunt of God's wrath in His body once and for all when He carried your sins. All of God's anger and condemnation fell on Him, consuming all your sins until God's wrath was exhausted.

Today, God is not angry with you. The body of Jesus absorbed everything — your sins, curses, and God's anger and condemnation. So live life expecting to see not the judgment, but the goodness and blessings of God!

Thought for the Day
Today, live life expecting to see not the judgment,
but the goodness and blessings of God.

Facts Change, but God's Word Remains

John 8:32
32"And you shall know the truth, and the truth shall make you free."

Consider the cold, hard facts that these three people faced: The aunt of a lady in our church saw her X-ray which showed that one of her two kidneys was cancerous. A couple in our church read their medical reports which said that they would never be able to produce a child. A lady in our church who acted as a guarantor ended up being asked by the finance company to pay it $34 million.

When such situations hit us and we allow the facts to settle in our hearts, we end up feeling greatly troubled. But when we let the truths of God's Word settle them all, we will sense the Holy Spirit bearing witness to the truths that we are believing. He is the Spirit of truth. (John 16:13.) He is not the Spirit of facts and does not bear witness to facts.

It may be a fact that you are sick. The doctorss say that you are sick. The X-ray film shows that you are sick. But God's Word says that by Jesus' stripes you are healed! (Isaiah 53:5.) That is the truth about your situation. What is the difference between fact and truth? Facts change, but truth — God's Word — remains!

When God's people choose to defy the facts and walk instead in His truths regarding their situations, the Holy Spirit in them will bear witness to the truths that they are believing.

The lady with the cancerous kidney underwent an operation to remove the organ. But praise God, she received supernatural restoration as later X-rays showed two healthy kidneys instead of one! God had formed a new kidney for her!

The childless couple received their miracle bundle of joy after seven years. Today, they are proud parents of not one, but four children!

The church member with the $34 million debt told the finance company that it was not being fair to her and that God would protect her. The company's management miraculously decided to cancel her debt!

The next time you are hit by disturbing facts, let God's Word settle the truth about your situation. And as the Holy Spirit bears witness to the truths that you are believing, the facts will change and you will receive your miracle!

Thought for the Day
Facts change, but truth — God's Word — remains!

By Jesus' Stripes You Are Healed

Isaiah 53:5
⁵… The chastisement for our peace was upon Him, and by His stripes we are healed.

You know, one of the biggest outcries against Mel Gibson's movie, *The Passion of the Christ*, was that it was too violent, especially the part where Jesus was scourged.

Let me tell you this: It was not violent enough! The Bible says that at the cross, Jesus' visage was marred beyond that of any man. (Isaiah 52:14.) In the movie, even after all the beatings, the actor James Caviezel, who played Jesus, still looked quite handsome.

But the reality is that when Jesus hung on the cross, He had "no form or comeliness… there is no beauty that we should desire Him" (Isaiah 53:2). He was beaten to a pulp until His face looked like jelly hanging out!

In the movie, when they scourged Him, only a small portion of His bones was exposed, so it was still quite tidy. But the messianic psalms say, "The plowers plowed on my back; they made their furrows long" (Psalm 129:3), and "I can count all My bones. They look and stare at Me" (Psalm 22:17). All His bones were exposed!

My friend, He was thinking of you when the soldiers tied Him to the scourging post. As they raised their whips, He said, "Let it all come on Me!"

But what came on Him was not just the whip stripping the flesh off His bare back, but your sicknesses and diseases. Each time He was whipped, every form of sickness and disease, including arthritis, cancer, diabetes, bird flu and dengue fever, came upon Him. "The chastisement for our peace was upon Him, and by His stripes we are healed."

Today, healing is your right because Jesus has paid the price for your healing. So if the devil says, "You cannot be healed," just declare, "Jesus has paid for my healing. Disease has no right to be in my body. I am healed in Jesus' name!"

Every curse of sickness that was supposed to fall on you fell on Jesus instead. He bore every one of those stripes, so that you can walk in divine health all the days of your life. The price has been paid so that you can rise up and get out of your bed of affliction!

Thought for the Day
Healing is your right because Jesus has paid the price for your healing.

See The Favor of God Multiplied in Your Life

2 Peter 1:2
²Grace and peace be multiplied to you in the
knowledge of God and of Jesus our Lord.

If you would like to walk in a greater measure of God's favor, 2 Peter 1:2 says that grace, which is the undeserved favor of God, and peace, can be multiplied to you. Peace is the word "shalom" in Hebrew. Its definition includes wholeness, health and prosperity. So when you walk in divine favor and peace, you will walk in blessings in every area of your life!

But how do the undeserved favor and shalom of God increase in your life?

It is not by your laboring or toiling to earn it. The Bible says that it comes as your knowledge of Jesus and His finished work increases. It comes as you learn more about and believe that through Jesus' one sacrifice at the cross, God removed all your sins, gave you His righteousness as a gift and put you in Christ to enjoy everything Jesus has. God's favor is multiplied in your life when you simply believe that the favor of God that is on Christ is also on you because of what Jesus' work at the cross has accomplished.

Today, you don't have to struggle for favor. Just release it by speaking forth God's Word in faith. On your way to work, say, "God's favor surrounds me as with a shield." (Psalm 5:12.) As you continue to speak God's favor over your life out of a revelation of Jesus' finished work, you will see more of it being released.

When I first entered the workforce, I began to declare the favor of God in my job. Every time I was given a new assignment, I proclaimed that the divine favor of God was on me. The company began to prosper and I was blessed financially. By the time I left the company to serve God full-time, my income had increased so that I was in the top 15 percent of earners in my age group in Singapore.

Today, in your workplace or at home, begin to declare the favor of God by faith. Expect to receive preferential treatment wherever you are. Say, "I am surrounded with the favor of God because of Jesus' finished work. I have favor before God and man!" And see God's favor work for you!

Thought for the Day
You don't have to struggle for favor. Just release it by
speaking forth God's Word in faith.

God Is for You, Not Against You

Romans 8:31
³¹What then shall we say to these things? If God is for us,
who can be against us?

Are you faced with challenges in your life right now? Are you having marital problems and financial woes? Maybe your child is going astray or an old illness has returned. What then will you say to all these things?

Do you know what God wants you to say? He wants you to say, "If God is for me, who can be against me?"

If you knew that the President or the Prime Minister was for you, you might believe that everything will be okay. But you have an even better backing! The Bible tells us that God, the Almighty, the Creator of the heavens and the earth, is for you! What problem can fasten its grip on you when the Almighty God is for you? Can the devil come successfully against you with God on your side?

If God is for you today, if God is for you right now, you don't have to moan, "If only I had this… If only I didn't say that…" And you don't have to worry about the future: "What if this happens… What if we don't have enough…" My friend, regretting the past and worrying about the future won't change anything. Look to your heavenly Father, instead. Because He is for you at this present moment, you can be confident that He will help you and provide for you.

Beloved, God sent His Son to die for you. And Jesus gave you a blood-bought right to an abundant life full of meaning and purpose! He gave you a blood-bought right to walk in divine health all the days of your life! He gave you a blood-bought right to prosperity even when the economy goes down!

You have all these things not because you deserve them, but because Jesus shed His blood and gave you the right to have them. All these blessings are yours today because God is for you. And if God is for you, who can be against you!

Thought for the Day
All blessings are yours today because God is for you!

The Teacher of All Things Is in You

John 14:26
²⁶But the Helper, the Holy Spirit, whom the Father will
send in My name, He will teach you all things....

If you are asking to whom or where you can go to get the help you need, ask no more. Just turn to God who has already promised you the Helper, the Holy Spirit whom He has sent in Jesus' name to dwell in you.

The Holy Spirit will teach you all things. Yes, teach you **all** things! Do you really believe that? Or are you like some who believe that you seek God's counsel only for spiritual things, but consult "professional" help for all other things in your life?

God does not want you to run to and rely on worldly wisdom. Now, there is nothing wrong with going to a doctor or engaging a financial consultant, but God wants you to come to Him **first** for counsel and direction. That is why He has sent the Holy Spirit, the Counselor (John 16:7, NIV), to teach you all things. The Holy Spirit is the Spirit of truth and He will guide you into all truth. (v. 13.)

The apostle John said, "But you have an anointing from the Holy One, and you know all things... the anointing which you have received from Him abides in you, and you do not need that anyone teach you; but as the same anointing teaches you concerning all things..." (1 John 2:20, 27).

So the way God teaches you is through the anointing within. It is a continuous anointing. In any particular situation, He is anointing you from within, teaching you by the presence or absence of His peace.

For example, a deal you are considering may sound very reasonable. But if you don't have the peace in your spirit, don't sign on the dotted line. Sign only when you have the peace. Be led by His peace and you will find that your heart will not be troubled, neither will it be afraid. (John 14:27.)

When you follow that peace which only God can give to you as an inward witness, good things and even miracles will come forth!

Thought for the Day
The Holy Spirit is the Spirit of truth and He will guide you into all truth.

God Wants You Cross-Conscious

1 Corinthians 2:2
*²For I determined not to know anything among you
except Jesus Christ and Him crucified.*

The apostle Paul, in his letter to the Corinthian church, said that he determined to know nothing among them except "Jesus Christ and Him crucified." In other words, Paul, who wrote two-thirds of the New Testament, had his mind full of Jesus and His finished work.

Beloved, God wants your mind full of the cross of Jesus. He wants you cross-conscious.

But what does it mean to be cross-conscious?

To be cross-conscious is to see Jesus, who loves you so much that He willingly died for you on the cross. To be cross-conscious is to look to Jesus, who offered His own body to be punished, so that your body can be free from all punishment.

To be cross-conscious is to fix your eyes on Jesus, who has provided for your deliverance and victory at the cross. At the cross, all your enemies were vanquished. All your diseases were destroyed. Your poverty was removed at the cross. Your sins were wiped out at the cross.

When the Israelites tasted bitterness in the waters of Marah, God showed Moses a tree, which he cast into the waters, making them sweet. (Exodus 15:23–26.) The tree represents the cross, which turned the bitter waters sweet. Today, Calvary's tree has turned your bitter situations sweet. Because of the cross, you can expect to see the bitter situations in your life made sweet!

When the Israelites were bitten by serpents in the wilderness, God told Moses to put a bronze serpent on a pole. The pole represents the cross and bronze speaks of judgment. Those who beheld the serpent on the pole lived because they saw their problem — the deadly serpent — nailed and put to death on the cross. (Numbers 21:6–9).

Today, you too will not die but live when you see all your sins judged at the cross, and with them, all your sicknesses, diseases, pains, failures and defeats. At the cross, all that is deadly in your life has been removed!

Thought for the Day
At the cross, your sins were judged, enemies vanquished, & (defeated)
diseases destroyed and poverty removed!

Your Father's Heart

Matthew 7:11
[11]If you then, being evil, know how to give good gifts to your children,
how much more will your Father who is in heaven give
good things to those who ask Him!

Let me tell you a true story I heard. There was a pastor whose young child was diagnosed with cancer. The day his boy was scheduled for an operation, this father cried out to God, "God, I'm almost 30 years old, but my boy is only about three months old. Why don't you just take some years off my life and give them to my boy?"

Then, from deep within him, he heard the voice of God say, "I am not like that." When the man heard that, he realized immediately that his son's sickness was not from God. He also realized that if he, who has faults, could want his child well, how much more his heavenly Father. So he changed his prayer and said, "Father God, I come against this sickness and I ask you for healing for my child." That day, on the operating table, the surgeons could find no trace of cancer in the child!

Today, God wants you to know that He is not the kind of Father who wants you sick and defeated, keeps you poor and wanting, refuses to provide for your needs and denies you your blessings.

When my daughter Jessica was younger, I bought a beautiful teddy bear for her. Teddy bears are her favorite toys and I could not wait to see her joy when she saw it. My joy is to see her happy. When she is sick and has difficulty sleeping at night, it hurts me to hear her cry. When she is crying, I cannot ignore her cries. I enter into her discomfort and pain even though I know that her sickness is something that will pass shortly. When she is in pain, I feel the pain too. When she is sad, I am sad too.

I believe that God gives us children to help us understand what His Fatherheart is like. His joy is to enter into your joy and see you happy. If you, in spite of your faults, know how to give good gifts to your children, how much more will your Father in heaven give good things to you when you ask Him! My prayer today is that you will know just how much your Father loves you!

Thought for the Day
God's joy is to enter into your joy!

Superabundant Supply in Your Area of Lack

Philippians 4:19
¹⁹And my God shall supply all your need according to His riches in glory by Christ Jesus.

A re you facing a lack in any area of your life, be it finances, health or relationships? Know that in that very same area, God has already prepared His superabundant supply which will abound toward you, and on top of that, His grace and more of His grace!

In John 6:1–13, Jesus was with a large crowd of people who were hungry. The problem then was a lack of food. But Jesus knew that where there is lack, there is superabundant supply in His Father's kingdom to overcome that lack.

His disciples, however, did not know that. They did not think the same way as Jesus did. They told Him that there was a boy with five loaves and two small fish, but they did not think that that would amount to anything. They said, "What are the five loaves and two fish among so many?" (v. 9).

They saw only the problem, the lack. But Jesus took the little, lifted it up as He looked to heaven and gave thanks to His Father, whose supply is so much more than we can ever ask for.

When Jesus started distributing the little that was in His hands, a miracle happened. Five thousand men, not counting women and children, ate as much as they wanted and for as long as they were hungry!

The supply kept flowing as long as the need was there. And after they were so filled, there were 12 baskets full of leftovers! That is God's superabundant supply. In God's kingdom, there is no such thing as the Father not having enough or not wanting to give abundantly to His children. No, He promises that He will supply **all** our needs according to His riches in glory by Christ Jesus!

My friend, God wants us to always be conscious of His grace abounding toward us and enveloping us. So let us, like Jesus, acknowledge God's superabundant supply by thanking Him for it and for whatever is in our hands. Let us believe that His superabundant supply will flow and multiply the little that we have, and fill us up to overflowing!

Thought for the Day
God's supply is so much more than we can ask for.

The Sure Symbol of God's Love

Romans 5:8
⁸But God demonstrates His own love toward us, in that
while we were still sinners, Christ died for us.

Imagine this scenario: Your car tire blows and you are late for work. At the office, you find out that someone else got the promotion you had been hoping for. Then, you receive a call from home informing you that your kitchen pipes are leaking again. Before long, you hear a voice telling you, "If God loves you so much, how come all these things are happening to you?"

Perhaps you are asking the same question today and wondering if God really loves you. Well, I want you to know that you must never judge God's love for you based on your circumstances. No, look at the cross instead! The cross is the sure symbol of God's love for you. It is at the cross that "God demonstrates His own love toward us, in that while we were still sinners, Christ died for us."

A teenager learned that the cross indeed spoke of how much God loves her. At one point in her life, she was contemplating suicide as the only way out of her loveless, messed-up life. She had intended to take some pills with a lethal dose of alcohol. She was all ready to die when she started clicking aimlessly on some MP3 songs on the Internet. And of all the songs that were on her screen, she picked a beautiful song written by one of our church musicians.

The lyrics of the song, sung by one of our church vocalists, spoke of being held by God's love and being treasured in His sight. They touched this teenager. Sensing that an awesome God with His amazing love was reaching out to her, she abandoned her plan to kill herself. Not long after that, she found our church and even met the person who had sung the song. She eventually came to know how much God loves her and how He has demonstrated His love for her through the cross.

Beloved, when you look at your life and find yourself wondering if God really loves you, look to the cross and see God's outstretched arms. It will remind and reassure you of how much He loves you!

Thought for the Day
Look to the cross and see God's outstretched arms —
that is how much He loves you!

Worship God As You Are

Ephesians 5:27
²⁷That He might present her to Himself a glorious church, not having spot or wrinkle or any such thing, but that she should be holy and without blemish.

Have you been to a worship service where you stood with your hands raised, ready to worship God, only to hear the worship leader say, "Before we worship God, let's all search our hearts"? Then, as you search your heart, before long, you dig up something that you don't like. The next thing you know, your hands are no longer raised and soon, you find yourself sitting down — you don't feel good worshiping God any more.

My friend, I have good news for you. Come and worship Him as you are. Come into God's presence Jesus-conscious, forgiveness-conscious and grace-conscious! Come into God's presence bringing only Jesus, the spotless Lamb of God, as your offering.

Your worshiping God is like the times God's people in the Old Testament brought their offerings to the priest. The priest examined the animal sacrifice to ensure that it was without blemish. The priest did not examine the sinner. If the animal was without blemish, God accepted the animal sacrifice as well as the offerer who brought the animal.

So when you come into God's presence, don't do any self-examination and be discouraged when you find faults in your life. God does not examine you. He sees you through the full value, and all the loveliness and acceptance of His Son. (Ephesians 1:6.) He sees you holy and without blemish!

Remember the woman who was referred to as a sinner, possibly a prostitute? She went to the house of the Pharisee who was hosting Jesus and wiped Jesus' feet with her hair. (Luke 7:36–50.) That was her act of worship.

She came to Him as she was. Yes, she knew that she had sinned, but she worshiped Jesus first because of who He is. She was Jesus-conscious. Then, she heard Jesus say, "Your sins are forgiven." (v. 48.) She received the forgiveness she needed from Him.

Whatever you need from the Savior, come to Him as you are. Worship Him for who He is and then you will hear Him say, "Go your way. Your restoration has come. Your prosperity is here. You are healed. You have been made whole!"

Thought for the Day
God sees you in Christ — holy and without blemish.

Everlasting Righteousness

Daniel 9:24
²⁴Seventy weeks are determined for your people and for your holy city,
to finish the transgression, to make an end of sins, to make
reconciliation for iniquity, to bring in everlasting righteousness....

On Sunday, we hear a message that says, "I am the righteousness of God in Christ." On Monday, we are still confessing, "I am the righteousness of God in Christ." But come Wednesday or Thursday, we begin to confess our sins! Then, when Sunday comes, we get a fresh revelation of our righteousness in Christ and we start to confess our righteousness again. Why do we do that?

It cannot be that on Sunday, we are righteous. Then, a few days later, we become unrighteous because of sin, but are "re-righteoused" when Sunday comes again. No, our righteousness is an "everlasting righteousness"! Jesus has obtained "eternal redemption" for us. (Hebrews 9:12.)

"But Pastor Prince, I have just sinned. How can I still be righteous?"

My friend, it is not what you do that makes you righteous. It is what Christ has done at Calvary. Romans 5:19 says, "For as by one man's [Adam] disobedience many were made sinners, so also by one Man's obedience many will be made righteous." It is the obedience of one Man — Christ — and not your obedience, that has made you righteous!

God wants you established in what Christ has done. He wants you conscious of your everlasting righteousness in Christ. How do you do that? You can listen to anointed messages that remind you of your righteousness in Christ. And don't just know it in your head. Speak it. Every morning, tell yourself, "I am the righteousness of God in Christ!" (2 Corinthians 5:21.)

You don't need a revelation of how sinful you are. You know it when you sin. The devil reminds you of your sins. Even your friends and loved ones sometimes point out your sins. What you need, instead, is a revelation of how forever righteous you are in God's eyes, especially when you sin.

And when you are conscious of this gift of righteousness that is everlasting, you will reign in life! (Romans 5:17.) You will reign over sin, bad habits, sicknesses, lack and everything that holds you back from a victorious life!

Thought for the Day
It is not what you do that makes you righteous.
It is what Christ has done at Calvary.

Boast in God's Grace for You

1 Corinthians 1:31
31... "He who glories, let him glory in the Lord."

If someone asks you, "What must I do to inherit eternal life?" you would probably tell him, "Believe in the Lord Jesus and you will be saved," wouldn't you?

Well, a rich, young ruler asked Jesus the same question, but instead of telling the man to believe in Him, Jesus gave him the law. (Mark 10:17–22.)

Jesus saw that the young ruler lived his life taking pride in his ability to keep the law to earn salvation and the favor of God. But because of His love for the man, Jesus had to show him that those who live by the law must realize that their self-efforts cannot save them.

He therefore reminded him, "You know the commandments: 'Do not commit adultery... 'Do not steal... 'Honor your father and your mother.'" The young ruler showed that his trust was in his law-keeping when he replied, "Teacher, all these things I have kept from my youth."

So Jesus had to tell him, "One thing you lack... sell whatever you have and give to the poor... and come... and follow Me." When the young ruler heard that, he walked away sorrowful.

When we boast of having kept the law, it will always point out something we lack or have failed to obey. The law is so holy and perfect that if we don't keep even one iota of it, it has no choice but to judge and curse us. (Galatians 3:10.) That is what the law was designed to do.

God does not want us to boast in our abilities to keep the law. If we are to have confidence in anything at all, if we are to boast in anything at all, it is in the grace of God. Only His grace can completely keep, save, heal, deliver and bless us.

So let's not boast in what we have done or are able to do, but boast in His grace for us — that He is our strength, health, favor, prosperity, wisdom, hope, salvation and glory. That is how we will see ourselves enjoying our inheritance of abundant life!

Thought for the Day
Only His grace, not our works, can save, keep, heal, deliver and bless us.

Believe and Act on the New Covenant

1 Samuel 17:45
⁴⁵Then David said to the Philistine, "... I come to you in the name of the
Lord of hosts, the God of the armies of Israel, whom you have defied."

Ever wonder why two people can hear the same thing and yet have very different responses? For one, what is said makes him afraid and discouraged. For the other, his heart is so filled with faith that he dares to come against the devil and what he is doing.

In the Valley of Elah, Goliath, the Philistine giant, taunted the armies of Israel for 40 days. When David came on the scene, he heard the same mockings of Goliath that the rest of the Israelites heard. But somehow, those same words that caused fear in the soldiers angered David. What did David know or see that the others failed to see?

David knew that he had a covenant with God. Now, King Saul and all the soldiers with him that day also had the same covenant with God, but only David believed the covenant. And he acted on his belief. So God caused his giant to come tumbling down.

If David had such a great victory even though he was under the old covenant, how much more you and I who are under the new covenant! Today, God is asking, "Where are my Davids who will believe the new covenant?"

What is the new covenant? It is the covenant of grace. And grace means unmerited, undeserved, unearned favor. God wants us to know that He has cut this covenant with us through Christ, our representative. And according to the covenant, we have His undeserved favor. We are blessed because Jesus took our beating. Because of what Jesus has done on the cross, we have victory over every giant.

Isn't that good news? Today, God wants you to stand before your "giant" and declare that in spite of what you are going through, in spite of what is happening, you believe that God is for you because of what Jesus has done for you. And then, before your very eyes, you will see the giants of accusation, intimidation, condemnation, disease and debt fall flat before you!

Thought for the Day
Because of what Jesus has done on the cross,
we have victory over every giant.

God Helps the Helpless

Psalm 63:7
⁷Because You have been my help, therefore in the
shadow of Your wings I will rejoice.

I have had people tell me, "Pastor Prince, please pray for me. I can't see a way out of the mess I am in. I know that this whole thing is my fault. Right now, I don't even know whether God will hear my prayers."

If you think about it, a whole lot of our troubles are of our own making. But it is when we deserve the punishment and not the blessing that we can receive grace — the undeserved favor and unmerited help of God!

When we stop trying to be deserving of God's help, we find God more than willing to be our Savior. But when we continue to try to work things out, we are trying to be our own saviors. God will say, "Save yourself because I can't help you when you don't need My help."

You might be thinking, *But Pastor Prince, don't you know, God helps those who help themselves?*

Contrary to popular belief, this saying that "God helps those who help themselves" is not in the Bible! God does not help those who help themselves. He helps those who are helpless and dependent on Him. He helps those who look to Him as their only source of help for their problem.

If you say, "My problem is that I am weak." God says, "That is not a problem. I am your strength." If you say, "Lord, my face is the problem. I am ugly." God says, "My face will shine on yours. I am your glory." If you say, "Lord, I am the problem. I am a nobody." God says, "I will make you a somebody."

Unfortunately, many of us are still trying to help ourselves, thinking that for certain matters, we don't really need God. But God says, "Without Me, you can do **nothing**." (John 15:5.) Do we really believe that? Or do we believe that without Him, we can still do some things to help ourselves?

Only when we realize that we can do nothing, and are nothing in and of ourselves, can we do all things **through Christ** who strengthens us. (Philippians 4:13.) Then, we will see the undeserved, unmerited help and favor of God deliver us from every evil!

Thought for the Day
God helps those who are helpless and completely dependent on Him.

Right Believing Produces Right Living

Luke 19:8
⁸Then Zacchaeus stood and said to the Lord, "Look, Lord,
I give half of my goods to the poor; and if I have taken
anything from anyone by false accusation, I restore fourfold."

Zacchaeus was a tax collector. He was despised because he was a deceitful man, cheating people of their money and resorting to false accusations to get what he wanted.

One day, Jesus visited him. The Bible makes no mention of Jesus rebuking him for his dishonest lifestyle the whole time they were together. Instead, Jesus showed him grace and honor by spending time with him. Before long, Zacchaeus stood up and declared to Jesus that he would restore fourfold to anyone he had taken from illegally, and would even give half of his goods to the poor.

A moment with Jesus completely changed Zacchaeus' heart. A moment with grace in person — without accusations, condemnation or judgment — caused such an inward transformation that in a short time, Zacchaeus was doing outwardly what was right and in a measure no man would have expected of him!

Many people want to live right. Their concern with right living makes them focus on themselves and the things they struggle with. But it is right believing that produces right living. If you are trying to break free from an addiction that has bound you for many years, believe that Jesus loves you so much that at the cross, He paid the price for you to be completely free from any addiction. Believe that by His stripes you are healed and delivered.

One member in our church had a smoking addiction. But each time he lit up a cigarette, he would believe that God was not judging or condemning him, and that he was still the righteousness of God in Christ. One day, he woke up impressed by the Spirit that that day would mark the start of a smoke-free life. Expecting to be assaulted by the usual cravings to smoke, he prayed this through-out the day: "Thank You, Jesus, for by Your stripes I am healed." Before he knew it, the day passed without him lighting up or suffering any withdrawal pangs! And since then, he has been totally free of this addiction.

Today, if you want to experience right living, find out what Christ has done for you and what you have in Him — and believe it!

Thought for the Day
Believe what Christ has done for you and what you have in Him.

Rejoice, O Barren!

Galatians 4:27
27... "Rejoice, O barren, you who do not bear!
Break forth and shout, you who are not in labor...."

B arrenness. What a painful and frustrating condition. Yet, in Isaiah 54:1 God's Word to those who are experiencing barrenness is to rejoice — "Sing, O barren"!

Why? Because in the previous chapter, it tells us that the chastisement for our peace fell upon Jesus. (Isaiah 53:5.) The word "peace" here in Hebrew means completeness, soundness, health and prosperity. In other words, all these benefits are yours today because Jesus has already been punished at the cross for your peace. That is why you can start rejoicing.

So God wants you right now, in whatever area you are barren, to start rejoicing as if the fruit or yield you want to see has already come. He wants you to start thinking, speaking and acting as if the barrenness is no more.

If you are financially barren, start planning for what you would do when your finances increase. I am not saying that you go out and spend recklessly, but start making plans for wealth and increase. The time to do this is when you are still in what your natural eyes see as a barren stage.

You may say, "Pastor Prince, you don't understand, the banks are chasing me!"

God says, "Rejoice because you are prosperous in Christ." In Christ, you are already blessed with every spiritual blessing, including prosperity. (Ephesians 1:3.) "For you know the grace of our Lord Jesus Christ, that though He was rich, yet for your sakes He became poor, that you through His poverty might become rich" (2 Corinthians 8:9).

If you are sick, start planning to do what you have not been able to do. Don't rejoice only when the healing manifests and the pain is no more. Rejoice now in your healing because Jesus has already borne your diseases and carried your pains, and by His stripes you have already been healed. (Isaiah 53:4–5.)

Whatever barren situation you are in, rejoice and tell God, "Father, because of the sacrifice of Your Son, I am blessed with all spiritual blessings in heavenly places in Christ. You have already given me everything. So I am going to act like it is so and rejoice!"

Thought for the Day
Start thinking, speaking and acting as if your barrenness is no more.

The Power of Your Words

Proverbs 18:21
²¹Death and life are in the power of the tongue,
and those who love it will eat its fruit.

M ost people, when they desperately want something, will say things like, "I am dying for that piece of cake!" Few will say, "I am living for that piece of cake!"

What is worse is that we are quick to mention death when things go wrong. We Singaporeans are quick to say things like, "Die lah! Die lah!" at the drop of a hat. Nobody says, "Live lah! Live lah!"

Yet, the truth is that every word you speak has power — to build or destroy hopes and dreams, to restore or cause loss, to heal or break the spirit, to bring delight or despair, to bless or curse — for God's Word says that death and life are in the power of the tongue.

So stop lining your words up with the negative circumstances. Instead, start lining your words up with God's Word and release the power of His Word to work for you.

For example, instead of speaking lack and poverty, say, "God's Word tells me that the good things are already here. I therefore pronounce my life blessed. I pronounce my life prosperous. I pronounce my life great. Darkness and gloom, poverty and sickness, defeat and depression, will not be in my life!"

Instead of speaking sickness and death, say, "I will live long. I will not die young. Jesus died young for me so that I can live long for Him. I am the righteousness of God in Christ and God's Word declares that no evil befalls the righteous. So no evil will come on me now and in the future!"

Instead of speaking fear over your children, say, "God's Word declares that the seed of the righteous shall be delivered. Therefore, my children are delivered from every curse, every power of darkness and every evil. In the name of Jesus, I call forth a great, bright and blessed future for my children!"

God wants you to have a life filled with good days and an abundance of every good thing. So say, "In the name of Jesus, I command blessings, favor, health, prosperity, protection, dominion and power to fill my life!"

Thought for the Day
Line your words up with God's Word and release the
power of His Word to work for you.

Jesus Is Willing, Be Healed!

Matthew 8:3
³Then Jesus put out His hand and touched him,
saying, "I am willing; be cleansed."

D
o you know that it is God's will for you to be healed? In fact, Jesus always healed the sick who came to Him. The blind, lame, maimed, mute, deaf and demon-possessed — He healed them **all**! (v. 16.)

The Bible says that he who has seen Jesus has seen the Father. (John 14:9.) You want to see what God is like? Look at Jesus! He never gave sickness to anybody. You never find Jesus looking at a person, a fine specimen of a man, and saying, "Come here. You are too healthy. Receive some leprosy!" In fact, when a leper came to Him for healing, Jesus, full of compassion, told the leper, "I am willing; be cleansed."

Unfortunately, there are some Christians who say, "It is God's will for me to be sick. God has some purpose, some mysterious purpose for my situation. It is all part of His divine plan and we shall all know in the sweet by and by, the reason why!" But these same people go to their doctors to get well. They take their medication and rest. Why do they do that if they really believe that God wants them sick? Doesn't make sense, does it?

Come on, what makes perfect sense is this: God wants you well. He wants you whole. His will is for you to be healed! In fact, He is so willing that He took **all** your sicknesses and diseases upon His own body, so that you don't have to suffer them today! He allowed Himself to be beaten and scourged, so that by His scourging — by His stripes — you are healed! (Isaiah 53:5.) Since He has already suffered the sickness on your behalf, why should you suffer it today?

So my friend, if you are sick, know that God did not give you the disease. Read every healing miracle that Jesus did in the Gospels and see how Jesus is the Lord who heals you. (Exodus 15:26.) Hear His gracious words, "I am willing, be healed," and know that they are as much for you today as they were for the leper!

Thought for the Day
Jesus took all your sicknesses and diseases upon His own body,
so that you don't have to suffer them today!

Discerning the Lord's Body

1 Corinthians 11:24
24and when He had given thanks, He broke it and said, "Take, eat; this is My body which is broken for you; do this in remembrance of Me."

Have you ever taken a close look at the Matzah bread that the Jews eat during their Passover meal? The bread, which is unleavened, is pierced with rows of little holes forming stripes. It is also slightly burnt. Many churches today use this bread for the Holy Communion.

Do you know why the bread is pierced, striped and burnt?

My friend, the bread that you hold in your hands when you partake of the Lord's Supper speaks of the body of our Lord Jesus Christ when He bore our sins and sicknesses on the cross.

Like the bread, He was pierced in His brow by the crown of thorns as well as in His hands and feet by the nails. He was also pierced in His side by a soldier's spear. The prophet Isaiah says, "He was pierced for our transgressions…" (Isaiah 53:5, NIV).

Like the bread, He was scourged on His back until His flesh was all torn and bloody, and His bones were exposed, so that today, you can say, "By His stripes I am healed!" (Isaiah 53:5.)

What about the burnt marks on the bread? The full fire of God's wrath fell on Jesus, burning up our sins into ashes, and at the same time, bringing out the fragrance of the offering of Jesus. Today, your sins and lawless deeds are but ashes, and your Father in heaven remembers them no more! (Hebrews 8:12.)

So the next time you partake of the bread during the Holy Communion, know that Jesus was pierced for your sins and scourged for your healing. He bore God's fiery judgment so that you will never be judged for your sins! He also bore your diseases and carried your pains so that you can walk in divine health!

When you discern these precious truths about our Lord's body, you are partaking of the Holy Communion in a worthy manner. And you will not be weak and sickly, nor die before your time. (1 Corinthians 11:27–30.) No, you will be strong and healthy, and you will live long!

Thought for the Day
Jesus was pierced for your sins and scourged for your healing so that you can walk in divine health!

God's Love Makes You Strong

Ephesians 3:19
¹⁹… know the love of Christ which passes knowledge;
that you may be filled with all the fullness of God.

If you were to thank God for something today, what would it be? For me, it would be thanking God for giving me Jesus. For when I see Jesus on the cross, I see the love of God overcoming everything for me. It causes me to say, "Thank You, Jesus! I love You, Jesus! I worship You, Jesus! Bless You, Jesus! Hallelujah!"

And as we worship and celebrate the love of Jesus in our lives, we will find ourselves changed, and we will see the mighty power of God displayed for us and through us.

This was the case in the life of David. His personal times of worship, of being absorbed in God's love for him, changed him from a mere shepherd boy to a lion killer, bear killer, giant killer and finally, a king over Israel.

Now, no one on earth, no matter how strong he is, let alone a youth, can come against a lion and pry open its mouth to snatch back his sheep which the lion had carried away, unless God's anointing is on him. And this was indeed what happened to David the shepherd boy who went after the lion, caught it by its beard, struck and killed it, and thus delivered the lamb from its jaws. (1 Samuel 17:34–37.)

My friend, no man can truly enjoy living in this world without God's strength in his life, God's favor in his work and relationships, God's protection for him and his family, God's increase in his finances, and God's health and healing for his body. Likewise, no woman can survive emotionally, socially or physically without God's tender touch, loving presence, sweet assurance and words of life in times of need.

Beloved, as you feed on Jesus' love for you, you will be filled with the fullness of God. Like David, God's anointing will begin to operate powerfully in your life. And when you encounter spiritual lions, even the devil himself — when he comes like a roaring lion against you, your loved ones or your possessions — you will grab hold of his mouth and tear him apart!

Thought for the Day
Feed on Jesus' love for you, and be filled with the fullness and
power of God to tear your spiritual lions apart!

Blessed Is Everything That Comes Forth From You

Deuteronomy 28:4
⁴Blessed shall be the fruit of your body....

The Bible records that Jesus' spit healed a blind man (Mark 8:23–25), Peter's shadow healed the sick (Acts 5:15), and handkerchiefs and aprons from Paul's body drove out evil spirits and diseases. (Acts 19:11–12.) This tells us that what comes forth from our bodies can be so blessed that it brings about blessings and miracles to others.

Indeed, God said, "Blessed shall be the fruit of your body..." He was not just referring to your children, or He would have simply said, "Blessed shall be your children." No, God meant that everything that proceeds from your body will be blessed. All that is of and from your body will be of top-notch quality!

This includes your health. So even if your doctor has said that you have a particular medical condition in your body, just believe that God calls your health, the fruit of your body, blessed. And expect to walk continuously in divine health!

God calls your thinking ability, the fruit of your body, blessed too. You will impress your teachers and schoolmates in school with your mental prowess, or your superiors and colleagues at work with your innovative ideas and solutions. Your mental faculties will be of quality par excellence!

If you are married, you will enjoy a truly blessed marriage and a fulfilling sex life with your spouse. A secular song that laments, "I can't get no satisfaction..." will never be true for you because God calls your marital relationship (both the emotional **and** physical parts of it), the fruit of your body, blessed!

If you are a parent, God calls your children, the fruit of your body, blessed. This means that they are special, having exceptional qualities. So the child you are taking care of is not just a child. You are holding a champion in your hands. He will grow up to be a general in God's kingdom!

Beloved, because Jesus has paid the price — His body was beaten, scourged and pierced for you, all these blessings are yours. Blessed shall be the fruit of your body!

Thought for the Day
Because Jesus has paid the price, everything that
proceeds from your body will be blessed.

The Lord Is Your Refuge

Psalm 91:1–2
¹He who dwells in the secret place of the Most High shall abide
under the shadow of the Almighty. ²I will say of the Lord,
"He is my refuge and my fortress; my God, in Him I will trust."

Every day, we are bombarded with news of conflicts, natural disasters, diseases and new strains of drug-resistant viruses. We also hear of people losing their loved ones in freak accidents. And we ask ourselves, "Is there a place where I can take refuge from a world gone mad?"

Yes, there is! God foresaw all these things and He has promised in His Word protection from every evil known to man. There is no trap set by the devil that our Father cannot deliver us from, if we trust in Him and take Him as our refuge. That is His promise in Psalm 91.

Whether it is an earthquake at midnight, a crazy sniper, an unknown virus or a terrorist attack, God says, "You shall not be afraid of the terror by night, nor of the arrow that flies by day, nor of the pestilence that walks in darkness, nor of the destruction that lays waste at noonday" (vv. 5–6).

Because you have made Him your dwelling place, angels are watching over you right now. (vv. 9–11.) They give heed to the voice of God's Word, so you should give voice to God's Word. This means that you should agree with and speak what God's Word says about His preserving and protecting you. Then, angels are sent to minister for you. (Hebrews 1:14.)

My friend, don't say, "If it can happen to them, it can also happen to me!" Say, "A thousand may fall at my side and 10,000 at my right hand, but it will not come near me!" (Psalm 91:7.) The world says that you cannot but expect danger all around. God says, "You are in this world but not of this world. You have My protection because you are of Me and in Me." (John 17:14–23.)

You have access by faith into the secret place of the Most High where no evil can touch you. There is no need to fear living in the end times because the Lord is your refuge and fortress. His Word says so. And those who trust His Word completely find His Word completely true!

Thought for the Day
The Lord is your refuge from every evil known to man.

Life Above the Sun

John 10:10
¹⁰... I have come that they may have life, and that
they may have it more abundantly.

When you are not enjoying abundant life, you will feel as if life is full of toil. In your heart, life is meaningless and empty. You feel like someone "grasping for the wind" (Ecclesiastes 2:11).

It seems as if nothing you do adds up to much. The Bible calls this life "under the sun" (v. 11). Someone who lives life under the sun may or may not know God, but God is either forgotten or not the center of things in his life. His thoughts are earthly and he does things to gratify his flesh. In the end, he finds life depressing and unfulfilled. Life under the sun is full of despair.

But this is not so with someone who lives life above the sun with God. For life with Him is filled with joy and pleasures at His right hand. (Psalm 16:11.) Life is abundantly full and good just as Jesus promised — "I have come that they may have life, and that they may have it more **abundantly.**"

When you live life above the sun, your thoughts are heavenward and you become Christ-occupied. You live for Him because you know that "all things were created through Him and for Him" (Colossians 1:16). When you live for His glory, your life takes on a new meaning and purpose.

God's Word says, "He is before all things, and in Him all things consist" (v. 17). The Greek word for "consist" means "held together." In Christ, all things are held together. And that is why when Christ is the central figure in your life, you will have it all together. Your mind will be held together. Your hopes and dreams will be held together. Your family will be held together by the cords of His love.

Your life will not be empty, but full of God's goodness because "Christ in you, [is] the hope of glory" (v. 27). It is a wonderful life — this life lived above the sun. And you will have an even more wonderful life to come in heaven!

Thought for the Day
When Christ is the central figure in your life, you will have it all together.

Beat the Odds With the Favor of God

Ruth 2:2
²So Ruth the Moabitess said to Naomi, "Please let me go to the field, and glean heads of grain after him in whose sight I may find favor." And she said to her, "Go, my daughter."

D o you look at yourself and see only lack in the natural? Do you say, "I don't have a good education," "I am poor," "I am too old" or "I am a divorcee"? I have good news for you. As a blood-bought believer and child of God, you have the supernatural favor of God!

In the Bible, Ruth was a poor Moabite widow who went with her mother-in-law to live in Bethlehem, a Jewish town where the inhabitants considered Moabites outcasts. But she did not wallow in self-pity and moan about being a poor widow of the wrong race in the wrong place. Instead, she believed that God would favor her and she declared, "I will find favor in the field that I glean from."

In the natural, Ruth had everything going against her. But because she trusted in the favor of God, she not only became the wife of Bethlehem's richest man when Boaz married her, she also became the great-grandmother of David and had her name included in the genealogy of Jesus Christ, even though she was not Jewish! That is what God's supernatural favor did for her. That is the kind of blessing God's supernatural favor can give you.

A church member shared how, due to unforeseen circumstances, she was late for a job interview. But she confessed God's favor on herself before the interview and miraculously, the interviewers shortlisted her for a second interview.

There were about 40 other applicants with the right experience. And though she lacked the relevant experience, by the favor of God, she got the job which came with better pay and a car allowance that fully subsidized her car loan. Her new company was even willing to pay for her gas and cell phone expenses — all because she believed and confessed that she had the favor of God!

Do not look at what you do not have in the natural and see lack. Trust in the favor of God and you will see blessings that your natural abilities cannot bring!

Thought for the Day
As a blood-bought believer and child of God, you have the supernatural favor of God!

God's Love Demonstrated

Romans 8:32
³²He who did not spare His own Son, but delivered Him up for us all,
how shall He not with Him also freely give us all things?

When we go through a trial, we tend to ask ourselves, "Does God really love me? How come I don't seem to see it?" When that happens, it is time to bring in the cross, for God's love for you is displayed forever at the cross.

God gave up His Son to suffer and die on the cross for you. Jesus was pierced in seven places for you — in His head by the crown of thorns, His two hands and feet by the nails, and His side and heart by the spear of a Roman soldier.

Jesus wore the crown of thorns on His head so that you can have a sound mind free from fears, guilt, depression, anxieties and stress.

When Jesus first showed His nail-pierced hands to His disciples, He said to them, "Peace be with you" (John 20:19–20). He wanted them to know that peace is found in His finished work, typified by His pierced hands. The more you see His finished work, which has bought complete forgiveness of all your sins, the more your conscience will be at peace and rest.

Jesus' feet brought Him to places where there was lack, diseases, rejection, condemnation and even death. And those feet were nail-pierced so that you do not need to be in such places yourself. He has rescued you from having to accept and suffer these things in life.

Blood and water flowed out of Jesus' side when it was pierced. (John 19:34.) Medical science will tell you that that means His heart had ruptured. Jesus died literally of a broken heart so that your heart can be filled with joy.

And just as Eve came forth from Adam's side when he was sleeping, the bride of Christ, the church, came forth from Jesus' pierced side and death. If He died to have you as His spotless bride, He lives today to care for you.

Beloved, the only man-made things in heaven today are those scars on His body. They will remain forever as tokens of His everlasting love and passion for you. So if God did not spare His Son, but delivered Him up for you, how will He not with Him also freely give you all things!

Thought for the Day
God's love for you is displayed forever at the cross.

The Gift of No Condemnation

John 8:11
11... "Neither do I condemn you; go and sin no more."

When Jesus was on earth, a woman caught in the act of adultery was brought before Him by the scribes and Pharisees, the religious mafia of His day. They tried to trap Him by posing a question that was difficult to answer: "Now Moses, in the law, commanded us that such should be stoned. But what do You say?" (v. 5).

Jesus answered, "He who is without sin among you, let him throw a stone at her first" (v. 7). The scribes and Pharisees began to leave one by one till none of them were left.

The people in the crowd who wanted to condemn the woman **could not**. But Jesus, the only One in the crowd who truly had the power to condemn her, **would not**. He then asked her, "Woman... Has no one condemned you?" (v. 10).

He spoke such words of grace to her because He loved her. Also, by asking her the question, He was giving her a chance to speak words of no condemnation to herself — "No one [condemns me], Lord" (v. 11).

Jesus not only spoke words of grace to her, He also gave her the gift of no condemnation — "Neither do I condemn you; go and sin no more." It was when she received the gift of no condemnation that she had the power to "go and sin no more."

Today, you have the gift of no condemnation because the Son of God was condemned for all your sins. (Romans 8:1.) Today, God cannot condemn you when you sin because He is faithful and just to what His Son has done.

So if the devil tries to convince you that God is angry with you when you blow it, just say, "God **does not** condemn me today because He has already condemned Jesus at the cross 2,000 years ago!"

Unfortunately, we still hear people saying, "Go and sin no more **first**, then I won't condemn you." Maybe you have been saying this to yourself too. But God says, "I don't condemn you. Go and sin no more." He gives you the gift of no condemnation, so that you have the strength to go and sin no more!

Thought for the Day
You have the gift of no condemnation because the Son of God
was condemned for all your sins.

You Are Perfect in God's Eyes

Hebrews 10:12, 14 KJV
¹²But this man, after He had offered one sacrifice for sins forever,
sat down on the right hand of God... ¹⁴For by one offering
He hath perfected forever them that are sanctified.

God sees you with no flaw, spot or imperfection, so honor His Word and the finished work of His Son by saying, "Amen!" Don't doubt your perfection in Christ.

To see yourself as being far from perfect is not modesty, but a failure to understand the perfect sacrifice that Jesus has made for you.

The Bible tells us, "For by one offering He hath perfected forever them that are sanctified." Did you get that? You have not only been sanctified, that is, made holy; but by the same offering of His body, you have been perfected. You are both holy and perfect in God's eyes!

Your sins have been purged perfectly. Today, Jesus is seated at His Father's right hand not because He is the Son of God (although that is true), but because His work of purging your sins is completely finished and perfect!

So instead of being conscious of your sins, which is to have an evil conscience (Hebrews 10:22), you can have a perfect conscience — a conscience that is free from the guilt and condemnation of sins.

When you find yourself conscious of your sins, just say, "Thank You, Lord Jesus, for Your wonderful work at the cross. It is a perfect work that has removed all my sins completely.

"Holy Spirit, thank You for convicting me of righteousness, not my own, but God's righteousness given to me as a gift. Keep on convicting me in the days to come, reminding me especially when I fail that I am still the righteousness of God in Christ."

My friend, God sees you perfect without any spot of sin. He sees you covered in the beautiful white robes of His own righteousness. He treats you as a righteous person because that is what He has made you. So expect good things to happen to you because blessings are on the head of the righteous! (Proverbs 10:6.)

Thought for the Day
To see yourself as being far from perfect is to fail to understand the
perfect sacrifice that Jesus has made for you.

Having All Things Added to You

Matthew 6:33
33But seek first the kingdom of God and His righteousness,
and all these things shall be added to you.

You are probably a responsible person who is concerned about providing well for your family — making sure that there is food on the table, money for the children's needs, comfort and education, and so on.

What does God have to say to us about these legitimate concerns? According to Matthew 6:31, He tells us, "Do not worry." Now, He is not saying that we don't need all these things because in the same portion of scripture He says, "For your heavenly Father knows that you need all these things" (v. 32).

So God cares about us having these things. He wants us to have all these things. In fact, He wants all these things added to us. And He tells us that the way these things are added to us is by us seeking first the kingdom of God and His righteousness. Therefore, our number one priority every day is to seek the kingdom of God and His righteousness. It is not to seek to add these things to ourselves.

But what is righteousness? Righteousness is not right behavior. It is right standing with the Father. It is the clearance of all your guilt, which makes you able to stand before God. It is not something you get through right behavior. It is a **gift** from God. Paul calls it "the gift of righteousness" (Romans 5:17). And to "seek" this gift is to be conscious of the fact that you have it, to confess that you are righteous in Christ.

So this righteousness we are told to seek is not right behavior, but right standing before God, which comes to us as a gift when we receive salvation. At the cross, Jesus didn't just remove our sins, He also gave us His righteousness so that today, we can come boldly before the throne of God and receive freely everything that He died to give us!

Today, if you want to provide your family with the good things in life, be assured that your heavenly Father knows that you need these things. Just seek His righteousness, not your own righteousness, and "all these things shall be added to you"!

Thought for the Day
Jesus gave us His righteousness so that we can come boldly before the throne of God and receive freely everything that He died to give us!

Your 'Work' Is to Enter His Rest

Hebrews 4:10–11
¹⁰... he who has entered His rest has himself also ceased from his works as God did from His. ¹¹Let us therefore be diligent to enter that rest....

A baby learns to sit first before he starts to stand and walk. The Christian life also begins with sitting. God "raised us up together, and made us sit together in the heavenly places in Christ Jesus" (Ephesians 2:6). How well we walk after that depends on how well we sit and rest in the finished work of Christ.

The promised land was a land of rest where God promised His people "large and beautiful cities which you did not build, houses full of all good things, which you did not fill, hewn-out wells which you did not dig, vineyards and olive trees which you did not plant" (Deuteronomy 6:10–11).

But for 40 years, God's people wandered in the wilderness because they refused to believe that God had given them a land where everything had been prepared — the work was finished. They could not believe that God had given them a land full of riches to enjoy, a land which just flowed with His goodness.

Today, there are believers who still cannot believe that the work of Jesus is truly complete and finished. They are trying to complete a completed work, finish a finished work and defeat a defeated devil.

There are believers today who are always working and trying to produce their healing, prosperity, success and victory. God wants us to stop trying and start trusting in His love for us. He wants us to stop working and struggling, and start resting and believing in His grace toward us.

The only "work" left for us to do today is to enter His rest. We are to labor every day to enter His rest. We are to rest inwardly and believe that the work is done because it is a finished work, and trust in God's undeserved favor toward us. We are to rest in Jesus our true ark, who will carry us through tempestuous waters.

So today, "if you will hear His voice, do not harden your hearts... be diligent to enter that rest" (Hebrews 4:7, 11). Let's enter His rest. Let's enjoy sitting together with Christ in the heavenly places; then we will run and not be weary! (Isaiah 40:31.)

Thought for the Day
How well we walk depends on how well we sit and rest in Christ's finished work.

Nothing Is Wrong With God, His Word and You

Song of Solomon 4:7
⁷You are all fair, my love, and there is no spot in you.

Sometimes, when we don't receive our healing, breakthrough, restoration or miracle child, we can't help but think that something is wrong with us. We tell ourselves, "Nothing's wrong with God, nothing's wrong with the Word, so something must be wrong with me!" My friend, if you think that your miracle depends on you, then you are on shaky ground.

In the old covenant, we see this "it's all up to me" demand put on man. God's part was to bless His people, but only if they played their part by obeying all of His laws. If they didn't do their part, not only would they not be blessed, but the curse would also come on them.

Most of the time, they ended up under the curse because they just could not keep all of God's laws. So God found fault with that covenant because though He wanted to bless man, man's sins made it difficult for Him to do so. Man himself was the weak link.

In the new covenant, man has no part to play except to believe and receive. The new covenant of grace was cut between God the Father and God the Son — both infallible and more than able to keep the covenant.

God the Son is man's representative. Jesus represents you and me. So in this covenant, how much we can receive from God depends on how good our representative is, how perfect His obedience is. Of course, Jesus is the perfect Man with perfect obedience. So in Him, we are qualified to receive all the blessings of God! We only need to believe and receive.

Jesus' blood has been shed for the remission of all your sins. You are now the righteousness of God in Christ. (2 Corinthians 5:21.) By His one perfect sacrifice, He has perfected you forever. (Hebrews 10:14, KJV.) There is no spot in you!

Today, the devil has no right to tell you that you cannot be blessed because there is something wrong with you. So as you are waiting for your miracle, say, "Nothing's wrong with God, nothing's wrong with the Word and nothing's wrong with me! I am going to receive my miracle!"

Thought for the Day
By Jesus' one perfect sacrifice for all your sins, He has perfected you forever.

Is Anything Too Hard for God?

Jeremiah 32:27
27 "Behold, I am the Lord, the God of all flesh.
Is there anything too hard for Me?"

D o you have a problem believing that the moment a sinner receives Jesus Christ as his Lord and Savior, he is saved? I believe that you will say, "No."

Let me then ask you which is harder for God (though in reality, we know that nothing is hard for God): to save a soul from hell or heal a sick body? Of course, it is "harder" to save a soul from hell because God had to send His Son to the cross.

So if God has already given you the greatest miracle that you can ever receive, which is to pluck you out of the clutches of eternal damnation and give you eternal life, what is healing your body, saving your marriage, turning your rebellious teenage son around or giving you that business deal to Him?

Therefore, don't think that when you come to God with a headache, He says, "No problem," but should you come to Him with cancer, He says, "Cancer? Wow! Not that easy. This is more problematic. I will need more power!"

No! It may appear more difficult to us, but with God, nothing is too hard for Him because He says, "Behold, I am the Lord, the God of all flesh. Is there anything too hard for Me?"

This was indeed the case for a church member who was suffering from ovarian cancer. After I had prayed for her, I told her, "This cancer is not a problem for God. Just believe that when God said that nothing is too hard for Him, it is so!" In a matter of weeks, she came back with tears in her eyes, testifying that she went back to the doctor and he pronounced her healed after he could find no traces of cancer in her.

Beloved, if it is a miracle you need, it is a miracle you will get. God has already given you the greatest miracle of eternal life, so why would He not give you all the other lesser miracles?

Thought for the Day
When God says that nothing is too hard for Him, it is so!

Convince Yourself, Not God

Mark 5:28
²⁸For she said, "If only I may touch His clothes, I shall be made well."

With a crowd thronging Him, Jesus was touched by a lot of people that day (v. 31), but only the touch of one woman drew a response from Him. And her touch sparked off instant healing in her body, releasing her from a sickness that had plagued her for 12 years.

Do you want to know how to touch God and receive the miracle you need?

When the woman heard that Jesus was coming by her village, she said to herself, "If only I may touch His clothes, I shall be made well." On her way to see Jesus, she probably told herself many times, "If I touch His clothes, I will be healed. I will be made whole." We don't know how long she had been saying that to herself, but she was convinced that Jesus would heal her.

If you are sick, convince yourself that Jesus is your healer and that by His stripes you are healed. You don't need to convince God. He is not the one who needs to be persuaded because His blessing is already on you! It is **you** who needs to be persuaded that God has already given you your miracle. That is the reason you confess His Word — to convince yourself, not God, to persuade your heart, not His.

Some people confess their faith to others to convince God indirectly. For example, if they are believing God for healing, they go around telling their friends, "I am believing God for healing." They are actually trying to convince or persuade God to heal them. They are telling God, "I've told so many people what I am believing You for. It would be very embarrassing if You don't make it happen." Their confession proceeds from unbelief and is used to manipulate God.

It is okay to tell others if you want to, so that they can stand in faith with you for your miracle. But don't do it to prove your faith to God and to convince Him. You just need to convince yourself that God loves you and delights in blessing you. Just say to yourself, "By His stripes I am healed. I will not suffer lack. I am greatly blessed, highly favored, deeply loved!" And let God take care of the rest.

Thought for the Day
**It is you who needs to be persuaded that God has
already given you your miracle.**

Receive As You Hear the Good News

Romans 1:16
¹⁶For I am not ashamed of the gospel of Christ, for it is the
power of God to salvation for everyone who believes....

If you have been to motivational seminars, you would probably have heard the speakers say, "If you follow these five steps, then you will come to a place of financial increase." They would probably have told you also that if you don't succeed, it is because you did not follow the steps correctly or diligently.

Thank God that the gospel or good news does not work like that! The minute you hear or read the good news, and you believe and receive it, His Word goes forth to *sozo* (the Greek word for "save") you, making you well, prosperous and whole, "for it is the power of God to salvation for everyone who believes."

What is the good news? It is that God loves us so much that He gave us His Son to take our beating so that we can have His blessings without having to work for them. Right now, as you are reading this devotional, listening to a preacher or watching a sermon DVD; as you hear God's Word, His power is released into your situation, working things out for you and turning your situation around for your good.

In Acts 14:8–10, we see Paul preaching the good news in Lystra. A man who was crippled from birth was listening to Paul. Paul, seeing that he had faith to be healed, said, "Stand up straight on your feet!" And the man leaped and walked! He heard the good news, believed it and was healed.

At a leadership conference in Oslo, Norway, where I was speaking, a pastor there shared how a well-respected businessman in his church was healed while listening to one of my sermon CDs. This man was deaf in one ear. And when he was listening to my teaching on the CD, his deaf ear popped open without anyone laying hands on him or praying for him! He was just listening to the good news when his ear opened. Now, that is what I call the power of God unto his salvation, *sozo*-ing him, making his hearing whole!

My friend, these miracles happen not because we follow some kind of formula faithfully, but because we hear the good news preached and simply believe it!

Thought for the Day
Miracles happen when we hear the good news preached and simply believe it!

Surely!

Isaiah 53:4
⁴Surely He has borne our griefs [sicknesses] and carried our sorrows [pains]....

While waiting for the manifestation of their healing, some people find it hard to believe that Jesus really took their sicknesses and pains, just as He took their sin and shame. If you are one of them, don't feel condemned. Your Father in heaven understands. That is why He put the word "surely" there when He said, "**Surely**, My Son has borne your sicknesses and carried your pains."

Once, my daughter Jessica was crying all night because she was not feeling well. She had been sick for a few days. In my study, I took out my Bible and the Lord led me to Isaiah 53:4 where it says, "Surely He has borne..." Now, I know the original Hebrew here and it says, "Surely He has borne our sicknesses and carried our pains." So I said, "Surely, He has borne Jessica's sickness..."

But it was like the verse was just not real to me. Her cries seemed more real. Then, all of a sudden, the Holy Spirit opened my eyes to a word in the verse that really revolutionized the way I saw the whole passage.

Notice the first word in the verse? It says, "Surely..." Surely, He has borne our sicknesses and carried our pains. Now, look at the next verse: "He was wounded for our transgressions..." (v. 5). Every Christian knows and believes that Jesus was wounded for our sins, yet the word "surely" is not put here but in the earlier verse. I think God knew that we would find it hard to believe that Jesus also bore our sicknesses and carried our pains, so He put the word "surely" there to help us believe!

When I saw that, I put my Bible on the floor, stood on it and said, "Father, you know I don't mean any irreverence, but I am standing on Your Word. **Surely**, Jesus bore Jessica's sickness and carried her pain! I don't care if I can still hear her crying. **Surely**, Your Son, Your beloved Son, bore her sickness and carried her pain! Hallelujah!" That night, the breakthrough came. That night, little Jessica was healed.

Are you or your loved ones suffering some sickness or pain right now?

Surely our Lord Jesus has borne your sicknesses and carried your pains. And as you believe this truth, **surely**, your healing and breakthrough will come!

Thought for the Day
Surely our Lord Jesus has borne your sicknesses and carried your pains.

Don't Give Up at Thirtyfold!

Mark 4:8
*8"But other seed fell on good ground and yielded a crop that sprang up,
increased and produced: some thirtyfold, some sixty, and some a hundred."*

Perhaps you have marveled at God's instantaneous healing miracles. Perhaps you believed that He would do the same for you. But now, when you see your own healing taking so long to manifest, you are tempted to give up.

My friend, when the manifestation does not come instantaneously, we are not to be discouraged because Jesus let us in on a secret when He shared the parable of the sower. (Mark 4:3–20.)

The parable of the sower teaches us that once we receive God's Word into our hearts regarding our situation, God's blessings will manifest in progression. When we receive our thirtyfold manifestation, it means that 70 percent of that condition is still there. But some of us give up at thirtyfold because we still feel more pain than relief.

We need to realize that we are thirtyfold better than before, and our sixtyfold is coming! Once we receive our sixtyfold manifestation, there is still 40 percent that is not well. But we are more healed than sick now, and we only need to get ready for the hundredfold manifestation!

For years, I had a skin condition. Medication did not help and, finally, after I had done everything I knew to do, I decided to take the Holy Communion and pray about it. I said, "Father, I have an infirmity. I don't know what is hindering the physical manifestation of this healing. Holy Spirit, I am trusting You to make perfect intercession regarding the manifestation of my healing."

That was how I prayed for my skin condition. Did I look into the mirror to see if it had left? Of course I did! I am like anyone else. But did I stop praying? No, I kept on praying until one day, I heard a voice within me say, "Look at your body." When I looked into the mirror, the skin condition was completely gone! I was totally healed, but the manifestation of the healing was gradual.

Today, if you have seen only a thirtyfold increase in your situation, don't give up. The sixtyfold, then hundredfold increases are on their way to you!

Thought for the Day
*If you have seen only a thirtyfold increase in your situation, don't give up.
The sixtyfold, then hundredfold increases are on their way to you!*

God Can Use Those Whom the World Rejects

1 Corinthians 1:26
²⁶For you see your calling, brethren, that not many wise according to the flesh, not many mighty, not many noble, are called.

You may think that you are a nobody, maybe even a has-been or a loser in the eyes of the world. Take heart because God's Word says that if you are not wise, not mighty or not noble according to the flesh, then you are a prime candidate for Him to call on! And when He begins to use you, you will see His favor, power and increase change your life.

In the eyes of the ancient world, Moses was the rising star of Egypt. The Bible tells us that in the first 40 years of his life, "Moses was learned in all the wisdom of the Egyptians, and was mighty in words and deeds" (Acts 7:22). But God could not use him then because he was too smart, strong and full of himself.

It was only 40 years later, after having been in the unglamorous desert of Midian, emptied of himself and thinking that he was a has-been, that God sent him to confound the might of Pharaoh.

The world may pass them by — the weak, the small, the forgotten and the losers, but God chooses them to confound those mighty in the world.

I know this to be true. As a little boy, I grew up facing rejection and ridicule because of my Indian-Chinese racial mix. And as a teenager, I was the butt of many jokes because of my stammering and stuttering.

When I was in my teens, I remember praying to God, "I don't know what I can do for or give You, but You got me — spirit, soul and body." I don't know how many times I prayed that prayer. But I knew that God heard me because He called me. Only God would dare choose me, a stammerer and stutterer, to pastor a church for Him that has since grown to more than 16,000 members today.

I know what I was and where I came from. I know I have done nothing and can do nothing apart from His anointing and grace in my life.

My friend, when you think that you are weak and small compared to others in the world, that is when God can use you to do great and wonderful things for Him!

Thought for the Day
God chooses the weak, the small, the forgotten and the losers to confound those mighty in the world.

Covered, Protected, Delivered

Exodus 13:21
²¹And the Lord went before them by day in a pillar of cloud to lead the way,
and by night in a pillar of fire to give them light, so as to go by day and night.

When the children of Israel were wandering in the desert, God led them by going before them in a pillar of cloud by day and pillar of fire by night.

By day, God spread the pillar of cloud as a covering over His people in the desert to prevent the scorching sun from striking them down. The people were shaded and kept cool. Today, you are also under His covering. He will not allow you to be struck down (Psalm 121:3–8), nor be oppressed by the heat of the day. (Isaiah 54:14)

At night, when the desert became dark and cold, God gave His people the pillar of fire to light the way for them, as well as to keep them warm and safe. Today, as you walk with God, you will not be overwhelmed by the cold, dark places in life because God's Word says, "You are all sons of light and sons of the day. We are not of the night nor of darkness." (1 Thessalonians 5:5.) You will not fear the terror by night or the pestilence that walks in darkness because God will deliver you from them. (Psalm 91:5–6.)

Like the children of Israel, who only needed to look up, and keep their eyes on the pillar of cloud and the pillar of fire, all you need to do today is to look up and keep your eyes on Jesus. When you need His direction for a situation, look to Jesus who has the words of eternal life. (John 6:68.) When you see symptoms of sickness in your body, look to Jesus who has borne away every disease and physical affliction. (Matthew 8:17.)

When the children of Israel were bitten by serpents in the desert, God told Moses to make a bronze serpent and put it on a pole — a picture of Christ being judged on the cross. (John 3:14.) Those who looked at the bronze serpent instead of their wounds were healed. (Numbers 21:9.) He who looks to Jesus lives!

Beloved, look to Jesus. He is your covering, protection and deliverance!

Thought for the Day
All you need to do today is to look up and keep your eyes on Jesus —
your covering, protection and deliverance!

What Is on Your Heart?

Hebrews 8:10
10"... I will put My laws in their mind and write them on their hearts...."

Many of us have been taught that we cannot trust our hearts. We quote verses like "The heart is deceitful above all things, and desperately wicked..." (Jeremiah 17:9), not knowing that Jeremiah was referring to the man who had not received Jesus as his Lord and Savior.

I have had people come to me and say, "Pastor Prince, I don't know what I should do with my life."

"What is on your heart?" I asked one of them.

"I would love to work among children."

"Then work among children!"

"But I am waiting on the Lord to tell me to do that."

"Well, He has given you the desire, so go and work among children!"

"But the desire comes from my heart. How do I know if it is of God?"

My friend, once you are saved, you have a brand new heart (Ezekiel 36:26), and you can trust the promptings of your heart because God dwells in you and He leads you from within. And don't worry because His promptings will never contradict His Word. It will lead you to good success.

Often, you find that when you follow your inner promptings, it is actually God who has put those desires in your mind and written them on your heart. I remember years ago when I approached one of our church leaders and told him, "I really think that you are called to be a full-time pastor." It turned out to be a confirmation of what he already knew on the inside. You see, God was already leading him from within. Today, he is one of our full-time pastors.

If you enjoy something and desire to do it, then go for it! Go with the flow. God Himself says that He will guide us from within. Let's not doubt Him. And don't worry about the outcome. Your part is just to follow the flow. God's part is to work in you both the willingness and the performance of it! (Philippians 2:13.)

Beloved, because God has given you a new heart, He will write His desires on it. And as you fulfill these desires, you will bring forth fruit, and not wither and die. Whatever you do will prosper!

Thought for the Day
You can trust the promptings of your heart because God
dwells in you, and He leads you from within.

The Antidote to Fear

1 John 4:18
[18] There is no fear in love; but perfect love casts out fear....

Experts tell us that babies have two natural fears: the fear of falling and the fear of loud noises. A study on fear was conducted on 500 adults of varying ages, backgrounds and lifestyles. The results showed that they shared some 7,000 different fears. This means that they must have learnt 6,998 fears since they were born. That is a lot of fears!

Actually, our bodies are designed for faith. Fear was foreign to man until Adam sinned against God. For the first time, Adam knew fear, and he hid from God and said, "I heard Your voice… I was **afraid**… I hid myself" (Genesis 3:10).

Since then, man has been living in the realm of fear — fear of the future, fear of what others might say, fear of diseases, fear of flying… Actually, every fear is born out of the feeling of being cut off from God. If you think that God is still mad at you, that He is out to punish you, how can you have faith that everything will be all right? How can you have faith for your miracle?

But I have good news for you. There is a sure antidote to fear. The apostle John says that "perfect love casts out fear." When you know that God so loves you that He gave His Son to take your beating so that you can take His blessings, you will stop fearing.

God so loves you that at the cross, Jesus was rejected so that you could become God's beloved. It was not the nails that kept Jesus on the cross. It was His love for you. And if God did not withhold Jesus, why do you think that He will withhold healing, finances or a blessed marriage from you? (Romans 8:32.)

Today, when you hear His voice, you will hear Him say, "You are My beloved child, in you I am well pleased." And you don't have to hide but you can run to Him without fear because He is not out to punish you. He is out to protect, prosper and provide for you, so fear not!

Thought for the Day
Run to God without fear because He is not out to punish you,
but to protect, prosper and provide for you.

God Is Not Judging You

Romans 8:33
[33] Who shall bring a charge against God's elect? It is God who justifies.

Some people see God as a judge who has exacting demands on man. When they fall short or when things go wrong in their lives, they think that God is judging them.

My friend, the truth is that if you are a believer, God does not bring any charge against you. Instead, He justifies you because of the blood of His Son. In fact, God's Word goes on to say that the One who has the right to condemn you, chose instead to die for you and is risen at the Father's right hand to be your righteousness! (v. 34.)

But what the devil tries to do is to get you to believe that God watches you with a critical eye and punishes you when you do wrong. He has deceived many sincere Christians into believing that if they have done something wrong, sickness or some other evil thing has a right to come upon them and their families. And when these things happen, he convinces them that they are suffering God's judgment because of their wrongdoings. In the meantime, these sincere Christians struggle with condemnation because they think that they are the cause of their problems.

Nothing could be further from the truth. Ever since the cross, where Jesus was judged in your place for every one of your wrong actions, thoughts and words, God no longer judges you, His child. You need not accept condemnation or evil things happening to you because Jesus took all your punishment at the cross.

So when you start to feel condemned for your actions or when you experience negative circumstances, say, "It is written: It is God who justifies me. I am completely forgiven and made righteous before Him. I refuse to accept any condemnation and I reject every symptom of the curse that I am seeing in my circumstances!"

Then, simply stand on the truth of God's Word, and watch Him deliver and bless you!

Thought for the Day
Don't accept condemnation or evil things happening to you because Jesus took all your punishment at the cross.

Be Established in God's Righteousness

Isaiah 54:14
14In righteousness you shall be established; you shall be far from oppression,
for you shall not fear; and from terror, for it shall not come near you.

Have you ever asked yourself why some Christians are constantly beset with overwhelming challenges, sicknesses and defeat if God's promise, "No weapon formed against you shall prosper" (v. 17), is true?

Well, this promise comes with a condition — "In righteousness you shall be established." When you are established in righteousness, you will be far from oppression and terror, and not a single weapon formed against you will prosper!

This condition is not hard to meet. For a start, you already have righteousness! When you received Jesus as your Savior, you received the gift of righteousness, which enables you to reign in life. (Romans 5:17.) This righteousness does not come from you but the Lord. (Isaiah 54:17.) And when you are established in **His** righteousness, no weapon formed against you will prosper.

But what does being established in righteousness mean? To be established in something is to have that something as your very foundation for security. So God wants you to know, be sure of and grow in the revelation that you are righteous by the blood of Jesus, by His perfect sacrifice at the cross.

When you feel as if you are in a storm, tossed here and there, and you begin to experience worry and fear, remind yourself of who you are in Christ. You are the righteousness of God in Christ and you have His righteousness!

As you do this, you will begin to notice the worry and fear slide off you, for when you are established in righteousness, "you shall be far from oppression, for you shall not fear; and from terror, for it shall not come near you"! That is why God wants you to be established in righteousness. He wants you to be free from fear, and far from oppression and terror.

So when the pressure is on, hold fast to the belief that you are the righteousness of God in Christ. That is where no weapon formed against you can prosper. As you keep believing and confessing your righteousness in Christ, revelation will break forth and you will experience the release of God's miraculous provision, divine protection and blessings into your life!

Thought for the Day
When you are established in His righteousness,
no weapon formed against you will prosper!

Live the 'Much More' Life

Romans 5:17
[17]For if by the one man's offense death reigned through the one, much more those who receive abundance of grace and of the gift of righteousness will reign in life through the One, Jesus Christ....

When God created man, He did not intend for man to grow old, become weak and powerless, suffer diseases and die — first the physical death, then the second or eternal death.

God never meant for man to go through all these and for death to reign. But because of one man's offense — that man being Adam — death reigns.

The ultimate death is the second or eternal death in the lake of fire. Before this death is physical death. Before physical death, you have diseases and illnesses. Not all diseases and illnesses lead to death, but they are manifestations of death. One step before diseases and illnesses is tiredness, weakness and powerlessness, which are signs and symptoms of death. Now, all these are forms of death. As you can see, death reigns!

Are you resigned to the fact that death can strike whoever, whenever and wherever it wishes? Are you allowing death to reign in your life and in the lives of your loved ones? Or are you allowing God's Word to tell you the truth about death?

"For if by the one man's offense death reigned through the one, **much more...**" Thank God for the "much more"! What Jesus, the last Adam, did is much more and far greater than what the first Adam did. We are those who have received the "abundance of grace and of the gift of righteousness." Therefore, our "much more" is that we will reign in life through Jesus Christ!

God considers death an enemy. He came to destroy death and give us eternal life. And the more we walk in the grace of God and His righteousness, the more we will reign in life. The more we believe in His grace or undeserved favor, and the more we know that we have been made righteous by His blood and not our good behavior, the more we will reign over all forms of death!

Thought for the Day
The more we believe in His grace, the more
we will reign over all forms of death!

Come As You Are And Receive

Matthew 15:27
*²⁷And she said, "Yes, Lord, yet even the little dogs eat
the crumbs which fall from their masters' table."*

Come as you are to the Lord with your need, and lean on His unfailing and unconditional love for you. You don't have to pretend to be more than what you are to receive the blessing you need from God. You don't have to pretend to be someone else to appear more deserving to receive from God.

A Canaanite woman desperately seeking healing for her demon-possessed daughter came to Jesus. (vv. 22–28) Knowing that He healed and did miracles among the Jews, she pretended to be a Jew, calling out, "O Lord, Son of David!" (Only the Jews addressed Jesus as the "Son of David.") Jesus did not answer her. His silence made her drop her pretense and cry out, "Lord, help me!"

Only when her pretenses had melted away did she see the grace of God extended to her. Jesus made a way for her to receive her miracle even though it was not yet time for the Gentiles to receive His blessings. He told her, "It is not good to take the children's bread and throw it to the little dogs."

Many people might be offended at being called a "dog." Actually, the Greek word used here by Jesus means "puppy," and is thus an affectionate rather than offensive term. So this woman was not offended. In fact, she knew then that she could receive healing for her daughter because even puppies get to eat what falls from their masters' table.

She saw that the crumbs under the Master's table were enough for a Gentile, a "little dog," like herself. You must understand that the Jews then considered Gentiles dogs. But what Jesus was trying to say was that He was called to the Jews first, not the Gentiles. Yet, He loved this Gentile woman and her daughter enough to provide a "loophole" for them to receive their miracle.

So when the Canaanite woman took her place by dropping the title "Son of David" and just leaned on Jesus' compassion for her, her daughter was healed from that very hour.

If God was willing to extend His grace to a Gentile, how much more you, His beloved child! You do not need to depend on pretensions to receive a miracle from Him. Come as you are and lean on His grace. If He has delivered Jesus up for us, "how shall He not with Him also freely give us all things?" (Romans 8:32.)

Thought for the Day
Just come as you are to receive all that you need from God.

The Clause That Makes It All Happen

Hebrews 8:12
*¹²"For I will be merciful to their unrighteousness, and their
sins and their lawless deeds I will remember no more."*

We are no longer under the old covenant. We are now under the new covenant. And in this new covenant, God says that He will do three things for us:

Lead us — "I will put My laws in their mind and write them on their hearts" (v. 10). These are the laws of faith, love and liberty to guide you in everything you do. It is a spontaneous, dynamic, active and intimate way to be led by God.

Work miracles for us — "I will be their God, and they shall be My people" (v. 10). The phrase "I will be their God" denotes a miracle-working God. So if you are sick and God says, "I will be your God," get ready for healing! If you are poor and God says, "I will be your God," get ready for prosperity!

Cause us to know Him effortlessly — "… all shall know Me, from the least of them to the greatest of them" (v. 11). The Greek word for "know" here is *eido*. It means to know intuitively without effort. This means that you will know God easily.

Do you want to experience all these blessings in your life today?

"Of course, Pastor Prince, I want to be led by God. I want Him to work miracles in my life. I want to know Him intimately without straining or striving."

Then, you need to know the clause that makes it all happen: "For I will be merciful to their unrighteousness, and their sins and their lawless deeds I will remember **no more**." The words "no more" in the Greek carry a strong double-negative sense. So God is saying, "I will never, by no means, remember your sins!"

Beloved, the more you believe this in your heart, the more you will see those blessings fulfilled in your life. When you realize how much God has forgiven you and remembers your sins no more, you will know Him, His ways and His will for you intimately and intuitively without effort.

So believe in your heart today the clause on which all these blessings hinge, and get ready for miracles and hopes fulfilled in the days ahead!

Thought for the Day
**When you realize that God remembers your sins no more, you will know Him,
His ways and His will for you intimately and intuitively.**

'I Will Be Your God'

Hebrews 8:10
¹⁰ ... and I will be their God, and they shall be My people.

When God says, "I will be your God," that is a declaration that He will work miracles in your life. So if it is a miracle you need, it is a miracle you will get!

If there is a huge sea blocking the way to your blessing and God says, "I will be your God," it means that He will open the sea for you so that you can receive your blessing.

If you are poor and God says, "I will be your God," it means that you will be well-provided for. Since God fed nearly three million Israelites in the wilderness every single day for 40 years, you can be sure that God will provide for you too.

If you are sick and God says, "I will be your God," it means that He is going to be "the Lord who heals you" (Exodus 15:26), and you will be healthy.

If you have incurred a huge debt and God says, "I will be your God," it means that He will bring about a supernatural cancellation of your debt.

But not only did God say, "I will be their God," He also said, "they shall be My people."

To be God's people means to be the protected ones. Not all on earth are God's people — only we who are redeemed by the blood of Christ. During times of uncertainties, God says to you, "You shall be My people." This means that you are protected from all pestilences, plagues, attacks and destruction.

Even when you hear people say that the economic crisis is coming, God says to you, "You shall be My people." This means that you don't have to worry or be anxious. The crisis will not affect you. Regardless of the situation in the world, you are protected and you will walk in the blessings of God.

God's power comes into every challenge you face when He says to you, "I will be your God and you shall be My people." You will experience the supernatural life. Your part is to believe what He declares and act like it is so!

Thought for the Day
God's power comes into every challenge you face because
He says that He is your God and you are His people.

You Have the Victory!

Romans 8:37
37Yet in all these things we are more than
conquerors through Him who loved us.

If God's Word says that we are more than conquerors through Christ, then we are. We are not going to become, we already are. We may be experiencing some failures or setbacks in life right now, but only good will come out of our situations because God says that "in all these things we are more than conquerors." We **have** the victory!

You see, God has placed us in Christ, whom He has exalted to the highest place in the universe. We are not trying to get to victory ground. We are already on victory ground. We don't confess God's Word to get victory. We confess His Word because we already have the victory. We don't fight **for** victory. We fight **from** victory.

The devil will try to steal our victory. He will come against us with lies and fears, and cause us to be conscious of our failures, weaknesses and symptoms in areas such as our health. But we are not trying to be healed. We are already healed because God's Word declares that "by His stripes we are healed" (Isaiah 53:5).

A sister in our church was seeing two psychiatrists. She had been under psychiatric care and medication for panic attacks for the most part of her life. She said that when she started coming to church and learning about Jesus, the truth of God's Word began to dawn on her.

She started believing that victory over her condition was already hers and began confessing it. From then on, all her fears were removed and her panic attacks ceased. Today, she has a sound mind, is free from all medication and knows that her life is greatly blessed through Jesus who loves her.

My friend, the moment you accept Jesus as your Savior, you are born again and the new person inside you is more than a conqueror. You are already on victory ground and you have victory over every challenging situation in your life!

Thought for the Day
We don't fight for victory. We fight from victory.

How Do You See God?

Luke 7:9
*⁹When Jesus heard these things, He marveled at him, and
turned around and said to the crowd that followed Him,
"I say to you, I have not found such great faith, not even in Israel!"*

The way you see Jesus, the revelation that you have of Him, will not affect God's acceptance of you. But it will affect your acceptance of what God has for you. It will affect how you receive from Him.

Consider the Roman centurion who told Jesus, "You don't have to come to my house. Just speak the word and my servant at home will be healed." (vv. 6–7.) Compare him with Jairus, the ruler of a synagogue, who told Jesus, "My daughter is dying. Please come to my house and lay Your hands on her, and she shall live." (Mark 5:22–23.)

Do you know that Jesus does not have to go to your house to heal you? So why did Jesus follow Jairus to his house? Jesus had to come down to Jairus' level of faith. Jairus believed that his daughter could be healed, but only if Jesus came and laid His hands on her.

The centurion was different. He said, "Lord, You don't have to come to my house. I know who You are." This centurion believed that Jesus did not have to come to his house for his servant to be healed. He believed that Jesus only needed to speak the word. He said to Jesus, "Just speak the word and my servant at home will be healed."

Do you know who Jesus is? The centurion had a greater understanding of who Jesus is than Jairus, the ruler of the synagogue, and he wasn't even a Jew!

Jesus asked his disciples, "Why are you so fearful? How is it that you have no faith?" (Mark 4:40). He even remarked, "O you of little faith" (Matthew 6:30). But to the woman whose daughter was demon-possessed, He said, "O woman, great is your faith!" (Matthew 15:28). And to the centurion, He declared, "I have not found such great faith, not even in Israel!"

My desire is for you to have an accurate understanding of who Jesus is because when your revelation of Jesus is big, you will know what has been freely given to you. And when you know what is yours in Christ Jesus, you will be rich in all things!

Thought for the Day
The size of your revelation of Jesus will affect how you receive from Him.

You Have It, So Say It!

Matthew 25:29
[29]'For to everyone who has, more will be given, and he will have abundance;
but from him who does not have, even what he has will be taken away.'

Have you come across people who have little, yet even that little is taken away from them? On the other hand, there are those who already have much, yet they receive even more.

Jesus said, "To everyone who has, more will be given. From him who does not have, even what he has will be taken away." Notice that Jesus doesn't go on to say what it is we have. He simply says, "But to everyone who has."

Jesus is talking about a firm belief in God's Word that gives one the courage to say, "I have it!" If you say that you have it, you have it, and more will be given to you. But if you say that you don't have it, when you actually do because God has freely given us all things (Romans 8:32), then even what you have will be taken away — not by God but by the devil! The devil does not want you to walk in God's blessings. So when you say that you don't have it, he can rob you of your blessings because he has your agreement!

When you need something, God says that you are to ask of Him. And when you ask, believe that you receive it. (Mark 11:24.) Say you already have it even if you don't see it in the physical realm yet, and one day, you will see it!

God is not saying, "Oh come on, pretend that you see it. And if you pretend long enough, you will have it." This is not a game! God is telling us to call forth those things which don't exist as though they do. (Romans 4:17.)

Today, we are talking about the haves and have-nots in the church. If you believe that it is yours, you will have it. You will see yourself possessing it and enjoying it, and more will be given to you. But if you say, "Well, I don't feel it and I'm not sure if it will come," in essence, you are saying that you don't have it when you actually do. Then, even what you have will be taken away. So say you have it today!

Thought for the Day
If you believe that it is yours, you will have it.

Redeemed From Every Type of Sickness

Galatians 3:13
¹³Christ has redeemed us from the curse of the law, having become a curse for us (for it is written, "Cursed is everyone who hangs on a tree").

The One who cleansed lepers, opened blind eyes and made the lame to walk took your sins, sicknesses and every curse when He hung on Calvary's tree. The curses that were meant for you because of your sins fell on Him instead. He was cursed in your place to redeem you from every curse that comes as a result of breaking God's laws.

What are these curses? They are listed in Deuteronomy 28. It is a long and detailed list. Don't get frightened when you read the curses, but rejoice because Christ has redeemed you from every single one of them, including those curses of sicknesses!

Are you stricken with tuberculosis, fever or inflammation? (Deuteronomy 28:22.) Christ has redeemed you from every one of these conditions!

Do you have painful boils, tumors or an itch which doctors say cannot be healed? (Deuteronomy 28:27.) Christ has redeemed you from every one of these conditions!

Perhaps yours is a serious and prolonged sickness. (Deuteronomy 28:59.) It doesn't matter. Christ has redeemed you from every prolonged sickness!

"Well, Pastor Prince, you have covered tuberculosis, fever, itch… but what about my disease? It is not covered in Deuteronomy 28. Did Jesus forget my disease?"

No, His work is perfect! Look at Deuteronomy 28:61: "Also every sickness and every plague, which is not written in this Book of the Law, will the Lord bring upon you until you are destroyed." That covers everything. So if Christ has redeemed you from this curse, then He has redeemed you from **every** type of sickness! I don't care what new type of sickness the world discovers because Christ has redeemed us from **every** type of sickness!

Now, if you have a particular sickness, say, "This (name the sickness) is part of the curse of the law. But Galatians 3:13 says that Christ has redeemed me from the curse of the law. Therefore, I have been redeemed from (name the sickness)!" Believe and confess that every day, and as surely as Jesus took every curse of sickness, your healing will break forth!

Thought for the Day
As surely as Jesus took every curse of sickness, your healing will break forth!

God's Superabounding Grace for You

2 Corinthians 9:8
⁸And God is able to make all grace abound toward you, that you, always having all sufficiency in all things, may have an abundance for every good work.

If you were in the same synagogue as the man with the withered hand (Luke 6:6–11), how would you see him and what do you think you would say to him?

Jesus was preaching in that synagogue when He saw the man with the withered hand. But He also saw superabounding grace around that hand for healing and wholeness. He sees differently from us. He sees the invisible. He sees that the kingdom of God is here, ever-present in any situation, with superabundant supply. We see only the visible, which is tangible, temporal and which seems so real to us.

But Jesus saw superabounding grace on that withered hand for healing because you do not tell a man with a withered hand, "Stretch out your hand," unless you see the supply, the superabundance for wholeness for that hand. Jesus called forth the superabounding grace to envelop that man's withered hand, and the hand was made whole.

It is possible for someone who is sick to have superabounding grace on him and yet that superabundance of grace does not heal his body. That is because he keeps acknowledging the lack or the problem he sees. He is more concerned with that which is visible and temporal.

Instead of calling forth, and acknowledging and confessing the superabundance of God's grace, he confesses his negative circumstance all the time. So even though the superabounding grace is there, it is there in vain. Isn't that sad?

Jesus called forth life, and life sprang into visibility. We must call forth what we want to see. Say, "Father, I thank You that right now, though my health is under attack, there is superabounding grace available for my healing and health. I call it forth and receive it now in Jesus' name. Amen!"

My friend, don't be conscious of what you see lacking or missing. Be conscious of God's superabounding grace for you and avail yourself of it!

Thought for the Day
See the kingdom of God ever-present in every situation,
with superabundant supply for you.

Nothing Shall by Any Means Hurt You!

Luke 10:19
¹⁹Behold, I give you the authority to trample on serpents and scorpions,
and over all the power of the enemy, and nothing shall by any means hurt you.

Years ago, while traveling on a domestic flight in the United States, I was seated next to a woman whose whole body was tense with fear. Concerned, I asked if I could help her in any way. Between sobs, she told me about her fear of flying. I told her, "Don't worry. I am on board. Nothing will happen to the plane." I did not say it with pride. I said it knowing that the Lord was on board the plane with me and that I would have a safe journey because He has promised that "nothing shall by any means hurt you."

Once, when Jesus was in the boat with his disciples, He told them, "Let us cross over to the other side." (Mark 4:35.) Believing that they would cross over to the other side, He fell asleep in the stern. A great storm arose, but it could not rouse Him from His sleep, only the cries of His terrified disciples did. They had forgotten what Jesus had said about them crossing over to the other side. They had also forgotten that with Jesus in the boat with them, there was no possibility of them going down. Nothing could by any means hurt them because Jesus was with them.

Even being thrown into a fiery furnace could not hurt three young Hebrew men because they believed that God would deliver them. They had proclaimed to the heathen King Nebuchadnezzar, "...our God whom we serve is able to deliver us from the burning fiery furnace, and He will deliver us from your hand, O king." (Daniel 3:17.) And in the midst of their fiery trial, their deliverer not only walked with them in the fire, He also delivered them from all harm. King Nebuchadnezzar even said, "Look!... I see four men loose, walking in the midst of the fire; and they are not hurt, and the form of the fourth is like the Son of God" (v. 25).

Beloved, in the midst of your storm or fiery trial, because Jesus is with you, nothing shall by any means hurt you!

Thought for the Day
Nothing shall by any means hurt you because Jesus is with you!

You Are Complete in Christ

Colossians 2:10
¹⁰You are complete in Him, who is the head of all principality and power.

When you look at yourself, what do you see? Do you see someone who is imperfect and lacking in many areas, or someone who is whole and complete in Christ?

There are believers who see themselves as incomplete. This is because they are conscious of their lack and imperfections. They say, "There are so many things imperfect about me! How can I be complete if there are so many things I am lacking in?" They see their weaknesses, condemn themselves and feel inferior to others.

The good news is that God does not see the way man sees. Man sees the flesh. God sees the spirit. He sees us already **complete** in Christ. In spite of our imperfections, He sees us as new creations, partakers of His divine nature and more than conquerors over our faults. And He wants us to see ourselves the way He sees us.

What we think we need or are lacking in, whether it is godly character traits or physical health, we already have in Christ.

I used to think that I had to ask God to make me more patient, until I realized one day that Jesus **is** my patience. Since then, I no longer ask God to make me wiser either, because Jesus **is** my wisdom. (1 Corinthians 1:30.) I am not waiting to receive more healing because Jesus **is** my complete healing at this moment. And I am not yearning for peace and rest one day because Jesus **is** my peace and rest today. Right now, I have everything because I stand complete in Christ!

My friend, you are not going to be complete in Christ some day — you are already complete in Christ! And what remains for you to do is to walk daily in that completeness by believing that it is true and confessing that what you need right now, Jesus is to you. He is your complete forgiveness, complete righteousness, complete favor and complete protection.

So don't focus on the lack you see in your life. Focus instead on how in Christ, you are complete in everything at this moment. And instead of weaknesses, lack and defects, you will see His strength, wholeness, soundness and completeness manifesting in you!

Thought for the Day
Don't focus on the lack in your life. Focus on how in Christ,
you are complete in everything at this moment!

Blessed Wherever You Are

Deuteronomy 28:3
³"Blessed shall you be in the city, and blessed shall you be in the country."

You may have heard of people who think that to have better "luck," they have to move to a new home, work for a certain company or even migrate to another country.

The truth is that it is not the place that gets you the blessings, but whether God's blessing is on you. And for you, child of God, you are already blessed with all spiritual blessings in Christ Jesus. (Ephesians 1:3.) He has paid for your blessings with His blood. So the blessing is not on the land but on the man!

It was in the city of Jerusalem that Jesus was whipped, cursed and spat on. And it was outside the city on Calvary's hill that He was pierced and crucified. That is why you are blessed in the city as well as outside in the country! In fact, you are blessed regardless of your location.

Perhaps you work in a non-Christian company and your boss doesn't quite like you. In fact, he sometimes mistreats you. But God can still bless you in spite of your boss. You get blessed because you believe God for it. It has nothing to do with your boss or the company.

Why then don't you seem to see the blessings?

My friend, if you don't see the blessings, check what you have been believing and saying. Some people complain and blame everyone and everything around them — their parents, race, gender, environment and government — for their lack of blessings. Beloved, I want you to believe and confess that you are blessed because of Jesus' finished work on the cross, not because you are of a certain race or work in a certain place.

It does not matter where you work or live, what color your skin is or what you do for a living. If God blesses you, you are blessed! And it is all because of Jesus. So say to yourself, "I am blessed wherever I am — blessed in the city, blessed in the country!"

Thought for the Day
God's blessing is not on the land but on the man!

The Blood of Jesus Protects

Exodus 12:13
¹³... And when I see the blood, I will pass over you; and the plague
shall not be on you to destroy you when I strike the land of Egypt.

For 400 years, the children of Israel were slaves in Egypt. Life for them was one of hard labor, pain, loss and even death. When Moses, their deliverer, came, what soon followed was one plague after another on the Egyptians. But none of the plagues caused Pharaoh to release the Israelites until they put the blood of a lamb on their doorposts. What nine plagues could not do, the blood did! The Israelites were finally set free because of the blood.

Are you under any kind of bondage? Are your loved ones held captive by the destroyer, who is bent on destroying them? Plead the blood of the Lamb of God over all that is yours and your family's. When nothing else seems to work, His blood always works!

When I was a teenager doing a stint as a relief teacher in a primary school, one of the girls in my class was absent from school one day. I didn't think too much about her absence until I returned home that afternoon. As I was praying, I was prompted by the Holy Spirit to pray for her protection and to cover her with the precious blood of Jesus.

It was revealed later on that she had been abducted by a notorious serial killer who had murdered a number of young children. My pupil recounted how she had been tied up and offered to the "deities" the killer had in his flat. Miraculously, he released her when the evil spirits found her to be an unsuitable offering.

Why was this pupil released unharmed? I believe that she was presented to the "deities" on the same afternoon that I pleaded the blood of Jesus over her. Of course, the evil spirits did not want her because the Most High God would not allow them to have her. God was protecting her. She was set free because of the blood of Jesus!

You see, when you plead the blood of Jesus, the destroyer cannot come near. When he sees the blood, he must respect the blood. He cannot touch what is covered by the blood. The blood of Jesus truly protects and sets you free!

Thought for the Day
When you plead the blood of Jesus, the destroyer cannot come near.

Let God Love You Instead

1 John 4:10
¹⁰In this is love, not that we loved God, but that He loved us and
sent His Son to be the propitiation for our sins.

"You have to love God more! You must have more passion for God!" You have probably heard this type of preaching and may have even tried your best to love God, only to fail miserably.

But what is the true definition of love? Let the Bible define it for us: "… this is love, not that we loved God, but that He loved us…" Yes, it is not about **our** love for Him, but **His** love for us!

"Pastor Prince, the Bible says that you must love God with all your heart, soul and strength!"

Yes, that is true according to the law (Deuteronomy 6:5), and even Jesus taught that as the great commandment when He walked on earth. (Matthew 22:37.) But that was before He died on the cross. At the cross, He became the very fulfillment of this law for us when **He** loved us with all His heart, soul and strength, by laying down His body and life on the cross for us.

Today, we are no longer under the law but under grace. And grace tells us that God loves us, not that we love God. Yet, we **will** love Him when we see how much He loves us. The Bible says that "while we were still sinners, Christ died for us"! (Romans 5:8.) That's how much He loves us!

Beloved, God has seen you trying your best to love Him. And because He loves you, He wants you to sit down and be still, and let Him love you instead. He wants to love you with all that He is and all that He has. He loves you unconditionally regardless of who you are or what you have done because His love is not dependent on you but on Himself. He will never stop loving you.

So let God love you today. Don't worry about loving Him. The more of His love you receive, the more you will fall in love with Him!

Thought for the Day
God loves you with all that He is and all that He has.

God Will Never Turn His Back on You

Hebrews 13:5
⁵… He Himself has said, "I will never leave you nor forsake you."

For six whole hours, the Son of God was suspended between heaven and earth. And at the height of His suffering on the cross, He cried out in the deep darkness, "My God, My God, why have You forsaken Me?" (Matthew 27:45–46).

For the first time, Jesus addressed His Father as "God." The Father had forsaken the Son. As Judge of the universe, God had to turn His back on His Son, who was carrying the filth of the world's sins, for His eyes are too pure to behold evil. (Habakkuk 1:13.)

If the Father had not turned His back on His Son, He would have to turn His back on you today when you call out to Him in your hour of need. But because Jesus has taken your place, today, you take His place, and you have God's face smiling on you always!

Right now, God's face is smiling on you. His countenance is shining on you. I can stand before you and declare, "The Lord make His face shine upon you" (Numbers 6:25–26). And it is all because Jesus has paid the price for God to never leave you nor forsake you. (Hebrews 13:5.)

As Judge, God turned His back on His Son. But as Father, He cried. His heart was broken because Christ was never more pleasing to Him than when He was on the cross. Christ's suffering was a sweet-smelling aroma to the Father. (Ephesians 5:2.)

Do you remember what Jesus said? "Therefore My Father loves Me, because I lay down My life that I may take it again." (John 10:17.) If you are a parent, you love each one of your children equally. But when one of them does something special for you out of love, it touches your heart, and you just want to run to him and hug him.

That was what happened at the cross, except that the Father could not embrace His Son. Instead, He had to turn His back on His Son because our sins had to be punished in His Son's body.

Beloved, when you cry out to the Father for help today, know that He hears you and will surely help you. Because of Jesus, He will never turn His back on you!

Thought for the Day
Because Jesus has taken your place at the cross,
God's face is always smiling on you!

God Can Turn Your Evil Day Into Good Days

Esther 9:22
²²... rest from their enemies... sorrow to joy... mourning to a holiday....

Today, many Jews still celebrate the feast of Purim. The name *Purim* is derived from "the lot" which a Gentile, Haman, cast concerning the fate of the Jews when they were in Persia under King Ahasuerus.

Haman, the villain in this story in the book of Esther, hated the Jews and sought to exterminate them. He got King Ahasuerus to allow him to issue a decree to annihilate all the Jews in one day — the thirteenth day of the twelfth month of Adar. But God used Queen Esther and her uncle Mordecai, both Jews, to turn the tables on Haman and save the Jews.

Haman was hanged on the very gallows that he had constructed for Mordecai! Then, the king allowed Queen Esther and Mordecai to issue a counter-decree to allow all the Jews to defend themselves and destroy their enemies in one day — the thirteenth day of the twelfth month of Adar!

So instead of the Jews being exterminated on that fateful day, their enemies were destroyed! God turned an evil day for the Jews into good days. He turned their mourning into rejoicing and gave them victory over their enemies.

My friend, God can do the same for you today. He only wants you to remain in your position of rest in Christ. You see, because of Jesus' finished work at the cross, you are seated in heavenly places in Christ, far above every principality, and evil assault the devil can throw at you. (Ephesians 2:6.) Just as Mordecai sat within the king's gate, and refused to stand up and bow to Haman, let's not "bow" to the devil by being persuaded to move from our position of rest in Christ. Don't allow him to get you worried, frantic and doing things to save yourself.

Queen Esther was also in a position of rest before Haman was executed. (Esther 7.) She was seated on a couch as Haman pleaded with her for his life. While doing so, he accidentally fell over the couch where the queen was. The king, thinking that Haman was assaulting his queen, sent him to the gallows!

Beloved, remain at rest in Christ's finished work, and He will turn your evil day into days of rejoicing and feasting!

Thought for the Day
Remain at rest in Christ's finished work, and He will turn your
evil day into days of rejoicing and feasting!

The Reason for the Resurrection

Romans 4:25
²⁵Who [Jesus] was delivered up because of our offenses,
and was raised because of our justification.

The Bible tells us that Christ was delivered up for our sins and raised from the dead for our justification. You may already know why Jesus died for our sins, but do you know the significance of God raising Him from the dead?

Let me give you an illustration to help you understand the significance of Jesus' resurrection.

Let's say that you are living in a foreign country. One day, you happen to break a major rule of the land. You appeal to the king for mercy. He says, "A rule is a rule. I cannot bend the rule for you. What will others say about my integrity? However, if you can find a substitute to take your punishment — three months in jail — I will allow it."

By God's grace, you find a willing substitute. He goes to prison on your behalf and you don't see him for some time. Days, weeks and months pass by.

Now, how or when will you know that your crime has been fully paid for? When will you be able to rest easy regarding your crime? It is when you see your substitute walking free again! When you see him out of prison, you will know that the sentence has been fully served. You will know that you are now justified and no one can bring a charge against you for your old crime. No longer will you be afraid of the king or his guards coming after you because you know that the one who was punished in your place is now walking free.

Beloved, Jesus, your substitute, paid the debt you could not pay. On the cross, He bore the sins of your entire life. God put it all on Jesus and then He punished Jesus for every single one of those sins until He was fully satisfied. And because He was so pleased with what Jesus had done, He raised Him from the dead.

Today, Jesus' tomb remains empty. He is not there for He has risen! His resurrection and empty tomb will forever be our assurance that we have been fully justified. You no longer have to be afraid of God judging you for your sins. His justice is on your side today!

Thought for the Day
Jesus' resurrection and empty tomb will forever be our
assurance that we have been fully justified!

See God As a Good Father

Luke 15:31
³¹"And he said to him, 'Son, you are always with me,
and all that I have is yours.'"

Faith is believing that we have a good God, and that He protects and provides for those who trust in Him. Remember the parable of the prodigal son? (Luke 15:11–32.) Jesus shared it to illustrate how good our heavenly Father is. The wayward son had squandered his father's inheritance before he decided to go home to ask his father to make him a hired servant.

But before he could reach home, his father saw him from afar, ran toward him and embraced him. And instead of making him a hired servant, the father turned to his servants and said, "Bring out the best robe! Get a ring and sandals for my son! Let's kill the fatted calf and celebrate!"

Now, when the older son returned from work and heard about the celebration, he became angry and refused to enter the house. When his father came out to ask him what was wrong, the older son complained, "Look, I've served you all these years. Yet, you never gave me a calf to celebrate with my friends. But as soon as this prodigal son of yours comes home, you kill the fatted calf for him!"

Notice what his father told him: "Son, you are always with me and all that I have is yours. We should celebrate because your brother was dead but is alive again. He was lost but is now found."

Can you see how the older brother perceived his father? He saw his father as a hard and stingy man. He believed that he had to work to get something good from his father. He didn't realize that he already had an inheritance! He could have killed the fatted calf any time for a celebration!

Like the father in the parable, God has already given you an inheritance in Christ. Don't fail to enjoy it by doubting God's goodness or by believing that you must work for it. See your Father's heart of love and goodness toward you, and celebrate your inheritance today!

Thought for the Day
Faith is believing that you have a good Father
who protects and provides for His children.

The King Is Not Angry With You

Proverbs 19:12
¹²The king's wrath is like the roaring of a lion,
but his favor is like dew on the grass.

The Bible tells us that the devil walks about like a roaring lion, seeking whom he may devour. (1 Peter 5:8.) But have you ever wondered why he acts like a roaring lion?

It has something to do with a lion's roar. In the Bible, the roaring of a lion speaks of the king's wrath — "The king's wrath is like the roaring of a lion." So when the devil walks about like a roaring lion, he is trying to give you the impression that the King is angry with you. And when you believe that God is angry with you, the devil knows that he has got you.

When you think that God is angry or displeased with you, you will not be confident of His love toward you. Instead, you will expect and fear punishment from Him. And you will want to stay away from Him because you do not wish to incur His wrath any further.

But the truth is that God is not angry with you, even when you fail or blow it, because all your sins have already been judged in the body of His Son at the cross. As the Lamb of God, Jesus became your burnt offering. That is why He said, "I thirst!" (John 19:28).

Those who heard Him say that at Calvary that day thought that His thirst was physical. Actually, His thirst was spiritual because He was being "burnt" by the fire of God's wrath. He was being judged for our sins. His body exhausted all of God's wrath until every claim of God's holiness was satisfied and His wrath appeased!

Now, there is a law called "the law of double jeopardy," which states that the same crime cannot be tried twice. Today, the fire of God's wrath will never fall on you as a believer because it has already fallen on His Son at the cross. He judged your sins then, but in the body of His Son.

So right now, you are not under the King's wrath but His favor. And His favor rains down on you like dew on the grass every morning!

Thought for the Day
You are not under the King's wrath but His favor.

Confessing Your Righteousness Pleases God

Romans 10:6
⁶... the righteousness of faith speaks....

Every time you confess, "I am the righteousness of God in Christ," God the Father is pleased. When you confess that you are the righteousness of God in Christ, it reminds Him of what His Son has done for you to become righteous.

Also, by making you righteous, God is showing Himself righteous — "to demonstrate at the present time His righteousness, that He might be just and the justifier of the one who has faith in Jesus" (Romans 3:26).

Each time Jesus hears you confess, "I am the righteousness of God in Christ," it brings much pleasure to His heart too, because you are laying hold of what He suffered and died to give you.

The Holy Spirit, who now indwells you to convict you of righteousness (John 16:7-8,10), also rejoices when you confess, "I am the righteousness of God in Christ." He is pleased when you flow with Him.

The delight of the Godhead is not the only thing you gain when you declare, "I am the righteousness of God in Christ." The Bible tells us that when you "seek first the kingdom of God and **His righteousness**... all these things shall be added to you" (Matthew 6:33).

Whether it is food, clothing or other necessities in life, "all these things" will be added to you. They will not just be given to you, but **added** to you as your inheritance when you seek first His righteousness.

You don't need to use your faith for every single need in life. You just need to use your faith for one thing — to believe that you are the righteousness of God in Christ, and it will cause all the blessings you seek to come after you and overtake you!

Thought for the Day
Use your faith to simply believe that you are the righteousness of God in Christ, and the blessings you seek will come after you and overtake you!

Your Sins Are Not Being Recorded

Hebrews 8:12
¹²"For I will be merciful to their unrighteousness, and their sins
and their lawless deeds I will remember no more."

I once read a comic book which showed how a man lusted after a woman, then died of a heart attack and went to heaven. In heaven, he saw a big screen showing everyone present a recording of all the sins which he had committed while on earth, including the last one. How embarrassing!

Don't worry, that is not going to happen to you in heaven. There is no big screen with front-row and circle seats for everyone to sit and watch your past sins. There is no video recorder in heaven recording your sins right now. Because your lifetime of sins has already been punished in the body of Jesus, God declares to you, "Your sins and lawless deeds, I will by no means ever remember!"

This is true even for the Old Testament heroes of faith such as Abraham, Moses and David. If you read Hebrews 11, which was written after the cross of Jesus, you will notice that there is no record of their sins or failures. Yet, their life stories tell us that they were far from perfect.

Abraham lied twice about his wife, Sarah. He told Pharaoh, and later, King Abimelech, that she was his sister to protect his own life. Moses killed an Egyptian who was beating a Hebrew, and hid the body in the sand. David committed adultery with Bathsheba and later arranged for her husband to be killed in battle. Yet, their sins were not recorded in Hebrews 11, only their deeds done in faith!

God is showing you that He does not record your sins or failures today. Instead, He records your faith confessions and deeds done in response to what His Son has done for you. Every time you sin, every time you waver in your faith, God does not record it. But every time you believe Him and respond in faith, He records it! That should not make you want to sin more. It should free you to love God more!

So don't be conscious of your failures. If God Himself does not remember them, who are you to remember them? Be conscious instead of your righteousness in Christ (2 Corinthians 5:21), and you will reign in life! (Romans 5:17.)

Thought for the Day
Don't be conscious of your failures because
God Himself does not remember them.

Jesus Delights in You
Drawing From Him

John 4:32
³²But He said to them, "I have food to eat of which you do not know."

When people make demands on you or keep depending on you, you may end up stressed, tired and irritable. But this is not the case with Jesus. When people draw from Him, He is strengthened and refreshed!

Jesus is, after all, God. And you honor God when you take your place as man and let God be God by drawing from Him. The One who said, "[I] did not come to be served, but to serve" (Matthew 20:28), loves it when you allow Him to minister to you.

The Bible tells us that when Jesus arrived at Sychar, He was wearied from the journey and rested at a well. A sinful Samaritan woman then came to the well to draw water. Jesus ministered to her and she left rejoicing with the promise of living water. The disciples, having returned with food for Jesus, found Him already strengthened and refreshed. When they wondered who had given Him food while they were away, He told them, "I have food to eat of which you do not know" (John 4:1–42).

Today, when you draw from Jesus and let Him minister to you, it is "food" for Him that "refreshes" and "strengthens" Him.

But it takes humility for us to allow Jesus to minister to us. We take pride in doing things for the Lord. We want to build our businesses, families and ministries for Him. All that is good, but without Jesus, we are spiritually bankrupt! We really have nothing to give to the Lord and His work. What we need to do first is to receive from Him because when we freely receive from Him, we are able to freely give. (Matthew 10:8.)

My friend, Jesus wants to minister to you. Don't try to minister to yourself. That is pride and self-righteousness. The Pharisees of Jesus' day, who felt that they did not need Him and that they could provide for themselves, were the ones who could not receive from Him. So bring to Him your needs and say, "Lord, I need to draw from You. I present my needs to You. Minister to me and meet my needs. I cannot, but You can. Thank you, Lord."

Thought for the Day
We need to first receive from Jesus before we are able to freely give.

God Says 'I Will' in the New Covenant

Hebrews 8:10,12
10"... I will put My laws in their mind... I will be their God...
12... I will be merciful to their unrighteousness...
their sins and their lawless deeds I will remember no more."

You may be feeling stressed at work today because your boss just gave you a list of things to do. Maybe he told you, "You have to type this letter. You have to meet this client. You have to write this report. You have to..." Wouldn't it be nice if your boss had, instead, said, "I will type this letter for you. I will meet this client for you. I will write this report for you. I will...?"

Well, your boss may not be that gracious, but your Father in heaven is! When He found fault with the old covenant and established the new covenant (Hebrews 8:7–8) in His Son's blood, His "Thou shalls" became "I wills."

You see, under the old covenant, the focus is on **you** — **Thou** shall not... **Thou** shall not... **Thou** shall not... It is all about your performance, your obedience, your works. But under the new covenant, God says, "**I** will put My laws in their mind... **I** will be their God... **I** will be merciful to their unrighteousness... their sins and their lawless deeds **I** will remember no more." It is no longer you working for God, but God working for you, in you, through you!

"Isn't there something for me to do?" you may ask.

My friend, the only thing for you to do is to believe God's "I wills." The more you believe His "I wills" or promises, the more you will see His heart for you and the more your faith will grow.

It is foolish for me to just tell you, "Come on, man, have faith!" You will still find it hard to have faith because I am not giving you anything to build faith in you. But if I were to tell you all about what God says He will do for you, faith will arise in your heart. Faith is a response to knowing what God says He will do for you.

So the best thing you can "do" under the new covenant is to not focus on what you must do for God, but what God says He will do for you!

Thought for the Day
The more you know what God will do for you,
the more faith will arise in your heart.

Receive By Grace Through Faith

Galatians 3:5
⁵Therefore He who supplies the Spirit to you and works miracles among you,
does He do it by the works of the law, or by the hearing of faith?

I magine that you are at a healing service. An alcoholic walks into the church reeking of alcohol. He sits behind the pianist, a nice elderly lady who has been serving in the church for 50 years. Both of them are suffering from rheumatoid arthritis. The healing power of God is present. In an instant, the alcoholic, who has never been in church before, gets healed. The pianist does not.

Most people, on hearing stories like this, would get upset and confused. They might ask, "Shouldn't God heal this nice old lady who has been serving Him faithfully all these years, and not that debauched drunkard?" You see, many people still believe that God heals only the deserving.

But that is not how God works. God looks at faith, not works. His power is made manifest in those who trust His goodness instead of their good behavior. So if we go back to the above example, God wants to heal both the alcoholic and the nice elderly pianist. All they need to do is to receive by grace, or unmerited favor, through faith.

You see, we cannot earn the blessings of God. We receive them by believing God's love and grace toward us. If we receive the greatest blessing — salvation — by simply believing that Jesus did it all for us and not by working for it, what makes us think that the other lesser blessings can be obtained by our works?

So if my daughter Jessica falls sick, I don't go to the Father and say, "Father, heal my daughter because I am Pastor Joseph Prince and I preach healing to the people." No, I go to Him by the blood of Jesus and say, "Father, I thank You that 2,000 years ago, Jesus bore Jessica's sickness in His body. On that basis alone and by Your grace, I pronounce her healed in Jesus' name."

When you simply believe that you receive your blessings based on Jesus' finished work and by His grace alone, you **will** receive your blessings!

Thought for the Day
God's power is made manifest in those who trust
His goodness instead of their good behavior.

Your Answer Is in His Word

Proverbs 4:20–22
²⁰My son, give attention to my words; incline your ear to my sayings.
²¹Do not let them depart from your eyes; keep them in the midst of your heart;
²²for they are life to those who find them, and health to all their flesh.

God has given us a sure way to receive the answers to our problems and challenges. It is His Word. Every answer or solution we need is found in the Bible.

Yet, many Christians are not walking victoriously in certain areas of their lives. This is because the devil continuously wages a war of distraction against them. He has managed to take them away from the one thing that can bring them victory — the Word. He will do everything possible to prevent them from opening the Bible because he knows that the Word will deliver them.

The distraction can be very subtle: a lot of things to get done, a lot of TV programs that interest you, or it may take the form of a big problem that makes you feel that you need to focus all your attention on it. The enemy knows that if he can get you to take your eyes off the Word of God, he can keep you from winning the battle.

When you are going through a tough time, it is not enough to know that God's answer to the problem is "somewhere in the Bible." Find the scripture in which God has promised the solution. Meditate on it until the truth of that scripture is revealed to you. When you do this, no demon or devil can prevent that word from God from bearing fruit in your life.

Even Jesus Himself used the Word to defeat the devil in the wilderness — **"It is written,** 'Man shall not live by bread alone, but by every word that proceeds from the mouth of God'"** (Matthew 4:4). The way to defeat the enemy is with "It is written…"

My friend, there is no substitute for the written Word. God tells us that we will find life and health if we give our attention to His Word and keep it in the midst of our hearts. So get into the Word and let God's promises abide in you.

Thought for the Day
Every answer we need is found in God's Word.

Time to Use Your Authority

Exodus 14:15–16
¹⁵And the Lord said to Moses, "Why do you cry to Me?
Tell the children of Israel to go forward. ¹⁶But lift up your rod,
and stretch out your hand over the sea and divide it....

The problem with the body of Christ today is not that we are not praying. We are praying. But many of us are praying desperate prayers. We are praying, "God, help… God, please… God, do something about my problem!"

If you are smiling a little by now, most likely, you know about such prayers and might have prayed a couple yourself. My friend, God does not want you to pray pleading prayers all the time. He wants you to use the authority He has given you to pray powerful prayers, to boldly command and to "stretch out your hand" and see miracles happen.

When Moses stood before the Red Sea with Pharaoh's army in hot pursuit, the Bible tells us that he cried out to God. But God told him, "Why do you cry to Me?"

There is a time for you to cry out to God and there is a time for you to use your authority. God told Moses, "Tell the children of Israel to go forward. But lift up your rod, and stretch out your hand over the sea and divide it."

The "rod" you have today is the name of Jesus. As you command in Jesus' name, your "sea" will open and you will go on dry ground through the midst of your problem.

Do you realize that Jesus did not say, "Go and pray for the sick"? He said, "Go and heal the sick." (Matthew 10:8.) So stop pleading and asking all the time, and start using the authority you have in Christ.

Jesus told the church, "All authority has been given to Me in heaven and on earth. **Go therefore…**" (Matthew 28:18–19). My friend, God wants you to go and use the authority that He has given you. And as you go, miracles will flow!

Thought for the Day
When you start using the authority you have in Christ, miracles will flow.

You Already Are, You Already Have

Mark 11:24
²⁴"Therefore I say to you, whatever things you ask when you pray,
believe that you receive them, and you will have them."

God's Word tells us that we can have what we ask for in prayer — by simply believing that we already have it! As you are praying, know that you already have your answer or breakthrough — "**believe** that you **receive** them." The Bible also tells us that we already have whatever we are praying for because we are already blessed with every spiritual blessing in heavenly places in Christ. (Ephesians 1:3.)

You were in Christ the moment you received Him as your Savior. So when you pray, you are actually releasing your faith to lay hold of what you already have in Christ. And as you keep saying that you already have it (Mark 11:23), you **will** see the manifestation of it in the natural realm.

In one of our church camps, a church member shared about the back problem she had had for 15 years as a result of a fall from her rooftop. She needed an operation to help stop the shooting pains in her spine. She had also been taking anti-stress pills for five years.

After coming to church, she realized that she had already received her healing through the finished work of Christ. Refusing the operation and even the pills, she would rebuke the pain, which kept coming back, saying, "In Jesus, I believe I am healed. I am not trying or going to be healed. I am already healed. I have a brand-new backbone for I am in Christ. As Christ is, so am I in this world." It was not very long before this sister saw the manifestation of her healing.

Sometimes, the symptoms of a sickness or of lack may return and you think that you still have not received your blessing. That is the time to release your faith and declare that you already have it. You are not confessing to get it. You are confessing because you already have it in Christ!

My friend, the Bible tells us that Christ is in us. (Colossians 1:27.) This means that right now, your healing, prosperity, wellness, family's well-being and everything your heart desires are in you. So say, "I have everything I need in Christ right now!"

Thought for the Day
Because Christ is in you, your healing, prosperity, wellness and
family's well-being are in you right now!

Power From Jesus' Body to Yours

Matthew 26:26
²⁶... "Take, eat; this is My body."

Can you imagine the Lord sick, nursing a cold or fever while He walked on earth? No, our Lord Jesus was never sick! He was vibrant, full of life and full of health. When He told His disciples, "Take, eat; this is My body," they could practically visualize what it meant because they had lived and walked with this Man. They had seen people without hands or feet made whole when they touched His body. (Matthew 15:30–31.)

Even His clothes were soaked with His health! A woman who had a bleeding condition for 12 years — no doctor could cure her — was healed immediately when she touched the hem of His garment. If the hem of His garment was soaked with His health, vibrancy, energy and divine radiance, how much more His body!

You know, some of the most encouraging verses in the Gospels are these: "And as many as touched Him were made well" (Mark 6:56); "for power went out from Him and healed them all" (Luke 6:19). I love those verses! That is our Jesus!

The Bible says that they put sick people along the streets, and Jesus walked around, touched them and healed them. Now, you see movie stars doing this: they run here and there, they slap their fans' hands, but nobody gets healed. But wherever Jesus walked, whoever He touched, He healed. Picture this: A trail of people. Those in front of Jesus are lying down, but those behind Him whom He has touched are leaping with joy and following Him! That is how Jesus healed the sick.

So that night, when He said, "Take, eat; this is My body," as He broke the bread and gave it to His disciples to eat, they knew what it meant. They were probably thinking, "We are going to ingest His health into our bodies! Hallelujah!"

That is what you must believe when you partake of the Holy Communion. It is not just a ritual or symbolic act. No, you must believe that He is the true bread from heaven who took your cancer, diabetes and heart disease, so that you can have His supernatural health! And when you eat of His broken body with this revelation, you will have life in abundance and the health of the Lord!

Thought for the Day
**Believe that Jesus is the true bread from heaven who took your cancer,
diabetes and heart disease, so that you can have His supernatural health!**

'I Am Who I Am'

Exodus 3:14
¹⁴And God said to Moses, "I am who I am."

Whatever your challenge is today, whether it is physical, emotional, financial or marital, the great I Am declares to you: "I am to you what you need Me to be."

Do you need healing? He says, "I am the Lord who heals you. (Exodus 15:26) And as you believe Me, you will see your healing manifest thirtyfold, sixtyfold and a hundredfold."

Are you groping in the dark, not knowing what to do? He says, "I am the light of the world. When you walk in Me, you will not walk in darkness, but will have the light of life." (John 8:12.)

Are you looking for a way out of a bad situation? He says, "I am your deliverer. I will reach down from on high, take hold of your hand and draw you out of the deep waters." (Psalm 18:2, 16.)

Are you wondering if there is more to life than merely existing from day to day? He says, "I am the resurrection and the life. (John 11:25) I came to give you life. And where there is life, there cannot be death. You will have life and life more abundantly." (John 10:10.)

Are you fearful of what is ahead of you? He says, "I am the good shepherd (v. 11), who leads you to pastures of tender green grass and waters of rest. You will not suffer lack." (Psalm 23:1–3.)

Are you confused by the opinions and reports of man? He says, "I am the Alpha and the Omega, the First and the Last. (Revelation 1:11.) I have the final word in your life. The doctors do not have the final word. The experts do not have the final word. I have the first word and the last word in your situation."

My friend, do not be fearful of the problems you face. The great I Am declares to you, "Fear not! For I am to you what you need Me to be!"

Thought for the Day
God declares to you, "I am to you what you need Me to be."

Point to Jesus, Your Qualification

1 Corinthians 1:30
³⁰But of Him you are in Christ Jesus, who became for us wisdom from God —
and righteousness and sanctification and redemption.

When the devil accuses us of having done wrong and tells us that we don't deserve God's blessings, what should we do? Well, the Lord showed me one day what we are to do. We are to point everything back to Jesus, who qualifies us for all of God's blessings.

So when the devil says, "You are not righteous enough," just look to Jesus and declare, "He is my righteousness!"

When the devil says, "You are not holy enough," just look to Jesus and declare, "He is my sanctification!"

When the devil says, "You don't deserve to be healed," just look to Jesus and declare, "By His stripes I am healed!"

When the devil says, "You don't qualify for the blessing," just look to Jesus and declare, "He is my qualification!"

Each time you point everything back to Jesus, the devil has nothing to say because Jesus qualifies you for all of God's blessings. In and of yourself, you do not qualify. Without Christ, there is nothing good in you which can qualify you.

But with Christ, your disqualification becomes your qualification for the un-deserved, unearned and unmerited blessings of God. And because God puts your life in Christ (Colossians 3:3), who is the all-deserving One, you become all-deserving. Because you are in Christ, you are qualified.

Jesus qualifies you because He died for you and gave you a blood-bought right to every blessing of God. You have a blood-bought right to a life full of meaning, purpose and abundance. You have a blood-bought right to walk in divine health. You have a blood-bought right to prosperity even when the economy is bad. You have a blood-bought right to preferential treatment because God favors you. You have a blood-bought right to the good life!

My friend, you have a right to all these blessings not because you are good, but because Jesus shed His blood and qualified you to have them. So don't let the devil or anyone tell you that you can't expect to walk in the blessings of God!

Thought for the Day
You have a right to all the blessings of God because Jesus shed
His blood and qualified you to have them.

Jesus — King and Lord Over the Storm

Matthew 14:27
²⁷But immediately Jesus spoke to them, saying,
"Be of good cheer! It is I; do not be afraid."

Are you going through a dark, difficult moment in your life? Perhaps the storm just rages on with no let-up and you are trembling in fear. You feel that any time now, you may just cave in and go under because you cannot beat this storm.

Be comforted that Jesus sees what you are going through and He always comes to where you are in your darkest hour. He did that for His disciples one stormy night on the Sea of Galilee. Jesus came, walking on the stormy waters, walking on top of the problem that was threatening to overwhelm them. He is indeed the King and Lord over the storms!

When your eyes are on Christ, even though the storms are raging and the winds are blowing, you will know that you are above your troubles and circumstances. When people ask you how you are doing under the circumstances, tell them, "I am not under the circumstances. I am on **top** of them because my God is above all!"

Don't be fearful. He will come to you walking on the stormy waters. Hear His comforting voice telling you, "Be of good cheer! It is I; do not be afraid."

And as you behold Jesus, you become like Him. You will find yourself doing things you did not know you could do. You will, like Peter, walk on water. (vv. 28-29.) This happens when you are occupied with the person of Jesus, with His resources, love, wisdom, ability, power and majesty.

My friend, even during the times when you take your eyes off Jesus, He never takes His eyes off you. And when you cry out to Him, He will immediately stretch out His hand to catch hold of you. You will not go under.

There may be times that you are not able to find your way back. Jesus will then hold your hand and walk you back to the boat. And like Peter, you will realize that with your hand in His, the storm will come to a standstill!

Thought for the Day
As you behold Jesus, you will find yourself doing
things you did not know you could do.

Your Advocate Always Wins Your Case

1 John 2:1
¹My little children, these things I write to you, so that
you may not sin. And if anyone sins, we have an
Advocate with the Father, Jesus Christ the righteous.

If you want a glimpse of some real-life celestial drama, picture this: God the Father sits as Judge of the universe with Jesus Christ at His right hand, who is not only your High Priest, but also your Advocate.

When your accuser, the devil, comes along and says, "You have done this wrong and you have not done that right," Jesus says, "Father, the devil is right, but My blood has paid for what the devil is accusing this person of."

Then the devil adds, "You have also not been reading the Bible or praying enough. And this morning, you told a lie."

Again, Jesus will say, "Father, the devil has indeed reported correctly, but My blood has paid for all these failures."

God the Father will then slam the gavel on the sound block and say, "Case dismissed! Next!"

You need to understand that God can justly declare you innocent and completely righteous because Jesus took your place at the cross, and shed His blood to pay for your sins and condemnation. (2 Corinthians 5:21.) God is simply being faithful and just to what Christ has done.

When Jesus rose from the grave, He rose as your Advocate, your lawyer. But unlike most earthly lawyers who take on cases because it serves their interests and wallets, He is a lawyer who is personally interested in your happiness and well-being. Unlike earthly lawyers who are not caught up in the feelings and sufferings of their clients, Jesus went through great sufferings for you and paid with His own life so that you can receive all the blessings of God.

As your Advocate, Jesus ensures that what He died and suffered to give you, you get! In heaven He defends and represents you to ensure that the healing, wholeness, protection and other blessings that He died to give you are enforced in your life. Beloved, have confidence in and rest in the ability of your Advocate!

Thought for the Day
As your Advocate today, Jesus ensures that you get
what He suffered and died to give you.

God Is Your Strength

Ephesians 6:10
¹⁰Finally, my brethren, be strong in the Lord and in the power of His might.

When you say, "I can manage this problem by myself, Lord," God says, "Okay, you do it then." But when you say, "Help me, Lord! I need You. I cannot do this on my own," God says, "Good, I have been waiting for you to say that. You cannot, but I can. Now, watch Me!" That is how God is — He loves it when you depend on Him.

You see, when you think that you are strong and don't need God, He cannot help you. But when you need Him and look to Him, He will not leave you weak and helpless. He comes and becomes the strength of your life. He becomes the breakthrough that you need.

A church member with a smoking habit came to me one day and said, "Pastor Prince, please pray that God will help me. I want to stop my smoking habit."

I told him simply, "You cannot, but God can."

He replied, "Yes, I know that I can't. But with God's help, I will discipline myself and try my best to quit the habit."

I told him, "No, you cannot, but God can." I repeated this to him a few times until he realized that it was not his self-discipline or willpower that would help him overcome his smoking habit, but the power of God. He finally understood that true deliverance from this destructive habit would not come by his own strength, but by "[being] strong in the Lord and in the power of **His** might."

When I saw him again a few weeks later, he said, "Pastor Prince, since that day, I didn't even try to stop myself from smoking. But each time I lit up, I told God, 'I cannot, but You can.' Then one day, the craving was gone! Jesus has completely delivered me from my bondage to nicotine!" This man experienced true deliverance, not just an outward form of discipline and willpower.

So when you say, "I can do something about it," you are still relying on your human strength. But when you say to God, "I cannot, but **You** can," you have just tapped into the real source of your strength — Jesus. And as you rest in His strength, you will see His power manifesting in your life!

Thought for the Day
As you rest in God's strength, you will see
His power manifesting in your life!

Count on God's Forgiveness

Hebrews 10:2
² ... For the worshipers, once purified, would have had
no more consciousness of sins.

What are you more conscious of today? Your sins or the fact that you have been forgiven? My friend, don't be conscious of your sins. Be conscious instead of Jesus and His finished work. The Lamb of God **has** taken away **all** your sins at the cross, so count on the fact that you are a forgiven child of God!

No matter what has happened or what you have done, God wants you to know that because of His Son's finished work, He will be merciful to your unrighteousness, and your sins and lawless deeds He will remember no more. (Hebrews 8:12.)

That is why you should not be conscious of your sins. In fact, when you are sin-conscious, the devil brings in condemnation, and the more you receive it and condemn yourself, the more you will find yourself unforgiving toward yourself and even others.

I was told by a pastor friend that when a lady, who had cancer on her face, asked for prayer for healing, the Lord revealed to him that it was self-hatred that was keeping her from receiving her healing. She could not forgive herself and was full of self-condemnation.

When she realized her problem, she counted on the fact that God was merciful to her unrighteousness and that she was already forgiven. She received the love of God. Then, right before the pastor's eyes, her whole face changed — she received her healing that very moment!

Something happens when you believe that you are forgiven. That is why God says to you, "I want you to believe that all your sins I will remember no more. I want you to believe that you are My child enjoying My mercy and that you can always count on My forgiveness."

Beloved, remember that all your sins have already been paid for by Jesus on the cross. And the more you count on the fact that you have the Father's forgiveness and that He does not condemn you because of Jesus' finished work, the more sin and its effects — sickness, hatred, lack and so on — will lose their grip on you. You will find yourself walking in a greater measure of God's grace and blessings!

Thought for the Day
Count on the fact that you are a forgiven child of God.

All That Jesus Is Before God, You Are

2 Corinthians 5:21
²¹For He made Him who knew no sin to be sin for us,
that we might become the righteousness of God in Him.

When an Israelite brought an animal as his sin offering, he laid his hand on it before killing it. (Leviticus 4:1–4.) By laying his hand on the sin offering, his sins were transferred to the innocent animal. The animal died for his sins and he went free.

In contrast, during the burnt offering, when the Israelite laid his hand on the animal (Leviticus 1:3–4), the beauty, worthiness and acceptance of the unblemished animal were transferred to him. God accepted the perfection of the animal sacrifice on his behalf to make atonement for him. Because God accepted the unblemished burnt offering, the offerer now had right standing before God.

Do you know that the two offerings speak of Jesus' one offering of Himself when He hung on the cross? He is both our sin offering and burnt offering — "For He made Him who knew no sin to be sin for us [as our sin offering], that we might become the righteousness of God in Him [as our burnt offering]." The moment you put your faith in Him, just by His one sacrifice, your sins were transferred to Him, and His righteousness was transferred to you. That is the grace of God toward you!

As our sin offering, He offered Himself once and for all. (Romans 6:10.) The sin offering was never a daily offering because God does not want His people to be sin-conscious. However, the burnt offering was both a morning and evening sacrifice (2 Chronicles 13:11) because God wants His people to be righteousness-conscious.

Beloved, God wants you to lay claim daily to Jesus as your burnt offering and say, "Father, I thank You that Jesus is my burnt offering. All that Jesus is before You — His righteousness, excellence, beauty and perfection — has been transferred to me. Jesus has Your unclouded favor, so I enjoy Your unclouded favor in my life. Jesus is the righteousness of God, so I am the righteousness of God in Christ. As He is before You, so am I."

Because Jesus became your burnt offering, what He is to the Father today, you are! That is what it means to be in Christ.

Thought for the Day
All that Jesus is before the Father — His righteousness, beauty
and perfection — has been transferred to you.

How You Know You Will Inherit It

Psalm 89:34
³⁴My covenant I will not break, nor alter the word that has gone out of My lips.

When God promises you something, do you take Him at His Word? Or do you, like Abraham, ask, "Lord God, how shall I know that I will inherit it?" (Genesis 15:8).

God did not reprimand Abraham for failing to take Him at His Word. That is how gracious God is to His people. He even came down to Abraham's level of faith and did something to assure Abraham that He would always keep His promises — He made a covenant with Abraham. (Genesis 15:9–17.)

God did not do it for His own benefit. God is a God of His Word. He does not break His Word. But He bound Himself to a covenant because He knew that Abraham needed to know in his heart that God would do whatever He had promised him.

Man finds it hard to just believe words. For example, when you buy a house, a contract is drawn up and signed by both parties, and lawyers are involved. You need a contract because you cannot trust the other person's words and he cannot trust yours either.

Likewise, we find it hard to take God at His Word. So God made a covenant with us, not because He cannot be trusted, but because He knows that we find it hard to just believe what He says. God knows that man will wonder, "What if God wakes up on the wrong side of His bed tomorrow and decides to fry me instead of bless me?"

But because God has made a new covenant with us, which is established by the blood of His Son, we can, like Abraham, not waver through unbelief regarding the promises of God, but be strengthened in our faith, being fully persuaded that God will do as He has promised. (Romans 4:20–21.) We have the assurance that God will not wake up one day and say, "Forget the new covenant. I want to remember your sins now and curse you instead of bless you!"

My friend, the new covenant blessings for you are guaranteed because God has bound Himself to the covenant. And He is a covenant-keeping God who is willing and more than able to do everything He has promised you!

Thought for the Day
Because God has made a new covenant with us, established by the blood of His Son,
we can be fully persuaded that He will do as He has promised.

God Still Performs Miracles

John 11:40
*⁴⁰Jesus said to her, "Did I not say to you that if you would
believe you would see the glory of God?"*

God, who parted the Red Sea, rained manna from heaven, caused the walls of Jericho to fall, shut the lions' mouths, healed the sick, raised the dead and calmed the sea, still performs miracles today.

However, some Christians doubt that God wants to work a miracle for them today. They believe that there were miracles when Jesus walked the earth, but they think that the day of miracles is over. And they talk about how everything will be perfect one day in the sweet by and by. But God wants us to know that He is still the God of miracles today.

Martha was like one of those Christians. She wondered if Jesus could perform a miracle when her brother Lazarus died. By the time Jesus arrived on the scene, Lazarus had already been dead for four days. So she thought that Jesus was four days too late. That is why she said, "Lord, if You had been here, my brother would not have died" (v. 21). And even when Jesus said that Lazarus would rise again, she said, "I know that he will rise again in the resurrection at the last day" (v. 24).

Martha believed that Jesus could perform miracles in the past and would do the same in the future, but she did not believe that He could give her a miracle when she needed it right then. You see, Martha was someone who lived wishing that the past could be changed and believing that the future would be better. But she did not believe that the "I Am" was there to meet her present need.

Today, God stands at the point of your need. What miracle do you need from Him? Believe that He is still the same miracle-working God today. Believe that you will see the glory of God. Believe and you will see your miracle!

Thought for the Day
The "I Am" is here to meet your present needs!

God Wants Your Household Saved

Acts 16:31
³¹So they said, "Believe on the Lord Jesus Christ,
and you will be saved, you and your household."

When God got you saved, He didn't just have you in mind. He had your whole family in mind. That is why His Word says, "Believe on the Lord Jesus Christ, and you will be saved, you and your household." Now, this does not mean that once you believe in Jesus, your family members are automatically saved. What it means is that you have opened a big door for God to move into your family's life and to touch every member of your family!

So don't worry about your unsaved parents or grandparents. God knows how to reach out to them. A relative of mine spoke only Cantonese, and could not go to church because she was very old and her legs were weak. But Jesus appeared to her in a vision and spoke to her in perfect Cantonese! She had never encountered Jesus, but knew that it was Him and understood what He said to her. After that, those who visited and spoke with her were amazed by her knowledge of Jesus.

Even up to the very last moment, God will reach out to your unsaved family members. This happened to my late maternal grandfather who used to make fun of me being a Christian. On his deathbed, he was gasping for air and in great discomfort. He couldn't die peacefully. My mother, who was with him, told him, "Dad, just say, 'God, forgive me.' Call on Jesus." My grandfather remained hardened and in great pain. But at the very last moment, he cried out, "Jesus, forgive me!"

You see, my grandfather had no time to pray the sinner's prayer. But God says that "whoever calls on the name of the Lord shall be saved" (Acts 2:21). Jesus will find every excuse to save a person. My mother saw the peace of God come upon my grandfather's face after he had called out to Jesus, and he passed away peacefully.

My friend, God's desire is for your entire household to be saved. Right now, your family may be giving you a hard time, but because you are a Christian, a big door has been opened for your Daddy God in heaven to touch them!

Thought for the Day
Once you believe in Jesus, you open a big door for God to move into
your family's life and to touch every member of your family!

Choose the Good Part and Profit

Isaiah 48:17
¹⁷… "I am the Lord your God, who teaches you to profit,
who leads you by the way you should go.

G od instructs us for our own benefit. He wants us to profit in every area of our lives — health, finances, career, marriage and family relationships. The Bible says that it is God who teaches us to profit. And it is He who leads us in the way that we should go.

God always has our best interests at heart. We only have to sit at His feet, listen to His Word and just have fresh, daily communion with Him, and He will make our way prosperous.

But we are constantly bombarded with things to do every day, like sending the kids to school, attending a business meeting or making a sales presentation. Likewise, in church, there are just as many important things to attend to — ministering to the needy, reaching out to the lost and healing the sick. But you know what? All these things will be taken care of when we sit at Jesus' feet and listen to His Word.

What was the Lord's response to Martha's complaint that her sister was sitting at His feet and listening to Him, instead of helping her with the many tasks? "Martha, Martha, you are worried and troubled about many things. But **one thing** is needed, and Mary has chosen that good part, which will not be taken away from her" (Luke 10:41–42).

Yet, many of us are like Martha. We worry about many things. And we are so busy that we have no time to sit at Jesus' feet to listen to His Word and enjoy communion with Him. When we fail to draw from Him, we end up running on our own strength, and relying on our own flesh and wisdom to get things done. Listen, you can never have a plan that is better than God's!

My friend, do you want to be led by God's wisdom and timing in your decision-making? Then, make it a point to choose the good part like Mary did. Spend time with Jesus, open your Bible and say, "Lord, speak to me." You will find that your heavenly Father takes care of your troubles, and teaches and leads you to profit!

Thought for the Day
When we sit at Jesus' feet to have fresh, daily communion with Him,
He makes our way prosperous.

Taught by God Himself

Hebrews 8:11
11 "None of them shall teach his neighbor, and none his brother, saying, 'Know the Lord,' for all shall know Me, from the least of them to the greatest of them."

As a parent or someone serving in Sunday school, you may think that the children under your care are too young to know the Lord. And you wonder if you are wasting your time reading Bible stories and singing hymns to them.

Or you may have been buying Mandarin and Hokkien sermon CDs for your dialect-speaking parents or grandparents, and you wonder if the Bible teachings are too difficult for them to understand.

My friend, don't underestimate the Holy Spirit. Many elderly folks in our Mandarin and Hokkien services, who first heard about Jesus through the recorded messages given to them by their children, are now born again and attending church regularly. And they are so full of Jesus that they cannot stop talking about Him to their relatives and friends.

Even for a young child like my daughter Jessica, when she was one year old, she would spontaneously raise her hands whenever she heard Christian songs, but not secular ones. My wife, Wendy, and I had never taught her how to recognize Christian songs. The only explanation we have is that Jessica was taught by the Lord Himself. (Isaiah 54:13.)

When Jessica turned two, she surprised us again. Wendy was tucking her in bed one night when Jessica looked at her and said, "Jesus died for Jessica because Jesus loves Jessica." No one taught her to say that. But I remember looking at her when she was younger and by faith saying, "You know, darling, Jesus died for Jessica." She just looked at me and I did not know whether she understood me then. I just believed that the Holy Spirit is a better teacher than I am.

So don't limit the Holy Spirit by saying things like, "The children are too young... My grandparents are not well-educated... My atheist friend won't be interested..." Just send God's Word into their lives by faith, and trust the Holy Spirit to do the teaching and imparting. For God says that no one has to teach anyone to know the Lord because all shall know Him, from the least, including little children, to the greatest!

Thought for the Day
***Just send God's Word into people's lives by faith and trust the
Holy Spirit to do the teaching and imparting.***

Receive the Word God Has Sent to Heal You

Psalm 107:20
20He sent His word and healed them, and delivered them from their destructions.

Your Bible will do you no good if you leave it on your bedside table, gathering dust. It will do you no good if you hold it like a teddy bear when you are facing your "giants." But God's Word will do you a lot of good when you receive it as truth and speak it as truth! Then, you will see your healing and deliverance from every evil condition that has been sent to destroy you!

The Bible says that "He sent His word and healed them, and delivered them from their destructions." Now, when God wants to heal you, what does He do? He sends His Word. Before God delivers you from your destruction, He sends His Word.

Are you still waiting to experience the blessing of healing that Jesus died on the cross to give you? Don't feel condemned. Your Father in heaven loves you and wants you well. But how does your healing come? By you receiving His Word on healing that He has already sent you. His promises of healing are all there in your Bible. But have you received them?

During one of our church services, a lady took out her cell phone and started sending text messages of every scripture and almost every key point that I was preaching that day to her friend who was at home dying of cancer. I was telling the congregation to keep confessing the healing scriptures over their bodies, no matter how bad their conditions were. I pointed them to Isaiah 53:5, which says, "By His stripes we are healed." The lady got so excited that she told her friend to keep believing and confessing it every day!

Her friend, on reading the text messages, simply received the Word of God and confessed it by faith. That very same week, when she went back to the doctor, the doctor could not find a single trace of cancer in her body!

Never underestimate the power of God's Word. The lady's friend was healed because she received God's Word by faith. She gladly read the messages that her friend had sent her, was encouraged by the Word, confessed it and received her miracle. God sent His Word and healed her, and saved her from her destruction!

Thought for the Day
When you receive God's Word as truth, you will see your healing and deliverance from every evil condition sent to destroy you!

Call It Forth!

Romans 4:17
¹⁷… God, who gives life to the dead and calls those things
which do not exist as though they did.

"**P**astor Prince, I feel the pain in my body. How can I go around saying that Christ has redeemed me from this sickness? How can I say that by His stripes I am healed?"

Well, God's way is to call those things that are <u>not</u> as <u>though they are</u>. And because you are made in God's image, you can also call those things that are not as though they are!

When God wanted to make Abraham a father of many nations, what did He do? He changed the way Abraham talked. At that time, Abraham did not even have a single child from his wife, Sarah, because she was barren. So how could he become a father of many nations?

God changed the way he talked. How? By changing his name from Abram to Abraham, which means "father of many nations" (Genesis 17:5).

Just imagine: From then on, every time he met someone, he would say, "Hi, my name is Father of Many Nations." Every time dinner was ready, Sarah would call out to Abraham, "Darling… Father of Many Nations… dinner is ready! Father of Many Nations…" You can just hear their neighbors saying, "They want a child so much they have gone mad!" But God changed the way Abraham talked so that he called forth what God saw him already blessed with.

You know, when Jesus saw the man with a withered hand, He didn't say, "My goodness! It is so withered!" He said, "Stretch out your hand!" (Matthew 12:13). He called forth what He wanted. He looked at the paralytic and said, "Rise, take up your bed and go home!" (Matthew 9:6.) He didn't see the way it was in the natural. He saw the way God meant it to be and He called it forth.

Genesis 1 tells us that in the beginning, there was darkness over the face of the whole earth. God saw the darkness and He said, "Light be!" And light was. God called forth what He wanted and it became so! If it had been me or you, we would probably have said, "Whoa! It is so dark!"

My friend, despite the pain, call forth your healing. It is pointless to state the obvious. So change the way you talk. See the way God meant it to be, and start calling forth your healing and wholeness!

Thought for the Day
God's way is to call those things that are not as though they are.

Prayers That Proclaim

Luke 13:12
¹²But when Jesus saw her, He called her to Him and said to her,
"Woman, you are loosed from your infirmity."

W hen you have a need, do you pray or do you plead? Do you begin your prayers with words like, "Please God, please! God, I beg You to have mercy!"

Prayers that plead and beg imply that your heavenly Father is not willing to do it. Yet, He is far more gracious and willing to give to you than you are willing to ask, think or imagine. (Ephesians 3:20.) He desires above all things that you prosper and be in health, even as your soul prospers. (3 John 1:2.)

In fact, long before you have a need, God has already met that need. Long before you knew you needed a Savior, He sent His Son to be your Savior. This is your God! He is a good God. So when you beg Him for something, you are actually saying that He is reluctant to give and needs to be persuaded strongly before He will move. Yet, He is not like that.

Jesus knew the heart of the Father. When He saw the woman bound with a spirit of infirmity, He did not pray, "Oh Father! She has been suffering for 18 long years! I beseech You, Father, have mercy on her. Please, please heal her!" No, when Jesus saw her, He immediately proclaimed, "Woman, you are loosed from your infirmity," because He knew the heart of the Father. He knew that the Father wanted her delivered from her crippling condition.

At the end of a church service, I don't stand and pray, "Oh God, please bless Your people. Oh God, do keep them. Oh God, be ever so gracious to them!" Instead, I proclaim, "The Lord bless you. The Lord keep you. The Lord make His face shine on you and be gracious to you!"

Beloved, when you pray, proclaim your healing, protection and provision because your Father's heart overflows with love for you. And when you declare it, He sanctions it. When you declare it, He establishes it!

Thought for the Day
What you declare by faith, God sanctions.

Don't Look Inside the Ark

1 John 2:2
²And He Himself is the propitiation for our sins,
and not for ours only but also for the whole world.

In the movie *Raiders of the Lost Ark*, the people who tried to look inside the ark were struck dead. What was inside the ark that brought judgment to those who looked into it?

The Bible tells us that the ark held the two tablets of the Ten Commandments, the pot of manna and Aaron's rod. (Hebrews 9:4.) These items were tokens of man's rebellion. The two tablets of the Ten Commandments represented man's rejection of God's standards. The manna represented man's rejection of God's provision, and Aaron's rod, man's rejection of God's appointed priesthood.

God did not want to look at these tokens of rebellion. He wanted to be merciful to His people, so He instructed them to place the items in the ark and to cover the ark with its mercy seat, which is also the place where the blood of the animal sacrifices was sprinkled.

Once a year on the Day of Atonement, the high priest would enter the Holy of Holies to sprinkle on the mercy seat the blood of the animal that had been sacrificed. The two cherubim on the mercy seat stood as guardians of God's righteousness and holiness.

Representing God's eyes too, they looked at the blood on the mercy seat. As long as the blood was there, the entire nation of Israel was forgiven. God's judgment passed over them and they were blessed for another year. (Leviticus 16.)

Today, the blood sprinkled on the mercy seat is not the blood of bulls and goats, but the precious, eternal blood of the Son of God! (Hebrews 9:12.) **Jesus** is our **"mercy seat"** for "He Himself is the **propitiation** for our sins, and not for ours only but also for the whole world." The word "propitiation" in the original Greek text is the same word as "mercy seat." (Romans 3:25, Hebrews 9:5.)

Beloved, God does not see your sins and count them against you because He sees His Son's blood. He sees His Son's perfect work that has more than satisfied Him. God does not want you to see your sins either. He does not want you to look inside the ark by focusing on your sins. He wants you to focus on Christ and His finished work!

Thought for the Day
Don't focus on your sins. Focus on Christ and His finished work.

Jesus, Our True Passover Lamb

Exodus 12:3
3 … every man shall take for himself a lamb, according to the house of his father, a lamb for a household.

Jews worldwide celebrate the Passover feast. The feast, which has been kept for generations, commemorates the deliverance of the Israelites from slavery in Egypt. (v. 14.) The night before the Israelites left Egypt, the destroyer went through the land killing the firstborn of man and beast. Only those households with the blood of the Passover lamb on their doorposts were spared.

God had told the Israelites, "Take a lamb, a lamb for a household." It was a lamb for each family. This tells us that the Lord Jesus Christ, who is our true Passover Lamb, is for whole families to be saved!

So your children are blessed once you receive Jesus. Your unsaved spouse and grandparents are blessed too, because Jesus is now the Lamb for your whole household. Your unsaved loved ones will enjoy the blessings of the saved. The Bible says that the sanctified will sanctify the unsanctified. (1 Corinthians 7:14.) Yes, they will still need to personally receive Jesus as their Savior, but God has marked them for salvation because you are saved!

Now, each household took a lamb which God said had to be without blemish. Why? Because the lamb typified Jesus, the true Lamb of God, who is without sin. John the Baptist said of Jesus, "Behold! The Lamb of God who takes away the sin of the world!" (John 1:29).

The lamb was then killed, and its blood put on the two doorposts and lintel of the house (Exodus 12:7), which speaks of the cross. Today, the destroyer has to pass over every family that believes in the finished work of Jesus at the cross and puts its faith in His blood, because there has already been a death. The blood proves it — the innocent Lamb for the guilty family!

Jesus also celebrated the Passover the night before He was crucified. But He was instituting the greater Passover. This time, it was not deliverance from Pharaoh and Egypt, but from Satan and his kingdom of darkness! It was not deliverance from slavery in Egypt, but from a life of bondage to sin to a life of liberty as free men in Christ!

Beloved, Jesus, the Lamb of God, sacrificed Himself to set you free. And when the Son sets you free, you are free indeed!

Thought for the Day
The destroyer has to pass over every family that believes in the finished work of Jesus at the cross and puts its faith in His blood.

Seek First God's Kingdom

Matthew 6:31–33
31 "Therefore do not worry, saying, 'What shall we eat?' or 'What shall we drink?' or 'What shall we wear?' 32 For after all these things the Gentiles seek. For your heavenly Father knows that you need all these things. 33 But seek first the kingdom of God and His righteousness, and all these things shall be added to you."

As a child of God, know that it is your Father's pleasure to meet all your needs. Jesus Himself tells us, "For your heavenly Father knows that you need all these things." But God does not want you to seek after things. He wants you to seek **first** His kingdom. And when you do that, all the things that you need will be **added** to you!

So your first priority every day is to seek His kingdom. The word "first" in verse 33 is the Greek word *proton*, which means "first in order or importance, holding the highest place in all our affections." My friend, God wants us to seek first His kingdom, and all things will fall gloriously in place.

We are not to seek after things the way Gentiles do. The word "seek" in "the Gentiles seek" (v. 32) is the Greek word *epizeteo*. It means "to seek with all their might with much sweat or with much stress." However, the way God wants us to "seek" in "seek first the kingdom of God" is the Greek word *zeteo*, which means "to hunger, to desire to worship." It is simply a hungering, a desiring for the kingdom of God, without any labor or toil.

But what is the kingdom of God? Romans 14:17 tells us that it is righteousness, peace and joy in the Holy Spirit. And the kingdom of God dwells within you because the Holy Spirit indwells you. So the kingdom of God is His righteousness, peace and joy in you.

Beloved, if you want to have peace and joy in the Holy Spirit flowing inside you, then seek every day to be conscious of your righteousness in Christ, not your own righteousness, but His righteousness given to you as a gift. Pursue Jesus first. Spend time with Him and listen to His Word. And when you do these things, you are seeking His kingdom and His righteousness, and all the things that you need will be added to you!

Thought for the Day
***When you pursue Jesus and His righteousness given to you as a gift,
everything you need will be added to you.***

When It Is More Blessed to Receive

Luke 10:42
[42]*"... Mary has chosen that good part, which will not be taken away from her."*

If Jesus came to your home, what would you do? Would you ask Him to sit down and then start serving Him? Or would you sit down and start drawing from Him? Would you let Him serve you and fill you up?

Jesus walked into the home of two sisters, Martha and Mary. (v. 38.) Martha saw His weariness. She knew that Jesus had been walking for miles, going about doing good, healing the sick and meeting the people's needs. Obviously, He must be tired, she thought, so she saw Him as someone she had to care for.

Mary, however, saw beyond Jesus' external weariness into His divinity. She saw that He was someone she needed to draw from. And by doing that, she made Him feel like God — the Savior who had come to serve her and not to be served by her. (Matthew 20:28.) Jesus even commended her for choosing the better portion!

Our human minds just find that hard to believe. Some people tell me, "But Pastor Prince, the Bible says that it is more blessed to give than to receive." (Acts 20:35.) When it comes to man, that is true. But when it comes to God, He wants to give. In fact, unless you learn how to receive from God, you will have nothing to give to man.

Which sister gave Jesus the sweeter feast and filled Him up? Martha who was busy preparing food for Him? Or Mary who sat still and drew deeply from Him? It was Mary. She made Jesus feel a sense of His divine glory. She allowed Jesus to be the giver, to be God.

Like Martha, we always reverse the roles. We somehow think that God needs our service, but He actually wants to fill us first. Mary's ears and heart were more precious to Jesus than Martha's hands and feet.

We use our ears and hearts to draw from Jesus. We use our hands and feet to serve Him, and there is a place for that. But our sense and appreciation of God's divine fullness is more precious to Him than all the service we can render Him. And when you draw from Him, you cannot help but become a great giver and server.

Thought for the Day
Unless you learn how to receive from God,
you will have nothing to give to man.

Start Using Your Measure of Faith

Romans 12:3
³… God has dealt to each one a measure of faith.

As children of God, we should never say, "I don't have any faith." To say this is to say that God is a liar because His Word already tells us that "God has dealt to each one a measure of faith."

Why then does the faith of some seem to be stronger than others?

Well, faith is like muscles. We are all born with a measure of muscles. But some of us develop our muscles better than others. Bodybuilders, for example, exercise their muscles very regularly to make them grow bigger and stronger.

Likewise, your measure of faith grows when you feed and use it. Each time you hear or read God's Word, you are feeding your faith. When you confess God's Word and expect good things to happen to you, you are using it. And the more you use it, the more your faith grows.

So use your faith. You could start with headaches, for example. When you have a headache, instead of always running straight for your painkillers, use your faith. Ask God for healing, and trust and thank Him for the healing.

Now, don't get me wrong, there is nothing wrong with taking medicine. And if you have to go to the doctor, don't feel condemned either. Just start using your faith at a level you are comfortable with. If you need to go to the doctor, then go in faith, praying, "Abba Father, I am going to the doctor. I am asking You in Jesus' name to give the doctor wisdom to give me an accurate diagnosis. My trust is not in him but in You."

And when you take your medicine, don't just pop in the pills. In faith, say, "Lord, sanctify this medicine," then take it. This is because some medicines have negative side effects. So when you ask God to sanctify it, He blesses that medicine. And what will be developing in you, growing bigger and possessing your body until it is too widespread, is divine health!

Beloved, you **have** been given a measure of faith. Start using it, believing that it is this measure of your faith that causes you to draw from the inexhaustible power of a faithful and loving God!

Thought for the Day
Your measure of faith grows when you feed and use it.

Let Jesus Wash Your Feet

John 13:8
⁸Peter said to Him, "You shall never wash my feet!" Jesus answered him,
"If I do not wash you, you have no part with Me."

C an you imagine the Lord wanting to wash your feet? Peter could not. His shocked reaction — "Lord, how can You wash my feet!" — would probably be ours too.

I want you to notice what the Lord said to him: "Peter, if I don't wash your feet, you have no part with Me." What the Lord was actually saying to Peter was, "Peter, you cannot flow together with Me, you cannot walk together with Me in ministry, in service and in effectiveness, if you don't let Me wash your feet." So Peter said, "Lord, [wash] not my feet only, but also my hands and my head!" (v. 9).

But Jesus answered him saying, "He who is bathed needs only to wash his feet, but is completely clean; and you are clean…" (v. 10).

Once we have accepted Christ as our Lord and Savior, we are bathed all over, and cleansed by His blood once and for all eternity! His blood has perfected us forever (Hebrews 10:14), and we only need to wash our feet because we walk in the world and our feet pick up dust and dirt, causing us to stumble.

So how is Jesus washing our feet today? Ephesians 5:25–26 tells us that "Christ also loved the church and gave Himself for her, that He might sanctify and cleanse her with the washing of water **by the Word.**"

We, the church, are cleansed with the washing of water by the Word. The more we come under anointed teaching that unveils Christ through the Word, the more the cleansing goes on. And as our feet are washed, instead of stumbling, we will be walking and even running!

Today, though high and lifted up in heaven, Jesus is dressed in a robe with a golden girdle around His chest. (Revelation 1:13.) Like a servant who uses his girdle as a towel to serve, Jesus wants us to sit down and let Him serve us — by washing our feet with a deeper revelation of Himself through His Word. Beloved, this is what gives us victory in our daily walk!

Thought for the Day
As we receive a deeper revelation of Christ through His Word,
we will see victory in our daily walk!

The Good Life Without the Sweat

Matthew 6:26
26 "Look at the birds of the air, for they neither sow nor reap nor
gather into barns; yet your heavenly Father feeds them.
Are you not of more value than they?"

Most people are of the opinion that the good life does not happen without hard work and buckets of sweat. They believe that to achieve success, you first need to have this educational certificate, that professional qualification, this particular job and that many years of hard work. I have good news for you: God has a better way.

We all must work, but the world wants you to believe that there is a natural process of sowing, reaping and gathering, accompanied by waiting, toiling and stress, before the good life actually comes. But God says, "My people do not need to go through this natural process to enjoy the good life for they are not of this world's system. They can operate out of My economy and I can give them the good life straightaway!"

In the same way that God feeds the birds which do not go through the sow-then-reap-then-gather system of the world, He wants to and will do much more for you!

Your heavenly Father wants you to know the generosity of His heart toward you and how much He wants to make you successful. A case in point is what happened to a church member who believed this truth. After leaving his previous job, he trusted God to provide him with a better one. Within just four months, he found himself heading two companies.

His newly formed distribution company not only clinched a major project in Singapore, but was also made the principal distributor in Southeast Asia for a popular line of products from the United States. His second company, which provided consultancy services, was given two projects by a Korean and a Hong Kong company for a six-figure consultancy fee in US dollars.

Today, God wants you to know that you are not of the world's system. You are of the kingdom of God — the same kingdom that feeds the birds that do not toil, but simply trust their Creator for all their provisions in life. Be convinced that you are of more value to your heavenly Father than the birds, and let Him give you the good life without the toiling and laboring of the world.

Thought for the Day
Operate out of God's economy by trusting His
heart for you, and enjoy the good life.

Don't Sweat Over Loss or Waste

Luke 15:22–23

22 "But the father said to his servants, 'Bring out the best robe and put it on him, and put a ring on his hand and sandals on his feet. 23 And bring the fatted calf here and kill it, and let us eat and be merry."

What would you say if your son, whom you had given a large inheritance to, came crawling home one day after wasting all his money on riotous living?

In the parable of the prodigal son (vv. 11–24), the father did not say one word about loss or waste, though his son had indeed wasted his inheritance on riotous living. The father only saw his son's homecoming as an opportunity to show him how much he loved him and to restore to him what he had lost.

Like the father in the parable, it is your heavenly Father's desire to embrace you and show you how much you are loved. And it is His good pleasure to restore to you what you have lost.

Perhaps you have lost something recently, or you are frustrated that something has gone to waste due to a bad decision you made. My friend, God does not see the finality of the loss or waste the way you do. When you come to Him with it, He sees it as an opportunity to restore to you what has been lost or wasted.

Even if, like the prodigal son, you feel far away from your heavenly Father, or you feel that you have disappointed Him, don't despair. The truth is that the moment you come to Him, He immediately restores to you the robe of honor to clothe your nakedness, the ring of authority to declare your position of power and dominion, and the sandals on your feet (which servants do not wear) to reinstate you as a son in His house.

He reassures you that you had never lost the position of sonship. And He celebrates your return to Him with the killing of a fatted calf because you are His beloved child whom He cherishes.

Beloved, in your Father's house, you not only come under His complete protection, but you also enjoy His inexhaustibly rich provisions and unconditional love!

Thought for the Day
It is your heavenly Father's desire to show you how much you are loved and to restore to you what you have lost.

There Is No Spot in You

Song of Solomon 4:7
⁷You are all fair, my love, and there is no spot in you.

Jesus tells us, His bride, "You are all fair, My love, and there is no spot in you." But our reply to Him tends to be, "Me? All fair and no spot? You don't know me, Lord!"

Do you really think that God doesn't know you?

God sees reality like no one else sees it. He sees the perfection of His Son's finished work in your life. By one offering of Himself at the cross, Jesus has perfected you forever! (Hebrews 10:14.) You have been made the righteousness of God in Christ. (2 Corinthians 5:21.) And you will never find any spot in this righteousness that Jesus died to give you.

So God wants you to see yourself righteous — all fair and spotless in Christ. Every day, be conscious of your righteousness in Christ. Say, "I am the righteousness of God in Christ. There is no spot in me whom He has perfected with His blood." When you do that, you are honoring Jesus and His finished work.

If you are conscious of your sins, then you are not honoring the work of Christ. You may think that you are being humble or holy by being sin-conscious. But do you know that the Bible calls sin-consciousness an "evil conscience"?

Hebrews 10:21–22 tells us that since we have Jesus as our High Priest, "let us draw near with a true heart in full assurance of faith, having our hearts sprinkled from an **evil conscience.**" What does the writer of Hebrews mean by "an evil conscience"? If you read the beginning of the same chapter, you will find that he is talking about a "consciousness of sins" (v. 2). Paul calls it a "conscience seared with a hot iron" (1 Timothy 4:2). The Greek word for "seared" here is *kauteriazo,* and it means to carry about with you a perpetual consciousness of sin.

So don't carry with you an evil or seared conscience. Your lifetime of sins has already been punished fully in the body of Jesus at the cross. Be conscious, instead, of your perfection and righteousness in Christ. Because of what Jesus has done for you, you can boldly declare, "I am all fair. There is no spot in me!"

Thought for the Day
See yourself righteous — all fair and having no spot in Christ.

Jesus, Your Good Shepherd and Door

John 10:7
⁷Then Jesus said to them again, "Most assuredly,
I say to you, I am the door of the sheep."

Jesus said that He is the "door of the sheep." What did He mean? Well, a sheepfold during Jesus' time had no door that could be opened and closed. The door of the sheepfold was just an opening. In this kind of sheepfold, after the sheep had entered it, the shepherd would sleep at the entrance. The shepherd became, effectively, the "door" of the sheepfold.

When Jesus told His disciples, "I am the good shepherd" (v. 11), He also assured them emphatically that He was the "door of the sheep." He was telling them and us, "Inside My sheepfold, My sheep are always safe, completely protected and kept close under My watchful eyes. And since I am just at the entrance of the sheepfold, nothing, not even the muffled bleat of one of My own, can escape My ears. Also, nothing evil outside the sheepfold can enter and touch My sheep without first coming through Me for I am the door of My sheep."

So when the fight of life comes knocking on your door and when panic threatens to rise within you, see yourself doubly protected! He is both the good shepherd and the door of His sheep. As your good shepherd, He gave His life for you to redeem you from poverty, sickness and every other curse.

As your door, He keeps out everything evil that He has redeemed you from. Because He shed His blood for you, you are covered and protected within the sheepfold by a blood-stained door. Disaster, destruction and death must pass over you and your family because of His blood on your door. Remember that on the night of the first Passover in Egypt, the destroyer could not enter the houses of the Israelites because of the blood of the lamb on their doors. (Exodus 12:13, 23.)

Today, you can live life untroubled and unafraid, knowing that Jesus, your good shepherd and door, protects and preserves you and your family. No evil will befall you or your loved ones because He is your dwelling place and refuge!

Thought for the Day
Jesus, your good shepherd and door, protects and preserves you and your family.

See God's Goodness in the Midst of Evil

Matthew 2:13
¹³ ... an angel of the Lord appeared to Joseph in a dream, saying, "Arise, take the young Child and His mother, flee to Egypt, and stay there until I bring you word; for Herod will seek the young Child to destroy Him."

God does not play a game of counterattack with the devil — the devil does something bad, then God steps in to bring something good out of it. The truth is, when something bad happens, it is the devil reacting to something good that God has started. The Lord once told me, "Tell My people that if they want to understand what I am doing, just look at what the devil is doing and see it in reverse. That is what I am doing, multiplied many times over."

I see this truth in the Bible. When Christ was born, soldiers were sent to kill all baby boys under the age of two in Bethlehem. The folks in Bethlehem then would have seen only evil. But there were those like Mary who saw God's goodness. They knew that God had sent a Savior into the world! The killing of the infants was just the devil's reaction to the gift of salvation that God had sent.

The Lord showed me that this was how we were to look at the bird flu when it hit our region in Singapore not too long ago. While I was pondering the significance of birds, the Lord showed me Matthew 6:26: "Look at the birds of the air, for they neither sow nor reap nor gather into barns; yet your heavenly Father feeds them. Are you not of more value than they?"

If God takes care of the birds, how much more will He take care of you! So, by attacking the birds with disease, the devil is, in essence, reacting to God's provision for His people. In other words, he saw that God's provision had already been released on His people in a big way!

With every new virus, or anything else that the devil throws at us, you must discern that the devil is trying to pervert and reverse what God is already doing. Then, you will know that something good is going to come out of it. You see, every new strain of virus tells us that God has already released a new anointing of health for His people. And I believe that He releases new levels of prosperity for His people too. So don't just see the evil. See the good that God is already doing!

Thought for the Day
Don't just see the evil around you. See the good that God is already doing!

Jesus' High Priesthood Is Forever

Hebrews 6:20
²⁰… Jesus, having become High Priest forever according to the order of Melchizedek.

Jesus is our High Priest **forever**. This "forever" aspect changes the way we are blessed and how we receive our blessings from God. As our High Priest, Jesus represents us before God. Since His priesthood is after the order of Melchizedek, which is one of righteousness, His righteousness becomes our righteousness forever. This means that we are forever righteous in God's eyes!

And because Jesus will never die, but continue as our High Priest forever, we have an everlasting righteousness, not merely a here-today-gone-tomorrow righteousness based on our works. No, we have a perpetual and everlasting righteousness because Jesus is our High Priest forever.

This also means that blessings are perpetually on your head because the Bible says that blessings are on the head of the righteous (Proverbs 10:6), and you are righteous forever!

Unlike the priesthood according to the Levitical order, which blesses as well as curses, the priesthood of Jesus according to the Melchizedek order only blesses. There is no cursing, only blessing — always and forever!

And because Jesus is our High Priest forever, the blessings do not come to us in intermittent drips, but stream into our lives in a never-ending flow. Because He is our High Priest forever, we can never stop His blessings.

By being our High Priest forever, Jesus also touches the blessings that He gives us with a forever effect. He touches our lives and we have eternal life. He touches our ministry and its impact becomes eternal. And the more we see His priesthood as having a forever effect, the more permanent our healing and prosperity will be.

Truly, there is nothing temporal about what Jesus our High Priest does. It is not a case of blessed today, cursed tomorrow. The blessings we receive are sure and steadfast because Jesus is our High Priest today, tomorrow and forever.

So rejoice because Jesus your High Priest changes how you are blessed forever!

Thought for the Day
God's blessings are sure and steadfast because Jesus is our High Priest
today, tomorrow and forever.

Jesus Is God's Satisfaction

Leviticus 1:9
*⁹… And the priest shall burn all [the pieces of the bull] on the altar
as a burnt sacrifice, an offering made by fire, a sweet aroma to the LORD.*

When Jesus was on the cross, He did more than just die for your sins. His one sacrifice did not just remove your sins, but it also clothed you in His righteousness and perfection. Jesus became the true "burnt sacrifice."

In the Old Testament, whenever someone offered a burnt sacrifice, the perfection of the animal came on him. In the same way, every perfect attribute of Jesus your "burnt sacrifice" comes on you when you take Him as your Savior. And because God sees you clothed with Christ, you have the same acceptance and favor with Him that Jesus has!

When Jesus was offered on the cross, the fire of God brought out His perfections like perfume to God. In that one sacrifice, Jesus' obedience and perfections rose as "a sweet aroma to the LORD," which is what is emitted when the offering is burnt. This "sweet aroma" speaks of a savor of rest to God. Jesus' perfect sacrifice gave God so much satisfaction that He rested.

You can also rest in the perfect sacrifice of Jesus, knowing that what He did, He did for you — "Christ also has loved us and given Himself for us, an offering and a sacrifice to God for a sweet-smelling aroma" (Ephesians 5:2). You can rest knowing that God the Father is satisfied with you because His Son's sacrifice has caused His heart to rest with regard to you. You can rest because Jesus is God's satisfaction for you.

Today, as you come before God, say, "Father, I thank You that Jesus is such a delight and joy to You. He satisfies Your heart completely. And what He did, He did for me. Because Jesus so satisfies You, I know that You are satisfied with me. Because Jesus is Your delight, I am also Your delight. Because Jesus so pleases You, I know I please You too. And because Jesus is my righteousness and perfection, I stand righteous and perfect before You."

Beloved, when you speak of Christ and His finished work, it goes up to God as a sweet-smelling aroma, a savor of rest. And if God can rest in the perfect sacrifice of His Son, you can too!

Thought for the Day
**You can rest because Jesus is God's satisfaction,
delight, righteousness and perfection for you.**

God Doesn't Remember
How Bad You Were

Hebrews 8:12
¹²"For I will be merciful to their unrighteousness, and their sins and
their lawless deeds I will remember no more."

Perhaps you have heard people say of others: "Oh, if only you had seen my husband in the early years of our marriage. He had such an explosive temper that I used to seek shelter in my mother's house!"

"No one would have ever guessed that she had such a promiscuous past."

"As a young boy, he would always lie through his teeth and not even bat an eyelid!"

Man looks at you and remembers what you were like in the past. But when God looks at you through the new covenant, He declares, "I will be merciful to your unrighteousness, and your sins and lawless deeds I will remember **no more**."

He states it plainly in His Word as if to assure us: "When you come to Me, don't think that I am thinking about your sins. Don't think that every time I look at you, I am reminded of your sins. Not only am I not keeping a record, but I am also not mindful of your failures and shortcomings. I am telling you that I will remember your sins no more, never again!"

God can say that all our sins He remembers no more because there was a time when He remembered them and punished every one of them — in the body of His Son at the cross. He punished every single one of them until Jesus cried out, "It is finished!" (John 19:30.) That is why today, God can justly say, "Your sins I will remember no more."

We all know that we sin from time to time. But the good news is that all our sins have already been dealt with at the cross. They have been washed away by Jesus' blood. Now, when we come into God's presence, He sees us without our sins. So beloved, forget your past failures. Believe that God remembers your sins no more and be the righteous person that you already are in Christ!

Thought for the Day
All our sins have been dealt with at the cross,
so we can come boldly into God's presence.

Jesus Has the Final Word

Revelation 1:8
⁸"I am the Alpha and the Omega, the Beginning and the End," says the Lord....

The doctor has just told you that you have an incurable disease. The X-rays and blood tests confirm it. Your worst fears have come true and you feel like your future has been sealed.

My friend, the doctor's report is not final. Jesus declares to you, "I am the Alpha and the Omega, the Beginning and the End." He has the first word as well as the final word in your situation. The experts and medical reports don't!

Alpha and omega are the first and last letters of the Greek alphabet. But Jesus did not speak Greek. He spoke Aramaic or Hebrew. So He would have said, "I am the *Aleph* and the *Tav*." *Aleph* and *tav* are the first and last letters of the Hebrew alphabet. So what Jesus is declaring to us is this: "I have the first word in your situation. And I have the final word in your situation!"

Each Hebrew letter has a corresponding picture. Interestingly, *aleph* is associated with an ox and *tav*, a cross. Together, they make up a beautiful picture of what Jesus did for us — He is the sacrificial "animal" on the cross. It was for us that He suffered, bled and died.

When Jesus hung on the cross, He took our infirmities and bore our sicknesses. (Matthew 8:17.) That is why your sickness does not have the final word in your life. Jesus does, because He took your sickness upon His body and paid for your healing with His blood.

When Jesus hung on the cross, He took our curse. (Galatians 3:13.) We were supposed to be cursed because of our sins, but He took our place and the curse fell on Him. Today, we take His place and His blessings fall on us!

So why settle for the curse of sickness or even poverty when the price for your healing and prosperity has been paid by Jesus? Sickness and poverty do not have the final word in your life. Jesus does because He redeemed you from every curse!

Beloved, when man says that it is impossible, Jesus says that it is possible. The Alpha and the Omega, the Beginning and the End, has the final word in your situation!

Thought for the Day
Jesus, the Alpha and the Omega, the Beginning and the End,
has the final word in your situation!

No More Sleepless Nights

Psalm 127:2
²It is vain for you to rise up early, to sit up late, to eat the bread of sorrows;
for so He gives His beloved sleep.

A re you one of those who have trouble sleeping at night? Perhaps just this morning you said, "I was up the whole night — my boy was running a high fever," or "I slept for only two hours — I was awake polishing up my presentation," or "I couldn't sleep at all — I was worried about the bills that are piling up."

God "gives His beloved sleep." Who are His beloved? You and I! Because we are in Christ, we are His beloved. (Ephesians 1:6; 2 Thessalonians 2:13.)

God says, "It is vain for you to rise up early, to sit up late, to eat the bread of sorrows..." In other words, it is pointless to worry and lose sleep because the truth is, "Unless the Lord builds the house, they labor in vain who build it; unless the Lord guards the city, the watchman stays awake in vain" (Psalm 127:1).

So let God be the One who builds your career and watches over your financial investments. Let Him be the One who guards your health, marriage and children. Don't worry and stay up late as if **you** are the source of the increase, or the one who has the power to make things happen and save the situation. No, God is the One and He says to you, "My beloved child, throw that care to Me and go to sleep." And while you are sleeping, He is working on your situation. He, who neither slumbers nor sleeps (Psalm 121:3–4), works the night shift for you as you sleep!

But because we are such doers and performers, it is hard for us to let go and let God take over. But when we actually do, casting all our cares, anxieties and worries once and for all into His hands, we will see how He cares for us affectionately and watchfully. (1 Peter 5:7.) We will see Him taking care of our problems and working things out for good. (Romans 8:28.)

Beloved, trust your Father's love for you. Cast your cares on Him and have no more sleepless nights!

Thought for the Day
Cast all your cares and worries into God's hands, and see how
He cares for you affectionately and watchfully.

Feed on Jesus and Live

John 6:57
⁵⁷"As the living Father sent Me, and I live because of the Father,
so he who feeds on Me will live because of Me."

Some time ago, I visited a friend of a church member who had cancer and wanted healing. He was all ears, lapping and soaking up everything I shared with him. Today, he worships with us in our church and is completely healed of cancer.

I remember being at another man's home at the invitation of his family members. He too was suffering from cancer. When I entered his home, the man had his television on. I started sharing Christ with him, but he was not at all interested in what I was saying. He continued watching the television program. I knew then that his healing was a lost cause because faith for healing comes by hearing God's Word, not by watching television, reading newspapers or listening to your favorite music.

Don't get me wrong. I am not against these things, but they are not going to heal you. When you are sick, what you want is God's healing flowing in your body. How does that happen?

One of the primary ways in which it happens is when you read your Bible, soaking up everything on Jesus. Before you know it, His divine health flows into your body, driving out every symptom of pain, sickness and disease. Even your discouragement dissolves effortlessly. You find yourself encouraged, refreshed and your darkness giving way to light. You see, there is no way you can feed on Jesus through reading and hearing His Word, and still remain the same. He said, "The words that I speak to you are spirit, and they are **life**" (John 6:63).

My friend, God wants Jesus to be food for you. We feed on Christ by seeing Him unveiled in the Word, by seeing and meditating on what the Holy Spirit reveals of His beauty and glory, and His finished work at Calvary. That is how we enjoy Jesus. It is like having a good meal. And when you do that, Jesus Himself promises that "he who feeds on Me will live because of Me"!

Thought for the Day
There is no way you can feed on Jesus through reading and
hearing His Word, and still remain the same.

The Mind of Christ Doesn't Grow Old

1 Corinthians 2:16
16... we have the mind of Christ.

Oh dear, my memory is not as good as it used to be. I must be getting old." Have you heard that before? Maybe you have even said it yourself a couple of times! But who says that as you grow older, you are supposed to forget things?

When the late Reverend Kenneth E Hagin was in his eighties, he was still healthy and strong. This amazing man of God would run around the platform as he preached. And those who have heard him preach would tell you that he had an amazing memory with which he could recall specific details such as the day of the week that a specific date fell on and even the time. Even at that age, the man's memory was superb!

He once shared how he had started to forget things when he was in his fifties. He had read a medical journal which said that every day millions of cells in our brains die. He didn't realize it, but those words got into his spirit and he started to forget things.

So he asked the Lord, "What is happening to me?" And the Lord said, "You read that article and you believed it." He repented and asked the Lord what he should do. The Lord said, "Confess My Word. My Word says that you have the mind of Christ, and the mind of Christ never forgets." He started to confess that he had the mind of Christ and that was how his memory remained sharp for the rest of his life.

My friend, the Word of God says that you have the mind of Christ. The mind of Christ is not old, slow or forgetful! I don't care how old you get. You don't have to become forgetful. Don't believe and confess what medical science or your friends say. Believe and confess the Word of God which brings life.

The power of life and death is in your tongue. (Proverbs 18:21.) So use your tongue for life. Don't sit around saying, "I am getting old and forgetful." Say, "I have the mind of Christ. My mind is sharp and quick because it is the mind of Christ!" Believe it, confess it, and see your thinking and memory live up to it!

Thought for the Day
You have the mind of Christ, which is not old, slow or forgetful!

Jesus' Blood Stops Evil in Its Tracks

Leviticus 1:11
¹¹He shall kill it [the burnt sacrifice] *on the north side of the altar before the Lord; and the priests, Aaron's sons, shall sprinkle its blood all around on the altar.*

The north of Israel has always been a source of evil for the nation. It was from Israel's north that destruction poured forth. (Jeremiah 1:14–15.) Israel's enemies always came from the north. (Jeremiah 6:1, 22–23.) Even today, the north of Israel is enemy-occupied land. The north is thus a picture of evil in the Bible.

Interestingly, the animal for the burnt sacrifice was killed "on the north side of the altar." The burnt sacrifice speaks of Jesus, who gave Himself as "an offering and a sacrifice to God" for us. (Ephesians 5:2.) Calvary, where Jesus was crucified, and the Garden Tomb, where His empty tomb is, are located to the north of Jerusalem. In other words, Jesus died in the north, from where evil comes against His people.

This means that Jesus' death stops evil in our lives when we, who are priests of the Most High God (Revelation 1:6), speak His blood over our lives, in the same way that Aaron's sons sprinkled the blood of the burnt offering all around on the altar.

This was the case for a church member who was serving in the army. He testified about how God preserved His life when a thunderstorm struck while he was carrying out sentry duty in a tower in his army camp. The rain kept him stranded in the tower, which had a metal-framed window.

Suddenly, a bright purplish flash lit up right next to him, stunning him completely and almost throwing him off balance. A bolt of lightning had struck the lightning rod on the roof and the electricity was conducted through the metal-framed window, causing the purple flash. But the blood of Jesus on him protected him from harm!

Praise Jesus, whose blood stops evil in its tracks! It does not matter what the devil sends your way. As long as you are covered with the blood of Jesus, no evil can harm you!

Thought for the Day
Jesus' death stops evil in our lives when we speak His blood over our lives.

How the Holy Spirit Helps Us

Romans 8:26
²⁶Likewise the Spirit also helps in our weaknesses. For we do not know
what we should pray for as we ought, but the Spirit Himself makes
intercession for us with groanings which cannot be uttered.

The Holy Spirit is not inside you to point out your faults or nag at you when you do wrong. God's Word tells us that He is inside us to help us in our weaknesses. In areas where we are without strength, He is there to help us. When we don't know what to pray, "the Spirit Himself makes intercession for us with groanings which cannot be uttered."

Now, don't read the verse and say, "Well, I don't know what I should pray for, and since the Holy Spirit makes intercession for me, I will leave the praying to Him."

If the Holy Spirit, without our participation, makes intercession for us, then every Christian would be living victorious lives automatically! But we know that there are many Christians who don't seem to be walking in the fullness of God's blessings. So obviously, Romans 8:26 is not saying that. What is it saying then?

In the first part of the verse, the word "helps" is *sunantilambanomai* in the original Greek text. It means "to take hold together against." Now, "together" means that our participation is required. In other words, the Holy Spirit *sunantilambanomai* or takes hold together **with us** against the problem.

So if you just sit back and don't take hold of the problem, the Holy Spirit has nothing to "take hold of" with you. If you don't pray, He has nothing to pray. If you keep quiet, then even if He wants to pray through you, He can't. But when you release your prayer in tongues, you are actually allowing Him to pray through you. And He will take hold together with you against the problem, and pray the perfect prayer through you because "He makes intercession for the saints according to the will of God" (v. 27).

And you can be confident that when you ask anything according to the will of God, He hears you. And if you know that He hears you, whatever you ask, you know that you have the petitions that you have asked of Him! (1 John 5:14–15.)

Thought for the Day
When you pray in the Holy Spirit, He takes hold
together with you against your problem.

Jesus Is Your Sweet Aroma to God

Leviticus 1:13
¹³"... the priest shall bring it all and burn it on the altar; it is a burnt sacrifice,
an offering made by fire, a sweet aroma to the LORD."

In Old Testament times, when a burnt offering was killed, its head was severed, the fat removed, and the entrails and legs washed. Then, everything was placed on an altar and burnt, and the sacrifice was a sweet aroma to God.

All this speaks of the death of Jesus, who has "given Himself for us, an offering and a sacrifice to God for a sweet-smelling aroma" (Ephesians 5:2).

The head of the sacrificed animal speaks of the mind of Christ offered as a covering for our minds. This means that although our minds are often clouded with unbelief, worries, foolishness, filth and human reasoning, God treats us as if we have the mind of Christ, without wrong or displeasing thoughts, bringing pleasure to Him like a sweet aroma.

The fat of the animal speaks of the riches of Christ, His best, for God equates the fat of something with the best of that entity. (Genesis 45:18.) The fat of the burnt sacrifice speaks of Jesus giving us His riches, His best, as our covering. So God does not see us in our lack, but in the riches and excellence of Jesus going up to Him as a sweet aroma.

The entrails or intestines speak of Jesus' motivations, feelings, affections and desires. We often feel fearful, anxious, stressed out or angry (and it affects our stomach and intestines). But God sees only Jesus' feelings and desires, which are always pure, beautiful and acceptable to Him — a sweet aroma.

The legs refer to Jesus' perfect walk — His power to serve and obey the Father — imputed to our weak and faltering walk. And the fact they are washed shows that even our crooked walk has been cleansed.

Beloved, God does not see your foolish mind, weak nature, inadequate feelings or faulty walk. Instead, He sees you in the perfection of His Son, who gave Himself up for you as a sweet-smelling sacrifice to God.

Thought for the Day
God does not see you in your imperfections, but in the perfections of His Son.

Don't Be Dust-Conscious

Luke 13:11
¹¹And behold, there was a woman who had a spirit of infirmity eighteen years, and was bent over and could in no way raise herself up.

Imagine being bowed over for 18 years. All you would see is the dust on the ground. That was the predicament of the woman in Luke 13. Dust was all her eyes fell on, all the time, everywhere she went, until she became dust-conscious. Thank God she finally saw the beautiful feet of Jesus, who brought her good news and raised her up.

Now, dust is the devil's food. The Bible tells us that God cursed the devil to eat dust all the days of his life. (Genesis 3:14.) Dust represents death. (Genesis 3:19.) The devil wants you to be like him — to fall flat on your belly, crawl and eat dust. To eat dust is to feed on your shortcomings and lack, until you constantly feel that there is so much in your life that you need to clean up. You may not be physically bowed over, but like the woman, you become dust-conscious and life every day is a struggle.

Having a dust-consciousness also affects the way you see others. You look at people's faults all the time. You point out their shortcomings and rake up their past failures. When you are dust-conscious, you find your relationships robbed of peace and joy.

And if you, like the woman, keep looking at the dust, before long, that inward position of dust-consciousness becomes so entrenched that you become the devil's food because dust is what he eats. God's Word describes him as being "like a roaring lion, seeking whom he may devour" (1 Peter 5:8).

If you don't want to be devoured by him, then lift your eyes above the dust! Instead of looking at your failures, look to Christ who has delivered you from every defeat. See yourself the way God sees you — righteous and holy in Christ. (Colossians 3:12; 2 Corinthians 5:21.) You are not dust because you are not in and of the flesh — you are in and of the Spirit. (Romans 8:9.)

My friend, the more you realize who you are in Christ, the more you will straighten up and walk the way God sees you — a new creation with His authority, power and overcoming Spirit!

Thought for the Day
**Instead of looking at your failures, look to Christ
who has delivered you from every defeat.**

Continue in God's Grace

2 Corinthians 3:6
⁶… for the letter kills, but the Spirit gives life.

To the Jews, the feast of Pentecost is a celebration of the giving of God's law. It takes place 50 days after the Passover feast. When God gave the Israelites the Ten Commandments at Mount Sinai, it was 50 days after they had celebrated their first Passover and come out of slavery in Egypt.

But what happened after God gave them the law on the first Pentecost? Three thousand people died! (Exodus 32:28.) Contrast this with another Pentecost in the New Testament. In the book of Acts, it says that when Pentecost had fully come, God gave not the law but the Holy Spirit, and what happened? Three thousand people got saved (Acts 2:41), which goes to show that "the letter [the law] kills, but the Spirit gives life"!

The law, which was "written and engraved on stones," ministered death. It killed 3,000 people. That is why the apostle Paul calls it "the ministry of death" and "the ministry of condemnation" (2 Corinthians 3:7–9). On the other hand, the Spirit ministered life — 3,000 people got saved.

My friend, when you come under the law by trying to keep God's commandments in order to be blessed, it will lead to death. There will be deadness in your marriage, ministry, health, career… in your life. But when you depend on the Spirit of grace, it will lead to life. You will see breakthroughs and miracles (Galatians 3:5), and manifest the fruit of the Spirit.

So if you want to be blessed, make sure that you are on the right mountain. You see, the law was given on Mount Sinai, but the Spirit on Mount Zion. That is why the Bible says that "you have not come to the mountain [Sinai] that may be touched and that burned with fire, and to blackness and darkness and tempest… But you have come to **Mount Zion** and to the city of the living God, the heavenly Jerusalem, to an innumerable company of angels" (Hebrews 12:18, 22). The Lord blesses you out of Zion (Psalm 128:5), and not Sinai!

Beloved, by grace you have been saved through faith. (Ephesians 2:8.) Now, continue in the Spirit of grace. Remain on the right mountain and He will continue to supply miracles in your life!

Thought for the Day
**When you depend on the Spirit of grace, you will
see breakthroughs, miracles and life.**

God Is Well Pleased With You, His Beloved

Ephesians 1:6
⁶… He [God] made us accepted in the Beloved.

S tudies have shown that in the heart of every child is a cry for his father's approval. Something happens when a father says to his boy, "Daddy is so proud of you." Or when a father says to his girl, "You will always be Daddy's favorite girl."

You can catch such a similar special moment in the Bible when God the Father displayed His approval of His Son — "This is My beloved Son, in whom I am well pleased" (Matthew 3:17). The Bible shows us that Jesus' ministry began with the approval of the Father, even before He had performed any miracle.

Now, you may think that God would naturally say that of Jesus, but not of us. My friend, the truth is that Jesus came for us and as us. He died for us and as us. He received the approval of the Father for us and as us. He came as our representative. And if that is not enough, God tells us in His Word that we are "accepted in the Beloved"!

Why did God specifically say "accepted in the **Beloved**" and not simply "accepted in Christ"? I believe that it is because He is calling to our remembrance what had happened at the Jordan river where He said, "This is My **Beloved** Son, in whom I am well pleased." God wants us to know that we are His beloved and that He is well pleased with us.

God sees us as His beloved because He has made us accepted in the Beloved. He wants us to wake up every day knowing that we are His beloved, unconditionally loved and wholly approved.

The more we know how much we are loved and treasured by God, the more we can expect good things to happen in our lives. We can expect to be healthy and whole. When we realize that we are the objects of God's love, instead of becoming easily frightened or threatened by anything or anyone, we become confident that we will win every fight of life.

That is exactly how your heavenly Father wants you to live. So live life today confident that you are God's beloved!

Thought for the Day
Like Jesus, you are God's beloved, unconditionally loved and wholly approved.

Jesus Overpaid Our Debt!

Hebrews 10:12
*¹²But this Man, after He had offered one sacrifice for sins forever,
sat down at the right hand of God.*

Do you know that we once owed God a huge debt? No, it was not a money debt, it was a sin debt. We owed God a sin debt, which we could never pay. But God so loved us that He came up with a plan to pay the debt — He gave us His Son to die on the cross for our sins. Jesus was without sin. So when He went to the cross as punishment for our sins, He paid for us a debt He did not owe.

My friend, the reality is that our sin debt has been more than paid in full. In fact, Jesus overpaid it! Jesus' sacrifice was an overpayment because it was not just a good man, revered for his saintly qualities and good character, who died for us. It was the Son of the living God, the Creator of the universe, the perfect Man, who died for us!

Because Jesus is God, His sacrifice is greater than the sacrifices of all good men — past, present and future — put together. His sacrifice avails for all who lived in the past, all who are currently alive and all who will live in the future. And His one sacrifice forever took away all our sins.

Jesus' sacrifice was also an overpayment because His blood is of far more value to God than the blood of bulls and goats used in the past to atone for the sins of the Israelites. His blood is the blood of God Himself, not of animals. Because His blood is eternal, His blood cleanses us forever, so we have eternal forgiveness!

My friend, the next time you are mindful of a bad deed, remember that Jesus, your sacrifice for sins, not only paid 100 percent for your sin, but His sacrifice was also an overpayment. You can therefore truly and completely rest in the presence of God, knowing that He is fully satisfied and completely at rest concerning you. He is not going to find some sin you had committed that Jesus' blood failed to cover.

Beloved, God can righteously give you His blessings and you can expect to receive them because Jesus overpaid your debt!

Thought for the Day
**Because Jesus overpaid your debt, you can truly and
completely rest in the presence of God.**

Consider the Lilies of the Field

Matthew 6:28–29
[28] "So why do you worry about clothing? Consider the lilies of the field,
how they grow: they neither toil nor spin; [29] and yet I say to you that
even Solomon in all his glory was not arrayed like one of these."

You may think that you must work very hard to provide for yourself and get ahead in life. But God wants you to consider the lilies of the field — they do nothing. They toil not, spin not and struggle not. Yet, they grow and are clothed by God while simply resting and basking in the sunshine of God's love! And when God clothes them, they look even more glorious than King Solomon, the richest king who ever lived.

Like the lilies of the field, God wants you to let Him take care of providing for your material needs, instead of you striving to do it yourself. When you let go and let Him, you will see Him bless you supernaturally, abundantly and generously!

This is what happened to one of our church members who had been looking for a job. Initially, he received only two calls for interviews after sending out 12 résumés. Refusing to be discouraged, he believed that God wanted to bless him not just with a job, but with a position of influence too.

God was faithful. This church member soon became the business manager of an engineering company even though he had no engineering background. He was offered a very attractive remuneration package and within his first week on the job, was asked to quote on two projects. He knew that this was God's doing because it was difficult enough just to secure an appointment with contract managers to discuss projects, let alone be asked to quote on not one but two projects. Before long, he was offered the position to run the entire Singapore subsidiary with only one other business development manager. He was then only 25 years old!

My friend, God can do for you what He did for this person. Just believe that if God clothes the lilies and grass of the field, which are here today and gone tomorrow, how much more will He clothe you, His eternal and precious child, with beauty and riches! All He asks is that you cease from your striving, allow Him to take over and just flow with Him!

Thought for the Day
When you let go and let God, you will see Him bless you
supernaturally, abundantly and generously!

Believe First and You Will See

Matthew 8:13
¹³... as you have believed, so let it be done for you....

You may have heard some people say, "How can I believe it when I don't see it? If I can only see it or feel it, I may just believe that something is happening!"

The woman with the issue of blood who came to Jesus could have felt the same way. For 12 long years, she had gone from one doctor to another, trying every conceivable cure they could offer. She not only grew worse, but ended up losing all her money to those doctors and their "cures."

Then, something happened to her when "she heard about Jesus" (Mark 5:27). She started believing that He could and would heal her to the extent that she said, "If only I may touch His clothes, I shall be made well" (v. 28). Acting on her belief, she made her way to Jesus and touched His garment. Immediately, her bleeding stopped and she felt in her body that she was healed of that affliction. Jesus, her true physician, also pronounced her healed.

Beloved, God wants you to know that when you believe Him, you will see your miracle. What you believe Him for, you will receive.

When a church member lost her wallet at a swimming pool, she prayed together with her husband, declaring their belief that God would restore the loss. One day later, not at the swimming pool but at her feet in the car, she found her wallet! She simply believed that God would restore her loss and she saw the restoration.

In another case, a lady who had skin cancer wore long sleeves all the time to conceal her condition from others. During one of our church camps, she went forward for prayer, believing God for her healing. After one of our pastors, Pastor Henry, prayed for her, she went back to her room, rolled up her sleeves and saw that all the cancerous scarring on her arms had disappeared! Her doctor later confirmed that she had been cured of skin cancer. She believed God for healing and saw it.

The world says, "Unless I can see it or feel it, I will not believe it." But God says, "If you will believe it, you will feel it. Indeed, if you will believe it, you will see it!"

Thought for the Day
If you will believe it, you will feel it and see it.

Scourged for Your Wholeness

Isaiah 53:5
⁵... and by His stripes we are healed.

Under Roman law in Bible times, a criminal was either scourged for a lesser crime and then set free, or crucified straightaway if guilty of a greater crime. But Jesus was **both** scourged and crucified. Pontius Pilate had hoped that after scourging Jesus and presenting His bloodied body to the people, they would be satisfied and willing to let Him go. But the people were not and demanded His crucifixion instead.

Don't think for a moment that the people had power to inflict such suffering on Jesus. It was all part of God's plan and the scourging was necessary for only by His stripes are we healed.

The Roman whip used for scourging was made of leather straps embedded with glass, bone and metal hooks. With just one strike, the instrument would have been wrapped around Jesus' body, causing the glass, bones and hooks to cut deep into His flesh. And as the whip was pulled back, the hooks would have stripped His flesh off, exposing muscle and bone. Indeed, the psalmist says, "They pierced My hands and My feet; I can count all My bones. They look and stare at Me" (Psalm 22:16–17), and "The plowers plowed on My back; they made their furrows long" (Psalm 129:3).

Although 39 was the maximum number of times one could be whipped according to Jewish law, I believe that Jesus was whipped more times than that because the Romans, who were not likely to regard Jewish law, carried out the scourging.

Whichever the case, His back would have been reduced to a mass of bloody, mutilated flesh. That day, Jesus' blood flowed freely from His body for your deliverance from every kind of disease and physical affliction. God allowed every one of those stripes to fall on His Son's body so that your body need not be scourged with diseases.

My friend, if you are sick or suffering from some physical condition, know that Jesus took the scourging as full payment for you to be free of that condition. He bore those stripes so that, today, there is no sickness, no disease left for you to bear. By His stripes you have been healed!

Thought for the Day
Jesus bore the terrible scourging to purchase for you
deliverance from every kind of disease.

Read the Good News Today?

Matthew 6:33
³³... seek first the kingdom of God and His righteousness,
and all these things shall be added to you.

God doesn't want you grabbing the newspaper first thing in the morning and reading all the bad news in the world. He knows that if you do that, your heart will be full of cares, anxieties and even fears.

This happened to a mother who read in the newspaper that children from China studying in our local schools were becoming top students. She wrote to the press, voicing her concerns about the stiff competition her child would face from these students, even for the top jobs in Singapore in the future.

When you are reading the newspapers, magazines, medical journals, economic reports, watching movies or surfing the Internet all the time, then you are getting your "nourishment" from these sources instead of God's Word. Now, I am not against these things. But if you constantly feed only on earthly things which cannot satisfy, you will fill your heart and mind with cares and worries.

Jesus doesn't want you to end up worrying about your life — what you will eat, drink or wear — as these are the things that the Gentiles (people of the world) seek. He says that your heavenly Father knows very well that you need these things. (vv. 31–32.)

That is why He promises you that if you would seek first His kingdom and His righteousness, all these things that the world seeks after will be added to you. It will not just be given but **added**, which means greater in quantity and quality!

If you are broke, don't pursue money. Pursue God, your prosperity. If you are faced with lack, don't pursue material goods. Pursue God, your provider. If you are sick, don't pursue the "cure." Pursue God, your healer.

My friend, don't grab the newspaper or call your friend first thing in the morning to talk about the latest bad news. Instead, grab your Bible and read all the good news God has for you for the day. And as you seek first the kingdom of God and His righteousness, all the things that the world is running after will be added to you!

Thought for the Day
Pursue God and His righteousness, and all the things that
the world seeks after will be added to you.

Thank Your Way to Greater Blessings

Luke 17:15
¹⁵And one of them, when he saw that he was healed, returned,
and with a loud voice glorified God.

People who have a grateful heart are always praising God. You often hear them say, "God is good!" They know that God is the reason for every blessing they get.

But there are those who look to God for blessings and when they get blessed, they just go on their merry way. Their hearts are captivated by the blessings instead of the One who has blessed them.

Jesus had an encounter with both these types of people when He walked into a village one day. Ten lepers cried out to Him, "Jesus, Master, have mercy on us!" (v. 13.) Now, when you call out to Jesus for mercy, He always hears you. On another occasion, when two blind men cried out to Him, "Son of David, have mercy on us!" He took the time to give them their miracles. (Matthew 9:27–30.)

So these ten lepers cried out to Him for mercy. He stopped, looked at them and said, "Go, show yourselves to the priests." And "as they went, they were cleansed" (Luke 17:14). But only one came back and fell at Jesus' feet, giving Him thanks. Notice the very sad words of Jesus that followed: "Were there not ten cleansed? But where are the nine?" (v. 17).

The other nine obviously knew that it was Jesus who had cleansed them. Yet, they did not bother to go back and thank Him. My friend, let it be said of you that when the blessings come, you remember to give God the praise, glory and honor, and acknowledge that He is the source of every blessing in your life.

Do you know that when the man came back to thank Jesus, he received the additional blessing of becoming whole? Jesus said to him, "Arise, go thy way: thy faith hath made thee **whole**" (v. 19, KJV). He was not just cleansed of leprosy, he got his missing fingers and toes back!

Beloved, when your heart is thankful toward God, you position yourself for even greater blessings!

Thought for the Day
When you praise God and give Him thanks for His blessings,
you position yourself for even greater blessings!

Moved by the Spirit, Not Human Honey

Leviticus 2:11
*[11]'No grain offering which you bring to the LORD shall be made
with leaven, for you shall burn no leaven nor any
honey in any offering to the LORD made by fire.*

Imagine yourself walking past the prodigal son sitting in the pigpen. (Luke 15:11–24.) You look at him and see him salivating for the pigs' food. Believing that it is good to show kindness, you give him money to buy food for himself.

That is human kindness which says, "I am a Christian. I should be kind, good and forgiving." Such human sweetness or kindness may be likened to honey. Interestingly, while we elevate it, God tells His people not to bring Him a grain offering with honey in it.

The grain offering speaks of Jesus' life on earth. Not mixing honey in the grain offering speaks of how the compassion and goodness we see in Jesus during His earthly ministry were all divine. There was no "honey" of human goodness that is tainted with human weakness.

In retrospect, the worst thing one could do for the prodigal son was to give him money when he was in the pigpen. Not only would he not have gone home, but what the Lord was doing in his heart would also have been spoiled. This is what happens when we go by the goodness of our human hearts instead of the goodness of God in our hearts, which is directed by His love, wisdom and perfect timing.

My friend, God does not want you to be moved by what you see but by His Spirit. There were many needy folks surrounding Jesus during His time on earth. But He did not heal every sick person around Him, feed every hungry stomach He passed or raise all who were dead. Isaiah 11:2–3 tells us that the Lord was not moved by what He saw or heard. He was moved only by the Spirit.

You too have the Spirit in you. (1 Corinthians 3:16.) Be moved by Him. Follow the peace that He puts within your spirit to do or refrain from doing something. That peace is the peace of God. Acting on that peace will cause God to be exalted, and His divine goodness and kindness to really be a blessing to you and others!

Thought for the Day
Don't be moved by the honey of human kindness but by God's Spirit.

Be Conscious of Your Position in Christ

John 15:5
[5] *"I am the vine, you are the branches. He who abides in Me, and I in him,*
bears much fruit; for without Me you can do nothing."

In this verse, Jesus says, "I am the vine, you **are** the branches." He did not say, "I am the vine, **try** to be the branches." In other words, He wants us to realize that we are already the branches. We do not have to struggle to become the branches.

As His branches, we only have to abide or remain in Christ, our vine. How do we do that? We do that by simply being conscious every day of our position in Christ. Because we have received Christ, we are in Christ and are accepted in the Beloved. (2 Corinthians 5:17, Ephesians 1:6.) God accepts us because we are in the Beloved and He is in us. And that is how God sees us today when we come into His presence.

What the devil wants to do then is to get you to focus on your **condition** instead of your **position** in Christ. The condition you are facing could be financial lack or deteriorating health. The devil wants you to focus on your condition and forget your position — that you are the righteousness of God in Christ and that you are seated with Him in heavenly places at the Father's right hand. (2 Corinthians 5:21, Ephesians 2:6.) He wants you to forget that you are an heir of God and a joint heir with Christ. (Romans 8:17.)

The devil knows that once you focus on your position in Christ, it will give you the power to change your condition and circumstances. John 15:5 says that you will bear "much fruit." This means that when you pray against any lack, abundant supply will flow. When you pray for healing, sickness will leave.

My friend, none of these things can happen by your own doing, but by Jesus' life which flows through you. Just as sap flowing through the branches of a vine will cause them to bring forth fruit, His life flowing through you will bring forth a bountiful harvest of prosperity, healing and miracles. You only need to remain conscious of who you are in Christ!

Thought for the Day
Remain conscious of who you are in Christ and you will bear much fruit.

Which Is Easier to Say?

Colossians 2:13
¹³And you, being dead in your trespasses and the uncircumcision of your flesh,
He has made alive together with Him, having forgiven you all trespasses.

Let me ask you a question which Jesus asked the Pharisees: "Which is easier, to say [to the paralytic], 'Your sins are forgiven you,' or to say, 'Rise up and walk'?" (Luke 5:23).

In the context of ministering to a paralytic, saying "Your sins are forgiven" is probably easier. Why? Because you don't need an outward manifestation to prove that his sins are forgiven. But when you tell him, "Rise up and walk," he must rise up and walk, or you will look very foolish! So that makes saying "Your sins are forgiven" easier than saying "Rise up and walk."

The truth is, what is seemingly more difficult for man in the natural is not so for God. With God, physical healing is clearly "easier" for Him than forgiveness of sins. The latter is the "harder" and greater miracle because it required God to deliver up His beloved Son to take on all our sins and shed His blood on the cross.

Yet, when faced with a loved one stricken with cancer, or when gripped by mounting debts after being jobless for a long time, we seem to find it harder to believe and say that God has already given us the breakthroughs we need, than to believe and say that our sins are forgiven. Saying that our sins are forgiven seems easier than saying that God has already given us the miraculous physical healing, supernatural financial breakthrough or divine favor at the next job interview.

But since God has done the "harder" and greater miracle of "having forgiven you all trespasses," there is nothing He will not do for you! (Romans 8:32.) In fact, if you think that there is something that God is withholding from you, you are implying that that something is greater than the forgiveness of sins which Jesus died to give you! But nothing can be greater than the perfect sacrifice of Jesus.

So hear the Lord telling you today, "Your sins have been forgiven you. You have perfect acceptance before God. Rise up and be healed! Rise up and walk in health, wisdom, favor, protection and wholeness!"

Thought for the Day
Since God has done the greatest miracle of having forgiven you
all trespasses, there is nothing He will not do for you!

God Will Surely Show You Kindness

2 Samuel 9:7
⁷So David said to him, "Do not fear, for I will surely show you kindness for Jonathan your father's sake, and will restore to you all the land of Saul your grandfather; and you shall eat bread at my table continually."

W hen the people in the palace heard that King Saul and his son Jonathan had died in battle, they panicked. Fearful that David was coming to seize the throne, and kill all the sons and grandsons of Saul, they ran for their lives. A nurse took Mephibosheth, Jonathan's son, and ran. But as she fled, the five-year-old boy fell and became lame in both feet. (2 Samuel 4:4.)

The poor boy would not have been crippled if they had known that David actually loved Jonathan and Saul, and would have looked after Jonathan's son because he had made a covenant with Jonathan. (1 Samuel 18:3.)

In this story, King Saul represents the human race. He is like Adam, who sinned against God and forfeited all that God gave to man. He had the position, but not the power anymore because of sin. Jonathan, who came after Saul, represents Jesus, who came as a human. Jonathan was not like Saul — he was good, just as Jesus is not like Adam — Jesus is the perfect Man. David represents God. So Jonathan's covenant with David speaks of Jesus' covenant with God. Mephibosheth represents believers today who are "lame" in some way — sick, depressed, fearful, poor and so on.

Now, Mephibosheth became lame because of bad news that was based on a lie. Many believers today are suffering needlessly because they believe the wrong things about God. They think, *My sin has found me out! God is coming after me!*

Well, I have good news for all Mephibosheths: David is not after your life! When David looked for Mephibosheth, it was to show him kindness, to take care of him and restore to him the land that had belonged to Saul, his grandfather.

Likewise, God is not out to get you. He knows all about your sins and still loves you. That is why He sent Jesus as the payment for your sins. And because of Jesus' covenant with Him, He says to you, "Don't be afraid, I will surely show you kindness. I will restore all to you and you shall always eat at My table!"

Thought for the Day
**God is not out to get you, but to show you kindness,
and to give you provision and restoration.**

Jesus Wore the Crown of Thorns for You

John 19:2
²And the soldiers twisted a crown of thorns and put it on His head....

If hard work is the formula for prosperity, then everyone who works hard should be prosperous. But this is certainly not the case. Many people who work very hard are still poor!

I am not advocating laziness. What I am saying is that working hard by the sweat of your brow is not how God's prosperity comes. In fact, if you have to work overtime all the time and are stressed out, you are probably operating under the curse.

What curse is that? It is this curse: "In the sweat of your face you shall eat bread..." (Genesis 3:19). And it refers to the stress, struggle and anxieties that come with working hard and yet producing little. Now, work itself is not a curse since God gave Adam work before the fall — Adam was to tend the garden of Eden. (Genesis 2:15.) It was only after he sinned that the land was cursed and it brought forth thorns, and man had to toil to eat of it. (Genesis 3:17–18.)

But praise God, Jesus wore the thorns on His head to show you that He has borne this curse for you and redeemed you from it. He wore the crown of thorns so that you can work stress-free and yet have the results. You don't have to be worried and stressed out day and night like the people of the world just to get ahead in life. Your heavenly Father can get you there without the worries and stress. (Matthew 6:31–33.)

Beloved, every curse that was supposed to fall on your head fell on Jesus' head, typified by the crown of thorns. He wore the crown of thorns for you so that you can have peace of mind. He wore the crown of thorns for you and took your curse so that you can wear the crown of glory and take His righteousness, and all the benefits of that righteousness!

Today, don't labor and toil like the people of the world. Instead, expect to see the blessings of God come into your life without blood, sweat and tears because Jesus wore the crown of thorns for you!

Thought for the Day
Your heavenly Father can get you ahead in life
without the toil and stress of the world.

Double for Your Trouble!

Zechariah 9:12
¹²Return to the stronghold, you prisoners of hope.
Even today I declare that I will restore double to you.

I am sure that you have heard the expression, "When life throws lemons at you, make lemonade!" Well, I want you to know that when the devil throws lemons at you, **God Himself** will make lemonade for you! After all, the Bible says that God works all things together for your good. (Romans 8:28.)

And He does it with style — He restores double for your trouble! Beloved, if you have lost a husband or wife through divorce, or a precious child through death, God can restore double to you, so that you end up having more than before, if not in quantity, then in quality!

Consider Job in the Old Testament. When he lost everything, his wife told him to curse God and die. (Job 2:9.) He refused and, instead, responded to God in faith, and "the Lord gave Job **twice** as much as he had before" (Job 42:10).

When David lost the child he had with Bathsheba, he stopped pleading and started worshiping God because he trusted in the mercies of God. (2 Samuel 2:15-20.) Later, God blessed David and Bathsheba with another son named Solomon, who became the wisest and richest king the world has ever known. (v. 24.)

Today, God promises to restore double for your trouble — "Even today I declare that I will restore **double** to you." If He declared it, He will do it! So you cannot but have hope that things will be even better than before. That is why in the same verse, He calls you "prisoners of hope." My friend, hope in the biblical sense means a confident expectation of good things happening in your life. You are a prisoner of that! You can't help but wake up feeling hopeful. You can't help but expect good things to happen to you!

So when trouble comes from the devil, don't give up and say, "It is hopeless!" Don't worry or get angry. Worship God like David did and see that trouble as an opportunity for God to bless you with more than what you originally had. And because God has declared it, be confident that you will get double for your trouble!

Thought for the Day
Because God has declared it, be confident that
you will get double for your trouble!

Let It Go!

Exodus 15:26
²⁶ "... *I will put none of the diseases on you which I have brought
on the Egyptians. For I am the LORD who heals you.*"

After crossing the Red Sea, the children of Israel came to a place called Marah. The waters there were bitter. That is why the place was called Marah, which means "bitter." The Israelites could not drink any of the water, so the Lord made the bitter waters sweet. (Exodus 15:23–25) Then, He brought up the subject of the diseases of Egypt and, for the first time, revealed Himself to His people as "the LORD who heals you."

Why did the Lord suddenly mention the diseases of the world (Egypt represents the world in the Bible) at a place called "bitter"? What do diseases have to do with bitter waters? I believe that it is because He wants His people to know that a major cause of diseases in their bodies is harboring bitterness and resentment!

Some years ago, a lady shared with me about her sister who had died of cancer at a young age. She said, "Pastor Prince, a number of years before she passed on, she went through a very bitter divorce. She was very bitter toward her ex-husband." Then, she asked me, "Is there a relationship between her bitterness and the cancer?"

I have studied the subject of healing for many years. I have read many books. I have listened to many sermons and I have sat under many healing ministries. And they all say the same thing: If you have unforgiveness in your heart long enough, that unforgiveness can sometimes translate into a disease in your body.

So if you have been bitter about something or someone, it is time to let it go! Your health, joy and life are more important. If you are already sick and you know that bitterness has something to do with it, let it go! See Jesus as your healer. He is standing at your place of bitterness today and He is saying to you, "My child, I can make your bitter waters sweet. I am the Lord who heals you."

My friend, let it all go and let Jesus heal not just your diseases, but your broken heart too!

Thought for the Day
Harboring bitterness and resentment is just not worth your health, joy and life.

Getting Filled With All
the Fullness of God

Ephesians 3:19
¹⁹To know the love of Christ which passes knowledge;
that you may be filled with all the fullness of God.

W e would all like to experience more health, prosperity and success in our lives. God, being God, has all of these things, won't you agree? So to be full of God is to be full of health, prosperity and success. But how does one become full of God?

In the past, I was told that to be "filled with all the fullness of God," I had to fast a certain number of days, pray a certain number of hours and speak in tongues incessantly! I am not belittling fasting, praying or speaking in tongues, but to be filled with all the fullness of God is not about what you do. It is not even about your love for Christ. It is actually about **knowing the love of Christ**! No one ever told me that if I knew how much God loves me and focused on His love for me, I would be full of Him.

When God made you, He designed you to run at optimal level when you are filled with His love, like a car that runs at its best when it is filled with the right kind of petrol or gasoline. When you realize how much God loves you and you feed on His love for you, you will be supernaturally filled with the fullness of God.

And to be full of God is to be full of everything God is to you and has for you. To be full of God is to come to a place of life, health, peace, prosperity — total wellness.

Also, when you are conscious of how much God loves you and you become filled with the fullness of God, what follows is the next verse — God doing exceedingly abundantly above all that you can ask or think, according to the power that works in you. (v. 20.) You will experience the tremendous blessings of God exploding in your life! You will become a blessing magnet!

So as God's beloved, continue to be nourished by His love for you, and experience more health, prosperity and success in your life!

Thought for the Day
Being filled with the fullness of God is not about what you do,
but about knowing how much God loves you.

God Remembers What You Say in Faith

Isaiah 55:11
¹¹ So shall My word be that goes forth from My mouth; it shall not
return to Me void, but it shall accomplish what I please,
and it shall prosper in the thing for which I sent it.

Some years back, I had a skin condition which refused to heal. I told God about it and began to take the Holy Communion believing and confessing that by Jesus' stripes I was healed. Nothing happened, or so it seemed.

But the Lord did not forget about my skin condition. One day, He prompted me to check my body to see if it was still there. I did so and realized that it had disappeared! God had not forgotten the Word which I had confessed in faith.

A mother and daughter, who had been listening to my sermon tapes, began to believe that as the righteousness of God in Christ, they attracted the blessings of God. At that time, the mother had entered her name in a number of lucky draw contests. Together, they believed for the grand prize of one of these contests, which was a $470,000 private apartment.

Soon after, the mother won two microwave ovens, a rice cooker and a $5,000 wristwatch. In the excitement of winning those prizes, they completely forgot about the grand prize. But God did not forget what they had believed Him for. Some time later, they received news that the mother was the winner of the private apartment!

Maybe you shared God's Word with a troubled friend a few years ago. You bump into him one day and he tells you, "Remember that day? You said something which transformed my life!" Your mind draws a blank because you have forgotten what you said. But God did not forget. He remembered what you said that day in faith.

You see, if the words you confess in faith for yourself or over your loved ones are God's own words, He says, "So shall My word be that goes forth from My mouth; it shall not return to Me void, but it shall accomplish what I please, and it shall prosper in the thing for which I sent it." Because what is promised to you is God's Word, you will see the manifestation of His promise. He will certainly watch over His Word to perform it! (Numbers 23:19; Philippians 1:6, KJV.)

Thought for the Day
God will certainly watch over His Word to perform it!

Safe Under God's Wings

Psalm 91:4
⁴He shall cover you with His feathers,
and under His wings you shall take refuge....

A farmer walked around his farm to take stock of his losses after a fire had destroyed it. When he came to the chicken coop, he noticed the charred carcass of a mother hen. He used his foot to turn the carcass over and to his surprise, live chicks ran out from under it! The mother hen had died protecting her chicks from the fire.

In the Bible, wings speak of protection. David said to God, "Hide me under the shadow of Your wings" (Psalm 17:8). Jesus Himself offered protection to the Jewish nation when He said, "O Jerusalem, Jerusalem, the one who kills the prophets and stones those who are sent to her! How often I wanted to gather your children together, as a hen gathers her brood under her wings, but you were not willing!" (Luke 13:34).

He wanted to gather the children of Israel under His wings to protect them, but they were not willing. That was why He wept over Jerusalem. He literally shed tears because He saw the destruction that would come upon His people. He saw the Roman siege of Jerusalem in AD 70, when the Romans burnt the city and holy temple, slaughtered many, took some captive and sold others as slaves. (Luke 19:41–44.) I believe that He also saw the Holocaust of World War II, which resulted in the extermination of six million Jews.

For us, because we have not rejected Jesus, but have received Him as our Savior, we have His protection, especially in these times of deadly pestilences, natural catastrophes and terrorist attacks.

Like the mother hen who spread her wings and died protecting her chicks, Jesus spread His wings of love and died on the cross for us. And after He had died to save us, He rose again and lives today to make sure that we are well taken care of.

Beloved, see yourself under the wings of your Savior, who has promised you this in His Word: "He shall cover you with His feathers, and under His wings you shall take refuge."

Thought for the Day
In these times of deadly pestilences, natural catastrophes and terrorist attacks,
see yourself protected under the wings of your Savior.

Jesus Has You Covered

Leviticus 1:4
⁴Then he shall put his hand on the head of the burnt offering,
and it will be accepted on his behalf to make atonement for him.

Imagine the perfection of Jesus covering you from head to toe in the sight of God every moment of the day. Does that sound like a dream? My friend, that is your reality today because Jesus became your burnt offering at the cross.

In the case of the burnt offering, when the offerer lays his hand on the animal sacrifice (vv. 3–4), the perfection and beauty of the unblemished sacrifice is transferred to him, and God sees and accepts him in the perfection of the animal.

In Hebrew, the word "accepted" implies being treated with favor, delight and acceptance. This means that you, for whom Jesus became a burnt offering, are treated by God with favor, delight and acceptance because the beauty and perfection of Jesus have been transferred to you. As your burnt offering, Jesus has made atonement for you on your behalf.

Jesus is your atonement or covering for sin. How precious Jesus is to the Father is how precious you are to the Father because when the Father sees you, He sees Jesus, your atonement, your covering.

So every day, take Jesus as your burnt offering. Come to God and say, "Father, I thank You that Jesus is my burnt offering. He covers me from head to toe with His righteousness. I thank you Father, that You see me without spot or wrinkle. You see me covered in all the value and perfection of the work of Your Son. What He is to You, I am. Who He is to You, I am. As He is now, so am I. I am in Him!" (1 John 4:17.)

Jesus has you covered. You don't appear before the Father with all your faults and shortcomings. Jesus proclaims to you what is right with you in spite of what is wrong with you because He has covered you with His perfection. Today, hear Him telling you, "Go, girl! I have you covered. There is nothing for you to worry about!" Hear Him saying to you, "Go for it, son! I am covering you. There is nothing for you to fear!"

Thought for the Day
You are treated by God with favor, delight and acceptance because the
beauty and perfection of Jesus have been transferred to you.

You Are a Blessing Going Somewhere to Happen

Deuteronomy 28:10
*¹⁰Then all peoples of the earth shall see that you are called by
the name of the LORD, and they shall be afraid of you.*

Today, we are called by the name of Christ — **Christ**-ians. Therefore, the blessing of Deuteronomy 28:10, which says, "Then all peoples of the earth shall see that you are called by the name of the Lord" is no longer just a promise but reality!

The second part of the verse — "and they shall be afraid of you" — is also true for you. People will respect you. Your boss will favor you and even your competitors will esteem you highly. They know that there is something special about you because good things happen when you are around!

I experienced this blessing when I first started working. I worked in a small third-floor office which constantly smelled of salted fish because there was a salted fish stall on the ground floor. It was in that small, dingy office that I kept on confessing that I was blessed by the Lord, and I experienced divine favor with my clients. My boss could see that there was something different about me.

The company's business flourished and before long, we moved out of that small office to a building which in the mid-eighties was considered an information technology hub. There, we occupied a couple of offices, and started specializing in computer software and courses. Soon, we occupied the entire floor! That was how much God was prospering us.

God was also blessing me tremendously. I was drawing a very good monthly income, enjoying the favor of my boss and was in his inner circle. A few years later, I decided to go into full-time ministry. When I broke the news to my boss, He cried. I never knew how much I meant to him until then. It was only then that I realized what a blessing I had been to him by the grace of God.

Beloved, because you are also called by the name of the Lord, wherever you go, you are a blessing. His blessing is on you. The people around you will look at you and know that you are a blessing going somewhere to happen!

Thought for the Day
**Because the blessing of the Lord is upon you,
good things happen when you are around!**

'Lord, I Cannot, but You Can!'

Philippians 2:13
¹³For it is God who works in you both to will and to do for His good pleasure.

Have you ever tried to break a bad habit on your own? You probably found that when you tried to stop it by sheer willpower, you saw improvement for a while, and then bounced back to square one. Worse, you found yourself binging on the very thing that you were trying not to do. And your condition was worse than before you started your "I'm going to quit" program!

The changes were temporary because it was **you** doing it.

A church member who had been a chain-smoker used to believe that with willpower, he could quit smoking. He would tell himself, "If there is a will, there is a way!" But he discovered that with willpower, he could stop smoking for a week or two, and then he would succumb to the pull of nicotine again.

When he turned his life over to God and learnt about God's grace, he told God, "I realize that I cannot stop smoking. I cannot, but You can break my habit, Lord." And every time he lit up, he would say, "Lord, I am trying to stop smoking, but I cannot. I am trusting You." He would even say, "I am still righteous because of Jesus' blood."

Well, in the very same year, all his cravings to smoke vanished! When asked how he succeeded, he would say, "It is entirely God and none of me! It is all by His grace." This man lost all the desire to smoke. That is true transformation.

When you receive the grace of God to do for you what you cannot do, you will experience effortless and permanent change on the inside, which in turn changes your actions on the outside. The Bible tells us that God works in us to give us both the will and ability to perform what He desires. It is God who removes the old want to's and gives us new ones. And He even gives us the power to carry them out!

Beloved, look to His grace to do what you cannot do. Say, "Lord, I cannot, but You can!" Then, what you experience will not merely be behavior modification, but true and lasting inward transformation!

Thought for the Day
It is God who removes your old want to's and gives you new ones.

God Is Not Punishing You for Some Sin

Ephesians 1:7
⁷In Him we have redemption through His blood, the forgiveness of sins,
according to the riches of His grace.

Some Christians believe that although you have forgiveness of sins, you are not free from the penalties of your sins. In other words, you can still expect punishment from God. For example, some married Christian couples have been told that they are childless because God is punishing them for having had pre-marital sex. So although God has forgiven them of that sin, He still has to punish them for it.

I am certainly not for pre-marital sex, but I want you to know that God, who is the only One who can fully appreciate the full value of His Son's blood and who is completely satisfied by His Son's sacrifice, is at rest in His heart today concerning your sins! That is why He is not against you even when you fail. Neither is He out to punish you when you sin. No, He still loves you, is for you and wants to help you overcome that sin.

In the Old Testament, the blood of bulls and goats could only "cover" sins and not take them away. (Hebrews 10:4.) But the blood of Jesus is not like the blood of animals! For by **one** sacrifice, the eternal blood of the Son of God has **forever** removed your sins (Psalm 103:12) and cleansed you of **all** unrighteousness! (1 John 1:9.) In fact, God is so satisfied with His Son's perfect work that He says to you today, "Your sins and lawless deeds I will by no means remember!" (Hebrews 10:17) And if God does not remember them, why would He punish you for them?

Beloved, you **have** "redemption through His blood, the forgiveness of sins, according to the riches of His grace." Because Jesus' work is complete, **all** your sins have been **completely** forgiven. And complete forgiveness means that the penalties for your sins can no longer fall on you because they had already fallen on Jesus at the cross. (Isaiah 53:5.)

So don't think for one moment that God is punishing you for some sin just because something bad happened to you. Look to the cross and know that all your sins have already been punished fully in the body of Christ. Believe that God is for you and expect victory!

Thought for the Day
Because Jesus' work is complete, all your sins have been completely forgiven.

See the Work Accomplished

John 19:30
³⁰So when Jesus had received the sour wine, He said, "It is finished!"
And bowing His head, He gave up His spirit.

What do you see when it comes to healing for your sick body, restoration for your failing marriage or breakthroughs for your financial woes? Do you see a finished work or a work that is yet to be completed?

God wants you to know that what you desperately need Him to do for you has already been done! Jesus' finished work at the cross so satisfied the Father's heart that from heaven's throne came the pronouncement, "It is done!" (Revelation 16:17) in response to Jesus' cry, "It is finished!" on earth. So God wants you to have this revelation that whatever you need Him to do for you has already been done because Jesus has accomplished it all for you.

If you need healing, know that your healing has been accomplished. If you need restoration for your marriage, know that your restoration has been accomplished. You are not going to die from any lack — you have been abundantly supplied. All these things have been accomplished, not by you, but by Christ alone!

My friend, if you are bothered by a pain in your body, God wants you to see your healing finished or accomplished for you by His Son's death on the cross. If it is a loss or debt you face, or a certain sin that you are struggling with, believe that your provision, restoration and deliverance have been accomplished for you.

Don't worry about what you see or feel, or the presence of contradicting reports. These are lying symptoms and though they may seem very real, they are temporal and not the truth. God's Word is the truth and it will remain because it is eternal. And when you believe that only what God's Word says about your situation is the truth, all the lying symptoms will eventually have to line up with His Word.

God the Son says, "It is finished!"

God the Father says, "It is done!"

What do you say?

Thought for the Day
**Whatever you need God to do for you has been done because
Jesus has accomplished it all for you at the cross.**

Be Anxious for Nothing

Philippians 4:6–7
⁶Be anxious for nothing, but in everything by prayer and supplication,
with thanksgiving, let your requests be made known to God;
⁷and the peace of God, which surpasses all understanding,
will guard your hearts and minds through Christ Jesus.

When faced with a challenge or crisis, our tendency is to get all anxious about it. But God does not want us to react this way. He does not want us to be anxious about anything. Instead, whatever the problem is, He wants us to go to Him in prayer and supplication, telling Him what we need and thanking Him for the answer. When we do that, His peace, which surpasses all understanding, will guard our hearts and minds from all worries, anxieties and fears.

"Pastor Prince, it is easy for you to say, 'Be anxious for nothing.' Try living with my husband for one day. Try disciplining that wayward teenager of mine. Look at the balance in my bank account! How can I not be anxious?"

Hold it! I am not the one who said, "Be anxious for nothing." The apostle Paul said it. Yet, it was not him — he was prompted by the Holy Spirit. And when Paul wrote that, he was a prisoner under house arrest in Rome. He had been sent to Rome because he had appealed to Caesar regarding his death sentence. The Jews in Jerusalem wanted him to be put to death. (Acts 28:16–20.)

Yet, under those trying conditions, he wrote these words: "Be anxious for nothing, but in everything by prayer and supplication, with thanksgiving, let your requests be made known to God."

My friend, if you are anxious or worried about something, remember those words. Let's say that you are anxious about a huge debt. Go to the Lord and pray, "Lord Jesus, I no longer want to be anxious about this problem. I hand it over to You and ask for supernatural cancellation of this debt. It is in Your care now. You are in charge. I thank You for taking care of it."

God is true to His Word. As you pray this prayer and cast your care to Him, you will find His peace setting your heart and mind at rest. So be anxious for nothing — let the One with whom nothing is impossible take care of it for you!

Thought for the Day
Cast your cares to God in prayer, and find His peace
setting your heart and mind at rest.

God Uses the Weak to Confound the Mighty

1 Corinthians 1:27
*²⁷But God has chosen the foolish things of the world to put to
shame the wise, and God has chosen the weak things of the
world to put to shame the things which are mighty.*

When you are faced with a big challenge, do you automatically look for the most powerful means to solve the problem? Well, that is not thinking the way God thinks. The Bible tells us that it pleases God to use what the world considers weak, foolish, base and despised to bring to nothing things which are mighty.

"What is that in your hand?" God asked.

"A rod," Moses said. (Exodus 4:2.) And with that rod, he performed miracles and confounded the might of Pharaoh.

"Five loaves and two fish," a little boy said. And with that little boy's lunch, Jesus fed 5,000 men, and his disciples gathered 12 baskets full of leftovers. (John 6:1-13.)

"The jawbone of an ass," Samson said. And with that, he slew a thousand Philistines, who were the enemies of God's people. (Judges 15:15.)

"Five stones and a sling," said David the shepherd boy. And with one of his stones and the sling, he brought down Goliath, the mighty Philistine champion.

At a recent conference for Hokkien-speaking pastors, Pastor Mark, our Hokkien and Mandarin services pastor, realized how his spoken Hokkien pales in comparison to the refined and flawless Hokkien spoken by the other pastors there. Yet, it pleases God to use Pastor Mark's colloquial Hokkien to lead many dialect-speaking folks, especially the elderly, to Christ.

Many of these elderly folks are testifying that for the first time in their lives, they are set free completely from fears of debilitating diseases, loneliness, deep-rooted superstitions, generational curses, the ravages of old age and even death.

My friend, don't despise what seems weak and insignificant to the world. God can use them to bring down the giants in your life!

Thought for the Day
*It pleases God to use weak, foolish, base and despised things of the world
to bring to nothing things which are mighty.*

Jesus Is Still Jehovah Rapha

Exodus 15:26
26 "… I am the Lord who heals you."

Do you know that the first compound name that the Lord revealed to the Israelites after they came out of Egypt was Jehovah Rapha, the Lord who heals you? It was as if He was telling them, as they began their new life with Him, that He had already healed them of all the diseases and pains they suffered when they were in bondage in Egypt. Indeed, when He brought them out of Egypt, "there was none feeble among His tribes" (Psalm 105:37).

Today, just as the Israelites were delivered from their bondage in Egypt and from slavery to Pharaoh, you have also been delivered from the bondage of sin and sickness, and from slavery to the devil, by the blood of the Lamb. And the Lord, who is the same yesterday, today and forever (Hebrews 13:8), still says to you, "I am the Lord who heals you."

A church member, who was experiencing pain in her womb for several months, looked to Jesus as her healer even as she went to see a doctor, who performed an ultrasound scan on her womb. When told that she had two big tumors and several blood cysts in her womb, she continued to look to Jesus as her healer. The doctor then had her blood tested to see if the tumors were cancerous.

Three days later, she saw the doctor again and was told that the tumors were not cancerous. Not only that, but a second ultrasound scan also showed that all the cysts and one of the tumors had completely disappeared! The other tumor had also shrunk. Although she had taken medication, the doctor told her that based on the original size of the tumor, it should have taken months to shrink that much. He commented that this was the quickest healing he had ever seen!

Beloved, if the doctor has given you a bad report regarding your health, don't despair. Look to Jesus and expect healing for your body. He is the same yesterday, today and forever. He is still Jehovah Rapha — the Lord who heals you!

Thought for the Day
Look to Jesus and expect healing for your body. He is still the Lord who heals you!

See Your Enemies Flee Because of Jesus

Deuteronomy 28:7
*⁷"The Lord will cause your enemies who rise against you to be
defeated before your face; they shall come out against you
one way and flee before you seven ways."*

S ome people think that Jesus and the devil are always confronting and fighting each other. But when I read my Bible, I don't see fights between the two. What I see is the devil having to flee whenever he encounters Jesus!

Consider the demoniac from the country of the Gadarenes in Luke 8:26–39. The demons in the man begged Jesus not to torment them or send them into the abyss, but to permit them to enter a herd of swine nearby.

You see, neither the devil nor his demons can stand before Jesus. They may be able to torment people for a while, but when Jesus comes on the scene, they know that that is the end of their stay. They will have to flee! All it took was just one word from Jesus, and the entire legion of demons had to come out of the man and flee into the swine.

As a child of God, you exude a spiritual fragrance that evil spirits can detect and which causes them to tremble. It is the life of Jesus inside you. And "He who is in you is greater than he who is in the world" (1 John 4:4). That is why no curse, spell, accusation, scandal or destruction planned against you can succeed. Your enemies may come against you one way, but the Lord will confuse them and cause them to flee before you seven ways!

Jesus paid with His life to give you this victory over your enemies. After His arrest in the garden of Gethsemane, the Jews and Gentiles were united for the first time with one common objective: torture Jesus and have Him killed. King Herod of the Jews and Pontius Pilate of the Romans were long-time enemies, but because of Jesus, they became friends. (Luke 23:12.)

My friend, Jesus' enemies were united and had "victory" over Him. But because He triumphed over them through the cross and rose again, today, your enemies will be scattered and you will have victory over them!

Thought for the Day
**Your enemies may come against you one way, but the Lord will
confuse them and cause them to flee before you seven ways!**

The Head and Not the Tail

Deuteronomy 28:13
*¹³And the Lord will make you the head and not the tail;
you shall be above only, and not be beneath....*

One of our church members saw his sales performance hit rock bottom by the middle of the year. As a result, he was ranked 320 out of the 420 financial advisers in his company.

Devastated and on the verge of giving up, he started listening to my messages and claiming God's promises such as "the Lord will make you the head and not the tail; you shall be above only, and not be beneath" and "many who are first will be last, and the last first." (Matthew 19:30.)

He committed everything to God because he believed that only God could turn things around for him. And God did just that.

By the end of that year, he was ranked second in his branch and 10th in the whole company! He qualified for a trip for two to Barcelonia, Spain, worth about $20,000. That was not all. For the first time in his 12 years as a financial adviser, he qualified for the Million Dollar Round Table Award. Only the top six percent of advisers in the entire industry qualify for this international award.

Beloved, when God makes you the head, you will end up on top of your circumstances. Consider the story of Joseph. (Genesis 39.) Even when he was a slave, he was the head and not the tail because God prospered everything that he did.

"But Pastor Prince, when I look at my life, there are times when I am up and there are times when I am down. Yet, the Bible says that I will be above only. I don't understand this."

What you are going through is only temporal. Keep believing that you are above only and not beneath, even when you have hit rock bottom. It is God who **always** causes you to triumph in Christ. (2 Corinthians 2:14.) You cannot cause yourself to triumph. Only God can and He has promised in His Word that you will be the head and not the tail, above only and not beneath. So believe His Word in spite of your circumstances and expect to see victory!

Thought for the Day
***Even when you have hit rock bottom, keep believing God's promise that
you shall be above only and not beneath.***

Release the Power in You!

Ephesians 3:20
²⁰Now to Him who is able to do exceedingly abundantly above all that
we ask or think, according to the power that works in us.

How much power is working in you right now? God's Word says that there is "power that works in us." It is a tremendous power that shakes the heavens and the earth because it comes from the throne of God, "who is able to do exceedingly abundantly above all that we ask or think"! The problem, however, is that many of us don't release that power.

God wants us to release that power because there are things that will not happen on earth until we do so. Jesus said that "whatever you bind on earth will be bound in heaven, and whatever you loose on earth will be loosed in heaven" (Matthew 16:19). What Jesus is saying is that what you permit to happen, heaven will permit. What you disallow, heaven will disallow!

So how do we release God's power in us? One way is to pray in tongues. When we allow His Spirit to make intercession for us (Romans 8:26), miracles happen.

Some time ago, the aunt of a church member underwent surgery to remove a diseased kidney. In spite of the surgery, the prognosis was poor. At home, the church member and his wife were prompted by the Spirit to release the power that works in them by praying in tongues for their aunt.

Back at the hospital, the aunt underwent further observation. When an X-ray of her abdominal area was taken, the doctor was shocked to find two healthy kidneys. Five other doctors were consulted who subsequently examined the aunt. At first, they thought that the surgeon who had performed the operation had made a mistake and did not remove the diseased kidney. But further investigation showed that the kidney had indeed been removed. They could not explain what had happened.

But the church member and his wife needed no explanation because they knew that when they released the power that worked in them, God did exceedingly abundantly above all that they could ask or think — He gave their aunt a new kidney.

Beloved, He can do the same for you when you pray in the Spirit and release the power that works in you!

Thought for the Day
When we allow the Holy Spirit to make intercession for us
by praying in tongues, miracles happen.

Jesus Met Every Claim of God on You

Leviticus 1:5
⁵He shall kill the bull before the LORD; and the priests, Aaron's sons,
shall bring the blood and sprinkle the blood all around on the
altar that is by the door of the tabernacle of meeting.

When the children of Israel were in the wilderness, God instructed them to set up a tabernacle as a place of meeting between Him and them. Near the door of the tabernacle was an altar. It speaks of the claims God makes on the righteousness of man. For this reason, an offering had to be killed, its blood sprinkled all around on the altar and its body burnt on the altar before one was counted worthy to go into God's presence.

The sprinkling of the blood of a bull or goat all around on that altar meant that the Israelites were under the covering of the blood of that animal. Even when they sinned, their sins were covered by the blood until the next sacrifice.

The blood speaks of Jesus' blood shed for us at the cross. Yet, His blood is worth so much more than the blood of bulls and goats because His blood is effective forever! In fact, His blood has met every single claim of God on man to the point that God is so completely satisfied that He now enjoys the savor of rest in what His Son has done.

You too can rest knowing that God is fully satisfied with you because of Christ's perfect sacrifice. Even if you fall into sin, you can turn to the blood of Jesus. Your sins are not merely covered by His blood, like how the blood of bulls and goats covered sins. No, your sins have been washed away by **His** blood! (Revelation 1:5.) In fact, your sins and lawless deeds God remembers no more! (Hebrews 8:12; 10:17.)

Jesus was your perfect offering placed on the altar of sacrifice. By just one offering of Himself, "He hath perfected forever them that are sanctified" (Hebrews 10:14, KJV). Jesus has not only sanctified you or made you holy, He has perfected you forever! Today, you can enter boldly into God's presence because He sees you the way He sees Jesus. He sees you perfected forever because you are in Christ!

Thought for the Day
Jesus has not only sanctified you or made you holy, He has perfected you forever!

The Son's Heartbeat for You

3 John 1:2, KJV
*²Beloved, I wish above all things that thou mayest prosper and
be in health, even as thy soul prospereth.*

L et's say that you are now in your nineties. Someone comes along and asks you, "You've been a Christian for a very long time. You have seen much and done much with God by your side. You have prayed all kinds of prayers too. So what would you place as top priority when you pray for people?"

I believe the apostle John was asked a similar question and his reply was, "Beloved, I wish above all things that thou mayest prosper and be in health, even as thy soul prospereth." When the apostle John wrote 3 John, he was already a very old man and probably the only disciple of the original 12 who was still alive. It had been so long ago since he last walked alongside his beloved Lord, and witnessed His crucifixion, resurrection and ascension.

The apostle John had also leaned on the Lord's bosom on the night of the Last Supper. And I believe that there on Jesus' bosom, he must have felt the heartbeat of the Son of God — that loving and compassionate heartbeat which had caused Him to go about "doing good and healing all who were oppressed by the devil" (Acts 10:38). In fact, two-thirds of Jesus' ministry on earth had to do with healing the sick.

And now, nearing the end of his life, and after all he had heard, seen and experienced, the apostle John prioritized, above all things, health as well as prosperity. He said, "I wish above all things that you prosper and be in health, even as your soul prospers." He knew the Lord's heartbeat. He knew that the Lord wants and will always want these for His people.

Jesus had prioritized divine healing during His earthly ministry. And Jesus, who is "the same yesterday, today, and forever" (Hebrews 13:8), will do the same for you today. His heart still beats for you. He will never miss an opportunity to do good to you, to heal you of your broken body, emotional scars and weary spirit, and to prosper you!

Thought for the Day
The Lord wants and will always want health and prosperity for His people.

God's Angels Are Watching Over You

Psalm 91:10–11
¹⁰*No evil shall befall you, nor shall any plague come near your dwelling;*
¹¹*for He shall give His angels charge over you, to keep you in all your ways.*

Don't you just sense your Father's love in these words? Like a mother hen that spreads her wings over her chicks to protect them, God will "cover you with His feathers, and under His wings you shall take refuge" (Psalm 91:4). So don't be fearful of accidents, terrorist attacks, diseases or tsunamis because your heavenly Father loves you and watches over you.

One of the ways He does this is with His angels. God has declared that **no** evil, plague or accident will befall you or even come near your dwelling "for He shall give His angels charge over you, to keep you in all your ways." When He says "no," He means "no-thing"! And if He tells His angels to "keep you in all your ways", it means round-the-clock divine protection for you!

Let me share with you a true story. A Christian was flying his plane when he realized that it was low on fuel. He contacted the air traffic controller and asked for assistance to land. But he was told that he could not land because there was a heavy fog. Then, the radio went silent and the plane entered the fog.

He was flying blindly when he suddenly heard over his headphones, "Pull up! Pull up!" He pulled up just in time to avoid hitting the expressway! Then, the voice said, "Follow my instructions and I will help you land safely."

He obeyed and landed perfectly. Thinking that it was the air traffic controller who had helped him, he immediately looked for him to thank him. But when he found him, the man said, "Listen, we lost contact with you when I told you that there was a heavy fog. None of us managed to speak to you after that." The pilot realized then that God had sent an angel to lead him to safety.

Beloved, your heavenly Father is watching over you. That is why no evil will befall you, nor will any plague come near your dwelling. And He has a host of angels to keep you in all your ways!

Thought for the Day
**Don't be fearful because your heavenly Father and
His angels are watching over you.**

See the Abundance Within You

Luke 17:21
²¹"... For indeed, the kingdom of God is within you."

When you were younger, were you often scolded for not finishing all your food or leaving the lights and fan on when you left your room? Were you constantly reminded that there are people starving in the world, that electricity costs a lot of money and that money doesn't grow on trees? Now, do you find yourself telling your child the same things?

We are naturally conscious of lack, but Jesus isn't. Even in the midst of lack, He was always conscious of abundance. Remember the little boy's five loaves and two fish? What did Jesus do when these were placed in His hands? Did He say, "What do you expect Me to do with so little?" No, His eyes were not on the natural, the visible, the lack. His eyes were on the kingdom of God where there is always abundance. So in His hands, the little boy's lunch was multiplied, and 5,000 men, not counting women and children, were fed that day! (John 6:1–13.)

God doesn't want you to be conscious of the lack in your natural circumstances. He doesn't want you to live by how much you earn or how much you have in the bank. Now, I am not encouraging you to spend foolishly beyond your means. I am saying that God wants you to be conscious of the abundance of resources in His kingdom.

"But Pastor Prince, where is that kingdom?"

As long as you have received Jesus as your Savior, that kingdom is in you!

Jesus said that "the kingdom of God is within you." This means that the kingdom of God is not some physical place. It is within you and it is where the abundance of resources is. So if you want to experience abundance in your life, be conscious first of the abundance inside you. Then, what is inside you will become a reality on the outside.

Beloved, God doesn't want you to be conscious of the lack you see outside you. He wants you to be conscious of the abundance within you because His kingdom is within you!

Thought for the Day
The kingdom of God, where there is always abundance, is within you!

The Blood Alone Saves

Exodus 12:13
¹³Now the blood shall be a sign for you on the houses where you are. And when I see the blood, I will pass over you; and the plague shall not be on you to destroy you....

On the night of the first Passover, many of the children of Israel were probably anxious. Imagine one Israelite asking another nervously, "Did you hear that the angel of death is passing through tonight?"

"Yes! We were told to put the blood of the lamb on the doorposts of our home and everything would be all right. Is that true?"

Like the Israelites, you might be wondering, "Can the blood really protect me? How much blood do I have to put on my doorposts? Will the angel of death get me if I am fearful?"

My friend, don't add to God's conditions. He said, "When I see the **blood**, I will pass over you; and the plague shall not be on you to destroy you." He did not say, "When I see the blood, plus your understanding, efforts, obedience, faithfulness and refusal to give in to fear, then I will pass over you."

It is the blood of Jesus alone that delivers you. If you think that it is because of your faith, then you will always be wondering, "Do I have enough faith?" No my friend, it is His blood alone that saves. And when God sees that you see that it is the blood alone that saves, He calls that faith in the blood, and every plague will pass over you!

God wants you to know that it is Jesus' blood **alone** that saves because every time you think that your deliverance depends partly on God and partly on you, you will not have a settled peace in your heart. But when you know that it is the blood alone that saves, you will have an unshakable peace.

It was the blood that saved the children of Israel from the destroyer on that Passover night and it is still the blood that saves today. And all you need to do for the blood to avail is to say, "Father, I thank You that the blood of Jesus alone covers me and my family. No evil, plague or disaster will befall me or my family because of the blood!"

Thought for the Day
When you know that it is Jesus' blood alone that saves, you will enjoy unshakable peace.

Have a Large Revelation of Jesus!

2 Peter 3:18
18... grow in the grace and knowledge of our Lord and Savior Jesus Christ....

In the Old Testament, three types of burnt offerings were brought to God. I believe that the rich brought offerings of young bulls (Leviticus 1:3), the not-so-rich brought sheep (v. 10) and the poor brought turtledoves. (v. 14.) Though of varying sizes and values, the different burnt offerings were all accepted as sweet aroma to the Lord. (vv. 9, 13, 17.)

These burnt offerings speak of Jesus and His perfect work at the cross. Today, to bring a "rich" offering means that you have a large revelation of Jesus and His finished work. To bring a "not-so-rich" offering means that you have a smaller revelation of Jesus and His finished work. But whatever the size of the revelation you have of Jesus, God accepts you just the same because Jesus is the only measure of your acceptance before God.

However, God wants you to grow in your revelation of Jesus because your well-being hinges on it. Before that first Passover night, all the children of Israel had received the same Word of God — "when I see the blood, I will pass over you" (Exodus 12:13). But I believe that some households lived through that night trembling in fear as they heard the loud wails outside their homes, while other households rested in God's Word, ate their Passover lamb and spent the night rejoicing in His protection, deliverance and love for them.

You see, as long as the households came under the blood, they were all saved, trembling or not! But when they didn't have a revelation of the power of the blood to save them from the destroyer, fear came in even though the blood availed for them. In the same way, God does not want you to struggle through trying times with fear, apprehension and stress. He wants you to enjoy and rest in a greater revelation of Jesus as your deliverer and salvation.

In 2 Peter 1:2, it says, "Grace and peace be multiplied to you..." God wants you to experience more of His grace and peace in your life. How? The verse continues, "... in the knowledge of God and of Jesus our Lord." The more knowledge of Jesus you have, the more God's grace and peace will rest on you!

Thought for the Day
Grow in your revelation of Jesus so that more of
His grace and peace will rest on you.

Condemnation Is the Root Cause

Romans 8:1, NASB
¹Therefore there is now no condemnation for those who are in Christ Jesus.

When you have a plant with sickly leaves, it would be foolish to just treat the leaves without knowing the root cause of the problem. Similarly, when "leaves" of sickness, poverty and destructive habits start sprouting in your life, you need to know what the root cause is.

Experts will tell you that it is stress. They may go a little deeper and say that it is fear — fear of the future, of rejection, of loss, of death and so on. But is fear really the root? Or is there something deeper than fear?

The Bible shows us that the most fundamental cause of problems in our lives is condemnation. With condemnation comes fear. Fear then induces stress which brings about the symptoms of the curse.

This is what happened to Adam. Long before he faced poverty, sickness and eventually death, he had stress. Because of his sin, God told him, "In the sweat of your face you shall eat bread till you return to the ground" (Genesis 3:19). Sweat speaks of stress. But before there was stress, there was fear because Adam told God, "I heard Your voice in the garden, and I was afraid because I was naked; and I hid myself" (v. 10).

But what made Adam fearful? Adam only feared when, seeing his nakedness, he realized that he had sinned against God. He felt so ashamed and condemned that he hid himself. God then asked him, "Who told you that you were naked?" (v. 11). There was no one else in the garden other than Adam and Eve, so we know that it was probably the devil who told Adam that he was naked.

My friend, condemnation is the root cause of the symptoms of the curse manifesting in your life. That is why you need to know that at the cross, God took all your sins, put them on Jesus and unleashed the full fury of His wrath against them until Jesus cried out, "It is finished!"

All your sins have been completely punished in the body of Christ who was condemned for you. The root cause of all your problems has been dealt with. This means that the devil cannot enforce the curse in your life apart from your receiving condemnation. So come to the place of no condemnation and no sick leaves will sprout in your life!

Thought for the Day
**Condemnation is the root cause of the symptoms of
the curse manifesting in your life.**

The Head and Body Are One

Colossians 1:18
18And He is the head of the body, the church, who is the beginning, the firstborn from the dead, that in all things He may have the preeminence.

God's Word says that Christ is the head and we the church are His body. So Christ and the church are **one**. Christ and you are one! You cannot say that God sees Christ, the head, perfect but His body imperfect. Or that Christ is accepted, but His body is not accepted. The measure of Jesus' acceptance with God is the measure of your acceptance with God!

So it makes no sense to say that the head is well, but the body is sick; that the head is rich, but the body is poor; or that the head is at rest, but the body is full of stress. My friend, what Jesus is before God, you His body are. As He is, so are you in this world! (1 John 4:17.)

Today, God wants you to lay claim on Christ being your head. Start believing that all His perfections, and the delight and joy that He brings to the Father's heart, He has set to your account. And you will begin to realize that as Jesus is a sweet-smelling aroma to the Father, so are you!

The more you begin to see that you are one with Christ, the more you will realize that whatever you need right now, He is dispensing to you. If you are sick in your body, Christ, your head, imparts His health and healing to you. If you lack wisdom, Christ, your head, freely imparts His wisdom to you. If you have any lack, Christ, your head, gives you His exceeding riches.

Beloved, have this rich revelation that Christ and you are one. You can never be separated from Christ, your head, from whom comes all the supply for your body — all the power, wisdom, prosperity and health. So declare, "As He is, so am I in this world!"

Thought for the Day
***The measure of Jesus' acceptance with God is
the measure of your acceptance with God!***

Grace and Peace Multiplied to You

2 Peter 1:2–3
²Grace and peace be multiplied to you in the knowledge of God and of Jesus our Lord, ³as His divine power has given to us all things that pertain to life and godliness, through the knowledge of Him who called us by glory and virtue.

Imagine if God were to visit you in a dream tonight and ask you what He could do for you. What would you say to Him? Would you ask Him to give you a deeper knowledge of Jesus our Lord?

God's Word tells us that when you receive revelation in the knowledge of Jesus, it will cause grace and peace to be multiplied in your life. It will cause you to receive all things that pertain to life and godliness.

What is grace? It is the unmerited, unearned and undeserved favor of God shown to us. There is nothing we can do to earn God's grace. But the more we learn of the beauty and love of our Lord Jesus, the more we see His perfect work on the cross, and the more we position ourselves to receive a multiplication of God's grace in our lives.

The verse says that peace too, is multiplied to us through the knowledge of Jesus our Lord. The peace of God sets our hearts free from fear, stress, worries, anxieties and cares. Wouldn't you want to have the peace of God presiding over your heart always?

God's divine power has given us all things that pertain not just to godliness, but to life as well. Wouldn't you say that health, money, a good job and a nice home for your family pertain to life? Well, all these things and everything else that God has already given is released to you through the knowledge of Jesus our Lord.

So let's ask God every day, "Father, give me wisdom and revelation in the knowledge of Jesus." For to know Jesus is to have grace and peace multiplied to us. To know Jesus is to receive all things pertaining to life and godliness!

Thought for the Day
The more we see Jesus and His perfect work on the cross, the more we position ourselves to receive a multiplication of God's grace in our lives.

Today's Bread Is Not for Tomorrow

Matthew 6:11
¹¹Give us this day our daily bread.

Doctors have discovered that worry, stress, fear and anxiety can cause stomach ulcers, high blood pressure and other health problems. The Bible says that "a merry heart does good, like medicine, but a broken spirit dries the bones" (Proverbs 17:22). It also says that God wants us to prosper and be in health, even as our soul prospers. (3 John 1:2.)

When our church was much smaller, I used to worry a lot about my sermons weeks before I even preached them! I was so stressed that I developed symptoms in my body. Two doctors checked me on separate days and found my blood pressure to be very high. Other tests found traces of blood in my urine. I even had mild panic attacks. I believe that the devil was trying to undermine my ministry and destroy me.

But praise God, He delivered and healed me, and taught me not to worry. Today, the church is a lot bigger and I have learnt by the grace of God not to worry. The verse that set me free was this: "Therefore do not worry about tomorrow…" (Matthew 6:34). You see, if you worry about tomorrow, you are trying to live tomorrow today!

My friend, God does not want you to do that. Jesus taught us to pray, "Give us this day our **daily** bread." He did not say, "Give us this day our weekly bread." God gives us daily bread, not weekly bread. God doesn't give tomorrow's bread today. And today's bread is not meant for tomorrow!

This means that God wants you to live today and not worry about what will happen or what you have to do tomorrow. He gives you sufficient grace for today, not tomorrow.

"But Pastor Prince, I have a very important presentation to give tomorrow!"

Beloved, when tomorrow comes, the bread — provision and grace — will be there. I am not advocating laziness and inactivity. By all means, do your homework, but don't worry about it. Just trust the One who wants you to give Him all your cares (1 Peter 5:7), and enjoy His peace and life today!

Thought for the Day
Don't worry about tomorrow for when tomorrow comes,
the bread — provision and grace — will be there.

See the Miraculous When You Give Thanks

John 11:41
⁴¹Then they took away the stone from the place where the dead
man was lying. And Jesus lifted up His eyes and said,
"Father, I thank You that You have heard Me.

Jesus lived a life of thanksgiving. He always thanked His Father for what He had and for always hearing Him when He prayed. That was how He released miracles in His life.

In the story of the feeding of the five thousand (John 6:1–13), Jesus' attitude was one of thankfulness. He took a little boy's lunch of five loaves and two fish, gave thanks and had them distributed. He gave thanks for the little that was there and the little multiplied. Not only did the people eat as much as they wanted, there were 12 baskets full of leftovers!

So when you see the meager balance in your bank account, thank the Lord for what you have. That's your "five loaves and two fish." When you give Him thanks that He is your provider and the source of your supply, in spite of the little you have, your little will become much, with leftovers!

Even when faced with the impossible, the solution was still, "Father, I thank You..." When Jesus stood outside Lazarus' tomb, and the people took away the stone that was covering the tomb, He did not see the situation as hopeless and impossible. He simply lifted up His eyes and said, "Father, I thank You that You have heard Me." Then, He proceeded to call forth Lazarus, and the man came forth alive once more!

The raising of Lazarus, who had been dead for more than four days, was one of Jesus' greatest miracles. And He accomplished this by saying, "Father, I thank You that You have heard Me." He thanked His way to an awesome miracle.

My friend, the next time you find yourself praying, "God, please do this for me! Please give me..." stop! Instead, say, "Thank You God, for hearing me. And because You have heard me, I thank You that I have what I asked for." And when you thank God, the little that you have will multiply. Your impossible situations will turn around to reflect God's provision. And resurrection life will hit you!

Thought for the Day
When you give Him thanks for the little you have,
your little will become much, with leftovers!

The Reason Believers Are Sick

1 Corinthians 11:29–30
²⁹For he who eats and drinks in an unworthy manner eats and drinks judgment to himself, not discerning the Lord's body.
³⁰For this reason many are weak and sick among you, and many sleep.

Have you ever wondered why some Christians are weak and sick, and die young? I thank God that the Holy Spirit gives us the reason as well as the solution. In 1 Corinthians 11:29–30, He tells us clearly that the **one** reason some Christians are weak and sick, and die prematurely, is that they don't discern the Lord's body when they partake of the Holy Communion.

Many believers don't understand that the pierced, striped and slightly burnt bread, which represents the Lord's body, is for their health and healing. And when they partake without discerning this truth, they partake in an unworthy manner. The reverse is true: if they discern accurately the Lord's body, then they will be strong and healthy, and live long.

Unfortunately, the church down through the years has misconstrued this teaching and taught that if you have sin in your life, you are unworthy and cannot partake of the Holy Communion, lest you become weak and sick, and even die! We have turned a blessing into a curse. Because of this, many Christians are afraid to come to the Lord's table and are therefore robbed of the health-giving power of the Holy Communion.

My friend, there is no such thing as a worthy person! The best of us still miss it and fail. So unworthy people are the only people who partake of the Lord's Supper. But because Jesus died for unworthy people, He has qualified those of us who take Him as our righteousness to partake of every benefit that He died to give us.

So it is not a matter of whether you are worthy or unworthy to partake, but **how** you partake. Come to the Lord's table with boldness and partake because Jesus has qualified you with His precious blood. Don't treat it as a ritual, but release your faith for health and healing as you discern that Jesus' body was broken so that yours can be healthy and whole today. When you partake like this, you are partaking in a worthy manner, and you will not be weak or sickly, or die prematurely!

Thought for the Day
The pierced, striped and slightly burnt Holy Communion bread,
which represents the Lord's body, is for our health and healing.

Look to the Word, Not Natural Facts

Numbers 21:9
⁹So Moses made a bronze serpent, and put it on a pole; and so it was, if a serpent had bitten anyone, when he looked at the bronze serpent, he lived.

"Pastor Prince, I know that God is my healer. But why is this sickness and pain still in my body?" If you have been looking at your sickness and pain all this while, stop looking at yourself and start looking at Jesus. Did He or did He not take upon Himself your sickness and pain?

God's Word declares, "Surely our sicknesses he hath borne, and our pains — he hath carried them..." (Isaiah 53:4, YLT). Since Jesus has already taken your sickness and pain at the cross, then He cannot "untake" them. Even if you find it hard to believe that Jesus has paid for your healing, especially when the pain is unbearable, the truth is that it is still paid for. It is a finished work!

God is not saying that your sickness does not exist, nor is He asking you to pretend that it is not there. He is asking you to **look away** from the sickness, painful as it may be, and look to the truth that it has already been judged at the cross in the body of His Son.

Once, while still in the wilderness, the children of Israel were bitten by deadly desert serpents. The serpents were real. The bites were painful and deadly. So God told Moses to point the people to the bronze serpent put on a pole — a picture of the cross. (John 3:14.) Bronze signifies judgment. In other words, the serpent — their problem — was already judged at the cross.

Those who kept their eyes on the bronze serpent lived. Those who focused on their wounds died. So stop looking at your sickness. Instead, look to the cross and see your sickness already judged in the body of Jesus. **Surely** He has borne your sicknesses and carried your pains! That is the truth of God's Word. And His Word supersedes natural facts.

My friend, you let natural facts rule or establish God's truths over your problem by what you choose to focus on. So decide today not to focus on the facts concerning your problem. Instead, establish the truth of God's Word and Christ's finished work over your problem — and live!

Thought for the Day
The truth of God's Word supersedes natural facts.

Make Your Temple a House of Prayer

Mark 11:17

17 Then He taught, saying to them, "Is it not written, 'My house shall be called a house of prayer for all nations'? But you have made it a 'den of thieves'."

It would be great if every time we prayed, the answers came quickly. Thank God for immediate results, but what do we do when the results are not immediate? The promises of God are there for us, but when they have yet to manifest in our circumstances, what should we do in the meantime?

Jesus showed us what to do. After He had cursed the fig tree, the tree did not wither immediately. (v. 14.) What did He do then? He went to the temple in Jerusalem and cleansed it, saying that it should be a house of prayer and not a den of thieves. (vv. 15–17.) After cleansing the temple, when the disciples saw the same fig tree the next day, it had dried up from its roots! (vv. 20–21.)

Today, you are the temple of God. (1 Corinthians 3:16.) And your temple should be a "house of prayer" or it becomes a "den of thieves." These thieves, or powers of darkness, will steal and rob from your temple, which is your body. (1 Corinthians 6:19.) They will steal and rob you of your strength, health, youthfulness, wisdom, hopes and dreams.

So make your temple a house of prayer by praying in tongues frequently. (Ephesians 6:18.) When you pray in the Spirit, you are praying perfect prayers. This is because the Spirit Himself makes intercession for you when He prays through you in tongues. (Romans 8:26.)

"Pastor Prince, how long must I pray?"

Well, how often in a day does the enemy attack you with fears, anxieties and worries? How often does that disease in your body remind you that it is there? How healthy and whole do you want to be?

Beloved, as you make your temple a house of prayer, the powers of darkness that have been stealing or robbing from you will be driven out of your life completely. You will see the manifestation of what you have spoken over your circumstances and you will see the withering of what you have cursed!

Thought for the Day
**Make your body, God's temple, a house of prayer by
praying in the Spirit frequently.**

God Gives You Power to Get Wealth

Deuteronomy 8:18
*18 "And you shall remember the LORD your God, for it is He who gives
you power to get wealth, that He may establish His covenant
which He swore to your fathers, as it is this day.*

The idea that poverty is holy and wealth a curse never came from God. It came from the devil, who wants you poor. He robs and steals from you (John 10:10), and even wants you to have a poverty mentality to keep you poor! God, however, wants you to prosper. And He does it by giving you the power to get wealth.

Having this power means that if you are a businessperson, you will find yourself full of innovative ideas that will bring in huge profits for your company. Even as a salaried worker, you will find yourself promoted quickly because your organization values your contributions highly.

God wants to prosper you in the same way He prospered Abraham — in all things (Genesis 24:1) — so that He can fulfill the covenant He made with Abraham. God gave Abraham the power to get wealth, and he became rich in "flocks and herds, silver and gold, male and female servants, and camels and donkeys" (v. 35). His son, Isaac, inherited his possessions and was also empowered by God to get wealth, so he became "very prosperous" (Genesis 26:13). God also gave Abraham's grandson, Jacob, the power to get wealth, and he grew "exceedingly prosperous" (Genesis 30:43).

God's promise that Abraham and his seed would possess the earth or be heirs of the world was not based on obedience to the law, but on the righteousness of faith. (Romans 4:13.) And because you are in Christ and righteous by faith, you are Abraham's seed and an heir of the Word according to the promise. (Galatians 3:29.) Are heirs of the Word poor? Of course not!

My friend, God wants you to be prosperous, not just inwardly but outwardly too. (3 John 1:2.) So today, even if you don't have a cent in your pocket, remember the Lord your God. It is He who gives you the power to get wealth, so that He may establish His covenant with Abraham!

Thought for the Day
God wants to prosper you in all things.

Done As You Have Believed

Matthew 8:13
¹³Then Jesus said to the centurion, "Go your way; and as you have believed,
so let it be done for you." And his servant was healed that same hour.

What are you expecting God to do for you today? Do you believe that God will respond according to your expectation? When Jairus, distraught at the sickness that was claiming his daughter's life, fell at Jesus' feet, he entreated Jesus to personally come to his house to lay His hands on his daughter so that she would be healed. (Mark 5:23.)

But do you know that Jesus can heal at a distance? He didn't need to go to Jairus' house to heal his daughter. Still, Jesus went and didn't even chide Jairus for his little faith. He met Jairus' expectation — his little daughter was raised from the dead that day. (vv. 41–42.)

Why do I say that Jairus had little faith? Because there was a Roman centurion who came to Jesus about his servant suffering at home. He recognized the power Jesus had and asked only that Jesus "speak a word, and my servant will be healed" (Matthew 8:8). Jesus told him, "Go your way; and as you have believed, so let it be done for you." True to the centurion's expectation, his servant was healed that same hour.

My friend, there is no particular level your faith must reach before God gives you what you are asking for. Your faith does not initiate God's giving. He has already given to you all things that pertain to life and godliness. (2 Peter 1:3.) His blessings are pressing on you already! Regardless of the level of faith you are at, He will respond. Jairus needed Jesus to go to his house to lay His hands on his daughter, and Jesus did. The centurion only needed Jesus to speak a word for his servant to be healed, and Jesus did. He met both their expectations.

My friend, don't fix your eyes on how much or how little faith you have. Fix your eyes on the One who loves you, who has already given you what you need. When you come to Him, simply believe that He is waiting to meet your expectation. He will say to you, "Go your way; and **as you have believed**, so let it be done for you."

Thought for the Day
Regardless of the level of faith you are at,
God will respond and meet your need.

Only Jesus Is Altogether Lovely

Leviticus 2:1
¹'When anyone offers a grain offering to the LORD,
his offering shall be of fine flour....

I love the symbolism of Jesus as fine flour. Even fine flour comes from wheat that has been pounded and beaten again and again, and sifted several times. Doesn't that remind you of Jesus' sufferings and sacrifice for you?

And like fine flour, there is nothing coarse about the person of Jesus. Everything about Him is in even proportions. Every word that He spoke when He was in this world, every thought of His, every action of His, was so fine! When He was kind, He was not soft. When He was assertive, He was not overbearing. He is steel and velvet, meekness and majesty. Like a perfect diamond, every which way you turn Him, you see flawlessness, beauty and brilliance. There is no one altogether lovely like Jesus!

What about Bible greats like Moses and Abraham, or Peter, John and Paul?

Moses, whom the Bible says was more humble than any man on the face of the earth (Numbers 12:3), was once so furious with his people that he struck a rock twice, something he was not supposed to do. (Numbers 20:1–12.) His temper got the better of him on that occasion.

Abraham, whom Christians regard as a man of faith (Hebrews 11:8–10), lied about his wife being his sister when a king coveted her. He endangered her life just to save his own skin. (Genesis 20:1–18.)

Peter, who was deeply zealous for Jesus, denied Him three times. (Matthew 26:33–34, 69-75.) John, the beloved disciple who leaned on Jesus' bosom, was all ready to call down fire from heaven to destroy the inhabitants of Samaria, who had rejected Jesus. (Luke 9:52–54.)

What about Paul, the apostle of grace, who blazed the missionary trail that future missionaries would follow? Even Paul went to Jerusalem when he was told not to by the Holy Spirit through some disciples and the prophet Agabus. (Acts 21:4, 10–15.)

Beloved, the best of us can miss the mark. The only One who is faultless, flawless and altogether lovely is Jesus. And because He never misses the mark, you can look to Him. He will never disappoint you!

Thought for the Day
Look to Jesus, who never misses the mark. He will never disappoint you!

Look Unto Jesus

Hebrews 12:2
²Looking unto Jesus, the author and finisher of our faith....

W hat does it mean to look unto Jesus? Well, we can think of it like this: if you are drowning and somebody walks past you, you do not look **at** him. You look **unto** him. When you look unto him, you are turning to him and expecting him to rescue you.

In the same manner, you look unto Jesus expecting Him to save, heal and protect you because you know His mighty power and sacrificial love for you. God's Word says that we are to keep "looking unto Jesus, the author and finisher of our faith." That is how God wants us to live.

So if you have a recurring migraine, keep looking unto Jesus. See Him taking that migraine upon His body on the cross and say, "Lord, I thank You that by Your stripes I am healed." (Isaiah 53:5.) As you keep looking unto Jesus, your healer, that migraine will have to bow to His finished work!

If you have a financial lack in your life, just keep looking unto Jesus with confident expectation that He will provide for you and deliver you from your lack.

"But Pastor Prince, is it really so simple? All I have to do is look unto Jesus and He will bless me financially?"

Yes, it is that simple. The problem with us is that we tend to look unto ourselves. But we cannot save or deliver ourselves. Even the apostle Paul struggled when he depended on his self-effort. That is why he said, "For the good that I will to do, I do not do; but the evil I will not to do, that I practice" (Romans 7:19). It was only when Paul looked away from himself and unto Jesus that he received his deliverance. (vv. 24–25.)

My friend, if you have been looking unto yourself, it is time to start looking unto Jesus. Look unto Him, the author and finisher of your faith. And soon, you will be looking at your healing and prosperity!

Thought for the Day
***Look unto Jesus, and expect Him to save, heal and protect you
because of His mighty power and sacrificial love for you.***

Working Out of Rest

Hebrews 4:3
³For we who have believed do enter that rest....

Naturally speaking, when we rest, we don't work. So what does working out of rest mean? Well, let me explain by sharing with you what the Lord had taught me.

Many years ago, when I first started preaching, I would prepare diligently for all my sermons. I fine-tuned my points and made sure that everything was in place. I would think to myself, *Man, I am going to share this... and that...*

But when I preached, I would forget to mention certain points. Because of that, I would get angry with myself. I would tell myself, *That was such a good point. Why didn't I remember to share it?*

Then, God began to speak to me. He said, "Son, your preaching is not out of rest. It is out of your memory." What He said next changed my life, not just in the area of preaching, but also in every other area, and I pray that it will bless you too. He said, "Prepare everything you need to. But when you stand in front of the people, whatever you need to say, I will give to you."

Yes, there must be preparation, whether it is your sermon or sales presentation. I am not telling you to be lazy and just do nothing. You need to prepare, but don't depend on your preparation. Just trust God and tell yourself that whatever you forget, God wants it forgotten. And whatever you didn't plan to say but said, it is because God wanted it said. Don't be stressed out and lose your rest by thinking, *I must know everything! I must remember everything and do everything I have prepared!*

No, believe God and be at rest. When the time comes, whatever you need to know, there and then, God will let you know. Whatever you don't need to know, you don't need to know. And don't worry about what you didn't say — believe that God didn't want it said.

My friend, when you live life like that — trusting God and resting in His love for you — you become cool and collected. And when you are peaceful and at rest in Him, what you do prospers!

Thought for the Day
When you are peaceful and at rest in God, what you do prospers!

Go Forth Neither Poor nor Feeble!

Psalm 105:37
³⁷He also brought them out with silver and gold,
and there was none feeble among His tribes.

When the children of Israel were slaves in Egypt, they lived in poverty and faced daily hardships from their cruel taskmasters. Scars and fresh lashes from their masters' whips covered their bodies. The blistering heat of Egypt caused excruciating sores to fester. Many of them were bent over because of the long hours spent carrying tons of bricks and mortar. Slaving away for long hours under harsh conditions added years to them. And with no proper nourishment, many of them were feeble and emaciated.

But something happened to them on the night of the Passover. (Exodus 12.) With the blood of the lamb applied on their doorposts, they came under God's protection. And inside their homes, as instructed by God, they ate the lamb roasted in fire.

I believe that those who were blind ate the eyes of the lamb, believing that the perfect eyes of the lamb would give them perfect vision. If they had heart conditions, they ate the heart of the lamb, believing that their hearts would beat strong again. And if they were lame, they ate the legs of the lamb, believing that they would be frisking like lambs.

And when morning came, something new and miraculous happened to them. They went forth with God no longer as slaves but free people. They were no longer poor and needy, but possessed silver and gold given to them by the Egyptians. And none of them — there were about 2.5 million of them — were feeble or sickly!

If this was what the children of Israel experienced after partaking of the Passover lamb, which was only a shadow or type of Christ, how much more will we who have come under the covering of the holy blood of Jesus, the true Lamb of God, experience such blessings?

When you put your trust in the Lamb of God, who was burnt by God's fiery judgment meant for us, you will go forth daily, neither poor nor feeble, but richly supplied and divinely strengthened in Christ!

Thought for the Day
Put your trust in Jesus and go forth daily richly
supplied and divinely strengthened!

Right Place, Right Time

Ecclesiastes 9:11
¹¹... the race is not to the swift, nor the battle to the strong,
nor bread to the wise, nor riches to men of understanding,
nor favor to men of skill; but time and chance happen to them all.

God's Word tells us that being faster, stronger and wiser does not automatically make you a winner in life. No, it is actually being at the right place at the right time that causes you to receive blessings. And God, who holds time and chance in His hands, is the only One who can put you at the right place at the right time.

He did this for Ruth. She trusted God for favor when she went looking for a field in which to glean. (Ruth 2:2.) Then, the Bible tells us that "she **happened** to come to the part of the field belonging to Boaz, who was of the family of Elimelech" (v. 3). Of all the fields in Bethlehem, she happened to end up in Boaz's field, and he was a close relative of Elimelech, her father-in-law. This meant that Boaz was her potential kinsman redeemer, someone who could redeem her from her plight as a young, childless widow in a foreign land.

Boaz also happened to be "a man of great wealth" (v. 1), and as it turned out, he was willing to redeem Ruth. (Ruth 4:9–10.) All these right happenings could only mean that God had placed Ruth in the right place at the right time.

I believe that the very day Ruth told her mother-in-law that the God of Israel would be her God (Ruth 1:16), God took note of it and made everything happen right for her.

Today, God also wants you to know that because you have said, "God, You are My God," He will be your God of divine happenings. He will place you at the right place at the right time, where you will meet the right people, do the right things and even escape danger!

You may not know where all the great opportunities are, but God does. He was the One who put in you the skills, talents and gifts that you have, and He knows where you need to be, when you should be there and what you need to be doing to be truly fulfilled!

Thought for the Day
God, who holds time and chance in His hands, is the only One
who can put you at the right place at the right time.

Rest and Find God's Grace

Luke 2:40
⁴⁰And the Child grew and became strong in spirit, filled with wisdom;
and the grace of God was upon Him.

The verse says that the grace of God was upon Jesus. The Bible also says that where sin abounds, grace abounds much more. (Romans 5:20.) And when you put the two together, you may find yourself asking, "If the grace of God was upon Jesus, does it mean that He sinned?"

No, Jesus did not sin. (2 Corinthians 5:21.) So there must be another explanation as to why God's grace was upon Jesus. There must be another explanation as to why someone can abound in God's grace even when he has not sinned.

Let's look at the word "grace" when it is first mentioned in the Bible. Genesis 6:8 says that "Noah found grace in the eyes of the Lord." Noah's name means "rest." So the verse is telling us that rest found grace. In other words, when you rest, you find grace!

So grace was upon Jesus because His life was a life of rest and trust in His Father. He said, "The Son can do nothing of Himself. He can do only what He sees His Father doing." (John 5:19.)

Likewise, grace comes upon you when you rest and trust God. If you have a wayward child, stop nagging at him and trust God to handle the problem. Say, "Jesus, I commit this boy into Your hands. I cannot control him. You can." If you have a persistent pain in your body, bring it to the Lord. Say, "Jesus, I hand all my worries about this pain to You. You work on the pain."

"Pastor Prince, what if nothing happens?"

Honestly, if after you have given the matter to Jesus and nothing happens, what can you do? If Jesus Himself can't do anything about it, do you think you can? But praise God, once the problem is handed over to Jesus, He **can** and **will** do a perfect work of taking care of it for you!

So live a life of rest. Have this attitude and tell the Lord, "I can do nothing of myself. I just rest in You Lord and I trust You." Beloved, what you will see is the grace of God upon you in every situation of your life!

Thought for the Day
God's grace comes upon you when you rest and trust Him.

Hope That Does Not Disappoint

Romans 5:5
⁵Now hope does not disappoint, because the love of God has been poured out in our hearts by the Holy Spirit who was given to us.

Today, we express hope as if we can't be sure what will really happen. We say, "I hope I will win that prize. I hope it won't rain tomorrow. I hope everything works out well."

But "hope" in the Bible is a confident and positive expectation of good. God wants you to have a confident expectation of good because as His child, He favors you. Because Christ is in you, the hope of glory (Colossians 1:27), you can expect the glory of God to shine into every area of your life, including your family, job, ministry, health and finances!

God's Word says, "Now hope **does not** disappoint, because the love of God has been poured out in our hearts by the Holy Spirit who was given to us." You may have experienced disappointed hopes, but there is a hope that does not disappoint when you are conscious of how much God loves you. It is a hope that springs from the heart of God, who loves you very much.

It is interesting that the first mention of the Holy Spirit in the book of Romans is tied up with the love of God. The book of Romans is considered foundational for Christians. Could it be that the first thing the Holy Spirit wants to do is to establish in our hearts that God loves us? Many people think that the Holy Spirit has come to teach us about power. But the truth is that the Holy Spirit has come not to reveal the love for power, but the power of love!

My friend, you may have just lost your job. But if you can say, "Jesus loves me this I know," you can also say, "I believe that I will get a better job tomorrow." Your sweetheart may have just left you for your best friend. But because you can say, "Jesus loves me this I know," you can also say, "I'll meet a better sweetheart."

When you believe that God loves you, you will have a positive expectation of good. You will have a hope that does not disappoint. So be careful what you hope for because you are bound to get it!

Thought for the Day
Being conscious of how much God loves you
gives you a hope that does not disappoint.

Satan Cannot Come Before God to Accuse You

Romans 8:33
33 Who shall bring a charge against God's elect? It is God who justifies.

The book of Job tells us that Satan came to God's throne and complained about Job. (Job 1:6–12) God's throne is the most holy place. So why did God allow Satan to come before Him?

Satan could come before God because Adam had given up his place when he bowed his knee to Satan in the garden of Eden. (Genesis 3.) So Satan had the right to take Adam's place and come before God.

But praise God, Jesus, the last Adam, has come! And the sprinkling of His blood has cleansed the things of heaven. (Hebrews 9:22–24.) His blood has cleansed and redeemed the unclean place where Satan walked and stood before God. There remains, therefore, no place in heaven for Satan. He cannot come before God any more to accuse you.

Who then, is in God's presence today? Jesus! He is there for us. (v. 24.) And since He is for us, "Who is he who condemns? It is Christ who died, and furthermore is also risen, who is even at the right hand of God, who also makes intercession for us" (Romans 8:34).

So what happened to Job cannot happen to you. Job longed for a mediator, but he had none. (Job 9:33.) His dream is our reality. Today, we have Jesus as our Mediator making intercession for us! (1 Timothy 2:5.)

However, since the devil cannot come before God any more, he comes to you on earth and accuses you in your conscience. His greatest tool is deception because he has no real power. (Colossians 2:15.) He has to deceive you into thinking that God is against you, that He is angry with you because you have failed Him, or that your sickness or poverty is God's punishment for your sins.

My friend, don't fall for the devil's lies. If it is God who justifies you, no one can bring a charge against you! Satan cannot come before God to accuse you. Instead, you have free access to God's throne of grace to "obtain mercy and find grace to help in time of need" (Hebrews 4:16). Jesus' holy blood has given you perfect standing in the presence of God!

Thought for the Day
If it is God who justifies you, who can bring a charge against you?

Seek God's Kingdom and He Will Solve Your Problems

Romans 14:17
17… the kingdom of God is not eating and drinking,
but righteousness and peace and joy in the Holy Spirit.

Are you troubled by many things today? For example, are you concerned about your rebellious teenager? Perhaps you see him as your problem, so you do your best to discipline him, only to end up with a heart full of worries and pain. And he is no better!

God says to you, "Don't focus on controlling your rebellious teenager. Instead, seek first My kingdom, which is righteousness, peace and joy in the Holy Spirit. Be conscious of the righteousness you have as a gift from My Son. Keep your inner man flowing with My peace and joy, and I will take care of your child."

We tend to think that the people around us are the problem. When we don't get the promotion we want, we blame our bosses and colleagues. When we lose our temper, we blame our wives and kids. However, God wants us to stop looking outside and to start looking within because His kingdom is within us. (Luke 17:21.)

The abundance of the kingdom of God is already inside you. As you seek first God's kingdom, and follow His righteousness, peace and joy, the abundance within you will flow out and become a reality in your circumstances. (Matthew 6:33.) You will find that God has not only taken care of what is troubling you, but has also added blessings to you, be it a promotion, well-behaved kids or a loving wife.

"But Pastor Prince, how do I keep my inner man flowing with righteousness, peace and joy?"

Be conscious of your righteousness in Christ. Don't be conscious of your sins and problems. Listen to anointed sermons that remind you of how righteous you are because of the perfect sacrifice of Christ. Peace and joy flow when you know that all your sins have been forgiven because of Jesus' finished work.

So the next time something troubles you, don't focus on correcting the problem. Instead, seek first God's kingdom and His righteousness. Make it a priority to have your inner man flowing with His peace and joy, and He will take care of that problem for you!

Thought for the Day
Have your inner man flowing with God's peace and joy,
and He will take care of that problem for you.

Be Mindful of Christ's Obedience at the Cross

2 Corinthians 10:5
⁵Casting down arguments and every high thing that exalts
itself against the knowledge of God, bringing every
thought into captivity to the obedience of Christ.

Have you ever felt condemned because of the bad thoughts you have had? You could be in the middle of a prayer meeting when suddenly a dirty thought enters your mind. Actually, it is the devil who puts such thoughts in your mind. Then, he steps back, looks at you and knocks you on your head, saying, "How can you call yourself a Christian and still think such thoughts?"

I used to be in bondage over the bad thoughts I had because I felt that I had to confess every one of them and seek God's forgiveness. But that is not what God's Word exhorts us to do. You see, God wants us to bring "every thought into captivity to the **obedience of Christ.**" Now, whose obedience are we to focus on? Christ's obedience and not our own obedience!

But what is "the obedience of Christ"? It is His obedience at the cross, where "by one Man's obedience many will be made righteous" (Romans 5:19). Jesus shed His blood for us at the cross. This means that when our thoughts condemn us, we are to focus our thoughts on Jesus' obedience at the cross.

My friend, the devil can only make inroads into our minds when he gets us to focus on **our** obedience instead of **Christ's** obedience. His strategy is to point us to our obedience or the lack of it to determine our standing before God. But just as our position as sinners is not based on what we **do**, but what the first Adam did, in the same way, we are forever righteous today not because of what we do, but because of what Christ, the last Adam, did on the cross.

So the next time your thoughts seem to condemn you, say, "I am righteous whether I have good or bad thoughts. My righteousness has nothing to do with my obedience. Jesus' obedience at the cross made me righteous." Then, go ahead and pray, knowing that you have access to God and His favor, and that He hears the prayer of the righteous. (Proverbs 15:29.)

Thought for the Day
**The devil's strategy is to point us to our obedience or the lack of it
to determine our standing before God.**

Rest and Receive Your Miracle

Hebrews 4:9
⁹There remains therefore a rest for the people of God.

In the healing of the paralyzed man at the pool of Bethesda (John 5:1–16), Jesus knew that for 38 years, the man had been flat on his back, unable to do anything for himself or others, no matter how hard he struggled.

In the case of the woman oppressed with a spirit of infirmity (Luke 13:10–13), Jesus knew that the woman had been bowed over for 18 years. And in that condition, she saw very little that was beautiful in life, only the dusty ground, dirty sandals and bruised feet.

What about the man with a withered hand? (Luke 6:6–10.) Jesus knew from His carpenter days how a useless hand could have easily given the man a very poor sense of self-worth.

I believe that all three of them must have struggled for so long to get back on their feet, to try to lift themselves up, to attempt to do something about their situations, only to be disappointed each time they failed. In fact, they got so frustrated with striving to get better that by the time they met Jesus, they had probably given up trying to change their situations.

It was then that Jesus came and extended His offer to turn their situations around. And when they embraced His offer, they received the miracles that they had sought for so long.

You too may have been struggling to get back on your feet, or to lift yourself out of the problem that has sorely weighed you down. You have attempted to do whatever you could, hoping that it would amount to something, but you have been frustrated time and again. My friend, God wants you to cease from all your struggling and accept the offer He extends to turn your situation around.

It is no coincidence that all three of them received their miracles on the Sabbath, the day of **rest** for the Jews. God's Word says, "There remains therefore a rest for the people of God." The day you cease from your own laboring and striving, and **rest** in the finished work of Christ, is the day you receive your miracle.

Jesus has done all the work. Whatever you need has been provided for at the cross. So just be at rest and receive your miracle!

Thought for the Day
God wants you to cease from all your struggling and accept the offer
He extends to turn your situation around.

Freely Receive What God Freely Gives

Romans 4:13
¹³For the promise that he would be the heir of the world was not to Abraham
or to his seed through the law, but through the righteousness of faith.

God promised that you would be the heir of the world. It is the same promise that He made to Abraham. And because you are Christ's, you are Abraham's seed and an heir "according to the promise" (Galatians 3:29).

When God made this promise to you, He made it so easy for you to receive — "through the righteousness of faith." All you have to do is believe that as the heir of the world every blessing is righteously yours because Jesus died to give them to you. He also rose from the dead to enforce them in your life.

So don't try to earn your blessings "through the law" — through your efforts or performance. Freely receive what God freely gives to you through Christ and His finished work at the cross.

When a church member was retrenched at 41 years of age, he refused to fret or think that he had to jostle with the rest of the people in the job market. Instead, he believed that by God's grace, he would get a better job with a higher pay. Indeed, through a mutual acquaintance, a new job came along with a pay packet that was 60 percent more than his previous one!

Another man was experiencing a strained relationship with his wife to the point that divorce was imminent. When he started attending our church, he realized that a happy marriage could be his, not by his trying to keep the marriage going or earning the love of his wife, but by believing that although he could see his own weaknesses, he was still the righteousness of God in Christ because of the blood of Jesus. Today, he and his wife are reconciled, and enjoying a blessed marriage.

Don't let the devil disqualify you by bringing you the law and saying, "How can you receive this blessing when just last night, you broke God's law?" or "Are you sure you deserve this?" Instead, say, "Father, I thank You that I receive everything freely by Your grace, Your unmerited favor in my life, because of the blood of Jesus!"

Thought for the Day
Freely receive what God freely gives to you through
Christ and His finished work at the cross.

Be Full of the Consciousness of God

1 Corinthians 2:12
¹²Now we have received, not the spirit of the world, but the
Spirit who is from God, that we might know the things
that have been freely given to us by God.

You are probably familiar with the story of how David, with a slingshot and a stone, slew Goliath, a 10-foot-tall Philistine warrior. But have you ever wondered why David succeeded while the others in the army of Israel did not even dare to face Goliath?

David's secret was that he was only conscious of victory and not defeat, because he knew a God who had rescued him time and again.

You can just imagine him saying, "One day, I was taking care of my sheep when a lion came and took one of them. I was not willing to settle for that! I went after the lion, caught it by its beard and smote it. The Lord delivered me from the lion's mouth. On another occasion, a bear came and took one of my flock. I went after the bear and smote it. So the Lord delivered me from the bear too. This same God, who delivered me from the paws of the lion and bear, will also deliver me from this Philistine." (1 Samuel 17:34–37.)

David was conscious of what God had done for him. He knew that God was for him, loved him, favored him and would give him victory again. My friend, you can also remind yourself that the same God, who did tremendous things for you in the past, will do the same for you again.

Be like David, who was conscious only of God's goodness and faithfulness. Don't be like the army of Israel. The men were conscious of the negative words of Goliath. I believe that they must have talked about his threats, repeating his words to one another, and as a result, filled their hearts with fear. (1 Samuel 17:11, 24.)

Beloved, don't feed on the negative words of man or the devil. It will only cause you to be anxious and fearful. Feed on God's Word by reading the Bible and listening to messages about who you are in Christ and what He has done for you. Pump yourself up with God's Word until you are full of the Spirit and consciousness of God, so that you might know the things that have been freely given to you by God!

Thought for the Day
The same God, who did tremendous things for you in
the past, will do the same for you again.

Thanking God at All Times

Hebrews 13:15
15 Therefore by Him let us continually offer the sacrifice of praise to God,
that is, the fruit of our lips, giving thanks to His name.

L ifting up your hands and thanking God is spontaneous and easy when you have just received a wonderful blessing: "God, I can't thank You enough for this miracle!"

"Thank You Father, for answering my prayer!"

"Father, thank You for the windfall!"

Perhaps you came close to being in a fatal accident, but God plucked you out of danger just in time. Or your grandmother, an unbeliever for many years, finally received Jesus as her Savior and got healed of a long-term disease.

But there are times when you don't feel like lifting up your hands to thank and praise God, yet you do it. Perhaps you feel very discouraged lately. Perhaps everything is going wrong for you and you feel like your life is in a mess. You can't hold back the tears. Yet, you make a conscious decision to lift your hands and thank God for being in the situation with you. You open your mouth and begin to praise Him even though you really don't feel like doing it.

In the midst of the trial that you are going through, you praise Him that He is your righteousness in spite of all the mistakes you have made. You thank Him that He is your Prince of Peace, and that His peace will arise in you and still the storms in your life.

My friend, God sees and appreciates such times when, despite feeling so discouraged, you offer a freewill thanksgiving offering to Him. In fact, your thanksgiving during such times is more highly prized by Him than your thanksgiving during those times when you are feeling joyful because you have just been blessed.

And when you choose to thank Him for His unfailing love, and His faithfulness to deliver, protect and provide for you even when you don't see the blessings yet, before long, you **will** find yourself experiencing and enjoying the blessings! So lift your hands and praise the Lord, for He is good, and His mercy endures forever! (Psalm 106:1.)

Thought for the Day
God sees and appreciates those times when, despite feeling so discouraged,
you offer a freewill thanksgiving offering to Him.

Your Words Carry Power!

Ecclesiastes 8:4
⁴Where the word of a king is, there is power....

In Bible times, a king's word carried tremendous power. What he decreed would come to pass. It would be done. For example, if he said, "Raise the taxes," the taxes would be raised.

Do you know that we are kings? The Bible tells us that Jesus has washed us from our sins with His blood and made us kings. (Revelation 1:5–6.) And as kings in Christ, our words carry power too.

When we place our hands on a sick person and say, "Be healed," the person is healed. When we lay hands on our children and say, "Be blessed," our children are blessed. There is power in our words because they are the words of kings!

When I was a young Christian in my teens, I wanted to practice what I had learnt about the power of my words. There was this particular plant near my home and whenever I passed by it, I would say to it, "Be cursed in Jesus' name!"

Many days passed. And I will never forget the day when I noticed that the leaves of the plant had turned brown! You may want to try this at home with your potted plants, but bless them instead!

Since our words carry power, can you imagine the harm we do when we say to our loved ones things like, "You are always so careless," "You are good for nothing" or "You are so stupid"? We are cursing them!

The devil is happy when you use the power of your words against yourself and your loved ones. He wants to see you defeated. So instead of saying, "I am always short of money," say, "The Lord is my shepherd; I shall not want." (Psalm 23:1.) Instead of saying, "I am so useless. I can't do anything," start saying, "I can do all things through Christ who strengthens me." (Philippians 4:13.)

Beloved, remember that as a king, what you say will come to pass because where the word of a king is, there is power. So learn to say what God says about you in His Word and see His promises come to pass in your life!

Thought for the Day
As kings in Christ, our words carry power. When we
speak God's promises, they will come to pass.

There Is Just Something Special About You

Isaiah 60:1
¹Arise, shine; for your light has come! And the glory of the LORD is risen upon you.

People might have said to you, "Why are you so lucky?" or "You seem to be looking younger and younger," or "There is so much bad news these days, yet you seem untroubled by them."

Now, the people of the world don't have spiritual discernment. They can only go by your physical appearance, behavior and what happens to you. In other words, if they notice something different about you, it is because they see the evidence of God's glory on your life — in your family and work life, health and finances.

Your friends and colleagues may have told you that you stand out from the rest as though a spotlight were on you. Indeed, this is so because of Christ in you, the hope of glory. (Colossians 1:27.) When God's glory rises upon you, your words carry weight, even if you are not eloquent. I should know. I stuttered and stammered right up into my teens. So when your words change people's lives, you know that it is not you. It is the Lord!

You don't have to be a straight-A student or someone able to speak the Queen's English. You may be foul-mouthed like the disciple Peter, but when God changes you and His glory rises upon you, and you stand up and preach, 3,000 people get saved! (Acts 2:14–41.) What is important is that God gives weight to what you say.

You might be a nobody like Joseph, who was a slave cast aside and forgotten in a dungeon. Yet, the greatest king on earth at that time sought Joseph out to have him interpret his dreams. In other words, God will give to you answers that the people of the world do not have.

Maybe it is your hands. When you lay hands on the sick, they recover. Maybe it is your ability to give counsel that is spot-on, or your ability to speak into their future with a word of knowledge or word of wisdom from God.

"The Gentiles shall come to your light, and kings to the brightness of your rising." (Isaiah 60:3). My friend, when you see this happening, it is because the people of the world are drawn to the glory of the Lord that has risen upon you!

Thought for the Day
**People of the world are drawn to the glory of
the Lord that has risen upon you!**

Round-the-Clock Protection

Psalm 91:5–6
⁵You shall not be afraid of the terror by night, nor of the arrow that
flies by day, ⁶nor of the pestilence that walks in darkness,
nor of the destruction that lays waste at noonday.

During World War II, German planes bombed London. Houses were leveled. But there was one that remained standing amidst the rubble. Its owner said that when she read Psalm 121:4, which says, "Behold, He who keeps Israel shall neither slumber nor sleep," she told the Lord, "Lord, since You don't sleep, then there is no point in both of us keeping awake. I will sleep while You keep watch." And she did, while the Lord protected her and her house.

In 2005, terrorists attacked London's public transport system. That day, a Singaporean girl found herself unexpectedly late for work and could not get to the train station in time to board her usual train. When she finally neared the station, she realized that it had been bombed just a few minutes earlier. Her mother, who worships in our church, believes that God protected her daughter that day.

God wants you to know that you have round-the-clock protection — "You shall not be afraid of the terror by **night**, nor of the arrow that flies by **day**, nor of the pestilence that walks in darkness, nor of the destruction that lays waste at **noonday**."

He protects you from "the terror by night," which could refer to evils such as rape, kidnap or murder. He promises you protection from "the arrow that flies by day." This could refer to bullets from a crazy sniper, drive-by shootings or homemade rockets fired into your territory.

God also shields you from "the pestilence that walks in darkness," referring to viruses which you cannot see. You don't have to be afraid of deadly viruses lurking somewhere or wonder if some deadly disease is developing in your body.

God also doesn't want you to be afraid of "the destruction that lays waste at noonday," such as a tsunami hitting the beach resort you are at, or a bomb going off in the shopping mall you are in.

You need not be afraid because God, who neither slumbers nor sleeps, is watching over you 24 hours a day!

Thought for the Day
Fear not. Trust in your heavenly Father who
gives you round-the-clock protection.

Down but Not Out

2 Corinthians 4:8–9
⁸We are hard-pressed on every side, yet not crushed; we are perplexed, but not in despair; ⁹persecuted, but not forsaken; struck down, but not destroyed....

Before you were a Christian, when something sad or bad happened to you, you cried until you had no more tears left. Your heart simply broke into pieces, and you felt trapped, depressed and totally defeated.

But after having become a Christian, when something bad happens to you, you may still cry, but you feel comforted inside. You are sad outwardly, but your heart isn't heavy. You don't understand why, but deep down inside you, there is something lifting you up. That something buoyant, which is rising from the inside of you, is the life of Christ in you!

You cannot be completely distressed because Christ in you is the Prince of Peace (Isaiah 9:6) who says to you, "Peace I leave with you, My peace I give to you; not as the world gives do I give to you. Let not your heart be troubled, neither let it be afraid" (John 14:27).

Yes, it may be a bad situation and you are in a tight spot, but Christ in you is the way, the truth and the life (John 14:6), and He says to you, "It will all be all right. I will provide a way out for you."

You know you are not defeated because Christ in you is your victory (1 Corinthians 15:57) and He says to you, "You are not fighting **for** victory, but fighting **from** victory because you already have the victory in Me."

Before you knew Christ, when you were down, you were out. But now, when you are down, you are not out because Christ in you is the hope of glory. (Colossians 1:27.) "Hope" in the Bible means a definite, positive expectation of good.

So Christ in you is the definite, positive expectation of a glorious marriage! Christ in you is the definite, positive expectation of a glorious family! Christ in you is the definite positive expectation of glorious health! Christ in you is the definite positive expectation of a glorious life!

My friend, Christ in you is the definite, positive expectation of all the glories of God revealed to you. No bad circumstance that you are in can or will ever cause you to be destroyed or forsaken by God!

Thought for the Day
Christ in you is the definite, positive expectation of
all the glories of God revealed to you!

Set Your Love Upon Jesus

Psalm 91:14
*14"Because he has set his love upon Me, therefore I will deliver him;
I will set him on high, because he has known My name."*

Jesus was in a house in Bethany when a woman came to Him with an alabaster flask containing very costly fragrant oil. She poured the oil on His head. (Matthew 26:6–7.) This woman loved the Lord. She had set her love upon Him.

But those who were present considered what she did a great waste because the oil could have been sold for an amount equal to one year's wages, and the money given to the poor instead. Even Jesus' disciples were indignant and asked her, "Why this waste?" (v. 8).

But Jesus defended her, saying, "Why do you trouble the woman? For she has done a good work for Me" (v. 10). Not only that, He accorded her the highest honor when He added, "Assuredly, I say to you, wherever this gospel is preached in the whole world, what this woman has done will also be told as a memorial to her" (v. 13).

Two thousand years have passed since this woman anointed Jesus with the expensive oil. She never expected in her wildest dreams that her act of love would be told down through the ages. Many kings and rulers have come and gone. Their great acts have faded from the memories of men. But what this woman did for Jesus is still told today around the world as a memorial to her!

When you get a revelation of how much Jesus loves you, you will set your love upon Him. And when you act out of love for Him, though others may see it as a waste of time, energy or money, He will defend you and deliver you from your critics. He will also set you on high. Your ministry will become powerful and life-changing. Your work will be highly esteemed among your peers. Your company will be prominent and highly successful. And it will not just be a job that you have, but a position of influence to impact many lives.

So set your love upon Jesus. Make Him the love of your life today, and He will defend, deliver and set you on high!

Thought for the Day
**When you set your love upon Jesus and act out of love for Him,
He will defend, deliver and set you on high.**

Supernaturally Multiplied Back to You

Hebrews 11:6
⁶But without faith it is impossible to please Him, for he who comes to God must believe that He is, and that He is a rewarder of those who diligently seek Him.

It pleases God when we believe that He is the giver, the blesser and that "He is a rewarder of those who diligently seek Him." Such was the faith of Ruth the Moabitess. When she decided to make the God of Abraham, Isaac and Jacob her God, she found Him to be her rewarder, who lovingly provided for her, divinely guided her, jealously protected her, gloriously redeemed her from her hopeless situation and richly restored her life. (Ruth 1-4.)

Today, this same God says to you that He is your rewarder. And when He is involved in your life, you will be amply rewarded. Peter, the fisherman, would testify to that. His fishing boat, which represented his life, caught nothing the whole night. But in the morning, when the boat was returned to him after he had loaned it to Jesus, it was no longer the same boat. It was anointed, blessed and so magnetized that a great number of fish was attracted to it. In fact, he received a net-breaking, boat-sinking load of fish! (Luke 5:1–11.)

Beloved, because God is your rewarder, if He borrows your "boat" even for a while, be assured that He will surely return it to you with a supernatural increase. Even if what you give Him is little, when placed in His hands, it will return to you blessed, anointed and multiplied.

This happened to the little boy who gave Jesus his lunch of five barley loaves and two fish. It must have thrilled the boy to see his small lunch supernaturally multiplied and satisfying not just him, but 5,000 men, not counting the women and children, and even leaving behind 12 baskets full of leftovers. (John 6:1–13.)

Beloved, believe that God is a rewarder. When you give Him your finances, time, possessions and abilities, know for sure that He will return them to you blessed, anointed and multiplied!

Thought for the Day
What you give to God will surely be returned to you with a supernatural increase.

Christ, the Power and Wisdom of God

1 Corinthians 1:24
24.... to those who are called, both Jews and Greeks,
Christ the power of God and the wisdom of God.

People today run after two things: miraculous signs and wonders, and knowledge. It was no different in Bible times. The apostle Paul acknowledged that "Jews request a sign, and Greeks seek after wisdom" (1 Corinthians 1:22).

So when Paul preached Christ crucified as God's solution to them, the message was "to the Jews a stumbling block and to the Greeks foolishness". (v. 23.) They didn't understand how getting a revelation of Jesus and His death could give them the miracles they needed or the wisdom they wanted.

Beloved, we don't have to run after miracles or wisdom today. We just need to run after Jesus because He is "the power of God and the wisdom of God." The more we know Christ and Christ crucified, the more we will have the power and wisdom of God.

Several church members have shared how they have seen the power of God blast financial debts out of their lives. Not knowing what to do about their debts, they looked to the Lord to deliver them. And the Lord was able to do so mightily because He is indeed the power of God.

So if you are facing a financial debt, Christ has the power to remove the debt. And because He is also the wisdom of God, He will show you where you went wrong and teach you how to stay out of debt!

Let me give you another illustration. Let's say a man, whose wife has left him, looks to Jesus to bring his wife back. Christ, the power of God, brings about a miraculous restoration of their marriage. But it is Christ, the wisdom of God, who will teach the husband how to keep his wife by showing him what he had done wrong and what to do to strengthen the marriage. If the husband does not have this wisdom, it will only be a matter of time before the same problems surface and his wife leaves him again.

My friend, Christ is both the power and wisdom of God to us. As the power of God, He removes obstacles in our paths. As the wisdom of God, He continually directs our paths!

Thought for the Day
As the power of God, Christ removes obstacles in our paths.
As the wisdom of God, He continually directs our paths!

Just a Groan Will Reach God's Throne

Romans 8:26
²⁶Likewise the Spirit also helps in our weaknesses. For we do not know what we should pray for as we ought, but the Spirit Himself makes intercession for us with groanings which cannot be uttered.

Once, when my father was hospitalized, I remember driving as fast as I could to the hospital to see him because his condition was deteriorating rapidly. I was just sobbing in my car on the way there. I didn't know what to pray. So I just cried and prayed in tongues, groaning in my spirit.

I believe that at that very low point, the Holy Spirit was helping me in my weaknesses — "For we do not know what we should pray for as we ought, but the Spirit Himself makes intercession for us with groanings which cannot be uttered."

The events that soon unfolded in the hospital convinced me that just a groan or sigh will reach the throne of our Abba Father.

I managed to reach the hospital just in time to clasp my father's hand before he was wheeled in for surgery. The surgeons came out of the operating theatre some time later to inform my mother that they didn't need to do anything after they had opened him up because they discovered that "surgery" had already been done on him!

Surprised, my mother answered, "He has never been operated on. I am his wife. I should know." Not convinced, the surgeons told my father when he regained consciousness, "We opened you up and found that surgery had already been done. Whoever did it did a perfect work."

Equally surprised, my dad told them, "I have never had surgery done on me."

"No, you have!" the surgeons insisted.

As my parents and the doctors continued arguing, I found myself thinking, "My goodness, I didn't even pray for a miracle on my way to the hospital. Yet, a miracle has just happened!"

My friend, when we who are God's children groan as we pray in the Spirit, the Holy Spirit makes intercession for us with groanings which will reach the throne of our Abba Father, and cause Him to move powerfully on our behalf!

Thought for the Day
Just a groan or sigh will reach the throne of your Abba Father and cause Him to move powerfully on your behalf!

Compassion With Action

Luke 7:13
¹³When the Lord saw her, He had compassion on
her and said to her, "Do not weep."

My friend, there is no trial, difficulty or challenge we face today that our Lord Jesus cannot identify with. The moment we experience a trial, right there and then, because He "was in all points tempted as we are" (Hebrews 4:15), He feels it too and is able to sympathize with our weaknesses.

Jesus' compassion for you is the same compassion He felt for the widow at Nain when He saw the dead body of her only son being carried out of the city gate to be buried. (Luke 7:11–15.) It must have been terrible for her to experience the death of her only son after having already experienced the death of her husband. What a horrible thought to be left all alone in the world with no means of support! When Jesus saw her, He was moved with compassion and said to her, "Do not weep."

Now, some religious leaders might also be moved to approach her, but only to say, "Look sister, something is terribly wrong. Your husband died. Now, your only son has died. You must find out what is wrong. You better ask God what sin you have committed and repent. Or perhaps there is a curse in your life that needs to be broken."

Isn't it beautiful that Jesus did not extend more confusion or condemnation toward her? He only extended His compassion to her, telling her, "Don't weep." This same Jesus will also come to you when you are most distraught and say, "Don't cry."

And Jesus' sympathy does not stop at "Oh, you poor thing! I am so sorry about what has happened to you." No, His sympathy will move Him to give you the miracle you need in your life. That is why He raised the widow's son back to life!

Beloved, rest in the truth that He who is seated at the Father's right hand today understands what you are going through and sympathizes with your weaknesses. The compassion of Jesus toward you causes Him to breathe life into your dead situation and turn it around for your good!

Thought for the Day
Jesus, who understands what you are going through,
will also breathe life into your dead situation!

Who Do You Say Jesus Is?

Mark 8:29
²⁹He said to them, "But who do you say that I am?"
Peter answered and said to Him, "You are the Christ."

D o you know that how you see Jesus determines what you receive from Him? If you see Jesus as your healer, you will receive healing. If you see Jesus as your refuge and fortress, you will receive protection.

The people of Nazareth, Jesus' hometown, saw Jesus in the natural. They said of Him, "Is this not the carpenter's son? Is not His mother called Mary? And His brothers James, Joses, Simon, and Judas? And His sisters, are they not all with us?" (Matthew 13:55–56). They saw Jesus in the natural. They did not see Him as God in the flesh. As a result, He could not do many mighty works there. (v. 58.)

Today, many people, including some philosophers, see Jesus of Nazareth as a good person who led an exemplary life. They feel that if all of us could live our lives like Him, the world would be a better place.

They don't see Jesus as the bread of God who came from heaven to give life to the world. (John 6:33.) They don't see Him as the One who came to give them living water, so that they would never thirst again. (John 4:14.) They don't see Him as the Lamb of God, who took away the sin of the world. (John 1:29.) They don't receive from Him what they need because they don't esteem Him rightly.

Jesus did not come just to set a good example for man to follow. He came to be our Redeemer. (Galatians 3:13.) He came to be our righteousness. (1 Corinthians 1:30.) He came to be our shepherd, so that we will not lack anything. (Psalm 23:1.)

Jesus asked His disciples once, "But who do you say that I am?" How you answer this question depends on how you see Jesus. And how you see Jesus will determine how and what you receive from Him. So see Him as your God, as everything He claims to be in His Word, and He will do mighty works in your life!

Thought for the Day
How you see Jesus determines how and what you receive from Him.

God Is a Giver, Not a Taker

Romans 8:32
³²He who did not spare His own Son, but delivered Him up for us all,
how shall He not with Him also freely give us all things?

Some Christians mistakenly believe that God gives and also takes away. At funerals, we sometimes hear the minister say, "The Lord giveth, and the Lord taketh. Blessed be the name of the Lord."

I remember an occasion when I was looking at a baby who was suffering from cancer. I heard one of his family members comment, "You can't be sure what God's will is. He may or may not heal." What that person meant was that although the Lord had given the parents this baby, He might later take the baby away from them.

Job displayed this very same attitude when he received the news that he had lost his property and children. Thinking that God was the source of his problems and not knowing that it was actually Satan who had come against him, he said, "Naked I came from my mother's womb, and naked shall I return there. The LORD gave, and the LORD has taken away; blessed be the name of the LORD." (Job 1:21.) Such a statement seems to honor God, but in reality, it reveals an erroneous view of our heavenly Father.

As children of God, we know what the Father's will is for us. He is a giver, not a taker! Jesus said, "Do not fear, little flock, for it is your Father's good pleasure to give you the kingdom" (Luke 12:32). It is the devil who is the thief. He comes to steal, kill and destroy. But Jesus came to give us life more abundantly. (John 10:10.)

Jesus met every need and healed every sickness brought before Him, and at the cross, He gave His own life. Never once did He take anything away from the people who came to Him. And the Bible says that whoever has seen Jesus has seen the Father. (John 14:9.)

Beloved, your heavenly Father wants you to know today that He is the One who gives you all good things. And if He has already given us heaven's best — Jesus — "how shall He not with Him also freely give us all things?"

Thought for the Day
If our heavenly Father has already given us heaven's best — Jesus —
"how shall He not with Him also freely give us all things?"

Nothing Can Stand Up to God's Love

Romans 8:35
³⁵ Who shall separate us from the love of Christ? Shall tribulation, or distress,
or persecution, or famine, or nakedness, or peril, or sword?

The pastor of our Hokkien and Mandarin congregations, Pastor Mark, used to suffer from certain health problems before he became a Christian. His doctor told him that he had to be on medication for life. He also had a huge financial debt. But when he caught hold of the teaching that he is God's beloved, he believed it totally. He also believed that nothing could be greater than God's love for him.

Today, Pastor Mark is off medication and completely delivered from that debt. God caused him to triumph over his sickness and debt because he cannot be defeated when he knows that he is God's beloved.

Tribulation, distress or persecution cannot stop your heavenly Father's love from working on your behalf. His love for you is bigger and stronger than your financial woes, marital problems or health concerns. And when God's heart of love moves for His beloved, He opens doors that no one can shut and He makes a way when there seems to be none.

Even during lean times, you will never find the righteous forsaken. King David said, "I have been young, and now am old; yet I have not seen the righteous forsaken, nor his descendants begging bread" (Psalm 37:25). Can famine or recession stop God's love from providing for His beloved? No! So don't think to yourself, *I must provide for my family. If I don't, who is going to take care of them? How are they going to survive?* God wants you to know that His love will continue to provide abundantly for you and your family.

What about deadly pestilences such as bird flu and mad cow disease, natural disasters such as tsunamis and earthquakes, or terrorist bombings? My friend, these things cannot devour you because God's love protects you. You will enjoy His protection when you know that you are His beloved.

Because God's love is greater than all the evil put together, we are more than conquerors through Christ who loved us. (Romans 8:37.) We always win in the fight of life not because of our love for Him, but because of His love for us!

Thought for the Day
We always win in the fight of life not because of our
love for Him, but because of His love for us!

Flow With Righteousness, Peace and Joy

Romans 14:17
17... the kingdom of God is not eating and drinking,
but righteousness and peace and joy in the Holy Spirit.

If we are supposed to seek first the kingdom of God every day (Matthew 6:33), then we should know what the kingdom of God is in the first place. I used to think that the kingdom of God was the mission fields and that to seek it meant doing missionary work.

Then, I realized that the kingdom of God was not something outside you flowing in — "the kingdom of God is not eating and drinking," but something inside you flowing out — "righteousness and peace and joy in the Holy Spirit."

So to seek first God's kingdom means to make it a priority every day to have your inner man flowing with righteousness, peace and joy in the Holy Spirit.

Righteousness is not your own righteousness based on what you do. It is not good works. It is a gift from Jesus, who is your righteousness. (Romans 5:17; 1 Corinthians 1:30.) God wants you to be established in the truth that you are the righteousness of God in Christ. (2 Corinthians 5:21.)

"Peace be with you" were the words that Jesus spoke to His disciples when He appeared before them after His resurrection. He also showed them His pierced hands and side. (John 20:19–20.) God wants you to know that His Son's finished work has given you peace. Your conscience can be at rest because your sin debt has been settled. You have peace **with** God and the peace **of** God.

Joy will come into your heart when you see Jesus in the scriptures, worship songs or anointed preaching. It is the same joy from the Holy Spirit that filled the disciples' hearts when they saw Jesus, His hands and His side. (v. 20.)

So every day, make it a priority to see yourself righteous in Christ. Don't be conscious of your sins. Instead, be conscious of your righteousness. And whether you are reading your Bible or listening to anointed preaching, see Jesus with His pierced hands and side, which speak of His finished work. See all your sins forgiven, and you will flow with peace and joy. When you do this, you are seeking the kingdom of God!

Thought for the Day
To seek God's kingdom is to have your inner man flowing with
righteousness, peace and joy in the Holy Spirit.

Believe Your Debt Is More Than Paid!

Hebrews 10:22
²²Let us draw near with a true heart in full assurance of faith, having our hearts sprinkled from an evil conscience and our bodies washed with pure water.

I would like you to imagine this scenario: You borrow a huge sum of money from a friend and promise to pay him back in six months' time. When the time comes, you feel really bad because you cannot repay him as you don't have the money. A year rolls by without you repaying a cent. Now you feel extremely guilty. You try to avoid your friend because you are too embarrassed and ashamed to see him.

Let's say that your best friend hears about your plight. Out of the goodness of his heart, he goes to your creditor and says, "Look, I understand that my best friend owes you money."

"Yes, he owes me $50,000."

"Here is $100,000. I am paying you on his behalf."

Your creditor says, "No, no, no! He owes me only $50,000."

Your best friend says, "I know. But take the $100,000 so that you can never say that he still owes you money."

Now your debt has been paid, in fact, more than paid. But if you don't know or believe this, that debt will still be on your conscience. You will still be afraid to see your creditor. And you will avoid him because he reminds you of your debt.

My friend, you need to know that Jesus was an overpayment when He offered Himself as your sin offering, because of the quality and worth of the Man Himself. He overpaid for your sins when He became your sacrifice on the cross.

But if you don't know or believe this, you will suffer as your unbelief will rob you of assurance, joy and peace. You will still have debt on your conscience. Even though God is not imputing sin to you (Romans 4:8), sin is still on your conscience. And as long as sin is on your conscience, you won't dare to draw near to Him.

Beloved, the truth is that your sins have been more than paid for. Jesus was an overpayment. So draw near to God today with no sin on your conscience!

Thought for the Day
**Jesus was an overpayment when He offered Himself as your sin offering,
so draw near to God today with no sin on your conscience!**

God Wants You Free From Worries

Matthew 6:25
25 "Therefore I say to you, do not worry about your life, what you will eat or
what you will drink; nor about your body, what you will put on.
Is not life more than food and the body more than clothing?"

Is your heart full of worries about your health, finances, family or future? Even when all is well, some people still worry because they have heard others say, "You should worry when everything is peaceful because something is wrong when the devil leaves you alone." So they worry even when there is nothing to worry about!

But Jesus does not want you to worry about what you will eat or drink, or about your body and what you will put on your back. He tells you not to worry about your daily provisions because God, who is your heavenly Father, knows that you need all these things and He wants to add these things to you. (vv. 32–33.)

God is the same God who took care of the children of Israel in the wilderness, feeding them with manna every day for 40 years! (Exodus 16.) Under His care, His people had no lack. When the people wanted meat for dinner, He simply rained quails on them. (Numbers 11:31–32.) The children of Israel only had to pick them up. If they had gone to look for meat themselves, they probably would not have found any in the desert.

The problem with us today is that we think that we must do something to help ourselves. Some of us may even think that it is easy for Jesus to say, "Don't worry. Take no thought for your life," because He does not understand the problems we face in life.

But the truth is that Jesus understands the problems we face in life. In fact, He faced what I would call the "final problem" — death. Death is the "final problem" because it puts an end to all our other problems. Jesus faced death at the cross, conquered it and rose from the dead. And because He conquered the problem of problems, we can trust Him when He tells us not to worry!

Thought for the Day
Don't worry. Jesus, who has conquered the
problem of problems, will take care of you.

God Is With You, Upholding You

Isaiah 41:10
¹⁰Fear not, for I am with you; be not dismayed, for I am your God.
I will strengthen you, yes, I will help you, I will uphold you
with My righteous right hand.

I t is easy to say, "Praise the Lord! Hallelujah!" when times are good. It is easy to believe that God loves you when you are on the mountaintop enjoying the sunshine. But what happens when you are down in the dark valley surrounded by your enemies?

Perhaps today, you are in the valley of marital, financial or bodily trouble, and you are asking, "Where is God?"

My friend, He is right there with you. The God of the valleys says to you, "Fear not, for I am with you; be not dismayed, for I am your God. I will strengthen you, yes, I will help you, I will uphold you with My righteous right hand."

When King Jehoshaphat was surrounded and outnumbered by his enemies, the Spirit of the Lord came upon Jahaziel and he said to the king, "Don't be afraid nor dismayed because of this great multitude, for the battle is not yours, but God's. You will not need to fight in this battle. Position yourselves, stand still and see the salvation of the LORD, **who is with you**…. Don't fear or be dismayed; tomorrow, go out against them, for **the LORD is with you**" (2 Chronicles 20:15,17).

What King Jehoshaphat did next was brilliant. He acted with wisdom from on high. Instead of putting his commandos in front, he put worshipers in front! What did the worshipers sing? They sang of God's love for them — "Praise the Lord for His **love** endures forever!" And God utterly destroyed their enemies! (vv. 21–23, NIV.)

Beloved, it is not the trials that make us strong, but our responses in those trials. The devil wants us to respond by asking, "Where is God?" But God wants us to respond with faith in His love for us. We are more than conquerors not because of our love for Him, but through Him who loves us. (Romans 8:37.)

So whatever valley you are in today, don't be afraid. God is there with you strengthening and upholding you. Just sing of His love for you and let Him fight your battles for you!

Thought for the Day
It is how we respond during trials — with faith in
God's love for us — that makes us strong.

Standing on No-Curse Ground

Genesis 8:4
*⁴Then the ark rested in the seventh month, the seventeenth
day of the month, on the mountains of Ararat.*

For 40 days and nights, it rained so hard that the whole world perished, except for Noah and those who were with him in the ark. At the end of 150 days, on the 17th day of the seventh month, the ark rested on the mountains of Ararat.

In Hebrew, the word "Ararat" means "the curse is reversed." The waters of judgment receded, causing the ark to rest on the mountains of Ararat, on new ground where the curse is reversed. And it happened on the 17th day of the seventh month on the Feast of Firstfruits — the exact date that Jesus rose from the dead 4,000 years later!

When Christ rose from the dead, we were raised together with Him. (Colossians 2:12). We who are in Christ, our true ark, stand on resurrection ground where the curse has been reversed (Galatians 3:13), where diseases, poverty and failures have no right to operate!

A church member shared how God delivered him from cervical spondylosis, a medical condition which causes the neck section of the spinal cord to deteriorate. An X-ray taken four to five years back showed that that area of his spinal cord was deteriorating fast. He was in pain and had to take medicine to manage the condition. And whenever he had a relapse, he would get depressed.

During his last relapse, he went to the doctor, trusting God that he was already healed, had another X-ray taken and was given some medication. He took the medication, still believing God that he was healed. The following morning, the pain in his neck was gone and he was able to turn his head. When he finally collected his X-ray results a week later, his doctor actually told him that his spinal cord looked better than the doctor's own! The doctor was very surprised because patients with this condition usually don't get better. God had reversed the curse of cervical spondylosis for him!

My friend, as a believer, you are on no-curse ground. You stand in the blessings zone where it is very easy for God's blessings to rain all over you!

Thought for the Day
***We stand on no-curse ground where diseases,
poverty and failures have no right to operate!***

God Blesses What You Touch

Deuteronomy 28:8
⁸"The Lord will command the blessing on you in your storehouses and
in all to which you set your hand, and He will bless you in the
land which the Lord your God is giving you."

Do you remember the story of King Midas and his golden touch? He made a wish that everything he touched would turn into gold, and his wish came to pass. He touched his food, the trees in his garden and his palace, and they all turned into gold! Then, he hugged his daughter whom he loved very much and she immediately turned into a gold statue!

God's way is better and it has no side effects. He wants to bless everything you touch. The Bible says, "The Lord will command the blessing on you... and in all to which you set your hand..." This means that whatever you touch, whatever you set your hands to, God will command the blessing upon it, be it a person, thing or business. So if you touch your child, he is blessed. If you touch your guitar, anointed music flows forth. If you touch your business, it prospers. When you touch a sick person, he gets healed. When you touch someone who is facing lack, his needs are met.

In the Bible, everything that Jesus touched prospered. He touched the eyes of two blind men and their eyes were opened. (Matthew 9:27–30.) He touched the open coffin of a widow's son, and the young man sat up and began to speak. (Luke 7:12–15.) He touched the leper and the leprosy departed. (Mark 1:40–42.) Under the old covenant laws, no one was supposed to touch a leper as lepers were considered unclean. If you touched the unclean, you became unclean. But Jesus touched the leper and the unclean became clean!

Everyone whom Jesus touched received a blessing. And because Jesus lives in you by His Spirit, what you touch will be blessed too. He paid the price for you to have this blessing. His loving hands which imparted blessings to so many were nailed to the cross so that today, God can command His blessing on all to which you set your hands!

Thought for the Day
Because Jesus lives in you by His Spirit, what you touch will be blessed.

The Power of the Body and Blood

1 Corinthians 11:26
²⁶For as often as you eat this bread and drink this cup,
you proclaim the Lord's death till He comes.

Some time ago, one of our church members developed deep vein thrombosis (DVT) while on a flight to Israel. As she was disembarking from the plane, she collapsed. She was rushed to the hospital. But on the way there, her heart stopped beating. Apparently, the blood clot in her leg had gone to her heart, causing it to stop beating. The doctors managed to revive her heart after a few attempts, but she remained unconscious.

When I arrived at the hospital with some of my church leaders a few days later, I was told that her condition had worsened. She was in the Intensive Care Unit (ICU). My leaders and I decided to partake of the Holy Communion in the ICU, proclaiming that Jesus had borne all her diseases, including DVT, and that His blood had already redeemed her from all curses, including diseases and death.

The next day, she regained consciousness! Her recovery was so supernatural that after a week of observation, she was discharged and was soon touring Israel with the next tour group that arrived there.

In another case, a church member's elderly mother underwent a series of operations and her condition deteriorated to the point where the doctor told the family to prepare for the worst. The family took Holy Communion in the ICU. They even put a small crumb in their mother's mouth and poured a little grape juice in. On the third day, something miraculous happened — their mother regained consciousness, got well and was discharged not too long after!

You see, each time you eat the bread and drink the cup, you proclaim the Lord's death for you. You discern that the Lord's body was broken so that your body can be whole. You discern that His healthy body has borne your diseases and pains, so that your body can be well. So when you eat the bread, you say that by His stripes you are healed. And when you drink the cup, you are drinking the life of Jesus which is in His blood.

Beloved, the life of Jesus is pain-free, disease-free and poverty-free. It attracts the favor and blessings of God. And because you have that life in you, it causes good things to happen to you!

Thought for the Day
Each time you eat the bread and drink the cup,
you proclaim the Lord's death for you.

Get God's Word for It

Matthew 4:4
⁴…He [Jesus] answered and said, "It is written, 'Man shall not live by
bread alone, but by every word that proceeds from the mouth of God.'"

When the devil tempted Jesus, Jesus turned the Word of God on him, saying, "It is written… It is written… It is written…" (vv. 4, 7, 10).

Likewise, should the devil remind you of the pain in your body, say what God's Word says: "It is written, 'By His stripes I am healed!'" (Isaiah 53:5; 1 Peter 2:24.) And tell Daddy God, "I have Your Word for it and I am standing on Your Word. I am not trying to be healed. My healing has already happened. I don't care what this body says. It has to line up with Your Word because by Jesus' stripes I am healed!"

And if the devil says to you, "Look at the meager balance in your bank account. How are you going to pay your bills?" just say, "I am not trying to be rich. I am already rich and I have God's Word for it. It is written, 'My God shall supply all my needs according to His riches in glory by Christ Jesus.' (Philippians 4:19.) It doesn't matter how much I have in the bank. God's Word tells me that as the need arises, the supply will be there!"

When fear grips you, don't say to yourself, "This fear is stupid. Come on, what are the chances of it happening to me?" Don't try to rationalize or reason your fear away. Instead, speak God's Word into the situation. Say, "It is written, 'For God has not given me a spirit of fear, but of power and of love and of a sound mind.'" (2 Timothy 1:7.) What if the fear returns? Speak God's Word again. Say, "It is written, 'For God has not given me a spirit of fear…'"

When the devil tries to deceive you, give him the Word of God. There is something about the Word of God that causes him not to want to hang around those who use it. It reminds him of Jesus, the Word made flesh (John 1:14), who rendered him powerless and of no effect when He said, "It is written…"

Thought for the Day
Turn the Word of God on the devil when he comes to
tempt you. You will render him of no effect!

'Now My Eyes See You, Lord!'

Job 42:5
5 "I have heard of You by the hearing of the ear, but now my eye sees You."

You may have heard of God from a friend or colleague. Perhaps you continue to hear of Him in church services on Sundays. Like Job, you say to God, "I have heard of You by the hearing of the ear." But God also wants you to be able to say to Him, "But now my eye sees You."

When Job told the Lord, "My eye sees You," he was not saying that he saw God physically. He was referring to the moment when he had a personal revelation of God.

Why was it so important for Job to have a personal revelation of God? You see, God wanted Job to know that without a personal revelation of Him, the devil could easily steal from him. But from the moment that Job had a personal revelation of God, things got a lot better for him, with God restoring to him double of everything that he had lost. (Job 42:10–16.)

There was a lady who was separated from her husband because he had an affair with his colleague. But when she came to our church and began to have a personal revelation of God's personal love for her, she believed God for the restoration of her marriage by the end of the year. She did not just hear of a God who "so loved the world" (John 3:16). She came to know the God who so loved her!

Not long after that, her estranged husband started dating her and was soon falling in love with her all over again. God also "took care" of the other woman — she resigned from the company. And on the first of January the following year, the couple moved back into their matrimonial home, their marriage now built solidly on God!

My friend, when you are reading your Bible or hearing God's Word being preached, and suddenly you exclaim, "I see it, Lord!" that is when your personal revelation of God has come. And you are now in a position to receive all that He has for you!

Thought for the Day
When you have a personal revelation of God, you are in a
position to receive all that He has for you!

The Lord Your Refuge Will Deliver You

Psalm 91:3
³Surely He shall deliver you from the snare of the
fowler and from the perilous pestilence.

Today, we hear of new strains of viruses which were unheard of only a generation ago. The world has yet to find cures for them and many people are afraid of being struck down by these viruses.

But as believers, we are not **of** the world, though we are **in** the world. (John 17:15–16.) So our protection is not of the world, but of the Lord. And when we say of the Lord, "He is my refuge and my fortress; my God, in Him I will trust" (Psalm 91:2), then what follows is not "maybe," but **surely** He willl deliver you from the snare of the fowler and from the perilous pestilence.

A couple in our church can testify that surely the Lord delivered and protected their two young children during a Hand, Foot and Mouth Disease (HFMD) outbreak, which claimed a few lives in Singapore not long ago.

When their four-year-old daughter started vomiting and running a fever, the mother brought her to their family doctor, who found ulcers in her mouth and small red dots on her hands and feet — symptoms of the HFMD. Naturally, the doctor prescribed medication for her.

Back home, however, the little girl continued to vomit throughout the day, throwing up everything including the medication. Her fever persisted. Not able to do anything for their daughter, the parents prayed, proclaiming Jesus as their healer, and partook of the Holy Communion many times with both their children.

That night, their daughter's fever broke and the vomiting subsided. They continued making the Lord their refuge and fortress. Within two days, their daughter was completely delivered from the disease. And all this while, their six-year-old son was completely protected from the infectious disease.

Beloved, you don't need to be afraid of deadly diseases which may have claimed the lives of others. You don't have to be fearful that you or your child may become victims of these super bugs. When the Lord is your refuge and fortress, surely He shall deliver you and your family from the snare of the fowler, such as the avian flu, and from all perilous pestilences!

Thought for the Day
Our protection is not of the world, but of the Lord, who delivers us
from the snare of the fowler and from the perilous pestilence.

Have You Taken Your Love Break Today?

John 15:9
⁹"As the Father loved Me, I also have loved you; abide in My love."

I n your workplace, you probably take coffee breaks, lunch breaks, tea breaks and definitely toilet breaks. Why not do the same in your spiritual life — take time out for breaks, especially love breaks?

What is a love break? It is the time you take to enjoy and feed on the love of Jesus for you. At any time during the day, wherever you are, find a quiet spot and feed on the love of Jesus. Just sit down and talk to Him. Say to Him, "Thank You, Jesus, for loving me. Nothing is going to happen to me that You don't already know about. Jesus, when I could not save myself, You died for me. You gave up Your life for me. What else will You not do for me!"

Such love breaks are typified in the Old Testament by Aaron the high priest and his sons eating the breast of the animal sacrificed. (Leviticus 7:31.) The breast of the animal speaks of the love of Jesus. Today, you are a priest to God. (Revelation 1:6.) So spend time feeding on the love of Jesus for you, and see yourself nourished, strengthened and sustained by His love. Jesus is our High Priest today. This means that His food is in loving us. He enjoys loving us and is also "nourished" by His love for us.

But do not forget that the breast was roasted by fire (Leviticus 7:35), which speaks of God's judgment on Jesus as He hung on the cross because He was carrying our sins. So as you feed on Jesus' love for you, see Him loving you at the cross. When things around you are not going well, do not allow the devil to say to you, "If God loves you, how come these things are happening to you?" My friend, interpret God's love for you based on the cross, not on your present circumstances.

During the day, when you are hard at work, when busyness sets in, when problems pile up or when discouragement comes, just stop everything and take a love break with Jesus! Let Jesus love you. Let yourself enjoy being loved by Him. Lean on His bosom, abide in His love and be nourished by His love for you!

Thought for the Day
Be nourished by God's love for you today!

God Justifies the Ungodly

Romans 4:5
⁵But to him who does not work but believes on Him who justifies
the ungodly, his faith is accounted for righteousness.

Boldness is what God wants you to have when you come to Him. He does not want you to be afraid to come to Him, feeling unworthy because of your sins. He wants you to come boldly to Him, knowing that the death, burial and resurrection of His Son Jesus Christ has justified you and qualified you to boldly receive from Him.

This was the kind of boldness that the woman with the issue of blood had when she touched Jesus. (Mark 5:25–34.) Now, by touching Jesus, she knew that she was breaking a Levitical law which states that anyone with a bodily discharge is unclean, and should not appear in public, let alone touch another person. (Leviticus 15.)

But she refused to feel condemned by the law. She believed what she had heard about Jesus, and was confident that there would only be love and compassion, not condemnation, from Him. She believed that Jesus would justify her and qualify her to receive the miracle she needed. That was why she boldly pressed her way into the crowd to touch Jesus, who indeed said to her, "Daughter, your faith has made you well" (Mark 5:34).

What was it about her faith that made her well? Romans 4:5 talks about faith that believes God justifies the **ungodly**. When you believe that God justifies the ungodly, it will give you boldness to come to God, even when you feel unclean because you have just blown it.

When you fail, don't run away from God. Run boldly to Him, knowing that you are justified by the blood of Christ and not by your good behavior.

The devil may say to you, "How can you do that? Who do you think you are?" Don't listen to him. Pick yourself up and thank God for the blood and the gift of no condemnation. (Romans 8:1.) If God justifies the ungodly, how much more you, His beloved child!

Thought for the Day
You are justified by the blood of Christ and not by your good behavior.

Don't Be Judgment-Focused

2 Corinthians 5:19
¹⁹… God was in Christ reconciling the world to Himself,
not imputing their trespasses to them….

On which two ancient cities did God rain brimstone and fire? If your answer is Sodom and Gomorrah, you are right. But if you think that God was all eager to destroy the two cities, you are wrong!

God wasn't willing at all. He was not on a sin hunt. He was on a righteousness hunt so that He could spare the cities. (Genesis 18:23–32.) And I believe that if Abraham had asked God, "What if You can find just **one** righteous man?" God's answer would have been the same: "I will not destroy the place for the sake of one righteous man."

Today, the righteousness of one Man — Jesus — has come. Jesus died for our sins and rose again for our justification. God was in Christ, reconciling the world to Himself, not counting our sins against us!

Therefore, no judgment will fall on you today because it fell on Jesus 2,000 years ago at Calvary. And if God was gracious enough to remove Lot and his family before the judgment fell (Genesis 19:12–22), how much more will He do for you who are no longer under judgment!

And because God does not judge you, don't be like Lot's wife, who became a pillar of salt when she turned around to look at the brimstone and fire. (vv. 24–26.) She wanted to see God's **judgment**, even though the angels had warned, "Don't look back, lest you be destroyed." (v. 17.)

So don't be judgment-focused and look back at the sins you have committed. God is not against you. He is for you and on your side. He remembers that He has already judged and punished your sins in the body of His Son. And because He is faithful to His Son and to what His Son has done, He will never judge or punish you. Any trouble that you might have today is not from Him. But He will show you a way of escape because He is on your side. He loves you and has your best interests at heart.

Beloved, God is not out to get you. He is out to bless you. And He wants you blessed more than you can ever ask or imagine! (Ephesians 3:20.)

Thought for the Day
Don't be judgment-focused because God is not
against you. He is for you and on your side.

God Can Qualify the Disqualified

Psalm 103:4
⁴Who [the Lord] redeems your life from destruction,
who crowns you with lovingkindness and tender mercies,

Four women are mentioned in the genealogy of Jesus. (Matthew 1:1–16.) Interestingly, they are not Sarah, Rebekah, Leah or Rachel, wives of the patriarchs of the Old Testament. Instead, they are Tamar, Rahab, Ruth and Bathsheba, women who had morally questionable backgrounds.

Tamar resorted to deception and prostitution to produce children through her father-in-law. Yet, it was from her line, the tribe of Judah, that the Messiah came. (Genesis 38.) Rahab was a Gentile and a prostitute in Jericho, who became a believer in the God of Abraham, Isaac and Jacob. (Joshua 2:1–21.) She also became the mother of Boaz, who married Ruth. (Ruth 4:13.)

Ruth was morally upright. But as a Moabitess, she was a Gentile and therefore considered unclean. Yet, she became the grandmother of David (Ruth 4:13–17), whom the Jews regard as their greatest king. Bathsheba committed adultery with David. (2 Samuel 11:4.) Later, she gave birth to King Solomon (2 Samuel 12:24), from whose royal line Jesus descended.

So what is God saying to us here?

He is saying that He is greater than our sins — where sin abounds, His grace abounds much more. (Romans 5:20.) His grace is greater than our sins, so that even when the world disqualifies us, He can qualify us to receive His blessings!

God is also saying that He is a God of many chances. These women's stories show us that even when our troubles are of our own making, they are neither final nor fatal. When we turn to Him, He will turn our situations around until we see His glory upon us!

Finally, God is saying that He is a God of supernatural positioning. Even when all our earthly connections are gone, the moment we turn to Him, He will find ways to turn our captivity into blessings.

My friend, don't look at your natural circumstances and be discouraged. Trust the One "who redeems your life from destruction, who crowns you with loving-kindness and tender mercies." Trust Him who qualifies the disqualified!

Thought for the Day
God's grace is greater than our sins, so that even when the world
disqualifies us, He can qualify us to receive His blessings!

God Is Easy to Take From

Exodus 3:8
⁸ So I have come down to deliver them out of the hand of the Egyptians,
and to bring them up from that land to a good and large land....

When the children of Israel provided for themselves in Egypt, they ate cucumbers, melons, leeks, onions and garlic. (Numbers 11:5.) These were types of food which required them to bend down close to the ground and pull out to eat — a backbreaking work.

But when God provided for them in Canaan, a land flowing with milk and honey (Numbers 13:27), He gave them grapes, pomegranates and figs. (v. 23.) These fruits were not found on the ground and the Israelites only had to pluck them to eat them.

God wants you to know that when He provides for you, you will see a flow of provisions coming your way, and all you need to do is to just stretch forth your hand and take from Him!

So if you are planning to get married, don't say to yourself, "Well, if I work harder and start saving now, I will have... oh my goodness, not much! The cost of the wedding banquet will wipe out everything! How can I get married?"

As a child of God, know that your Daddy God is excited about your upcoming wedding, and He is very rich! I have not seen a single couple in our church lacking on their wedding day. What I have seen is money coming in on the wedding day itself. And before the last drop of champagne is drunk, everything is paid up. So instead of trusting your efforts to have enough for your big day, God wants you to fix your wedding date and put your trust in Him to provide for you richly.

Are you faced with a financial debt? How much do you think you can save by working overtime and taking on a second job? Some of our church members will testify that God simply turned their financial situations around. In fact, Pastor Mark, our Hokkien and Mandarin services pastor, had a sizeable debt before he became a Christian. After he got saved, he handed his debt problem over to God. Within two years, his debt was supernaturally cleared and he even had a surplus!

My friend, faith is the hand that takes from God. And He is easy to take from!

Thought for the Day
Faith is the hand that takes from God, who provides for you richly.

What Have You Been Saying?

Proverbs 18:21
²¹Death and life are in the power of the tongue....

M any things in life can cause us to fear — losing our jobs, deadly diseases, terrorist attacks and so on. When these things confront us, we tend to give in to worry and fear, and start talking about our fears.

Job was no different. He constantly feared that God would punish him and his family because he kept thinking that his sons had sinned against God. He would get up early in the morning to offer burnt sacrifices, saying, "It may be that my sons have sinned and cursed God in their hearts." And the Bible tells us that he did this "regularly." (Job 1:5.)

So Job kept confessing the sins of his sons and fearing that something terrible would happen to him and his family. In fact, his sin-consciousness didn't just produce fear, the Bible tells us that he "greatly feared." (Job 3:25.)

It is important that we understand that it was Job's sin-consciousness that opened the door to Satan. His preoccupation with sins that his family may have committed gave Satan the opportunity to bring death and destruction into his life. God had a hedge of protection around Job. But when he started being sin-conscious and having a fearful expectation of judgment, the hedge was removed and Satan could attack him. (Job 1:9–12.)

My friend, today, if you have sinned, don't say, "I have failed again. I deserve to be punished by God." Know that you already have forgiveness of sins because Jesus was punished and condemned in your place! (Ephesians 1:7.) So say, "I am the righteousness of God in Christ. Jesus, You are my holiness and perfection." (1 Corinthians 1:30; 2 Corinthians 5:21.)

We must be mindful of what we believe and say regularly because "death and life are in the power of the tongue." So when you hear of a deadly virus taking many lives, don't say, "I'm next because I have not been a good Christian!" Instead, say, "Jesus, You are my righteousness and protection. Surely You shall deliver me from the snare of the fowler and from the perilous pestilence!" (Psalm 91:3.)

Beloved, such believing and confessing not only please God, but they also shut the door on Satan so that he cannot make any inroad into your life!

Thought for the Day
Be mindful of what you believe and say regularly because
death and life are in the power of the tongue.

Blessed With Every
Pneumatikos *Blessing*

Ephesians 1:3
³Blessed be the God and Father of our Lord Jesus Christ, who has blessed us with every spiritual blessing in the heavenly places in Christ.

Some people think that the term "spiritual blessing" refers to only non-visible and intangible blessings like peace and joy. To them, God's promise of "every spiritual blessing" excludes the tangible blessings of health, prosperity, a healthy marriage and so on. They say things like, "Don't expect God to remove this tumor because our blessings are only spiritual."

Beloved, do you know what the word "spiritual" here means? In the original Greek text, it is *pneumatikos*, which in this context means having properties and characteristics belonging to the Spirit of God. So if you have the *pneumatikos* blessing of health, for example, it means that it is of the Spirit of God, and therefore does not depend on your exercising or dieting.

A church member had high blood pressure which did not normalize even after he started exercising and eating well. So he stopped being preoccupied with his exercise and diet regimes, and simply rested in the truth that a normal blood pressure was a *pneumatikos* blessing from God already given to him. In a short time, his blood pressure came down to a healthy level!

The same goes for the *pneumatikos* blessing of prosperity. It is of the Spirit of God and does not depend on our toiling seven days a week or monitoring the stock market closely.

A church member, who owns a small company, received her *pneumatikos* blessing of prosperity when she believed that God would cause her small company to be publicly listed. He did. In fact, the company was over-subscribed seven times within the first week! Later on, it even made inroads into Dubai in the Middle East. For a woman to find favor in a male-dominated society like Dubai, it can only be the *pneumatikos* blessing of favor, which is not subject to the laws of man.

My friend, believe that you have received every *pneumatikos* blessing, and you will find yourself enjoying blessings that are eternal, just as God is eternal, and of a quality that only the Spirit of God can give!

Thought for the Day
**You have received every pneumatikos *blessing and each one*
*is of a quality that only the Spirit of God can give!***

Pray Perfect Prayers in the Spirit

Romans 8:27
²⁷Now He who searches the hearts knows what the mind of the Spirit is, because He makes intercession for the saints according to the will of God.

Wouldn't you like to pray effective prayers that are always in line with the will of God and that always hit the mark? Well, when you pray in the Spirit, you can.

You see, when we pray in English or our known language, and according to our limited understanding, we can pray amiss. Sometimes, our heads get in the way and we find ourselves asking, "Isn't it selfish of me to pray like this?" or "Am I praying in line with God's will?"

My friend, that is why God gives us the gift of praying in tongues. When we pray in tongues or in the Holy Spirit, we can never pray out of God's will because the Holy Spirit "makes intercession for the saints according to **the will of God.**"

In other words, we pray perfect prayers in line with God's will when we pray in tongues. And the Bible goes on to tell us that "if we ask anything according to His will, He hears us. And if we know that He hears us, whatever we ask, we know that we have the petitions that we have asked of Him" (1 John 5:14–15).

Isn't it wonderful that God has put in you the Holy Spirit who prays perfectly? He knows the heart of God and precisely what you need. And He makes intercession for you because He loves you very much.

The Holy Spirit is like your lawyer or legal counselor. He knows what belongs to you legally. He knows what your blood-bought rights are in Christ. Best of all, He knows exactly how to enforce them in your life!

Beloved, when you pray in tongues, you allow the Holy Spirit to pray perfect prayers through you. He pleads your case before God. He knows where you have gone wrong and what the root of the problem is. He also has the wisdom, solution and power to win your case. With the Holy Spirit on your side, you cannot but come out victorious!

Thought for the Day
We pray perfect prayers in line with God's will when we pray in tongues.

God Is in It With You

Romans 8:28
²⁸And we know that all things work together for good to those who love God,
to those who are the called according to His purpose.

D o you feel misunderstood and forsaken by the people you love? Have you been falsely accused and stripped of everything, without a dime to your name? Maybe today, you feel that you have hit rock bottom and you wonder if you can ever rise again.

Joseph, who was sold by his brothers into slavery (Genesis 37:28), went through all these experiences and emotions. Still, he was conscious that God was in it with him every step of the way. Though his life was a "mess," he believed that it was not an accident. Though the things that were happening to him were not good, he believed that God was making all things work together for his good. And it was indeed so — Joseph eventually rose to occupy the most powerful position in Egypt, second only to Pharaoh. (Genesis 41:40.)

Probably, this consciousness that God was in it with him was the reason he forgave his brothers when he met them again later in his life. Joseph told them, "But now, do not therefore be grieved or angry with yourselves because you sold me here; for **God** sent me before you to preserve life" (Genesis 45:5).

So like Joseph, whatever you are facing now, be conscious that God is in it with you. Be Jesus-conscious. Though you may have nothing or not much now in the natural, the truth is that you have everything when you have Jesus!

The same Jesus who went around enriching others with 12 baskets full of leftovers, a net-breaking, boat-sinking load of fishes, and who never impoverished anybody, will empower you to prosper and succeed in life. The same Jesus who went about doing good will cause good to explode in your life. The same Jesus who went about healing the sick and never giving anyone sickness will keep you in divine health and protect you from harm.

Beloved, because "Jesus Christ is the same yesterday, today, and forever" (Hebrews 13:8), as He was with Joseph, He is with you right now. And He will empower you to live the high life — the abundant life in which you will see God's promises manifest!

Thought for the Day
God is with you every step of the way and making all things work for your good.

Fresh Grace Every Day

Matthew 6:34
³⁴Therefore do not worry about tomorrow, for tomorrow will worry about its own things. Sufficient for the day is its own trouble.

I am concerned about the big business deal that I have to close tomorrow." "I am worried about tomorrow's job interview." "My medical test results will be out tomorrow. I am afraid it won't be good."

God does not want you to worry about tomorrow. He wants you to know that He gives you all the help you need for today, and when tomorrow comes, so will fresh help from Him.

This is God's principle even in the Old Testament. When the children of Israel were in the desert, God gave them fresh manna from heaven every morning. (Exodus 16:13–16, 31.) They did not have to worry about tomorrow because when tomorrow came, there was fresh manna again. He was their provision every day.

Today, God's manna is the grace He gives you every day. If you are worried about a situation tomorrow, know that there will be sufficient grace for that situation when it comes. God wants you to simply rest in His ability to heal, deliver, protect and provide for you every day.

In the Old Testament, when the armies of Moab and Ammon came against King Jehoshaphat, God told the anxious king, "Do not be afraid nor dismayed... for the battle is not yours, but God's... You will not need to fight in this battle... stand still and see the salvation of the LORD..." (2 Chronicles 20:15,17).

When the next morning came, King Jehoshaphat saw how God caused such confusion to come upon his enemies' camp that it brought about their own slaughter. Amid all that fighting in the enemy camp, God's people merely stood still and saw Him fight the battle for them just as He had promised.

My friend, when you see a problem looming in your tomorrow, don't be afraid or dismayed. Look to the Lord, and see His grace and salvation deliver you.

God wants you to live a stress-free life, not one filled with worries about tomorrow's problems. When tomorrow comes, His grace will be there for you as your help, protection, favor and enabling!

Thought for the Day
God gives you all the help you need for today.
When tomorrow comes, so will fresh help from Him.

Jesus Understands What You Are Going Through

Hebrews 4:15
¹⁵For we do not have a High Priest who cannot sympathize with our weaknesses, but was in all points tempted as we are, yet without sin.

D o you sometimes wonder if God really knows what it is like to be poor, rejected by people or sick with aches and pains. Perhaps you are asking, "Does God really understand what I am going through?"

My friend, Jesus was no stranger to emotional or physical pains, poverty or hardships. He was born into a poor family. He had a smelly manger for His birthplace. (Luke 2:7.) From an early age, as a carpenter, He knew all about working hard with His hands, standing on His feet all day long and returning home with aches in His body.

The religious leaders of His day made life difficult for Him. They challenged His authority (Matthew 21:23) and tested His teachings. (Matthew 19:3.) They also called Him a glutton, winebibber, friend of tax collectors and sinners (Matthew 11:19), and blasphemer. (Mark 2:7.)

They said that He was demon-possessed and mad (John 10:20), put Him on the spot when they brought an adulterous woman to Him (John 8:2–11), attempted to stone Him (John 8:59, 10:31–39) and accused Him of perverting the nation. (Luke 23:2.)

Have you been chased out of your home because of your Christian beliefs? Jesus understands what you are going through. He was chased out of His own hometown. (Luke 4:29.) Have you been rejected by someone you love? Jesus also experienced the pain of being denied by a loved one (Luke 22:54–62) and betrayed by one considered close to Him. (vv. 47–48.) He also knows all about the sickness you are suffering because He bore your sicknesses and pains on the cross. (Isaiah 53:4.)

Jesus certainly understands all that we are going through because being born fully Man, He was "in **all** points tempted as we are." He endured His sufferings for our sakes, so that we can have His peace and the anointing to rise above the troubles we are facing!

Thought for the Day
Jesus understands all that we are going through because being born fully Man, He was in all points tempted as we are.

Nothing to Do, Only Believe

John 6:28–29
[28]... "What shall we do, that we may work the works of God?"
[29]Jesus answered and said to them, "This is the work of
God, that you believe in Him whom He sent."

When I was a young Christian, I attended a seminar on what we must do to "work the works of God." I was told that we had to pray more, fast more, know our enemy and so on. I came away from the seminar confused. Then one day, I found the same question in the Bible. But the answer was very different!

In the Gospel of John, we find Jesus being asked the same question by the multitude who had been awed by His miracles — "What shall we do, that we may work the works of God?" The people had seen Jesus healing the sick, and feeding 5,000 men with only five loaves and two fish.

Notice how Jesus answered them: "This is the work of God, that you believe in Him whom He sent." My friend, the greatest doing is believing — believing in Jesus, the sent One, who has done it all for you at the cross!

If you are asking, "What must I do to receive my healing?" the answer is this: believe in Jesus, who "Himself took our infirmities and bore our sicknesses" (Matthew 8:17). We have seen members of our church delivered from life-threatening conditions such as cancer and kidney failure. They had simply believed that Jesus bore their diseases on His own body. There was nothing for them to do, except to believe.

When the jailer asked Paul and Silas, "Sirs, what must I do to be saved?" they said, "Believe on the Lord Jesus Christ, and you will be saved, you and your household" (Acts 16:30–31). The greatest miracle in your life happens not by you working and trying to save yourself, but by you simply believing in Jesus, who died to save you from eternal damnation and to give you eternal life. Why then, should the lesser miracles of healing or financial breakthroughs be any different?

Beloved, what is the miracle you need today? There is nothing left for you to **do**, but everything for you to **believe**, because Jesus has done it all for you!

Thought for the Day
The greatest doing is believing — believing in Jesus
the sent One, who has done it all for you!

What Do You See?

Mark 11:24
²⁴Therefore I say to you, whatever things you ask when you pray, believe that you receive them, and you will have them.

A blind lady was led to a great healing evangelist for prayer. After he had prayed for her, he asked her, "Now, tell me what you see." She opened her eyes only to be told, "Close your eyes. Tell me what you see." She opened her eyes again only to be told, "I didn't say to open your eyes. I asked you what you saw. Close your eyes! Now, tell me what you see."

This went on for a while, until the lady realized that the evangelist was asking her what she saw on the inside. Did she see herself seeing? When she understood that, she said, "I see myself with sight." Then, the evangelist told her, "Now, slowly open your eyes." That moment, she opened her eyes to perfect vision!

When you prayed just now, what did you see inside you? Were you praying for someone's healing, but seeing that person in a coffin? Were you praying for a financial breakthrough, but seeing the banks pursuing you till you were bankrupt?

You see, you don't get what you pray for. You get what you believe you receive when you pray. Jesus said, "Therefore I say to you, whatever things you ask when you pray, believe that you receive them, and you will have them."

Beloved, "whatever things" covers your every need. And believing that you receive them comes before having them. Jesus once told a centurion, "Go your way; and as you have believed, so let it be done for you." The centurion's servant was healed that same hour. (Matthew 8:13.) The centurion believed that he received his miracle even before he saw it in the natural.

So when you pray, what do you really believe and see on the inside?

"Well, Pastor Prince, I really can't see it."

Then don't pray yet. Change your vision on the inside first. Start seeing yourself with the answer. See yourself healed. See yourself living in the bigger house that you need. See yourself enjoying more than enough. When you can see it and believe it, then pray in faith, and you will have whatever you ask for!

Thought for the Day
You don't get what you pray for. You get what you believe and see yourself receiving on the inside when you pray.

Every Curse in Your Life Destroyed

Galatians 3:13
¹³Christ has redeemed us from the curse of the law, having become a curse for us
(for it is written, "Cursed is everyone who hangs on a tree").

Many believers probably know that when Jesus died, our sins were forgiven because He shed His blood. Without the shedding of blood, there is no forgiveness of sins. (Ephesians 1:7, Hebrews 9:22.) But why did Jesus have to die on the cross, since the capital punishment of Israel during the time of Christ was stoning and not crucifixion?

Jesus hung and died on the cross because He knew the law which says that "he who is hanged is accursed of God" (Deuteronomy 21:23). He wanted to redeem us from every curse of the law, so He went to the cross, "having become a curse for us." Jesus took all our curses at the cross, so that we can take all His blessings!

The moment you received Jesus, every curse in your life was destroyed. And the way you experience this is to simply believe and confess what Jesus has done for you. Say, "Because of Jesus, I am blessed." The more you say it and believe it, the more you will experience it.

So if there is an area in your life in which you feel oppressed, for example, a skin condition that refuses to heal, say, "Christ has redeemed me from this skin condition. I refuse it and reject it in Jesus' name because by His stripes I am healed!" (1 Peter 2:24.) Believe it and say it until you see it!

"But Pastor Prince, my father died of cancer. His father died of cancer. And I have been told by my doctor that there is a likelihood that I might get it too. It's in our blood!"

My friend, the blood of Christ shed at the cross has redeemed you from **all** curses, including diseases like cancer! God put the curse of cancer on Jesus at the cross. And He put **all** the blessings of Jesus on you. Therefore, expect only the blessings of Jesus to come upon you and overtake you!

Thought for the Day
The moment you received Jesus, every curse in your life was destroyed.

You Have the Same Favor Jesus Has

Romans 4:16
16 Therefore it is of faith that it might be according to grace, so that the promise might be sure to all the seed, not only to those who are of the law, but also to those who are of the faith of Abraham, who is the father of us all.

God's grace is His undeserved, unearned and unmerited favor. And because it is undeserved, unearned and unmerited, all of us qualify for it. But how do we walk in it?

Just as a password gives you access to a computer program, faith enables you to walk in God's unmerited favor. Now, faith has nothing to do with what you do or what you can do. Faith is simply believing and declaring what God has done and is doing for you.

When you believe that the favor of God is on you because of Christ's finished work, His promises of provision, healing and restoration become sure to you. They are not just sure to the Jews, but also to you and me because we are "of the faith of Abraham."

Ruth was a Gentile widow who put her faith in God's grace. She believed and declared that God's favor would lead her to the right field in which to glean, where she would find favor in the owner's sight. (Ruth 2:2.) Because she depended on God's unmerited favor, God not only placed her in wealthy Boaz's field, but also in the genealogy of Jesus! (Matthew 1:5.)

Ruth's faith in God's favor opened up a whole new world for her. She went from poverty to wealth, widowhood to marriage, and from being childless to having a complete family. She also became a respected member of the community. (Ruth 4:13–15.)

If Ruth, a Gentile who was under the old covenant, enjoyed God's favor, how much more will we who are under the new covenant of grace enjoy the blessings that the unmerited favor of God brings! In fact, because God sees us in the Beloved today, we enjoy the same favor that Jesus has! (Ephesians 1:3–6.)

My friend, when you believe that you have the same favor that Jesus has, a whole new world will open up to you — a world where all of God's promises are "Yes" and "Amen" in Christ! (2 Corinthians 1:20.)

Thought for the Day
When you believe that the favor of God is on you because of Christ's finished work, His promises of provision, healing and restoration become sure to you.

Fight From Victory, Not for Victory

Ephesians 6:11
¹¹Put on the whole amour of God, that you may be
able to stand against the wiles of the devil.

God does not need you to defeat the devil today. Jesus has already done it and given you the victory. (Colossians 2:15, Romans 8:37.) Your part is to enforce the victory by simply standing your ground, which is victory ground. In other words, you "fight" **from** victory ground by standing. You don't fight **for** victory.

In Ephesians 6:10–18, the passage on spiritual warfare, the word "wrestle" appears only once (v. 12), while the word "stand" appears four times — "**stand** against the wiles of the devil," "**withstand** in the evil day," "having done all, to **stand**," "**Stand** therefore" (vv. 11, 13–14). Four times the Holy Spirit tells us to stand. Yet, many Christians are focusing on wrestling their way to victory!

My friend, you are already on victory ground. You already have everything in Christ. (1 Corinthians 3:21, 23.) You are already blessed with every spiritual blessing in Christ. (Ephesians 1:3.) The devil knows this. And that is why his tactic is to deceive you and make you think that you don't have the victory.

So when he attacks you by saying, "Look at that small sum in your bank account! How are you going to pay the bills?" stand your ground. Declare, "I am not trying to be rich, I am rich. In Christ, I am rich!" It doesn't matter how much you have in the bank. You are rich because you are in Christ. And as the need arises, the supply will be there if you believe that you are already rich.

It is the same with healing. The devil will try to attack you with symptoms in your body. He will try to put pain in your body, and make you feel weak here and there, so that you think that you are still sick. He is trying to make you believe that you don't have your healing. That is the time to be conscious of Jesus' finished work and declare, "I am not trying to get healed, I am healed! I am standing on the victory ground which Jesus has given me!"

Beloved, it makes a world of difference when you fight **from** victory and not **for** victory!

Thought for the Day
You are already on victory ground. You are already blessed
with every spiritual blessing in Christ.

Speak Blessings Over Your Family

Psalm 5:12
12For You, O LORD, will bless the righteous; with favor
You will surround him as with a shield.

What do you believe and say to your loved ones every day? For orthodox Jews, on Friday evenings in their homes, the father lays his hands on his children and pronounces God's blessings over them. No wonder Jewish children grow up to be winners in the fight of life! They become some of the world's greatest inventors, bankers, musicians and entertainers.

Although a minority race, the Jews have produced the most number of Nobel Prize winners. I believe that it is because they bless their children in the same way the patriarchs of the Old Testament did. Abraham, Isaac and Jacob released God's blessings upon their children by laying hands on them and speaking forth the blessings. (Genesis 27:27–29, 38–40; 48:14–16.)

In the New Testament, the apostles pronounced blessings over the churches they were preaching to. To the church in Philippi, Paul declared, "And my God shall supply all your need according to His riches in glory by Christ Jesus" (Philippians 4:19). John released a powerful blessing upon Gaius when he said, "Beloved, I pray that you may prosper in all things and be in health, just as your soul prospers" (3 John 1:2).

Even Jesus pronounced a blessing of deliverance on the daughter of the Syro-Phoenician woman — "go your way; the demon has gone out of your daughter" (Mark 7:29). This was a blessing of deliverance by proxy. The woman took it by faith and found that her daughter was well when she reached home. (v. 30.) Likewise, the centurion took the blessing by faith and healing came upon his servant back home. (Matthew 8:8–13.)

The parents of a little girl did the same thing while worshiping in our church. Their daughter was in the hospital in the final stages of cancer. When I pronounced the blessing of healing that Sunday, they received it and pronounced it over their daughter. She was soon discharged from the hospital healed!

My friend, bless your loved ones. Declare over them, "The Lord blesses you and surrounds you with His favor as with a shield." Speak forth your own blessings by declaring, "Thank You, Lord, that You prosper me and I am in excellent health!"

Thought for the Day
Pronounce God's blessings over your children and they will
grow up to be winners in the fight of life.

Remain Steadfast in the Faith

1 Peter 5:8–9
[8]Be sober, be vigilant; because your adversary the devil walks about like a roaring lion, seeking whom he may devour. [9]Resist him, steadfast in the faith....

W hen I was a teenager, I was taught that if I wanted to resist the devil, I had to rebuke him. So whenever an evil thought came to my mind or I was tempted, I found myself saying, "I resist you, devil, in Jesus' name! I bind you, devil! Go away from me, devil! I rebuke you in Jesus' name!"

This went on until God showed me one day that though I had "resisted" the devil, I had spent more time talking to him than to God! I was more conscious of the devil than of God throughout the day.

I checked the Word of God and realized that we resist the devil not by focusing on resisting him, but by being established in **the faith** that we are made right with God through Jesus' blood, that we are the righteousness of God in Christ. (2 Corinthians 5:21.)

Yes, the devil will continue to remind you of your mistakes, failures and sins. And he will tell you that because of these things, you cannot receive your healing, that you will have to pay for your mistakes or that something bad will happen to your family. He will accuse you, condemn you and try to persuade your heart to believe that he can do bad things to you.

But the truth is that the devil cannot enforce anything in your life if he cannot persuade your heart. And your heart cannot be persuaded if it is "steadfast in the faith," if it is established in righteousness. God says that once you are established in righteousness, "You shall be far from oppression, for you shall not fear; and from terror, for it shall not come near you" (Isaiah 54:14).

So now that my heart is established in righteousness, I can boldly declare, "Yes, I may have these problems in my life, but I am not guilty in God's eyes. I am justified in His eyes by faith because of what Christ has done. I am righteous by Jesus' blood!" Beloved, that is how you resist the devil and become undevourable!

Thought for the Day
We resist the devil not by focusing on resisting him, but by being established in the faith that we are the righteousness of God in Christ.

From 'Deliverance' to 'No Evil Shall Touch You'

Job 5:19
¹⁹He shall deliver you in six troubles, yes, in seven no evil shall touch you.

God will deliver you from all your troubles. (Psalm 34:19, 2 Timothy 4:18.) But deliverance is actually not the best that God has for you because it implies that you are in trouble. God's best for you is the place where no trouble or evil can touch you. And with His help, you will come to that place because the Bible says, "He shall deliver you in six troubles, yes, in seven no evil shall touch you."

This does not mean that God will only deliver you six times. It just means that as you keep believing God's promises of protection, after some time, you will come to a place where no evil will touch you!

So when trouble comes, God does not want you to be discouraged. He wants you to know that it is only the devil trying to steal His Word from your heart. The devil is afraid of leaving God's Word in your heart for even one second because he knows that it will lead you to a place where no evil will touch you. That is why he comes immediately to steal God's Word from your heart.

He will do so by telling you, "Look, your child is sick. Where is God now?" You must not respond by saying, "Well, I guess it does not work. Maybe God's promises of deliverance are not for my family."

No, you must continue to stand on God's promises. Say, "The previous flu my child had did not stay. God promises me deliverance and He did deliver my child then. So I will live life believing His promises of deliverance because His Word is true. And I will come to a place where no evil can touch me and my family!"

Beloved, even if in the next moment you happen to stub your toe against something hard, don't be discouraged and wonder why God did not protect your toe. The devil had meant to cause greater harm to you, but thank God that he could not because God is watching over you. And keep standing on His promises until you come to the place where no evil will touch you!

Thought for the Day
***Keep believing God's promises of protection and
come to a place where no evil will touch you!***

Much Better Than Before

Isaiah 61:7
⁷Instead of your shame you shall have double honor, and instead of confusion they shall rejoice in their portion. Therefore in their land they shall possess double; everlasting joy shall be theirs.

God says in His Word that you will receive double for your trouble. If the devil has given you one trouble, then for that one trouble you can expect to receive a double-portion blessing! And if that trouble has caused you to experience shame, God's promise to you is this: "Instead of your shame you shall have double honor." God wants to give you a **double-portion** blessing for every trouble you go through!

And don't think that God is behind your troubles. The devil is the real culprit. Sometimes, it could be the one you see in the mirror every morning! But the moment you respond to God in faith, He gets involved in your restoration. And He does not restore to you the same amount that you have lost. You always get more than before, if not in quantity, then in quality. You will be at a higher place than before. You will be stronger, healthier, wealthier, wiser or more at peace!

This was the case with Job. Satan was behind Job's troubles, but when Job responded in faith, God took it upon Himself to restore to Job all that he had lost. The Bible tells us that Job received double in terms of quantity — from 7,000 sheep to 14,000 sheep, 3,000 camels to 6,000 camels, 500 yoke of oxen to 1,000 yoke of oxen and 500 female donkeys to 1,000 female donkeys. And for the children he had lost, God restored in terms of quality — his daughters were the fairest in all the land. (Job 1:2–3, 13–19; 42:12–15.)

If Job, who was not under the new covenant, could be blessed with double for his troubles, how much more we who are under the new covenant! In fact, God will not only restore double but triple, fivefold or even sevenfold! Such was the restoration experienced by one of our pastors, who was cheated of some money. In the end, he received a sevenfold restoration!

My friend, for everything that you have lost, get ready for God's restoration. Expect to receive double and even more for every trouble!

Thought for the Day
If Job, who was not under the new covenant, could be blessed with double for his troubles, how much more we who are under the new covenant!

Life With God Is Easy and Light

Matthew 11:28
²⁸Come to Me, all you who labor and are heavy laden, and I will give you rest.

It always warms my heart to know that Jesus sees the cares we carry in our hearts. He knows the worries you have for your family and for the future. He feels the heaviness in your heart as you struggle with the sickness in your body. He says to you, "Come to Me, all you who labor and are heavy laden, and I will give you rest."

Jesus wants to give you rest. And He says that the way you receive rest is to be yoked with Him, for His yoke is easy and His burden is light. (vv. 29–30.)

What does it mean to be yoked with Jesus? Imagine a pair of oxen yoked together. The younger ox sees what the lead ox does and follows. If the lead ox turns left, the younger ox turns left. If the lead ox stops, the younger ox stops. When the lead ox starts moving again, the younger ox follows. Likewise, Jesus wants us to follow His leading and flow with Him.

It is not hard to flow with Jesus because He will not lay anything heavy on you — "For My yoke is **easy** and My burden is **light**" (v. 30). When you are yoked with Him and you flow with Him, you will find that there is nothing heavy-hearted, ill-fitting or burdensome from the Lord. When you flow with the Lord, you will find that things fall into place. You will not be weighed down, anxious or distressed.

You might say, "But Pastor Prince, God has given me this heavy burden. It is weighing heavily on my heart!"

My friend, if the burden is heavy, it is not from God because Jesus said that His burden is **light**. The devil has probably given you the burden to crush you!

"Oh, Pastor Prince, you are making light of how serious my burden is."

No, I am not. Jesus did say that His burden is **light** and His yoke **easy**. So a life yoked with Him is anxiety- and worry-free.

Beloved, follow His leading and flow with Him, and you will find rest for your soul!

Thought for the Day
The way you receive rest is to be yoked with Jesus,
for His yoke is easy and His burden is light.

Watch What Jesus Does

Luke 1:37
³⁷"For with God nothing will be impossible."

Y ou may have heard from friends or seen in Christian books the popular question, "What would Jesus do?" It is a question Christians are taught to ask themselves when faced with a problem.

But when you ask yourself, "What would Jesus do?" in any situation, it is subject to your own interpretation and theology. For example, if you are from a church that doesn't believe that Jesus heals today, you may think that this is how Jesus would pray for the sick, "O Father, give him patience to endure his sufferings," and proceed to pray that way for a sick person. So when you try to think of what Jesus would do, you are going back to your flesh!

Maybe the reminder should be, "Watch what Jesus does." When I preach, I watch what Jesus is doing or leading me to do. If He prompts me to say or do something, I say or do it. I know that I am not in the pulpit to manifest Pastor Prince or his flesh, but to manifest Jesus Christ, with whom nothing is impossible!

One Sunday service, prompted by God, I shared with the congregation that He wanted to restore lost items. The following week, a church member wrote, "Last Sunday, Pastor Prince, you mentioned that the Lord would help us recover lost items. I knew that the word was for me. My diamond bracelet and ring had been missing for weeks… Praise God, when I returned home that day, my maid placed the lost items in my hands. She found them at 10:30 that morning while I was still worshiping in church."

On another occasion, I was praying for a wheelchair-bound lady when I felt God telling me to pull her up from her wheelchair. Boy, was I glad that before I realized what I was doing, she was standing up on her feet unaided! Now, if I had taken some time to think — "My goodness, what am I doing?" — my thinking could have obstructed my obedience to God's prompting.

So when you are led to talk to someone, watch what Jesus does. When you pray for your child, watch what Jesus does. When you confess God's Word into your situation, watch what Jesus does! Keep your eyes on Jesus, with whom nothing is impossible!

Thought for the Day
Watch what Jesus is leading you to do and experience the miraculous.

Nothing Is Too Hard for God

Jeremiah 32:17
17'Ah, Lord GOD! Behold, You have made the heavens and the earth by Your great power and outstretched arm. There is nothing too hard for You.

Our minds tend to see our problems as big or small. Even when we pray for the sick, we say things like, "You have a headache? No problem. Let's pray for your healing." But when it is cancer, we say, "Oh, let's tell the senior pastor about it. It would be better if he prayed for you." We think of headaches as small problems and cancers as big ones.

But that is not the way God thinks. There is nothing too hard for Him who made the heavens and the earth! With God, there is no such thing as a "big" problem. In fact, the "bigger" the problem, the "easier" it is for Him! In the feeding of the 5,000, it took only five loaves to feed the multitude. (Matthew 14:15–21.) But in the feeding of the smaller multitude of 4,000, it took seven loaves. (Matthew 15:32–38.)

In man's scheme of things, it should take more loaves to feed more people. But this is not so with God. It took fewer loaves to feed more people. This is God's way of telling us that the "bigger" the problem, the "easier" it is for Him. I am not saying that small problems are hard for God. But it is so encouraging to think that it is "easier" for God to heal cancers than headaches!

Imagine coming to God with a big problem. "So, what is your problem, My child?" God asks. You say, "Father, it is a huge financial debt — not thousands but millions!" He says, "Easy. It is already cancelled."

In another scenario, God asks, "So, what is your problem, My child?" You say, "Father, I have lost my job and I can't find a new one. I am already in my fifties and I don't have the necessary qualifications." He says, "No problem. Consider yourself employed. And in this new job, you won't just have a job, you will have a position."

Beloved, with God, it is never a problem because there is nothing too hard for Him!

Thought for the Day
**With God, your problem — small or big — is never a problem
because there is nothing too hard for Him!**

One Thing Is Needful

Proverbs 4:20–21
²⁰My son, give attention to my words; incline your ear to my sayings.
²¹Do not let them depart from your eyes; keep them in the midst of your heart.

George Müller, who lived in the 1800s, cared for more than 2,000 orphans in his five large orphanages. But he never allowed his huge responsibility to take him away from the Word of God. He said that every day, he would set aside time to study the scriptures until his inner man was happy in the Lord.

Once, Müller met a man who worked between 14 and 16 hours every day. He told the man, "You are destroying your health. You don't have time for your family and, most importantly, you don't have time to nourish your inner man with the Word of God."

The man replied, "I hear you, but I can't see how I can cut down my working hours and spend time in the Word because even with the 14 to 16 hours I put in each day, I still can't put enough bread on the table for my family."

As the man walked away, Müller said, "He doesn't believe that if he gives time to God's Word first, God will take care of all his needs."

Likewise, do you really believe that every day, only one thing is needful? Even if the bills don't get paid, the children are not making any headway in their studies and the office work is not completed, all these things can wait. Only one thing is needful — that you spend time in the Word of God.

When Martha complained to Jesus that her sister Mary had left her to serve alone (Mary was sitting at Jesus' feet and hearing His Word), Jesus defended Mary by saying, "Martha, Martha, you are worried and troubled about many things. But **one thing is needed**, and Mary has chosen that good part, which will not be taken away from her" (Luke 10:41–42).

My friend, you will not lose out when you take time to sit down and listen to God's Word. Even your health and well-being will be blessed. (Proverbs 4:22.) So take time today to meditate on His Word. It will make your way prosperous (Joshua 1:8–9), and give you divine health and good success!

Thought for the Day
You will not lose out when you take time to sit down and listen to God's Word.

No Death, Only Life!

Proverbs 12:28
²⁸In the way of righteousness is life, and in its pathway there is no death.

God does not want us to worry about whatever happens in the world. We don't need to be affected by whatever is causing the world to be afraid because we are the righteousness of God in Christ. (2 Corinthians 5:21.) And the Bible says, "In the way of righteousness is **life**, and in its pathway there is no **death**."

The patriarchs of the Old Testament did not suffer during the famines that occurred in their lifetimes. Abraham remained very rich in livestock, silver and gold. (Genesis 12:10, 13:1–2.) Isaac reaped a hundredfold in the land he sowed. (Genesis 26:1, 12–14.) Joseph, with his entire family, was richly provided for in Egypt. (Genesis 47:11–13, 27.) They weren't just spared from suffering — they prospered exceedingly!

So even if our nation or the world enters a recession, we need not suffer. As long as we keep our eyes on Jesus, our righteousness, we will prosper!

This proved true for a church member whose boss told everyone to expect a substantial pay cut during an economic downturn. But while her colleagues received pay cuts, she received a substantial increment! As the righteousness of God in Christ, she saw prosperity in a time of lack.

In the midst of fearful news such as terrorist attacks, deadly pestilences and natural calamities, God says, "In the way of righteousness is life, and in its pathway there is no death." In fact, He protected an entire coastal town in South India during the Asian tsunami in 2004.

A pastor who lived in that coastal town was praying that morning when he felt prompted by the Holy Spirit to plead the blood of Jesus over his entire town. So he did just that. When the tsunami struck, his town was untouched while five other towns, which were further inland, were wiped out by the devastating flood.

My friend, God protects us when the world is experiencing evil because we are the righteousness of God in Christ. His Word declares that "in the way of righteousness is life, and in its pathway there is no death"!

Thought for the Day
You don't need to be affected by whatever is causing the world to be afraid because you are the righteousness of God in Christ.

The Spirit's Rest and Refreshing

Isaiah 28:11–12
*¹¹For with stammering lips and another tongue He will speak to this people,
¹²to whom He said, "This is the rest with which you may cause the
weary to rest," and, "This is the refreshing"....*

To counter stress, many people resort to tobacco, alcohol or tranquilizers. These things, besides having harmful side effects, are costly and often lead to addictions.

God has something better for us. It is powerful, costs us nothing and has no harmful side effects. He calls it "the rest" and "the refreshing." What is He referring to? Speaking in tongues — "For with stammering lips and another tongue…"

One of our church members was on medication for nine long years for a host of problems: severe depression, suicidal thoughts, insomnia, chronic sinusitis, gastritis and panic attacks. Every day, he had to take up to 30 tablets to keep these conditions under control.

He suffered from such bad sinusitis that he had to visit the hospital regularly to drain the mucus. He could not sleep much — at most three hours — even with sleeping pills. And because of his panic attacks, he could not go to work and seldom left his house. His wife had to look after him and their three kids. The side effects of the long-term medication also caused his physique to balloon.

One day, he felt God prompting him to pray in tongues as often as he could. He obeyed. The moment he started to pray in tongues, even though it was just a few syllables, he felt a rest, a peace. This encouraged him to pray in tongues more. And the more he prayed in tongues, the more rest and peace he felt.

His sinuses began to clear up and he was healed of gastritis. Slowly, the fears and panic attacks left him too. He also started to have quality sleep without the sleeping pills! The Lord even taught him how he was to eat — two meals a day, but to eat whatever he wanted. Today, he is back to his normal weight!

Through praying in tongues regularly, God delivered this man from a host of long-term illnesses. My friend, this is the rest and the refreshing which God has promised us. So start praying in tongues regularly, and let His rest and peace saturate your entire being!

Thought for the Day
**Pray in tongues regularly and let God's rest and
peace saturate your entire being.**

Healthier, Stronger Each Day

Acts 2:46
⁴⁶So continuing daily with one accord in the temple, and breaking bread from house to house, they ate their food with gladness and simplicity of heart.

Back then in the early church, Christians would meet each other every day, either corporately in the temple or from house to house in smaller groups. And when they met in their homes, the Bible tells us that they would **break bread**. That's the Holy Communion, and they took it every day!

Now, I am not saying that you must take the Holy Communion every day. But if you feel led to and you want to, go ahead! The thing about taking the Holy Communion daily is this: If you are sick, you can be made well on a gradual basis. This means that you get healthier and stronger from day to day — first thirtyfold, then sixtyfold, then a hundredfold!

You see, while you can receive healing through the prayer of faith (Mark 11:24), it sometimes puts pressure on you because it requires you to believe that you receive it all — complete healing — the moment you pray. There is nothing wrong with the prayer of faith, but you may find yourself saying, "I must believe I receive it all, now! I must believe I have it all, now!"

But the Holy Communion allows you to receive a measure of healing every time you partake in faith, so that you get better and better. The more you take it, the better you become. There is no pressure to believe that you receive it all at once. Isn't God good? He meets you at your level of faith!

Now, there are cases I know of in our church, in my family and in my own life, where the manifestation of healing is immediate and complete. If it happens that way, praise God! But if not, don't worry. The more you partake, the better you will become.

I know of people who take the Holy Communion three times a day, just like they would medicine! Why not? My friend, if you are very sick and you are diligently taking your medication three times a day, why not give the Lord's Supper the same amount of attention? Why not boost your recovery rate? And the next time you eat the bread and drink the cup, you may just find your disease totally gone!

Thought for the Day
If you are diligently taking your medication three times a day, why not give the Lord's Supper the same amount of attention?

Jesus Makes All Things New

John 1:3
³All things were made through Him, and without Him
nothing was made that was made.

Any electronic product that you buy usually comes with an instruction booklet that says, "Send only to authorized dealers for maintenance and repairs." Similarly, when something in your body or life breaks down, you go back to Jesus, your Creator and Maker. You go to Him because God's Word tells us that "all things were made through Him, and without Him nothing was made that was made."

The Bible says that in the beginning, God created everything by speaking (Genesis 1), and Jesus was the Word who caused everything to come to pass. (John 1:1–2, 14.) So when relationships in your family break down, when your finances are low or when some part of your body isn't working properly, you go to Jesus who can fix it and even make it better than before!

A mother from our church testified of how God gave her a brand-new daughter who used to be a very rebellious teenager. The day the girl gave her life to Jesus marked the start of a new life with her family. She also became the face to look out for in the national swimming arena. When asked by reporters about her record-breaking feats, she told them that it was Jesus who did it all for her!

A lady once approached me and said, "Pastor Prince, I don't know if you still remember me, but I came to you before when I was a divorcee. This is my husband — the same man I divorced some years ago. We remarried and these are our children!" Now, this doesn't usually happen in cases where divorce has taken place, but this couple looked to Jesus and saw their broken family made whole!

When man puts something that has been broken back together, it is usually not as good as before. But when Jesus does it, all things become new! (2 Corinthians 5:17.) The One who made the heavens and the earth is more than able to make it better than it was before!

Thought for the Day
When something in your body or life breaks down,
go back to Jesus, your Creator and Maker.

Jesus' Priesthood Never Curses

Hebrews 5:9–10
⁹And having been perfected, He became the author of eternal
salvation to all who obey Him, ¹⁰called by God as
High Priest "according to the order of Melchizedek."

When Jesus died and rose again, He became our High Priest. But notice that Jesus' priesthood is "according to the order of Melchizedek." Why the Melchizedek priesthood?

The Melchizedek priesthood **gives** to man (whereas the Aaronic priesthood **takes** from man). We see this when Melchizedek gave bread and wine to refresh a tired Abraham after his battle with the enemy kings. (Genesis 14:14–20.) So if Jesus' priesthood is according to the Melchizedek order, then it is one in which we can come boldly into His presence to receive from Him! (Hebrews 4:16.)

Moreover, the first word from Melchizedek's mouth was "Blessed" — "Blessed be Abram…" (Genesis 14:19). The Melchizedek order is just that — blessings. In other words, Jesus' priesthood is one which blesses and never curses us!

So are we conscious of Jesus, our High Priest, giving to us every day? Are we alert to all His blessings coming from heaven toward us on earth?

Now, it is easy for us to believe God for His blessings in creation. For example, we have no difficulty believing that the sun will rise every morning. But while we have no problems believing the work of creation, we have problems believing the work of redemption. We sometimes find it hard to believe God for healing, prosperity, favor, protection or restoration — blessings that Jesus died to give us. We don't really believe that every day, the Lord will take care of us, keep our bodies healthy and provide for all our needs.

Yet, creation is fallen. It can be a blessing as well as a curse. Sometimes, a storm arises, and powerful winds and rains destroy thousands of homes and lives. Sometimes, dark clouds hide the sun and make the whole day gloomy.

My friend, we can't put our trust in creation, but we can certainly put our trust in redemption. And unlike creation, the blessings of redemption are all good! The work of Jesus is not subject to the weather or anything else. The work of redemption is as sure as Jesus Himself. He died and rose again to be our High Priest who daily showers us with blessings!

Thought for the Day
Jesus' priesthood, which is according to the order of Melchizedek,
is one which blesses and never curses us!

You Are a Son and an Heir of God

Galatians 4:6–7
*⁶And because you are sons, God has sent forth the Spirit of His Son into
your hearts, crying out, "Abba, Father!" ⁷Therefore you are no longer
a slave but a son, and if a son, then an heir of God through Christ.*

Perhaps these questions have been popping into your head lately: "If you are a Christian, why are you sick? If your heavenly Father is so wonderful, why do you have so many problems? Doesn't your God help you, His child?"

And if you have been tempted to ask, "God, I am Your child. Why is this happening to me?" know that Jesus knows exactly how you feel because 2,000 years ago, the devil played the same trick on Him — "If You are the Son of God..." (Matthew 4:3). You see, the devil's intention was to make Jesus doubt His Sonship, and the devil wants to do the same thing to you today.

He wants to destroy the Spirit of sonship in you and in the body of believers. He knows that once you really believe that you are a son of God, something happens — you begin to live life as "an heir of God through Christ."

As a son and an heir of God, you inherit all the blessings of God that Jesus died to give you, including salvation, healing, prosperity, wholeness, favor, intimacy with God and answered prayers. And Jesus rose from the dead to make sure that what He died to give you, you get. He is alive today to enforce this rich, blood-bought inheritance in your life!

My friend, you are an heir of God through Christ. This means that you are joint heirs with Jesus. (Romans 8:17.) So His inheritance is your inheritance too!

What is prosperity when you are an heir of God? All the diamonds and gold came from Him. What is provision when you are an heir of God? He owns every beast in the forest and the cattle on a thousand hills. (Psalm 50:10.) What is healing when you are an heir of God? He is your Creator and the very breath of your life.

Beloved, enjoy every bit of your inheritance in Christ, not because you deserve it, but because it was paid for by Jesus' blood!

Thought for the Day
As joint heirs with Christ, His inheritance is your inheritance too!

Release the Anointing Into
Your Situation

Leviticus 2:1
*¹'When anyone offers a grain offering to the LORD, his offering shall be of
fine flour. And he shall pour oil on it, and put frankincense on it.*

The grain offering in the Old Testament speaks of Jesus' sacrifice, and oil in
the Bible speaks of the anointing of the Holy Spirit. So the grain offering
of fine flour, which had oil poured on it, speaks of Jesus' humanity being
anointed by the Holy Spirit.

Jesus is fully God. But when He came to earth, He literally emptied Himself,
taking the form of a servant. (Philippians 2:7.) That is why He needed to be
anointed of the Holy Spirit before He could begin His ministry. (John 1:33.)
Though fully God, He did things by the power of the Holy Spirit.

Jesus was anointed to bring the blessings of God into the lives of people. He
first spoke of His anointing when He was preaching in His hometown — "The
Spirit of the LORD is upon Me, because He has **anointed** Me to preach the gospel
to the poor..." (Luke 4:18).

Today, Jesus' anointing has come upon you. (1 John 2:20.) The Bible says that
"the anointing which you have received from Him abides in you" (v. 27). But how
is this anointing in you released?

My friend, it is when you call upon Jesus' name. In Song of Solomon 1:3, the
virgins, representing the church, love His name, which is like ointment poured
forth when **spoken**. When they called upon His name, His fragrance was released
and the anointing was poured forth.

So when you call upon the name of Jesus, you are releasing His anointing. Call
upon His name when you are feeling down and His anointing will lift your spirit
up. If you are feeling dry and empty, just say, "Jesus, Jesus." Before you know it,
a river of refreshing will gush forth as His anointing flows. Call upon His name
when you need a breakthrough and His anointing will release it to you.

Romans 10:13 says that "whoever calls on the name of the LORD shall be
saved." So call on Jesus' name and watch His anointing release your deliverance,
healing, protection and prosperity, and make you whole!

Thought for the Day
**The anointing which you have received from Jesus abides in you and
is released into your situation when you call upon His name.**

God of the Small Things Too

John 21:9, 12

⁹Then, as soon as they had come to land, they saw a fire of coals there, and fish laid on it, and bread... ¹²Jesus said to them, "Come and eat breakfast."

Like many parents, Wendy and I pray for our daughter Jessica every night before she sleeps. When Jessica was two years old, we decided to pray that her diapers would not overflow during the night. Her diapers not overflowing might be a small thing, but we knew that it would give our little girl a comfortable sleep every night. And after we started praying for this, we noticed that her diapers did not overflow.

That incident made me realize that our God is not just interested in the big things that affect us. He bothers and cares about the minor things that affect us too. There is nothing too insignificant for Him. So don't be like some religious people who have this idea that God only wants us to bring the big issues to Him, and that He doesn't want us to bother Him with small issues.

Nothing could be further from the truth. God cares about everything that you experience, from the small ulcer in your mouth to your concerns about the world's economy. Even when you tell Him about the inconvenience that might arise if the bus is late, He takes note of that too. In fact, when you come to Him often about anything and everything in your daily life, you compliment Him because you are telling Him that He is your Daddy God who watches over you.

Jesus represented the Father's heart and will when He was on earth. (John 5:19.) He cared when His disciples were out at sea the whole night, cold and shivering. He cared when they caught nothing that night. (John 21:3.) He cared that they would not have fish to sell. So He gave them a huge catch early the next morning. (vv. 5–6.) He knew that they were cold and hungry, so He prepared breakfast for them, served over a fire of coals to keep them warm.

Jesus showed us that God is our loving heavenly Father who cares about the big and small things that happen every day in our lives. Nothing escapes God's eyes because He loves you!

Thought for the Day
God is not just interested in the big things that affect us.
He bothers and cares about the small things too.

Jesus, the Measure of Your Righteousness

2 Corinthians 5:21
²¹For He made Him who knew no sin to be sin for us,
that we might become the righteousness of God in Him.

God wants us to seek His righteousness and not our own righteousness. When we seek our own righteousness, we will always end up feeling miserable because we can never be righteous by our works, no matter how hard we try. That is why our loving Father wants us to remember that righteousness is not right behavior but a person — Jesus (1 Corinthians 1:30), and that we have "become the righteousness of God in Him."

I know of a lady who, before coming to our church, attempted to establish her own righteousness by confessing all her sins to "clean" herself up. But she found that the more she confessed her sins, the more sins she discovered in herself. She became guilt-ridden and miserable. Feeling stressed out and weary of confessing her sins all the time, she eventually left the church she was attending. In fact, she never stepped into another church again for the next 10 years.

One day, someone gave her my message tape entitled *You Will Never Lose God's Everlasting Righteousness Given to You* and she started listening to it. Once she learnt that Jesus was the measure of her righteousness and acceptance before God, she began to seek God's righteousness by seeing Christ as her righteousness. Before long, peace and joy came flooding back into her life.

Today, she worships in our church. She testified of how God has supernaturally healed her of a long-term medical condition she had. Even her husband, once balding, found hair sprouting supernaturally! God was adding all these things to her according to His promise — "But seek first the kingdom of God and **His righteousness**, and all these things shall be added to you" (Matthew 6:33).

Beloved, seeking God's righteousness means that you see Jesus as someone who knew no sin but became sin for you, so that He could give you His righteousness and make you the righteousness of God in Him! As you proclaim daily the truth that you are the righteousness of God in Christ, you will see "all these things" (Matthew 6:33) added to you without even asking for them!

Thought for the Day
Righteousness is not right behavior but a person — Jesus.

God Wants His Children Well and Joyful

John 14:9
⁹Jesus said to him, "… He who has seen Me has seen the Father.…

Imagine the following scenario: A father tells his little girl, "Come here, girl. Mummy says that you have been playing by the roadside. Is that true?" "Yes, Daddy. I am sorry." "Sorry? How many times have I told you not to play near the road? Come here! Lie down on the road and stretch out your legs!"

Daddy drives his car over his little girl's legs. You can hear the sound of bones being crushed and the poor girl screaming in pain!

"Now, darling, you know that Daddy loves you. And Daddy did that to teach you a lesson, that playing by the roadside is dangerous."

You are probably shaking your head in horror by now, wondering which sick father would do that. Yet, there are many Christians who believe that our heavenly Father does the same thing. They say that He gives people sicknesses, accidents, earthquakes and death to teach them lessons.

But Jesus said, "If you have seen Me, you have seen the Father." Jesus is the nature of God in action. Throughout the Gospels, we see Jesus or God going about healing the sick. If God wants some people sick, then there should be at least one incident in the Gospels where you see Jesus saying, "Behold, your complexion is too lovely, receive leprosy," or "Blindness is good for you. Remain blind." But no, never once! In fact, Jesus "went about **doing good** and **healing all** who were oppressed by the devil" (Acts 10:38). That's the heart of God.

As a father, if your child is sick and in pain, your heart just wants him well. How much more your heavenly Father! My friend, God does not give your child a sickness to teach both of you some lesson or to glorify Himself. To think so is to talk out of a warped mind bound by religion! And Christianity is not a religion. It is a loving relationship with your Father in heaven.

Beloved, hear God speaking this to your heart today: "I will never punish you for your sins because they have been punished in My Son's body. I do not wish you ill. I will not take away your child or give you a car wreck to teach you some lesson. My heart always wants My children well and joyful!"

Thought for the Day
If God wants some people sick, then there should be at least one incident in the Gospels where Jesus gave sickness to or refused to heal someone.

Turn Your Cares Into Prayers

Philippians 4:6
⁶Be anxious for nothing, but in everything by prayer and supplication,
with thanksgiving, let your requests be made known to God.

My friend, God doesn't want you to be fearful, fretful or anxious. Instead, He wants you to "be anxious for nothing, but in everything by prayer and supplication, with thanksgiving, let your requests be made known to God."

So when you have a care or worry, straightaway, turn that care or worry into prayer. That is supplication. And when you are troubled by a care or worry that you don't know how to pray for, pray in the Spirit or tongues. And in the midst of that prayer, thank God that He is already your healing, provision, prosperity, good success and victory. That is thanksgiving.

"Pastor Prince, if I am worried about something, how long should I pray?"

Keep on praying. Pray in the Spirit until the worry lifts or dissipates, "and the peace of God, which surpasses all understanding, will guard your hearts and minds through Christ Jesus" (Philippians 4:7).

This was what one of our church members did when he found himself anxiously trying to access some important data in his USB flash drive. After a whole day at it with no results, he finally stopped himself from being anxious and instead, turned his worry into prayer, asking the Lord to settle it for him. As he prayed in tongues, he was also thankfully repeating in his heart that having the Holy Spirit — the Helper — with him was to his advantage. (John 16:7.)

Later that evening, using his wife's computer, he succeeded in accessing the data in his flash drive after a few attempts. He quickly backed up the data. It was only when subsequent attempts to use the flash drive on his wife's computer failed did it suddenly dawn on him that God had "resurrected" his flash drive that one time, just for him to recover his data!

Beloved, I believe that we would all worry a lot less and enjoy our lives a lot more if only we realized this truth: Our Abba Father is so strong that there is nothing He cannot do, and He is so loving that there is nothing He will not do for us!

Thought for the Day
Our Abba Father is so strong that there is nothing He cannot do,
and He is so loving that there is nothing He will not do for us!

Total and Complete Forgiveness

Ephesians 1:7
⁷In Him we have redemption through His blood, the forgiveness of sins,
according to the riches of His grace.

People have said to me, "Pastor Prince, I was taught that only my past sins — from the day I was born until the day I became a Christian — have been forgiven, and that my future sins are not forgiven until I confess them and seek forgiveness."

My friend, when Jesus died on the cross, how many of your sins were future?

Unless you are more than 2,000 years old, all your sins were future then! Jesus took them all upon Himself, nailed them to the cross and declared, "It is finished!" (John 19:30.) So if you are not forgiven of **all**, then you are not forgiven at all.

"You mean Jesus also died for the sin that I have just committed?"

Yes!

"And also for the sins which I will commit?"

Yes! That is why He said, "It is finished!"

But many of us are inconsistent in our believing. One part of us says, "God has forgiven me of all my sins." But another part says, "Yes, but I must still confess my sins to be forgiven of them." Are you like that?

Beloved, you are forgiven not because of your work of confession. Your confession **cannot** wash away your sins. You are forgiven because of the blood of Jesus shed for you. His blood **alone** cleanses you.

You cannot believe that you are forgiven of your past, present and future sins, and still think that there is something for you to do to make that forgiveness complete. If you do, then it becomes your work too, not Jesus' alone.

Is there a place for confession of sins? Yes! If you have just sinned, you can always tell God about it without feeling condemned because you know that you **already have** forgiveness and that Jesus was condemned in your place. But you don't confess your sins to God in order to be forgiven. You already have total and complete forgiveness because of the blood of Jesus!

Thought for the Day
You are forgiven because of the blood of Jesus shed for you.
It is His blood alone that cleanses you.

God's Grace Is Unmerited

Galatians 5:4
⁴You have become estranged from Christ, you who attempt to be
justified by law; you have fallen from grace.

What is the grace of God? Simply put, the grace of God is God blessing, healing, delivering and prospering you because of Jesus. The grace of God is His unearned, unmerited and undeserved favor toward you simply because of Jesus' finished work at the cross.

Because God's grace is based on Jesus' work and not yours, the only way you fall from this grace is by believing that you can earn, merit and deserve it through your obedience and good works.

For example, you fall from grace when you say, "God has to answer my prayer because I have prayed long enough." You also fall from grace when you think that because you are serving in church or you have kicked a bad habit, God is pleased with you and He has to bless you.

When you think that it is by your efforts and obedience that you receive God's blessings, you become like the Pharisees. They believed that their law-keeping justified them and ensured that God would bless them. But the truth is that when you believe like them, "you have become estranged from Christ, you who attempt to be justified by law; you have fallen from grace." This means that you are cut off from Christ, who is your salvation, Redeemer, healer and provider. Christ has become of **no effect** to you!

My friend, surely you would want Christ to be of effect to you. People to whom Christ is of effect receive from Him the miracle they need. When He is **of effect** to them, He is their healer and they get healed. He is their wisdom and they are wise before man. He is their good success and they experience good success in all that they do.

Beloved, for Christ to always be of effect to you and to never nullify the grace of God operating in your life, just remember and believe that it is because of Christ and His finished work — His blood, His stripes, His death, His obedience — that you are justified, healed, prosperous and blessed!

Thought for the Day
The only way you fall from God's grace is by believing that you can earn,
merit and deserve it through your obedience and good works.

Don't Put Your Faith in
Diets and Exercise

Psalm 118:8
⁸It is better to trust in the LORD than to put confidence in man.

A lot of people think that the way to get healthy is to watch what they eat. For example, many people say that the Mediterranean diet is a very healthy one. I agree, generally. But do you know that the people whom Jesus healed were also on a Mediterranean diet? They did not eat pork and prawns, for example, because they were Jewish and these things were not kosher for them.

I know that you want to walk in divine health. But God does not want your focus to be on food — what to eat, what not to eat — or even exercise — how to exercise, when to exercise. All these are natural means which the people of the world trust in. It is better to trust in the Lord and His finished work, than to put your confidence in the latest man-made diet plans and exercise regimes.

At the cross, Jesus took your sicknesses and carried your pains, and by His stripes you were healed. (Isaiah 53:4–5.) The Bible even tells us how to escape sickness and premature death — by discerning the Lord's body when we partake of the Lord's Supper. (1 Corinthians 11:29–30.) But instead of focusing on these truths, many of us prefer to focus on dieting and exercising.

Now, I am not against eating well or exercising. I myself exercise and I do watch what I eat. For example, I don't like to eat oily stuff because it makes me feel uncomfortable. And when I have to preach, I do my best not to eat foods that make me burp!

But I eat generally healthy stuff not because I trust dieting to make me healthy. I exercise not because I trust exercising to make me healthy. No, I trust the finished work of Christ to make me healthy. I eat well because I like to feel good and I exercise because I enjoy the rush, the sweat!

God wants you to be free when it comes to eating and exercising. Don't make laws for eating and exercising, and then trust these laws to give you "divine" health. Trust in the finished work of Christ. Discern His body when you partake of the Holy Communion. And just enjoy your food and workout!

Thought for the Day
It is better to trust in the Lord and His finished work, than to put your
confidence in the latest man-made diet plans and exercise regimes.

God Favors You Because He Loves You

1 John 4:19
19 We love Him because He first loved us.

Have you ever found yourself receiving such exceeding favor that you wonder why? My friend, it is because God is lavishing His grace — unearned, undeserved, unmerited favor — on you. And He does it because He loves you.

I love reading the Old Testament story of Ruth, a young Moabite widow, because it speaks of God's amazing grace. The moment Ruth depended on God's grace or favor, she had full access to His blessings. Of all the fields in Bethlehem, His grace led her to the field that belonged to Boaz, who was not only a wealthy bachelor, but also a relative of her father-in-law. (Ruth 2:3.) Boaz was therefore her potential kinsman-redeemer — someone who could redeem her from her plight as a poor and childless widow.

Boaz favored Ruth from the moment he laid eyes on her. Ruth was not even Jewish, yet he cared for her safety by telling her not to glean in another field and to stay close to his young women. He even commanded the young men working for him not to touch her and to allow her to drink the water which they had drawn.

During mealtimes, he sat her beside the reapers although she was just a lowly gleaner who picked up what they had missed or dropped. On top of that, he gave her parched grain, making sure that she ate and was satisfied, and that she had leftovers to bring back to her mother-in-law. (Ruth 2:1–18.)

Ruth simply believed that she would find favor in the field and God placed her at the right place at the right time, so that He could open a big door of blessings to her.

Do you know that Boaz is a beautiful picture of our Lord Jesus? The Bible says that "He first loved us." Jesus saw you and loved you first, long before you knew Him or loved Him. And He favors whom He loves.

Beloved, there is no need to fight or strive to qualify for God's favor and blessings. His favor is all over you because He first loved you. Just trust in His love for you and you will see His favor bringing an abundance of blessings into your life!

Thought for the Day
God is lavishing His grace — unearned, undeserved,
unmerited favor — on you because He loves you.

The 12 Wells and 70 Palm Trees

Exodus 15:27
²⁷Then they came to Elim, where there were twelve wells of water and
seventy palm trees; so they camped there by the waters.

Would you like to know an important biblical key to divine health? It is found in today's verse, which comes right after God says, "I am the Lord who heals you" (v. 26). He said this to His people after He brought them out of Egypt.

The wells of water and palm trees speak of refreshment. They paint a picture of an oasis in the desert. The Israelites rested and were refreshed there. But why the numbers 12 and 70?

There are no insignificant details in the Bible. The 12 wells of water and 70 palm trees represent anointed ministries that refresh you with God's Word. So if you want to know Jesus as the Lord who heals you, sit under anointed preaching of God's Word because when His Word goes forth, it will heal you. His Word is medicine to all your flesh! (Proverbs 4:22.)

How did I make that connection? Let the Bible interpret the Bible. Matthew 10:1 says that when Jesus had "called His **twelve** disciples to Him, He gave them power over unclean spirits, to cast them out, and to **heal** all kinds of sickness and all kinds of disease." He sent out the 12 and said to them, "And as you go, preach, saying, 'The kingdom of heaven is at hand.' **Heal** the sick, cleanse the lepers, raise the dead, cast out demons..." (vv. 7–8).

Then, in Luke 10:1, the Lord "appointed **seventy** others also, and sent them two by two before His face into every city and place where He Himself was about to go." He also said to the 70, "And **heal** the sick there, and say to them, 'The kingdom of God has come near to you'" (v. 9).

In other words, Jesus anointed the 12 and then the 70 disciples to preach God's Word and heal the sick. Today, if you want refreshment, if you want health and healing, don't sit under ministries that tell you that God doesn't always want to heal and that He sometimes gives you diseases to teach you lessons. Instead, sit under anointed ministries that preach the good news and practice healing the sick. Beloved, that is how you can begin to walk in divine health!

Thought for the Day
For refreshment and health, sit under anointed ministries that
preach the good news and practice healing the sick.

Give God's Word Priority and
See Good Success

Joshua 1:8
*⁸This Book of the Law shall not depart from your mouth, but you shall
meditate in it day and night, that you may observe to do according to
all that is written in it. For then you will make your way
prosperous, and then you will have good success.*

In life, there is **good** success and **bad** success. Bad success is the kind of success which robs you of time with your family, friends and church, and destroys your health and relationships. With good success, on the other hand, you see prosperity in every area of your life.

God wants you to enjoy good success and the key to this lies in what God told Joshua when he took over the reins following the death of his leader Moses — "This Book of the Law shall not depart from your mouth, but you shall meditate in it day and night, that you may observe to do according to all that is written in it. For then you will make your way prosperous, and then you will have **good success.**" Spending time in God's Word daily will give you godly wisdom, which will make your way prosperous and give you good success.

Look at how Joshua's life turned out in the end. When Joshua died, "they buried him within the border of his inheritance at Timnath Serah, which is in the mountains of Ephraim, on the north side of Mount Gaash" (Joshua 24:30). Joshua had a whole mountain for his inheritance! This means that he was prosperous and successful!

It was also said that Israel served the Lord, not idols or other gods, all the days of Joshua's life. (v. 31.) This means that while Joshua was around, people were impacted for God's glory.

And at the end of his life, a fulfilled Joshua had this to say, "But as for me and my house, we will serve the LORD" (v. 15). Having your family loving God and serving Him with you is the most important success and greatest prosperity that you can ever have.

Beloved, when God's Word takes priority in your daily life, not only will your finances be blessed, your ministry and family life will also be blessed!

Thought for the Day
**Spending time in God's Word daily will give you godly wisdom, which will
make your way prosperous and give you good success.**

What Have You Been Saying?

Psalm 91:2
²I will say of the LORD, "He is my refuge and
my fortress; my God, in Him I will trust."

When a great storm arose as Jesus and His disciples were in a boat on the Sea of Galilee, He did not say to His disciples, "The storm is here to teach us courage." Instead, He took authority over the storm and said, "Peace, be still!" and there was a perfect calm. (Mark 4:39.)

When He met the widow of Nain whose only son had died, and on another occasion, the two sisters whose brother Lazarus had died, He didn't tell them, "God wanted to take him home." No, He spoke to the dead son: "Young man, I say to you, arise" (Luke 7:14). And standing outside Lazarus' tomb, He said, "Lazarus, come forth!" (John 11:43). And both men came back to life.

What have you been saying about your situation?

When you feel the pain in your body, don't say of the Lord, "God wants me sick to teach me to trust Him more." Instead, say, "Lord Jesus, I thank You that by Your stripes I am healed." (1 Peter 2:24.)

While trying to make ends meet, don't say of the Lord, "The Lord keeps me poor to keep me humble." Instead, say, "The Lord is my shepherd; I shall not want" (Psalm 23:1).

And if you have an intimidating boss at work, don't say, "The Lord is my patience, I will endure." Instead, say, "The Lord is my helper; I will not fear. What can man do to me?" (Hebrews 13:6).

We are living in the last days when there are terrorist attacks and deadly viruses lurking around, and the world is afraid. But we will not speak negative words and be fearful like the people of the world. Instead, we will speak God's Word and reign over these things. Like the psalmist, we will say of the Lord, "He is my refuge and my fortress; my God, in Him I will trust."

So find out what God's Word says about your situation, believe it and declare it. And because God's Word cannot return to Him void (Isaiah 55:11), you will see what you believe and confess come to pass!

Thought for the Day
**Speak God's Word and reign over the things that the
people of the world are afraid of.**

Kept in All Your Ways by God's Angels

Psalm 91:11–12
¹¹For He shall give His angels charge over you, to keep you in all your ways.
¹²In their hands they shall bear you up, lest you dash your foot against a stone.

You are about to step onto the road when something pulls you back just in time to avoid being hit by a speeding car. You are shocked. When you come to your senses, you ask yourself, "Could it be that an angel just saved me from a fatal accident?"

I believe that angels walk with us. The verse tells us that God has given His angels charge over us to keep us in all our ways. And in their hands they will bear us up, so that not even a stone will trip us up.

But we may not know it when we encounter an angel. (Hebrews 13:2.) This was probably the case with a couple in our church who were holidaying at a beach resort on Penang Island when a tsunami struck at about 12:30 p.m. on December 26, 2004.

It was slightly past 11 a.m. when the wife suddenly had a craving for food from the mainland. The couple decided to check out earlier, so that they could reach the mainland in time for lunch. While loading their luggage into their car at the hotel driveway, a man impatiently motioned to them to hurry up and get moving.

Annoyed by his impatience, they quickly loaded their stuff and drove off. The minute they reached the mainland, they heard that a tsunami had struck Penang Island at the same beach where they were just a while ago. While thanking God for their narrow escape, it suddenly dawned on them that the impatient man could have been an angel charged by God to hurry them off!

God tells us that we have "an innumerable company of angels" (Hebrews 12:22). And He has given them charge over us to protect us from accidents, natural disasters, terrorist bombings and other dangers. So don't fear these things and lock yourself at home. Go for that holiday! Go for that lunch appointment! Believe that God loves you, and thank Him for His angels who walk with you and watch over you!

Thought for the Day
Don't fear what the world fears because God loves you,
and His angels walk with you and watch over you!

It Shall Not Come Near You!

Psalm 91:7
⁷A thousand may fall at your side, and ten thousand at
your right hand; but it shall not come near you.

Your doctor or insurance agent may ask you, "Do you have a family history of cancer?" If you say, "Yes," they will probably tell you that you might get some form of cancer too.

Now, if you are without God, you would probably agree with them and start worrying about your health. But you are not without God! In fact, His Word tells you, "A thousand may fall at your side, and ten thousand at your right hand; but it shall not come near you." Therefore, even if you have a family history of cancer, and your family members have died of cancer, you can have the confidence to declare that it will not come near you!

My mother had this attitude. After a thorough medical check-up, the doctor was surprised and told her that she did not have high blood pressure or heart disease, although these two conditions have plagued her father and siblings. You see, my mother had already firmly declared that no deadly, family-related disease would come near her.

Praise God for my mother's trust in God's Word because I am the generation after her! In fact, after my mother told me about the results of her check-up, I randomly opened my Bible only to read about Rahab the harlot who by faith "did not perish with those who did not believe" (Hebrews 11:31).

Beloved, God wants you to know that even though you are **in** this world, you are not **of** this world. You belong to Him. You don't have to get caught in dire situations along with the people of the world. Because God is on your side, "He shall deliver you from the snare of the fowler and from the perilous pestilence" (Psalm 91:3).

Even when it comes to generational diseases, you can boldly declare, "That disease stops here!" because you have God and His Word. And when you believe God and His Word, you will see His promises come to pass for you — "A thousand may fall at your side, and ten thousand at your right hand; but it shall not come near you"!

Thought for the Day
A thousand may fall at your side and ten thousand at
your right hand, but it shall not come near you.

Sow Where You Want a Harvest

Genesis 26:12
*¹²Then Isaac sowed in that land, and reaped in the same
year a hundredfold; and the LORD blessed him.*

When you sow apple seeds, you get apples. When you sow seeds of friendship, you get friends. If in the natural, you receive in the area in which you sow, how much more will you receive in the supernatural when God blesses you!

The Bible tells us that when Isaac sowed in the land, he reaped a hundredfold even though there was a famine in that land. (v. 1.) The reason was that "the LORD blessed him."

So if you are believing God for a breakthrough in a particular area, sow in that area. That was how our church went about setting up our first childcare center years ago. One of the first things we did was to sow a childcare center for a Christian organization in Thailand.

And within the first month, our childcare center in Singapore made a very handsome profit. This was amazing considering the fact that we took over the premises of a previous childcare center that had closed down because it was making losses. It could only be the Lord blessing us. And He "is able to do exceedingly abundantly above all that we ask or think" (Ephesians 3:20).

Whatever money or time you give to the Lord, He will multiply it back to you. For example, you have 24 hours a day like everyone else, but the Lord can make your day very fruitful. And even after doing all that needs to be done, you will find that you still have time left to rest.

Even when you have nothing to give but prayers, your prayers will not return to you void. God can answer them exceedingly above what you have asked. When Job lost everything that he possessed, he prayed for his friends, and the Lord not only restored his losses, but He also "gave Job twice as much as he had before" (Job 42:10).

So start sowing seeds in the area that you are believing God for, and know that before long, you will be reaping your harvest!

Thought for the Day
***If you are believing God for a breakthrough in a
particular area, sow in that area.***

Christ, Your Wisdom, Will Prosper You

1 Corinthians 1:30
30But of Him you are in Christ Jesus, who became for us wisdom from God....

It is believed that there has never been a wealthier king than King Solomon. God gave him wisdom that not only made him wise in matters of justice, but also brought him gold and silver. (1 Kings 3:12–13.)

According to a report by the Illinois Society of Architects in 1925, the cost of Solomon's temple in terms of existing values would have been about $87 billion! The priests wore garments costing more than $10 million! These amounts only cover what Solomon spent on the temple and not his personal assets.

We can go on talking about the riches of King Solomon, but the Bible tells us that there is one greater than Solomon. (Matthew 12:42.) His name is Jesus, and He is the most prosperous Man who ever lived and who will ever live.

If there was a need to feed the hungry, He simply multiplied whatever food was placed in His hands. On one occasion, He multiplied five loaves and two fish to feed 5,000 men, not counting women and children. And incredibly, there were 12 baskets full of leftovers. (Matthew 14:15–21.)

If any of His own faced lack, it was not long before abundant provision flowed to them. Once, when His disciples caught nothing after a whole night of fishing, He merely spoke a word of command and schools of fish obeyed, swimming toward His disciples' boat so that they received a net-breaking, boat-sinking load of fish. (Luke 5:1–7.) In another incident, He provided the money for the temple tax, even if it took a fish to bring it to them! (Matthew 17:24–27.)

My friend, this same Jesus has become for you wisdom from God. If you are a businessperson, with Christ in you, you have wisdom that is greater than the wisdom of all the world's business gurus put together. And if you are a student, Christ in you will manifest wisdom that is greater than all the wisdom of the brilliant minds in the academic world.

Beloved, believe that because Jesus, God's wisdom, is in you, there is no reason you cannot prosper today, and astound the world in the same way Solomon did!

Thought for the Day
**Because Jesus, God's wisdom, is in you, there is no
reason you cannot prosper today.**

Jesus Can Identify With Your Pain

Leviticus 2:4
⁴"And if you bring as an offering a grain offering baked in the oven,
it shall be unleavened cakes of fine flour mixed with oil,
or unleavened wafers anointed with oil.

Private pains, deep hurts, shameful addictions. You may think that nobody understands what you are going through, but God does. He can identify with all your pains and is able to help you. (Hebrews 2:18; 4:15.)

In the Old Testament, the grain offering brought to God speaks of Jesus' life on earth. The fine flour, which the grain offering is made with, is flour that has been pounded, ground, beaten and sifted through to get it consistently even and fine. Therefore, it typifies the humanity and sufferings of Jesus.

One of the ways the Jewish women prepared the grain offering was to bake it. The baking done in the depths of the oven speaks of the "hidden" sufferings that Jesus went though. I believe that Jesus faced sufferings that we cannot fully understand. Even as a young boy, He must have gone through sufferings that prepared Him to die for all humanity at the cross. And during His ministry years, it must have grieved Him when time and time again, He found unbelief not just in the people around Him, but even in His disciples.

Jesus also suffered at the hands of men — slanderers who misunderstood Him. Once, the Pharisees insinuated that He was born out of wedlock because His mother was with child before she married Joseph. (John 8:39, 41.) That scandalous remark, probably not the first, must have hurt Him.

Consider also the temptations He faced. There were not only three. God's Word says that He was tempted for 40 days! (Luke 4:2.) Not all the temptations were recorded. Those 40 days must have tried Him sorely.

What do all these mean?

My friend, Jesus went through all those temptations and sufferings for you, yet He did not sin. (Hebrews 4:15.) There is no temptation or suffering that you are going through that He cannot identify with. So come to His throne of grace today and receive His superabounding grace to face and overcome those trials in your life!

Thought for the Day
There is no temptation or suffering that you are going through that Jesus cannot identify with or give you His superabounding grace to overcome.

What You Are Conscious of Will Manifest

1 John 4:4
⁴You are of God, little children, and have overcome them,
because He who is in you is greater than he who is in the world.

If you have been to a circus performance or watched one on television, you would be familiar with the act involving a lion and its trainer. But have you ever wondered why, besides holding a whip, the trainer would arm himself with a stool and point its legs toward the beast?

The whole idea is to distract the lion. You see, as powerful as the beast is, it can be immobilized by distractions. If this man-eater is not distracted from time to time, it might just decide to maul the trainer to death!

The devil is like the trainer. He knows that you have God's power inside you because the Lion of Judah is in you, and "He who is in you is greater than he who is in the world." So what the devil tries to do is immobilize you with distractions.

For example, he may bring to your attention a pain in your body to distract you. And you find yourself going to a few medical journals or the Internet to find out more about the symptoms. You also decide to consult more than one doctor. And because you know of someone who has the same condition, you talk to him about it.

In the end, you are distracted by the pain, the symptoms, your findings, the doctors' reports and your friend's experience. And you find it hard to believe and focus on God's Word about your healing. You have become immobilized, powerless and fearful.

So the devil's trick is to get you to focus on your condition. When you are conscious of the symptoms in your body and your findings, you will see sickness manifest. But God wants you to focus on who you are and what you have in Christ. When you are conscious that you are the healed in Christ, you will see healing manifest.

My friend, what you are conscious of will manifest. So be conscious of Christ, who is all the power of God inside you, and you will see that power manifest!

Thought for the Day
Be conscious of Christ, who is all the power of God inside you,
and you will see that power manifest!

You Are Perfect in God's Eyes

Hebrews 10:12, 14, KJV
¹²But this Man, after He had offered one sacrifice for sins forever, sat down on the right hand of God... ¹⁴For by one offering He hath perfected forever them that are sanctified.

God sees you with no flaw, spot or imperfection, so honor His Word and the finished work of His Son by saying, "Amen!" Don't doubt your perfection in Christ.

To see yourself as far from being perfect is not modesty, but a failure to understand the perfect sacrifice that Jesus has made for you.

The Bible tells us, "For by one offering He hath **perfected forever** them that **are sanctified.**" Did you get that? You have not only been sanctified, that is, made holy, but by the same offering of His body, you have been perfected. You are both holy and perfect in God's eyes!

Your sins have been purged perfectly. Today, Jesus is seated at His Father's right hand not because He is the Son of God (although that is true), but because His work of purging your sins is completely finished and perfect!

So instead of being conscious of your sins, which is to have an evil conscience (v. 22), you can have a perfect conscience, a conscience that is free from the guilt and condemnation of sins.

When you find yourself conscious of your sins, just say, "Thank You, Lord Jesus, for Your wonderful work at the cross. It is a perfect work that has removed all my sins completely.

"Holy Spirit, thank You for convicting me of righteousness, not my own, but God's righteousness given to me as a gift. Keep on convicting me in the days to come, reminding me especially when I fail that I am still the righteousness of God in Christ."

My friend, God sees you perfect without any spot of sin. He sees you covered in the beautiful white robes of His own righteousness. He treats you like a righteous person because that is what He has made you. So expect good things to happen to you because blessings are on the head of the righteous! (Proverbs 10:6.)

Thought for the Day
To see yourself as far from being perfect is to fail to understand the perfect sacrifice that Jesus has made for you.

Like Father, Like Son

Romans 8:16
¹⁶The Spirit Himself bears witness with our spirit that we are children of God.

Everything produces after its kind. Dogs give birth to puppies, cats give birth to kittens and tigers give birth to tiger cubs. In the same manner, when you are born again, you are born of God. You are a child of the Most High God. He is your Father and He doesn't see you in the flesh. He sees you in the Spirit. And His Spirit bears witness with your spirit that you are His child.

So when the devil comes to you and says, "Well, your father died of cancer, his father died of cancer and you are going to die of cancer too, just like your father," just know in your heart that you **are** like your Father — your Father in heaven! Declare, "I am a child of the Most High God. He doesn't have cancer, so neither do I!"

My friend, when you are born of God, you are born to win. Because your Daddy God is a winner, you are one too! When you wake up in the morning, say, "I am a winner because God is a winner!"

When you say that you cannot afford to buy something that you need, you have forgotten which family you now belong to. You have been born again into a very rich family — your Father owns every beast in the forest and the cattle on a thousand hills! (Psalm 50:10.) You have a Daddy God in heaven who is well able to supply all your needs. (Philippians 4:19.) Even if you don't have much money now, don't worry. Just ask God for the supply because your heavenly Father is rich.

When someone talks to you about a problem and asks, "What are we going to do about it?" you should say, "Don't worry. Let's talk to Daddy God about it. It is not a problem for Him, so it will not be a problem for us."

Beloved, even when all around you is going under, your Daddy God is still the same heavenly Father who kept Noah's world afloat, his loved ones safe and sound, and his possessions intact. Your world will never go under because you are God's beloved child!

Thought for the Day
Because you are born of God, you are born to win.

Quench the Enemy's Fiery Darts

Ephesians 6:16
16Above all, taking the shield of faith with which you will be
able to quench all the fiery darts of the wicked one.

I believe that when you pray in the Spirit, that is, in tongues, a shield goes up all around you — a **watery** shield. But why do I call it a "watery" shield? Let me share with you what the Lord showed me.

Once, I was meditating on Ephesians 6:16 — "above all, taking the shield of faith with which you will be able to quench all the fiery darts of the wicked one." At first, I thought of a Roman soldier's wooden shield. But three words kept repeating themselves in my mind: "quench" and "fiery darts." Then, the Lord said, "Son, if it is a wooden shield, the fiery darts will burn it up." He showed me a watery shield instead, one which was able to **quench** the fiery darts.

You may ask, "Where did the water come from?"

Remember that Jesus said, "He who believes in Me, as the Scripture has said, out of his heart will flow rivers of living water" (John 7:38). The next verse says, "But this He spoke concerning the Spirit..." (John 7:39).

Jesus was speaking about the Holy Spirit, which He likened to rivers of living water flowing out of us. So when we pray in the Spirit, rivers of living water will flow, quenching the devil's fiery darts thrown at us!

This happened one day when I was having supper with a church member. Now, I don't often pray in tongues when I say grace over my food. But that night, I felt prompted by the Spirit to do so. So I prayed in tongues as I laid my hands on my packet of *nasi lemak* (coconut-flavored rice).

Soon, we were tucking into our food and talking when suddenly, I bit on something hard. I spat it out quickly and realized that it was a nail! Then, I realized that this was the reason the Lord wanted me to pray in tongues. Though the devil was trying to "nail" me, he failed!

My friend, put up the watery shield that God has given you. Pray in the Spirit and quench the enemy's fiery darts!

Thought for the Day
Pray in the Spirit and quench the enemy's fiery darts!

Don't Let Your Past Rob You

Philippians 3:13–14
¹³Brethren, I do not count myself to have apprehended; but one thing I do,
forgetting those things which are behind and reaching forward to
those things which are ahead, ¹⁴I press toward the goal for the
prize of the upward call of God in Christ Jesus.

A re you living a life of regrets thinking, "If only…"? "If only I had that college education… If only I had married the right girl… If only I had taken up the other job… If only I had not made that stupid mistake…"

Is your past robbing you of the joy of today? Then forget your past!

You might say, "But Pastor Prince, you do not know what I have done in the past!"

Consider Paul. If the devil had anything to bring against Paul, it would be reminders of how he had persecuted the early church and caused the deaths of many, including Stephen, the first Christian martyr.

Paul had done horrendous things that were hard for him to forget. But he had such a revelation of God's awesome forgiveness that he could say, "forgetting those things which are behind… I press toward the goal for the prize of the upward call of God in Christ Jesus."

Beloved, God has forgiven you of all your sins. He has completely forgiven you and declared, "Your sins and lawless deeds, I will remember **no more**." (Hebrews 10:17.)

Like Paul, you can forget your past, the wrongs you have done and the hurts you have caused others or been through yourself. God can take the tears of yesterday and transform them into the miracles of tomorrow. He can restore to you in all abundance what you have lost. He can cause all things, even the painful events of your past, to work together for your good. (Romans 8:28.)

God's Word says, "The glory of the LORD shall be your rear guard." (Isaiah 58:8.) His glory will cover your past. Wherever you go, His glory covers your past. It is no longer the same past that you know of because His glory has descended on it. Your past is past. It has been wiped out. It is gone! So don't let your past rob you of today's joy any longer!

Thought for the Day
Because God's glory covers your past, you don't
have to let your past rob you of today's joy!

Believe That God Is Your Rewarder

Hebrews 11:6
⁶But without faith it is impossible to please Him, for he who
comes to God must believe that He is, and that He is a
rewarder of those who diligently seek Him.

Most people quote only the first part of Hebrews 11:6 — "without faith it is impossible to please Him." Yet, it goes on to say, "for he who comes to God must believe that He is, and that He is a rewarder of those who diligently seek Him." In other words, the faith that pleases God is the kind of faith that believes that God exists and that He is a **rewarder**.

The Bible also says that "faith is the substance of things hoped for, the evidence of things not seen" (Hebrews 11:1). So even in times of difficulty, when we don't see good things happening in our circumstances, we are to believe that God will turn things around and reward us.

God turned things around for Ruth, the Moabite widow, when she believed the Lord and made Him her God. (Ruth 1:16.) The Bible tells us that she was given a "full reward" by the Lord when she came under His wings for refuge. (Ruth 2:12.) Not only did He give her protection, He also gave her abundant provision, exceeding favor and a glorious redemption. (Ruth 2:9–17, 3:11, 4:10–13.)

When Rahab, the harlot of Jericho, heard reports of how the Lord had opened up the Red Sea for the children of Israel, she believed that "He is God in heaven above and on earth beneath" (Joshua 2:9–11). Though Rahab had not personally witnessed the miracles, she believed God and hid the Jewish spies from their pursuers. (vv. 4–6.) Because of her faith, she not only did not perish with those who did not believe (Joshua 6:25, Hebrews 11:31), but she was also given a place in the "hall of faith" in Hebrews 11.

God was so pleased with the faith of these two Gentile women that He not only blessed them in their lifetimes, but He also put them into the genealogy of His Son Jesus Christ, the great Redeemer and rewarder.

Beloved, when you come to the Lord with your needs, believe that He is God, and that He is a rewarder. God has pleasure in this kind of faith. He wants to be the rewarder of your faith in Him!

Thought for the Day
The faith that pleases God is the kind of faith that
believes God exists and that He is a rewarder.

Speak God's Word and Activate His Angels

Psalm 103:20
²⁰Bless the LORD, you His angels, who excel in strength,
who do His word, heeding the voice of His word.

Notice that the verse says that angels are "heeding the **voice** of His word." Now, who gives voice to God's Word? We do! Each time we speak God's Word, we give voice to His Word. And when angels hear His Word given voice, they respond!

The Bible says that at the end of Daniel's three weeks of fasting and praying for an answer from God, the angel Gabriel appeared to Daniel and said to him, "I have come because of your words" (Daniel 10:12).

So when angels hear you saying, "Thank You, Father, no evil shall befall me nor shall any plague come near my dwelling" (Psalm 91:10), they will come to your aid because you are giving voice to God's Word. Even if you cannot quote the verse perfectly, they can still come to your rescue.

This was what happened to a lady in the United States. While walking home after an evening church service, she was attacked from behind by a man and dragged toward a dark corner in an alley. In that frantic state, she remembered only one word from that evening's sermon. So she shouted, "Feathers! Feathers!" Her attacker released her and fled!

Feathers? What did she mean? She was actually referring to Psalm 91:4 — "He shall cover you with His **feathers**, and under His wings you shall take refuge." In that state of panic, she remembered only one word — "feathers," and it was enough to cause her attacker to flee. You see, it is not your ability to quote an entire verse perfectly that releases God's power, but faith in His Word and His love for you. And one word from Him is enough to send your enemies scurrying away.

However, if you know God's Word by heart but refuse to proclaim it, the power of His Word cannot be released. The Bible does not say that angels heed His Word. No, it says that "His angels, who excel in strength, who do His word, heeding the **voice** of His word." So beloved, give voice to God's Word and see His angels respond. His angels are activated for your benefit when you speak His Word!

Thought for the Day
One word from God released through your mouth is
enough to send your enemies scurrying away.

You Have a Double-Portion Inheritance

Isaiah 61:6–7, NIV
⁶And you will be called priests of the Lord... You will feed on the wealth of nations, and in their riches you will boast. ⁷Instead of their shame My people will receive a double portion... they will inherit a double portion in their land....

You are called "priests of the Lord" because Jesus has cleansed you with His blood and made you kings and priests to God. (Revelation 1:5–6.) And as priests of the Lord, God says to you, "You will feed on the wealth of nations, and in their riches you will boast." And you will "inherit a **double portion** in their land."

This promise came true for a church member who received his double portion while working for one of the top American companies in Singapore. Within a short time, he received two pay increments. And within just two years, he received an unexpected promotion to a senior position in the company. It was unexpected because the norm to qualify for such a promotion in the company was four years.

He was also named the recipient of a privileged stock award worth a five-figure sum, the net value of which was likely to double, judging by the then prevailing bullish stock market. He acknowledged that it was certainly God's favor because past awardees were a very small number of top management personnel who had made significant contributions to the company. And only an even smaller percent of their worldwide employees had ever received this prestigious award. He was only the second recipient, besides his boss, in the Singapore office to receive it.

This church member literally inherited a double portion — two pay increments, a promotion within two years and a stock award which was likely to double in value. Indeed, he was feeding on the wealth of the nations and boasting in their riches!

Beloved, believe God when He says that His people will receive a double portion. This double portion includes blessings of favor, fruitfulness, success, riches and health. In fact, the people around you will look at you and your descendants, and acknowledge that you are a people that the Lord has blessed!

Thought for the Day
As priests of the Lord, you have a double-portion inheritance.

A Greater Blessing Is in Store for You

Romans 8:31
³¹ What then shall we say to these things? If God is for us, who can be against us?

Whenever the devil throws something at us, we need not lose hope. In fact, we can be sure that God will turn it around for our greater blessing because He is for us.

When God first made man, He gave man dominion over everything on earth. (Genesis 1:26.) But when Adam fell, sin and death entered the world, and man lost his authority to the devil.

So did the devil win? No, God executed His redemption plan by sending His Son Jesus to die for us. And He wants us to know that Jesus' death did more than just restore us to the same position that Adam had — it placed us in a much higher position!

When the Father raised Jesus from the dead, we who are in Christ were raised with Him. In other words, we are now seated with Him at God's right hand in the heavenly places, "far above all principality and power and might and dominion, and every name that is named, not only in this age but also in that which is to come" (Ephesians 1:21)! Adam never had this position. So through Jesus' death and resurrection, we have received so much more.

In the Old Testament, we read of how God brought the Israelites out of bondage in Egypt into a land flowing with milk and honey. The devil thought that he could foil God's plan by putting giants in the promised land to stop the Israelites from inheriting it. But God outsmarted the devil. He allowed the giants to build their homes and cities, dig wells and cultivate crops until the right time came. Then, He brought the Israelites into the land and evicted the giants!

So the Israelites ended up inheriting large beautiful cities which they did not build, houses full of all good things which they did not fill, hewn-out wells which they did not dig, and vineyards and olive trees which they did not plant! (Deuteronomy 6:10–11.) Although the devil tried to prevent God's plan for His people from coming to pass, they ended up receiving so much more!

Beloved, the devil may throw obstacles and evil circumstances at you, but God will turn those evil schemes around for your greater blessing because He is for you!

Thought for the Day
**When the devil throws something at you, God will turn it around for
your greater blessing because He is for you.**

Let the Lord Be Your Defense

Psalm 94:22
²²But the LORD has been my defense, and my God the rock of my refuge.

Imagine being a poor widow, a stranger in the land and holding one of the lowliest jobs in society. That was Ruth's situation, so it would have been easy for her to feel vulnerable and defenseless. But because she trusted the Lord (Ruth 1:16), He placed her under Boaz's protection.

Boaz, the owner of the field she worked in, commanded his young men saying, "Let her glean even among the sheaves, and do not reproach her" (Ruth 2:15). What he was saying to his men was this: "She might be a gleaner, but because I care for her, treat her with respect and make sure she is not put to shame."

Boaz is a picture of our Lord Jesus. If you are feeling vulnerable and defenseless right now, imagine Jesus commanding His angels, "Watch over this one who belongs to Me. Make sure he is treated with respect and not put to shame because he is someone I love and someone whom I died for."

God's Word tells us that if God is for us, who can be against us? (Romans 8:31.) No one who has set himself against us can prevail because when God is for us, His protection is upon us. That is why I have never answered any of the poison email messages which I have received in the course of my ministry.

My attitude is this: Jesus is my defense. If He does not defend me, it means that there are things in my life that are not to be defended, and I would be glad to find out about them now rather than later. On the other hand, because I take the Lord as my defense, and He defends me, what can those who are against me do to me?

When you defend yourself, you have only your two hands and your own human resources. But when you let Jesus take up your defense, He defends you with His nail-pierced hands and His legions of angels! The results will be amazing.

Beloved, the Lord is your defense and refuge. Trust Him to defend and protect you!

Thought for the Day
If the Lord is your defense, what can those who are against you do to you?

Lift Songs of Praise to the Lord

Ephesians 5:17
¹⁷Therefore do not be unwise, but understand what the will of the Lord is.

God wants us to walk as wise men and women, and not as fools. (v. 15.) Now, He will not tell us to walk in wisdom without showing us how. That is why His Word goes on to say, "Therefore do not be unwise, but understand what the will of the Lord is."

So what is the will of God? The next two verses tell us how to identify it: "And do not be drunk with wine, in which is dissipation; but be filled with the Spirit, speaking to one another in psalms and hymns and spiritual songs, singing and making melody in your heart to the Lord" (vv. 18–19).

As you allow yourself to be filled with the Spirit by lifting songs of praise to the Lord, singing or speaking (God knows some of us can't sing!) psalms, hymns and spiritual songs, and making melody in your heart to the Lord, God promises that you will know what His will is for your situation. You will then have the wisdom to decide wisely what to do next.

I have found this to be true in my own life. Whenever I face a difficult situation, the more I think about it, the more confused I get. The more I try my best to come up with a smart solution, the further the answer seems to get from me. But when I turn away from my problem and turn to God, singing in the Spirit and praising Him, I get a clearer perspective of the problem when I come back to it later. I also find an inner prompting to make certain decisions which in the end, turn out to be better than anything I could have come up with on my own.

So my friend, lift up songs of praise to the Lord, whether times are good or bad. For when you fill your mouth with praises to God, He will lead you and guide you in all the affairs of your life. Even if you are stuck with a problem, He will show you the way to go or make a way out for you. Either way, you will get the wisdom and help that you need!

Thought for the Day
When you fill your mouth with praises to God, He will lead you and guide you in all the affairs of your life.

Which Righteous Man Do You Want to Be?

Genesis 24:1
¹Now Abraham was old, well advanced in age;
and the LORD had blessed Abraham in all things.

The Bible says that Abraham was righteous. But do you know that his nephew Lot was righteous too? (2 Peter 2:7–8.) Yet, both men lived very different lives. Although they both lived under God's grace some 400 years before the law was given, Abraham was very blessed, whereas Lot lost a great deal!

Both men had large herds and flocks. When their herdsmen started quarrelling over space, Abraham took the initiative to make peace. He even let Lot pick the lands that he wanted. Both men were righteous, but one was more gracious than the other.

Lot picked the well-watered plain of Jordan, where the cities of Sodom and Gomorrah were. He dwelt there and pitched his tent as far as Sodom. Eventually, he lived in Sodom. Now, Sodom and Gomorrah in the Bible represent a sinful lifestyle. Some Christians think, "Since I am righteous by faith and under God's grace, I can live a sinful lifestyle."

Well, let's learn from Lot. He first saw Sodom, then his feet walked toward it and finally he went into it. I like what a great man of God said: "Sin will take you farther than you want to go, keep you longer than you want to stay and cost you more than you want to pay." What did Lot end up paying?

He was captured when four kings plundered Sodom and Gomorrah. And even after Abraham rescued him with the help of God, he did not learn his lesson. He went back to Sodom. Some Christians live from one bail-out to another. God delivers them from, say, debt, and they go right back to borrowing money or gambling! Sodom and Gomorrah were eventually destroyed. Lot escaped with only the clothes on his back and even lost his wife in the process.

Beloved, you **are** the righteousness of God in Christ. When you truly understand what Jesus did to make you the righteousness of God, it will cause you to fall out of love with sin and fall in love with God. Then, it will not be hard to have a heart for God, as Abraham did, and like Abraham, be blessed in all things!

Thought for the Day
As the righteousness of God in Christ, choose to live a life that pleases God, and like Abraham, you will be blessed in all things!

Our Help in Time of Need

Hebrews 4:16
*¹⁶Let us therefore come boldly to the throne of grace, that we may
obtain mercy and find grace to help in time of need.*

I f you are facing a challenge right now, I want you to know that you have a standing invitation from your heavenly Father to come boldly to the throne of grace to "obtain mercy and find grace to help in time of need."

The phrase "help in time of need" means that you get healing when you are sick, provisions when you are in lack, restoration when your relationship with a loved one breaks down, and favor when news of job cuts or bad prospects are rife.

"Pastor Prince, how can I come boldly when I have been a lousy Christian?"

You can come boldly because you come to God by the blood of Jesus Christ and not by how you have lived your life. So whenever you come into God's presence, you don't have to be afraid that your sins will be exposed because the blood of Jesus has removed every one of them. God does not see even one speck of sin in you because He sees only the blood of His Son, which has been shed for your total forgiveness and acceptance.

My friend, when you have failed and need mercy, God's Word assures you that you will find mercy when you come boldly to God. Mercy means that you don't get the bad things you deserve, such as condemnation, poverty, failure, loss and even death.

And mercy is not the only thing that you will obtain when you come boldly to God. You will also find grace. Grace means that you get the good things that you don't deserve, such as health, protection, anointing, favor, good success and life more abundant.

So come boldly to the One who loves you passionately, unconditionally and with an undying love. Come boldly to Him who knows everything about your situation and has the solution. He has wisdom far beyond that doctor you highly respect, that lawyer you greatly honor and the best experts you can consult. Beloved, come boldly to the throne of grace to obtain mercy and grace to help in your time of need!

Thought for the Day
**Come boldly to God who knows everything about
your situation and has the solution.**

The Lord Is Able and Most Willing

Matthew 8:3
³Then Jesus put out His hand and touched him, saying, "I am willing;
be cleansed." Immediately his leprosy was cleansed.

When you see someone receiving a miraculous healing or financial breakthrough, do you ask, "What about me, Lord?" I believe that the leper who came to Jesus must have asked the same question.

He must have heard or seen from a distance, since he was not permitted to be in public places by the law, how Jesus had healed the sick. So he had no doubt that Jesus **could** heal him, but he was not sure if Jesus **would**. He said to Jesus, "Lord, if You are willing, You can make me clean" (Matthew 8:2). He was confident of the power of God, but not the love of God for him.

Like the leper, maybe you don't have a problem believing that God **can** give you your miracle, since He is Almighty God. But you are wondering if He **will** do it for you. My friend, let Jesus' actions and answer to the leper settle this question once and for all. He stretched forth His hand, touched the leper and said, "**I am willing**; be cleansed." And immediately, the leper was healed.

I want you to notice that Jesus touched the leper. He could have healed him from a distance with just a spoken word. He had healed others this way as in the case of the centurion's servant and the Syro-Phoenician woman's daughter. So why did He touch the leper?

Jesus knew that for so many years, the leper had been cut off from his family and society, so he must have been feeling dehumanized. I believe that Jesus touched him to make him feel human again, to make him feel loved and accepted again. His touch was His love language to the leper.

Can you see God's heart of love here? Can you see how much He loved the leper? That is how much He loves you! The day that you come to know God's heart of love and believe that He wants you blessed more than you want to be blessed is the day that you receive your miracle!

Beloved, catch a glimpse of God's heart of love, and you will believe that He is not only able, but also willing to make you whole!

Thought for the Day
God is not only able, but also willing to make you whole!

A Brand New Body at The Blast of a Trumpet!

1 Thessalonians 4:16
¹⁶For the Lord Himself will descend from heaven with a shout,
with the voice of an archangel, and with the trumpet of God.
And the dead in Christ will rise first.

All over the world, Jews celebrate Rosh Hashanah, the Jewish New Year. Occurring usually in the month of September, this feast is celebrated with the blowing of trumpets — the shofar or ram's horn. That is why it is also called the Feast of Trumpets.

The Jews observe seven feasts: The Passover, Unleavened Bread, Firstfruits, Pentecost, Trumpets, Atonement and Tabernacles. The first four have been fulfilled literally by Jesus. He was the Passover Lamb (1 Corinthians 5:7), the bread of life (John 6:35) and the firstfruits of those who have fallen asleep. (1 Corinthians 15:20.) And when Pentecost had fully come after His ascension, He sent us the Holy Spirit. (Acts 2:1–4.)

So the next feast that we are waiting for Jesus to fulfill literally is the Feast of Trumpets. Why is this feast significant to us? Because when Jesus fulfills it, it means that we are going up to meet Him in the clouds!

I am talking about the rapture of the church. When the trumpet sounds, "in the twinkling of an eye," we who are alive will be changed. We will put on new bodies that will be like Jesus' body! Those who are dead in Christ will rise and also receive new bodies. They will go up first followed by us who are alive, and we will all meet the Lord in the air. (1 Corinthians 15:51–55.)

This means that there is a possibility that you might not see death! The Bible says, "Then we who are alive and **remain** shall be caught up together with them in the clouds to meet the Lord in the air" (1 Thessalonians 4:17). It is one thing to happen to be alive, but quite another to **remain** alive.

I believe that there is a generation of Christians who know the resurrection power of the Lord. They know how to walk in their inheritance and put off sickness and death until the coming of the Lord. My friend, may you be counted as one of them as you take the Lord Jesus and His finished work as your victory over sickness and death!

Thought for the Day
When the trumpet sounds, we who are alive will put on new bodies like Jesus' body!

Not Satisfied With Just Being Saved

Genesis 12:7
⁷Then the LORD appeared to Abram and said, "To your descendants I will give this land." And there he built an altar to the LORD, who had appeared to him.

I don't know about you, but I am not satisfied with just knowing that I am righteous by faith. I also want to get to know the One who made me righteous. I want to have an intimate relationship with my Savior!

Abraham was such a man. He was righteous by faith, but he also had a close walk with God and was blessed by God in all things. (Genesis 24:1.) His nephew Lot, on the other hand, although righteous too (2 Peter 2:7–8), had no heart for God. He ended up losing a lot when Sodom, the city he dwelt in, was destroyed along with Gomorrah. He was saved by the skin of his teeth!

My friend, do you want to be a Christian like Lot, righteous but always finding yourself in trouble, or do you want to be a righteous-and-blessed Christian like Abraham? Then, like Abraham, have a heart for God.

From place to place, Abraham would build an altar to the Lord. And in between altars, he grew very rich! (Genesis 13:2.) There is no biblical record, however, of Lot ever building an altar to the Lord.

What is an "altar" in today's context? It is a place where you know that you have a close relationship with God. For example, when my late father was in the hospital, I was worried and did not know what to do. I remember driving down the road and crying. After a while, I just threw my cares to the Lord. When I reached the hospital, I just laid my hands on my father and said, "Be healed in Jesus' name." And he was healed!

Till today, I can remember the place where I had cast my cares to the Lord and leaned on His love for me. That is my "altar." And it is not the only one.

We have got to have this kind of relationship with God, one full of "altars" that remind us of His love, goodness and faithfulness. Let's not live the Christian life like Lot, saved by the skin of our teeth. Let's walk closely with God as Abraham did, and be richly blessed in every area of our lives!

Thought for the Day
Choose to have an intimate relationship with the One who made you righteous.

God Is Your Abba, Father

Galatians 4:6
⁶And because you are sons, God has sent forth the Spirit of
His Son into your hearts, crying out, "Abba, Father!"

Have you ever realized that God was never known as "Father" until Jesus came to earth and revealed Him as such? In His prayer to His Father, Jesus said, "And I have declared to them Your Name, and will declare it, that the love with which You loved Me may be in them, and I in them" (John 17:26). What name was Jesus referring to? It was the name "Father." If there was anything close to Jesus' heart, it was to introduce God as "Father" to us.

In the Bible, Jesus said, "Therefore do not worry, saying, 'What shall we eat?' or 'What shall we drink?' or 'What shall we wear?'... For your heavenly **Father** knows that you need all these things" (Matthew 6:31–32). Once, He said, "If you then, being evil, know how to give good gifts to your children, how much more will your **Father** who is in heaven give good things to those who ask Him!" (Matthew 7:11).

Jesus wants you to always have this image of God in your mind — that He is your Abba, Father. Why? Because He wants you to know that there is nothing more important or too insignificant for the Father when it comes to His children.

Imagine a father playing with his five-year-old son, when he notices a splinter embedded in his little boy's thumb. The concerned father asks, "When did you get this?"

"A few days ago," the boy answers.

"Why didn't you tell Daddy about it?"

"I thought you were too busy and that I shouldn't bother you."

If you were that father, wouldn't it break your heart to hear your child say this to you?

A splinter in one's thumb may be a small thing, but there is nothing too small when it concerns your child because if it affects him, it affects you too. Now, no matter how old you are today, you are still God's child, so don't think that your problem is too small for God. If it is important to you, it is important to your Father too. Beloved, always remember that He is your Abba, Father!

Thought for the Day
If it is important to you, it is important to your Abba, Father!

Jesus Has Given You His Peace

John 14:27
27 Peace I leave with you, My peace I give to you;
not as the world gives do I give to you....

In Israel, Jews greet each other with the words "shalom, shalom." Unlike the English word "peace," "shalom" does not just mean peace of mind, but also wholeness for your entire being — spirit, soul and body. It means having a sense of completeness and soundness. In other words, shalom encompasses your prosperity, health and total well-being.

When Jesus spoke to His disciples in John 14:27, He did not use the English word "peace." He would have used the Hebrew word "shalom," saying, "Shalom I leave with you, My shalom I give to you..." Interestingly, the word "leave" here actually means "bequeath," the way a rich man bequeaths his estate to his beneficiary.

The disciples must have been excited when they heard that Jesus was bequeathing them His shalom. They must have known that to receive His shalom was to have His health because they had never seen Him sick. To have His shalom also meant never being in lack because He was never broke. Whenever He needed money, money was there. For instance, once, money to pay the temple tax came in the mouth of a fish! (Matthew 17:24–27.)

The disciples also understood that having Jesus' shalom meant having His abundance because they had seen Him meeting the needs of thousands with plenty of leftovers. They saw him feeding 5,000 men (not counting the women and children) with 12 baskets full of leftovers! (Mark 6:34–44.)

Jesus wanted His disciples to know that His peace was different from the peace that the world offers. His peace would change whatever trying circumstances that beset them. Even if it was a mega storm, it would have to bow to His peace. The Prince of Peace merely spoke, "Peace, be still!" and the winds and the sea obeyed Him. (Mark 4:39.) His peace changed the mega storm into a perfect calm.

Beloved, that is the kind of peace that Jesus has bequeathed to you. Therefore, believe that His shalom, which He has left with you, will change all your difficult situations, bringing you from sickness, lack and mental anguish to health, prosperity and total wellness!

Thought for the Day
Jesus has bequeathed you His shalom, which does not just mean
peace of mind, but also wholeness for your spirit, soul and body.

The Light of the World Exposes Your Perfection

John 8:12
12 Then Jesus spoke to them again, saying, "I am the light of the world.
He who follows Me shall not walk in darkness, but have the light of life."

When I was a teenager, I heard preachers saying this: "Jesus is the light of the world. So don't think for one moment that you can do things behind His back. His light will expose all the bad things that you have done!" So I was afraid to come near God, fearing that His glorious light would show up my faults, weaknesses and shame.

But is this what "the light of the world" does?

The truth is found in the context of the verse. Jesus declared that He was the light of the world right after He had told the woman caught in the act of adultery, "Woman, where are those accusers of yours? Has no one condemned you?"

When she said, "No one, Lord," He said to her, "Neither do I condemn you; go and sin no more." Then, the Bible tells us that "Jesus spoke to them again, saying, 'I am the light of the world…'" (vv. 10–12).

How wonderful it is to know that when Jesus said, "I am the light of the world," His light was not to show up the woman's sin because He had just told her that He did not condemn her.

This tells us that we don't have to be fearful when we come into God's presence. He is not there waiting to punish us for our mistakes and failures. His light is not for exposing our sins and shame, or for condemning us. No, His glorious light is for showing us how perfectly His Son's blood has washed away our sins! That is why Jesus could tell the woman that He did not condemn her — because He would be condemned for her sin as well as ours at the cross.

Beloved, Jesus' light unveils the truth that our sins have been completely removed. It reveals how perfect and spotless we are because of Christ's perfect work at the cross. When you know this, you can go boldly into God's presence, knowing that you have the light of life that gives you grace and hope!

Thought for the Day
Jesus' light unveils the truth that our sins have been completely removed.

Life Under the New Covenant

Hebrews 8:10
¹⁰... I will put My laws in their mind and write them on their hearts....

What laws was God referring to when He said, "I will put My **laws** in their mind and write them on their hearts"? He was certainly not referring to the Ten Commandments, known as the laws of the old covenant, since He said that He found fault with that covenant and declared it obsolete. (vv. 7–9, 13.)

The laws that God puts in our minds and writes on our hearts refer to the royal law of love (Matthew 22:37–40), the perfect law of liberty (James 1:25) and the law of faith. (Romans 3:27.) These are the laws of the new covenant.

You live according to the laws of the new covenant when you are conscious of how much God loves you. And the more you are conscious of His love for you, the more your heart is filled with love. When that happens, you will love God and the people around you supernaturally and effortlessly. That is God writing on your heart the royal law of love — that we love because He first loved us. (1 John 4:19.)

Secondly, when you know that you are perfectly accepted by God because of Jesus' sacrifice, you can have the courage and liberty as a child of God to come boldly into the presence of your heavenly Father. And in His presence, He is able to write on your heart new desires. You will find yourself wanting to do the right thing at the right time. You will live life victoriously from the inside out. This is the perfect law of liberty operating in your life.

Thirdly, when you sense what God is writing on your heart and putting in your mind, and as your faith is activated causing you to trust Him and His love for you, He calls it obeying the law of faith. When that happens, whatever you believe, you receive!

My friend, God has made it easy — and you will find that it is exciting — to live life under the new covenant!

Thought for the Day
You live according to the laws of the new covenant when
you are conscious of how much God loves you.

Take, Take and Take More!

1 Corinthians 2:12
[12]Now we have received, not the spirit of the world, but the Spirit
who is from God, that we might know the things that
have been freely given to us by God.

As a child of the Most High God, God wants you to know the things that have been freely given to you. He wants you to receive them freely although it cost Him His Son. He paid the price, but He wants you to receive the blessings freely. That is His love toward you.

Perhaps you are asking God, "How is it that I don't have this blessing? And why do I have so little of that?"

I believe that He is saying this to you: "What do you lack, My child? Health? Take it! It has been paid for with the life of My Son.

"Do you need peace of mind? My Son wore the crown of thorns on His head to give it to you. Take it!

"Lack wisdom? Take My wisdom!

"Need victory? Victory is not something you attain. It is a gift to be received. Take it!

"Take My prosperity! Take My favor! Every time you come into My Presence, take, and take some more!"

God, your heavenly Father, wants you to receive like the prodigal son, who deserved nothing, but received everything. (Luke 15:11–24.) God delights in giving freely. And He delights in you receiving freely because it shows that you value and appreciate His Son's sacrifice.

You miss it when you are busy trying to earn what has been freely given to you, when you think that you must do more for God to bless you, or that you must pay the price for it. God cannot give it to you based on your works because if it is by works, it is no longer by grace. When you try to work for it, you frustrate the grace of God and make light of Jesus' work at Calvary.

My friend, the days of trying, striving and earning are over. The days of take, take and take more have come. Take and you will bring pleasure to God's heart!

Thought for the Day
God delights in you taking freely from Him because it shows that
you value and appreciate His Son's sacrifice.

God Is Behind Your Increase

1 Corinthians 3:7
⁷So then neither he who plants is anything,
nor he who waters, but God who gives the increase.

Sometimes, we think that the increase or success which we enjoy is the result of our own efforts or hard work. Now, I am not advocating laziness, but the truth is that **God** is the One behind our increase.

We see this truth when we read the story of Ruth, a young widow from Moab, who worked as a gleaner in a barley field from morning till evening. Now, we could attribute the entire ephah — a substantial 10-day supply — of barley she collected at the end of the day to her hard work. After all, she did work all day in the field.

But when we read about how Boaz, the owner of the field, had secretly told his reapers to "let grain from the bundles fall purposely for her; leave it that she may glean" (Ruth 2:16), we know that it was because of Boaz's intervention that Ruth ended up with so much.

I believe that Jesus, our heavenly Boaz, does the same thing for us today. He causes people to favor us and "drop" blessings on us because He loves us. Then, He causes us to "pick up" these blessings. Often, it happens so seemingly naturally we forget that it is the Lord who has blessed us with the increases.

A church member who runs a florist business shared that once, God caused someone who needed a lot of flowers to "drop" a huge order with her. She also shared that she was hardly making any money even though she had been working hard for many years. But when she became a Christian after coming to our church, she began to confess every day that God's favor was on her. Within a few weeks, that big order worth $14,000 came in. Only God could have given her such a supernatural increase.

My friend, your hard work is not behind your increase. The Bible tells us that it is "God who gives the increase." He is the One who is behind your increase and He delights in blessing you because He loves you!

Thought for the Day
God is the One behind your increase and He delights in
blessing you because He loves you!

Proclaim the Lord's Death

1 Corinthians 11:26
²⁶For as often as you eat this bread and drink this cup,
you proclaim the Lord's death till He comes.

In the Old Testament, whenever the children of Israel sacrificed a lamb for a burnt offering as they faced a strong enemy, victory was theirs. For example, in 1 Samuel 7:7–11, when the Philistines were coming against them, the prophet Samuel offered a lamb as a burnt offering. As it was being offered, the Lord came like a loud thunder on the Philistine army, confusing them. This led to victory for the Israelites.

Every time something bad happened to the children of Israel, by offering a lamb sacrifice, they were proclaiming the Lord's death, and the battle would turn in their favor.

Today, when we are faced with an enemy, how do we offer our "burnt offering"? How do we proclaim the Lord's death and come out victorious? Do we ask Jesus to come down to where we are at and die on the cross all over again?

Of course not. Jesus died **once** for **all** our sins — past, present and future. (Hebrews 10:12.) His work is perfectly perfect and completely complete, so He doesn't have to die for us again. Today, we proclaim His death simply by partaking of the Lord's Supper.

Every time you partake of the bread and wine, you declare to the principalities and powers of darkness that the Lord's death avails for you. Every time you partake, you are saying that because Jesus has been judged and punished in your place, you cannot be judged and punished. Because Jesus died young in your place, you will live long. And because He conquered death and stripped the devil of his powers, you will not be defeated. The victory is already yours!

That is why the psalmist David said, "You prepare a table before me in the presence of my enemies…" (Psalm 23:5). The Lord's table is prepared for you in the presence of your enemies because when you partake of the bread and wine, you will see your enemies tremble and scatter! Why? Because when you proclaim the Lord's death through the Holy Communion, you are reminding the devil and his cohorts of their humiliating defeat at Calvary's cross! (Colossians 2:15.)

Thought for the Day
Every time you partake of the bread and wine, you declare to the powers of darkness
that the Lord's death avails for you and that the victory is already yours!

Only Christ's Atonement Satisfies God

1 John 2:1–2
¹... if anyone sins, we have an Advocate with the Father, Jesus Christ the righteous. ²And He Himself is the propitiation for our sins....

Today, Jews still observe Yom Kippur or the Day of Atonement. As the name suggests, it is a day set aside to make atonement for one's sins. But for Christians, this beautiful feast points to Jesus and what He did for us on the cross. Because of His sacrifice, all our sins have already been perfectly atoned for. That is why, should we sin, we know that "we have an Advocate with the Father, Jesus Christ the righteous." And He Himself is the propitiation for our sins.

Now, it does not say that if anyone **repents**, we have an Advocate with the Father. It says that if anyone **sins**, we have an Advocate with the Father. The moment a child of God sins, straightaway, his Advocate, Jesus Christ, goes into action to pray for and protect him.

What about repentance then?

The word "repentance" is *metanoia* in the Greek, which means to change one's mind. For example, you used to believe that Jesus was just a good man. Then one day, you repented and believed that He is the Son of the living God, who died for your sins and rose again on the third day, and you gladly took Him as your Savior.

Bible repentance is not this idea of hitting or punishing yourself to atone for your sins. Don't turn it into a human work, like the man who went to a priest to confess his sins. When they were done, the priest asked the man, "By the way, what do you do for a living?" The man replied, "I'm a contortionist," and proceeded to give a demonstration. Another man came along wanting to confess his sins. When he saw the contortionist all twisted up on the ground, he said, "If this is repentance, forget it!" and ran off!

My friend, there is no need to climb the Himalayas or whip your back bloody to atone for your sins. No amount of self-punishment or crying can atone for them. Your sins have already been punished fully in the body of Jesus. Only His finished work satisfies God. So change your mind and simply believe that Jesus alone is the propitiation for your sins!

Thought for the Day
No amount of self-punishment can atone for your sins. Just rest in the truth that Jesus alone is the propitiation for your sins!

Pronounce Yourself Clean!

Matthew 8:3
³ Then Jesus put out His hand and touched him, saying, "I am willing;
be cleansed." Immediately his leprosy was cleansed.

Most of us are familiar with the healing of the leper in Matthew 8. It is a beautiful account of God's willingness to touch and heal the sick, no matter how unclean they may be. Whenever we doubt God's willingness to heal us, we should listen to the words of Jesus again: "I am willing; be cleansed." He is the same yesterday, today and forever!

Since the Bible is clear about God's willingness to heal, why do we still have problems with our health? Why do we still experience symptoms in our bodies?

I believe that the answer is found in what Jesus told the leper to do next. He told him to go and show himself to the priest. (Matthew 8:4.) This was the law then for lepers who were healed. (Leviticus 14:2–3.) And he was to hear the priest pronounce the word "clean" over him. (v. 7.)

You see, as believers, when we received Jesus, His blood cleansed us from sin as well as sickness. (Isaiah 53:4–5.) But we keep hearing people pronounce sin, sickness, poverty and death over us. We keep hearing people tell us that we are unclean, undeserving, poor, weak, and that it is only natural that we grow old and sickly, and die.

God is waiting for a priesthood that will rise up and pronounce His people clean!

"But Pastor Prince, where can I find such priests?"

Who are the priests today? You and I! In fact, we have more authority to pronounce good things than the Levitical priests of the Old Testament. They were just priests. But we are **king-priests** by the blood of Jesus! (Revelation 1:5–6.) Where the word of the king is, there is power. (Ecclesiastes 8:4.) And by the word of a priest, every controversy and every assault shall be settled. (Deuteronomy 21:5.)

Beloved, God has cleansed you, so pronounce yourself clean! Right now, put your hand on your heart and pronounce good things over yourself. Say, "I pronounce myself clean, righteous, healed, whole and prosperous by the blood of Jesus!" By your word as a king-priest, every assault against you shall be settled!

Thought for the Day
Because you are a king-priest by the blood of Jesus, you can pronounce
good things over yourself and see them come to pass!

Jesus Is Your Qualification for God's Blessings

Deuteronomy 28:2
²And all these blessings shall come upon you and overtake you...

God loves to bless you. He has even declared that "blessings shall come upon you and overtake you." This means that you can't run fast enough to escape them! When you turn one corner, there is a blessing waiting for you. When you turn another corner, you run smack into another blessing!

Now, you may think that you don't qualify for God's blessings because of the preceding verse which says that these blessings will come to pass only if you diligently obey God's voice and keep **all** of His commandments. You know that no matter how hard you try, you just cannot keep all of God's commandments. In fact, the Bible says that if you fail to keep just one commandment, you fail to keep all. (James 2:10.)

My friend, I have good news for you: Jesus is the One who qualifies us for every single blessing because **He** has kept all of God's commandments. When He died for us on the cross, He not only fulfilled all of God's commandments, He also redeemed us from the curse of the law. (Galatians 3:13.) Note that He did not redeem us from the blessings of the law, so the blessings are still ours today!

As you read the list of blessings in Deuteronomy 28, starting with "Blessed shall you be in the city... in the country... the fruit of your body... your basket... when you come in... when you go out..." (vv. 3–13), I believe that Jesus is saying to you, "Like the blessings? Then take them by faith!"

You may say, "But I don't deserve them." Yes, you don't deserve them, but you still get them because of Jesus. That is God's grace! The law says, "You must deserve the blessings." But the law is no longer here. Grace is here. So take the blessings by grace through faith. Believe God for the blessings.

Today, it is no longer a question of how much or how well you have kept God's commandments. It is a question of how much you can **believe** God for His blessings. All the promises of God in Christ are "Yes," and because you are in Christ, you can say "Amen!" to His blessings! (2 Corinthians 1:20.)

Thought for the Day
Jesus is the One who qualifies us for every single blessing
because He has kept all of God's commandments.

Joint Heirs With Christ Jesus

Romans 8:16–17
*16 The Spirit Himself bears witness with our spirit that we are children of God,
17 and if children, then heirs — heirs of God and joint heirs with Christ....*

As long as you are born again, you are no longer a "slave," but a son of the Most High God. And God does not just call you His son. He also calls you "an heir" through Christ. (Galatians 4:7.) In fact, Romans 8:17 says that you are "joint heirs" with Christ.

As a joint heir with Christ Jesus, you inherit everything that He is. How precious Jesus is to the Father, is how precious you are to the Father. The way the Father loves Jesus, is the way the Father loves you!

How accepted are you by God today? Look at Jesus. That is how accepted you are! Christ is the measure of your acceptance. How favored are you by God? Look at Jesus, who is seated at the Father's right hand. You enjoy that same favor today because whatever Christ enjoys, you enjoy!

As a joint heir with Christ Jesus, you also inherit all that He has obtained from the Father. How much Jesus has, is how much you have. How prosperous is the One who made all things, and who put the gold, silver and diamonds in the earth? So are you in this world! (1 John 4:17.)

I used to read the Bible to find out how to be a rich, successful and victorious Christian. But now, I read it to find out more about Jesus because I know that when I find Him, I find my every blessing in Him. (Ephesians 1:3, 2 Peter 1:3.)

My friend, all that Jesus is in heaven today, you are in this world. All that belongs to Him belongs to you. That is why it is in your interest to know Him more, to see Him in all His glory and beauty. And because Jesus is so rich and glorious, it will take you a lifetime to discover everything that He has done for you and has for you.

Beloved, you are an heir of the Most High God. You are a joint heir with Christ Jesus. So find out all the blessings that your rich inheritance includes and start walking in them today!

Thought for the Day
All that Jesus is in heaven today, you are in this world.

Christ Is Our Mercy Seat

Psalm 91:1
¹He who dwells in the secret place of the Most High shall
abide under the shadow of the Almighty.

In the Old Testament, there was a place where God met with His people. In Exodus 25:22, God said, "And there I will meet with you, and I will speak with you from above the mercy seat, from between the two cherubim which are on the ark of the Testimony..." This place was above the mercy seat of the ark of the covenant, under the wings of the two cherubim. The psalmist calls it "the secret place of the Most High... under the shadow of the Almighty."

The mercy seat covered the ark which contained the three emblems of man's rebellion: the golden pot of manna — man's rebellion against God's provision, two tablets of stone on which God wrote the Ten Commandments — man's rebellion against God's standard, and Aaron's rod — man's rebellion against God's authority. Once a year on the Day of Atonement, the high priest would sprinkle the blood of the sacrificed animal on the mercy seat and so make propitiation for the sins of Israel.

Today, it is not the blood of animals that makes propitiation for our sins, but the holy blood of the Son of God. (Romans 3:24–25.) The word for "propitiation" in the original Greek text is *hilasterion*, which actually means "mercy seat." So Christ is our mercy seat. His blood speaks for us and puts God on our side. God does not see our rebellion. He sees the blood of His Son and accepts us!

That is why we can come boldly to the secret place of the Most High, in Christ, and feel secure that we have every right to be in God's presence. We can come boldly to Him to obtain mercy and find grace to help in time of need. (Hebrews 4:16.)

And because Christ, our mercy seat, covers us with His blood, we are under God's protection. We are in the secret place of the Most High, abiding under the shadow of the Almighty. Here, no evil will befall us, nor will any plague come near our dwelling. (Psalm 91:9–10.) In the secret place of the Most High, we are favored and kept safe from all harm!

Thought for the Day
Because Christ, our mercy seat, covers us with His blood,
we are under God's protection and favor.

God Commands His Blessing on Your Storehouses

Deuteronomy 28:8
⁸The LORD will command the blessing on you in your storehouses...

W hen Jesus walked on earth, He had no bank account or credit card. Yet, He was rich, lacking nothing. He had whatever He needed for Himself as well as for the people around Him. When they needed healing, He provided it. (Matthew 12:15.) When they needed food, He provided it. (Matthew 14:13–21.) As long as they had Him, they had whatever they needed.

Likewise, when you have Jesus, you have an anointing within that makes you rich, even though in the natural, when you look at your finances, there may not be much. God Himself has promised that He will command the blessing on you in your storehouses. Notice that He said "storehouses." This means that He will command the blessing on your bank accounts, investment plans and everywhere that you put your money! Your storehouses will be blessed because when God commands the blessing, the blessing has no choice but to come on your storehouses!

We saw this happen to one of our church's storehouses — our investment in Marine Cove, an open-air, seaside shopping-cum-dining-cum-leisure resort complex. We invested in the place because we wanted to multiply the Lord's money. We did not want to leave the money in the bank where the interest rate then was less than one per cent. We prayed about it and the Lord led us to invest in Marine Cove.

And since day one, we have been making money from that investment. In fact, our highest annual return was 11 percent net! When SARS hit Singapore in 2003, people were avoiding the air-conditioned malls and coming to Marine Cove. The place was packed. Only God could have known how things would turn out. We even made money from the parking charges! That was how much the Lord was multiplying His money through our investment.

Beloved, just believe God when He says that He will command His blessing on you in your storehouses. Get your storehouses ready and make room for the blessings. Position yourself to capitalize on the opportunities that He is sending your way!

Thought for the Day
**Your storehouses will be blessed because when God commands the blessing,
the blessing has no choice but to come on you in your storehouses!**

God Will Cause Your Gift to Prosper You

Proverbs 17:8
*8A present is a precious stone in the eyes of its possessor;
wherever he turns, he prospers.*

When we see something moldy, we throw it away. But when Alexander Fleming saw his culture dishes contaminated with mold, he discovered penicillin. You see, he had a gift which prospered him.

Joseph, a Hebrew slave in Egypt, had nothing except his gift of interpreting dreams. But look at what that gift did for him. It prospered him. He interpreted Pharaoh's dream and became the most powerful man in Egypt after Pharaoh. (Genesis 41.)

"But Pastor Prince, what if I don't have any gift?"

My friend, don't let anyone tell you that you don't have any gift. God has given each person a gift which can open doors of opportunities and bring in great blessings.

Maybe you are just not aware of that gift you have inside you, or perhaps it has profited you nothing thus far as you have not found out how best to use it. You need to take your gift and ask God for wisdom to cultivate it until it becomes such a powerful tool or "precious stone" that wherever you turn, you prosper.

This was the case with a church brother who was tremendously gifted in the creative arts. For a long time, he lacked the confidence and boldness to leave the security of his police job and step out on his own. But when he began to seek God's wisdom for his situation, God gave him boldness to leave his job and go back to school to pursue the creative arts. In school, he prospered, becoming one of its top students and impressing the principal so much with his creative gift that he was offered a teaching position in the school even before he graduated.

Now, please don't go and quit your job after reading this. What you should do is ask God for wisdom regarding your gift. For when the wisdom of God is added to your gift, that gift becomes "a precious stone in the eyes of its possessor; wherever he turns, he prospers."

Thought for the Day
**Ask God for wisdom to cultivate your gift until it becomes such a
"precious stone" that wherever you turn, you prosper.**

Jesus, Your High Priest, Intercedes for You

Hebrews 7:25
²⁵... He is also able to save to the uttermost those who come to God through Him, since He always lives to make intercession for them.

The verse says that Jesus always lives to make intercession for us. Once, I used to think that this meant that Jesus is seated at the Father's right hand today, praying all the time for us, waiting and hoping that the Father will do something for us.

But that is not true. Look at what Jesus prayed when He stood before Lazarus' tomb. He declared, "Father, I thank You that You have heard Me" (John 11:41). He prayed these words even before Lazarus came forth from his tomb alive. Jesus knew that what He said would come to pass because the Father always hears Him. (v. 42.)

So what does "He always lives to make intercession for them" mean?

Because Jesus is our High Priest (Hebrews 4:14), we get a picture of what happens when we pray when we understand what the high priest in the Old Testament did with the burnt offering of a bird. (Leviticus 1:14–17.)

The birds brought to the high priest are a picture of our prayers "flying" to the Lord Jesus because we pray to the Father in Jesus' name. Now, just as the high priest removes the bird's feathers after killing it, Jesus removes all that is superfluous and unclean from our prayers, such as unbelief and self-centeredness.

Then, just as the high priest offers the bird as a burnt sacrifice, a sweet aroma to the Lord, Jesus our High Priest adds His perfection, beauty, excellence and fragrance, which the Father so delights in, to our prayers. That is how He presents our prayers to the Father. That is how He lives to make intercession for you.

My friend, you don't have to run to a church leader to get him to pray "more powerfully" for you. You can pray yourself. Then, take advantage of Jesus' intercession for you and say, "Lord Jesus, I don't know what else to say... please intercede for me." And when Jesus gives His personal touch to your prayer, you can be sure that it will be answered!

Thought for the Day
***Jesus removes all that is superfluous and unclean from our prayers,
and adds His perfection, beauty, excellence and fragrance to them!***

Behold the Glory of Jesus in You

2 Corinthians 3:18
*[18] But we all, with unveiled face, beholding as in a mirror the
glory of the Lord, are being transformed into the same image
from glory to glory, just as by the Spirit of the Lord.*

When you look in a mirror, what do you see? Of course, you see yourself. But God does not want you to see yourself in the natural. You may be sick, weak, broke and depressed, yet God wants you to see yourself the way He sees you — healed, strong, rich and whole because Christ is in you. (Colossians 1:27.)

God wants you to behold as in a mirror the glory of His Son, who is in you by His Spirit. As you do this, His Word says that you are being transformed from glory to glory — from poor to rich, sick to healed, loser to winner!

The world may say to you, "It can't be that easy. You can't be transformed just by beholding the glory of Jesus. No, you must do something about you. If you don't put in effort, nothing will happen. If you don't start making changes, nothing will change."

But the world will never understand that as you are beholding the glory of the Lord, who is the successful One in you, you are being transformed from a failure to a success. And this is not accomplished by any effort of yours to get ahead in life, but by the Spirit of the Lord! (Zechariah 4:6.)

As you behold the glory of the Lord who is the healthy One in your sick body, you are transformed from sickness to health. And this is not accomplished by any effort of yours to keep fit and eat well, but by the Spirit of the Lord!

My friend, what can be easier than beholding the beauty of the Son? So stop focusing on yourself and your efforts. Look away from these things and begin to behold the glory of Jesus, who is in you right now, and you will begin to behold the miracles that you need!

Thought for the Day
***As you behold the glory of Jesus, who is in you by His Spirit, you are being
transformed from poor to rich, sick to healed, loser to winner!***

Heir of the World Today

Romans 4:13
13 For the promise that he would be the heir of the world was not to Abraham or to his seed through the law, but through the righteousness of faith.

God promised Abraham that he would be the heir of the world. Now, don't be too quick to say, "Well, that promise was made only to Abraham and not me." The verse says, "For the promise that he would be the heir of the world was not to Abraham or to **his seed** through the law, but through the righteousness of faith." So the promise was not just made to Abraham, but to "his seed" as well; that is, you and I who belong to Christ — "And if you are Christ's, then you are Abraham's seed, and heirs according to the promise." (Galatians 3:29.)

Notice that God did not say that you would be the heir of the country you are living in, but heir of the world! The Greek word for "world" here is *kosmos*, which means the universe as well as the whole circle of earthly goods, endowments, riches, advantages and pleasures. All these are yours to inherit through the righteousness of faith in Jesus and His finished work at the cross. This righteousness is given to you as a gift from God, so you don't have to earn it through good works.

For God to fulfill His promise, He has to prosper you. You can't be the heir of the world and be poor or in debt! Not only that, He must keep you healthy because you can't inherit the world when you are sick and always flat on your back.

Don't listen to people who tell you that you will only get to enjoy these blessings when you get to heaven one fine day. Why would you need riches in heaven? There, even the streets are made of pure gold. (Revelation 21:21.) And why would you need healing in heaven? There is no sickness there. So you need the health and wealth in the here and now!

Beloved, God wants you to be the heir of the world **today**. So lay hold of your rich inheritance today. Jesus paid for it with His blood. Don't push it all to the sweet by and by!

Thought for the Day
You are an heir to the universe as well as the whole circle of earthly goods, endowments, riches, advantages and pleasures.

'All That I Have Is Yours'

Luke 15:31
31 ... 'Son, you are always with me, and all that I have is yours.'

After running a few errands for his parents, a little boy went to his father and said, "I know why you and Mommy had me." "Why?" asked his father. "So that you guys would have someone to run errands for you!" exclaimed the boy.

Like the little boy, do you see God as a Father who demands obedience and service from you? Have you ever felt that unless you obey Him and keep all His commandments, you don't have a right to be blessed by Him?

Jesus shared the story of the prodigal son to show how some of us call God "Father" and yet don't know His heart. There are two sons in this parable. We know what happened to the prodigal son, but we can also learn something about the older son. This is what he said to his father when he discovered that his father had thrown a party to celebrate the return of his irresponsible, spendthrift brother: "Lo, these many years I have been serving you; I never transgressed your commandment at any time; and yet you never gave me a young goat, that I might make merry with my friends" (v. 29).

Now, this son believed that his father had brought him into the world to serve him. He saw his father as someone issuing commandments to him all the time. And he saw himself as someone who had to obey those commandments to enjoy his inheritance. But the truth is that the father had already given him his inheritance. (v. 12.) The father even reminded him lovingly: "Son... all that I have is yours." And I am sure that that inheritance included more than one goat!

Have you, like the older son, failed to understand your Father's heart? Your heavenly Father already gave you a rich inheritance in Christ when you became His child. He wants you to know that you have received the Spirit of sonship. (Romans 8:15.) So call out to Him, "Abba, Father!" and know how much He loves you. Because you are His heir, all that He has is yours to enjoy today!

Thought for the Day
Your heavenly Father has already given you a rich
inheritance in Christ when you became His child.

You Are God's Beloved

Ephesians 1:6
⁶To the praise of the glory of His grace, by which He made us accepted in the Beloved.

At the Jordan River, Jesus heard His Father say to Him, "You are My beloved Son; in You I am well pleased" (Luke 3:22). Later, in the wilderness, Jesus heard the devil say to Him, "If You are the Son of God…" (Luke 4:3).

Notice that the devil not only questioned Jesus' sonship, but he also dropped the word "beloved" when he said to Jesus, "If You are the Son of God…" You see, the devil cannot remind you that you are God's beloved because when you know this truth, whatever he wants to bring against you will not succeed!

Many girls are giving away their virginity because they need to feel wanted and loved. And young boys join gangs to feel accepted because they have been rejected and made to feel worthless by others.

But when you know that you are God's beloved, no temptation can succeed against you, not even the "giants" who may taunt you. Consider David, who slew Goliath. "David" in Hebrew means "beloved." It takes a David to knock down a giant. In other words, it takes someone who knows that he is God's beloved to win the fights of life!

You are God's beloved not because of what you do. Christ did everything. He is God's Beloved. But God put you in Christ. That is why you are "accepted in the Beloved." And what God said to Jesus, He says to you today: "You are My beloved son. In you, I am well pleased."

So if the devil tells you, "Hey, you call yourself 'God's beloved' after what you just did?" have the assurance that it is not based on what **you** have done, but what **Christ** has done. And you are still God's beloved because you are in Christ!

When you say that, I believe the devil screams in frustration because he has no power over you when you are conscious that you are God's beloved. There is truly a place of safety when you know that you are His beloved.

My friend, we are not being proud when we call ourselves God's beloved. How can we boast when we know that it is God's grace that has made us accepted in the Beloved!

Thought for the Day
It takes someone who knows that he is God's beloved to win the fights of life!

The Promise of the Father

Acts 1:8
[8]"But you shall receive power when the Holy Spirit has come upon you;
and you shall be witnesses to Me in Jerusalem, and in all
Judea and Samaria, and to the end of the earth."

Before Jesus went back to heaven, He told His disciples to "wait for the Promise of the Father" (v. 4). There are thousands of promises in the Bible, so which promise was He referring to?

The early church knew which promise Jesus was referring to because He had told His disciples, "Do not leave Jerusalem, but wait for the Promise of the Father, which you have heard Me speak about. For John truly baptized with water, but you shall be **baptized with the Holy Spirit** not many days from now." (vv. 4–5.) Jesus was referring to the baptism in the Holy Spirit with speaking in tongues. (Acts 2:1–4.)

Jesus wants you to know the value of the Promise of the Father because He said, "You shall receive power when the Holy Spirit has come upon you; and you shall be witnesses to Me..." He did not say, "You shall **do** witnessing," but "You shall **be** witnesses." In other words, your very person will be a witness to Him!

This is because the power you receive when you are baptized in the Holy Spirit is the same power that so anointed Peter that the sick were laid on the streets for his shadow to fall on them and heal them. (Acts 5:15.) Even handkerchiefs and aprons from Paul's body were so saturated with the anointing of the Spirit that when they touched the sick, people witnessed diseases and evil spirits leaving the sick! (Acts 19:12.)

That same power caused a Holy Spirit-baptized church member, who prayed in tongues, to experience God's healing power when he laid hands on his mother who was in an advanced stage of cancer. And because she was healed, she became a witness of the love and power of God to her friends and unbelieving relatives.

Beloved, when you are baptized in the Holy Spirit, you will be a witness to others that no problem, trial, disease or sickness is a match for the power of the Spirit in you!

Thought for the Day
Your very person will be a witness to Jesus when
you are baptized with the Holy Spirit.

Let Not Your Heart Be Troubled

John 14:27
²⁷Peace I leave with you, My peace I give to you…
Let not your heart be troubled, neither let it be afraid.

The night before Jesus died, He gave His peace to His disciples — "Peace I leave with you, My peace I give to you…" This peace was not just for His disciples, but also for us today. We have His peace.

The moment you believe in Jesus Christ, He who is the Prince of Peace comes to live inside you. And when the Prince of Peace resides in you, every blessing that you will ever need pertaining to your soundness and wholeness is already inside you.

"Pastor Prince, if this is true, then why do I still see problems in my health, finances, family and relationships?"

The answer is a troubled heart. That is why after Jesus said, "Peace I leave with you," He said, "Let not your heart be troubled, neither let it be afraid."

A troubled and fearful heart works like fingers that clamp down hard on a water hose. The supply of water is flowing from the tap, but little or nothing is coming out at the other end of the hose. God's ever-present supply of blessings toward you is like the water flowing freely from the tap. But you don't see the blessings when you allow your heart to be gripped by worry or fear.

So when fearful, anxious thoughts come, remind yourself of Jesus' words: "Let not your heart be troubled, neither let it be afraid." Even when things appear to get worse, say, "Lord, I refuse to worry about this. In the midst of all this, I see the finished work of Christ. He said, 'It is finished!' So my child's healing is accomplished. My marriage is blessed. My debts are cleared. I will let not my heart be troubled by these things."

Beloved, I cannot "let not" for you. Your family and friends cannot "let not" for you. Only **you** can "let not your heart be troubled." So guard your heart from being troubled. You don't have to guard your career, reputation, children or even health. When you guard your heart, God will guard everything else for you!

Thought for the Day
When you guard your heart, God will guard everything else for you!

See Yourself in Christ

Ephesians 1:3
³Blessed be the God and Father of our Lord Jesus Christ, who has blessed
us with every spiritual blessing in the heavenly places in Christ.

I remember going through a terrible time of depression when I was 18 years old. Believing that I was demon-possessed, I sought out a great man of God to have him cast the devil out of me. But when this man of God laid hands on me, he began to prophesy over me. He said, "Joe, I see you preaching to thousands and used by God to impact thousands of lives. Joe, you are called by God and the devil is attempting to stop you."

What? I came here for deliverance! I am only interested in saving my own life, not preaching nor impacting lives, I thought to myself then.

You see, what happened was that at that moment, God allowed this man to step into the timeless zone He exists in to bring my future before me. As far as God was concerned, my future had already happened, though I was only 18 years old then. Today, I am a pastor of a church that has more than 16,000 members. Today, I am seeing what was told to me long ago.

God does not see as we see. Abraham was a childless, 100-year-old man. His wife, Sarah, at 90 years old, was doubly dead in her womb. (Genesis 17:17.) Yet, God saw him and talked to him as if he were already the father of many nations.

My friend, God wants you to see the way He sees. Right now, you may see yourself going through a trial in your marriage, work, finances or health. But God sees a blessed marriage, success at work, supernatural increase in wealth and a healed body because He tells you that you are already blessed with every spiritual blessing in the heavenly places in Christ.

You see, God sees you in Christ. So when you see yourself in Christ, who is outside time, you step into the timeless zone. In that timeless zone in Christ, whatever needs and trials of yours are already removed, repaired, restored or resurrected! In that timeless zone in Christ, you are already blessed with every spiritual blessing in the heavenly places!

Thought for the Day
See yourself the way God sees you — in Christ and blessed with
every spiritual blessing in the heavenly places!

God Has Seen Your Future and It Is Good!

Isaiah 54:2
²"Enlarge the place of your tent, and let them stretch out the curtains of your dwellings; do not spare; lengthen your cords, and strengthen your stakes.

At the end of 2004, during one of our services, the Lord told our church this: "I your God have gone ahead of you and I have already been to your future. I have seen it. And I declare that it is good."

Although this word was given through me to our church, I believe that it is not only for our church, but also for every member of the body of Christ.

I tell you, when God declares your future good, it will be good! It will be filled with many wonderfully good days!

So what do you do when the Lord tells you that you are going to have a good future loaded with His blessings? You prepare for it! In other words, before the blessings come, before the increase comes, He wants you to enlarge the place of your tent and stretch forth the curtains of your dwellings.

For example, if you are believing God for a child, start reading books on babies and preparing the baby's room. In fact, prepare to have more than one child. Start looking for a bigger place for your family for God says, "Enlarge the place of your tent, and let them stretch out the curtains of your dwellings; do not spare; lengthen your cords, and strengthen your stakes." Get ready for expansion!

My friend, God wants you to get ready, and expect such favor and increase in the days ahead that "you shall expand to the right and to the left, and your descendants will inherit the nations, and make the desolate cities inhabited" (v. 3).

Because God has declared your future good, know that you stand on favor ground today. Expect good things to happen to you. Expect to see the favor of God on you and your family. Expect the blessings and increase of the Lord. Expect many good days to show up in your life!

Thought for the Day
Get ready for expansion because the Lord has been to your future and He declares that it is good!

True to Your Assessment

Leviticus 27:12
¹²... the priest shall set a value for it, whether it is good or bad;
as you, the priest, value it, so it shall be.

Your colleague says that this week is going to be a lousy one because the new boss is mean. You disagree and say that it is going to be a blessed week. Both of you will go through the same week, but with very different outcomes. While your friend's week will indeed turn out to be a lousy one, yours will be filled with the favor of the Lord!

In the Old Testament, when someone brought what he had to the priest for a valuation, whatever the priest assessed the value of the item to be, it was so. If he assessed it to be of good value, then it was of good value. If he assessed it to be of poor value, then it was of poor value.

Today, you are also a priest because of Jesus' blood. (Revelation 1:5–6.) And "as you, the priest, value it, so it shall be." If you assess your year to be one of financial breakthroughs, so it will be for you. If you assess your life to be filled with divine health, so it will be for you.

There was a stroke patient who was bedridden. While listening to my recorded sermons, he assessed that with God as his salvation, his life would be long and satisfying. (Psalm 91:16.) He believed that God would help him walk again. Not too long after his assessment, he was able to walk and was no longer bound to the bed! The next assessment he made about his health was complete recovery with God as his helper.

Actually, you have more authority than the Levitical priests of the Old Testament. They were of the old priesthood of mortal men. But you are of the greater and "forever" priesthood of Jesus! (Hebrews 7:8, 17.) Not only that, you are a king-priest. (Revelation 1:6.) In other words, you are a king as well! And as a king, your assessment is also binding because where the word of a king is, there is power! (Ecclesiastes 8:4.)

My friend, this means that you have a double portion of assessment power. Therefore, boldly assess good things for your life, and it will be so for you!

Thought for the Day
As you, the priest, assess your situation, so it shall be.

Forgive and Let God Do the Rest

Ephesians 4:32
³²And be kind to one another, tenderhearted, forgiving one another,
even as God in Christ forgave you.

People like to say, "I can forgive, but I cannot forget." Have you heard that before? Now, in the first place, nowhere in the Bible does God tell you to forgive and then to **forget**. It is not in the Bible! The devil is adding something here to make the whole thing burdensome.

God only tells us to forgive because God in Christ has forgiven us a debt we cannot pay. When we do this, we do ourselves a favor because harboring bitterness and unforgiveness can sometimes destroy our health!

So just forgive and let God take care of the rest. When you really forgive, sometimes, He makes you forget. But sometimes, you still remember the incident because it was a major thing in your life. Yet, when you look back at it, the pain is no more there. The sting is gone and you are not bitter.

Joseph had forgiven his brothers before they came and bowed down to him. He remembered what they did to him, but he did not remember it with bitterness. (Genesis 50:15–21.) So you may remember the incident, but the bitterness is gone because you have put the cross in the picture — "God in Christ forgave me. Daddy, I forgive you. Mama, I forgive you. My cousin, I forgive you."

When you forgive, forgive by faith, not by your feelings. We walk by faith, not feelings. (2 Corinthians 5:7.) Some people are waiting for feelings — "I am waiting, Father, for the right emotion to come on me to forgive that person." That "right emotion" may never come!

No, forgive by faith, and do it once and for all. Spend time in prayer. Take out your diary and write it down: "Father, I bring this person before You. You know what he did to me. Father, as You forgave me through Jesus' cross, even though I did not deserve it, by faith, I now forgive this person and I let my anger against him go in Jesus' name. Amen!"

Once you forgive by faith, you will see the sting of bitterness removed from your heart. You will experience the peace and joy of God filling your mind, and see a greater measure of wholeness in your body!

Thought for the Day
When we forgive others, we free ourselves from bitterness and
unforgiveness, which can destroy our health!

The Life of Jesus Is in You

John 10:10
¹⁰... I [Jesus] have come that they may have life,
and that they may have it more abundantly.

Though Jesus is completely God, He was born completely human. He went through temptation after temptation and conquered every one of them. (Hebrews 4:15.) And all that overcoming power is found in His life. And He put that life in you — the life of Christ is in you!

During Jesus' ministry on earth, He conquered sickness, the winds and waves, the powers of darkness and death. It is His life that brings victory over the devil and all his works. And He put that life in you — the life of Christ is in you!

Finally, Jesus went to the cross. And that life in Him put an end to everything that was natural of the Adamic race — sickness, poverty, failures, pains, curses and death. All that was natural ceased to be in that life of His. But all that was supernatural remained in Him. And He put that life in you — the life of Christ is in you!

Then, Jesus rose from the dead. And in that life of His was added the power of resurrection. And He put that life in you — the life of Christ is in you!

After His resurrection, Jesus went back to heaven to His Father. Today, He is seated at the right hand of God, resting in His finished work, occupying a place of the highest authority. And He put that life in you — the life of Christ is in you!

And because Jesus went back to the Father, the Holy Spirit came to indwell you (John 16:7), so that you will live life with His anointing in you and walk in His overcoming power.

All that Jesus is, God meant for you to be. All that He has, God meant for you to have. All the exciting things that you read in the Bible about Jesus, all the treasures of Him hidden in the Old Testament and the unsearchable riches in Him that you find in the New Testament, all of that life of His, is not out there somewhere. God has deposited all of it in you, so that you can live the abundant life that Jesus came to give you!

Thought for the Day
All that Jesus is and all that He has, God has deposited in you so that
you can live the abundant life that Jesus came to give you!

Blessed in More Ways Than One

Romans 5:1
¹Therefore, having been justified by faith, we have
peace with God through our Lord Jesus Christ.

We are not trying to get peace with God. We already have peace with God, having been justified by faith through our Lord Jesus Christ. This peace **with** God brings us the peace **of** God, which guards our hearts and minds. (Philippians 4:7.) Then, the peace of God **inside** us will also translate into the peace of God **outside** us — in all our outward circumstances.

Firstly, we will find that what would normally cause us much care and anxiety will no longer be the case. Secondly, not only will everything turn out well, but we will also be blessed in more ways than one. This is what happens when Jesus, the Prince of Peace, is our peace.

A church member, though stricken with cancer, enjoyed the peace of God, knowing that He was her healer. She later received confirmation from two different doctors that she had been completely healed of cancer. In addition to receiving her blessing of complete healing, she also received from her insurance company a critical illness claim of $50,000!

Another church member, upon hearing news of her retrenchment, committed the matter to God, believing that He would work all things out for her, especially her loss of a regular income. Shortly after, she received her retrenchment package — a substantial five-figure sum. And within days of her retrenchment, she received calls from her contacts in the industry, offering her jobs, two of which were jobs in well-known multinational corporations (MNCs).

At that time, she had not yet started looking for a job, so the calls were unexpected but welcomed. She finally opted to work for one of the MNCs — a dream come true for her — at a salary that was 30 percent more than her previous one! When she simply prayed, "Abba Father, I trust You to look after me," and rested in His love and peace, she was abundantly blessed.

Beloved, because Jesus is your peace, you are blessed in more ways than one. Your soul will prosper. Your health will prosper. Your finances will prosper. Your loved ones will be taken care of. Your relationships will flourish. You will enjoy the favor of God. All because you have the Prince of Peace!

Thought for the Day
Because you have peace with God and the
peace of God, you are abundantly blessed!

Clothed With Jesus' Robe of Righteousness

Leviticus 1:6
⁶And he shall skin the burnt offering and cut it into its pieces.

D o you know who first clothed man with coats of skin? It was God Almighty Himself, when He found Adam and Eve hiding behind the bushes because they were afraid of Him. They had become fearful and conscious that they had sinned against God. In their sin-consciousness, they realized that they were naked and that the glory of God, which had been their covering, was gone.

So God killed an animal to clothe Adam and Eve with coats of skin. (Genesis 3:21.) An animal had to die and its bloodied skin became their covering. This speaks of the blood of Jesus that covers you when He became your burnt offering. The Lamb of God did not just take away your sins. He also gave you His righteousness.

Beloved, you are covered by Jesus' blood. You are righteous by His blood. God has clothed you with the robe of righteousness, which was paid for by Jesus' blood. I am not talking about a physical robe made of cloth. I am talking about the robe of righteousness that was on Jesus when He said to the storm, "Peace, be still!" and there came a perfect calm (Matthew 8:23–27), when healing flowed from Him to the sick and when He raised Lazarus from the dead. (John 11:38–44.)

When you believe that you are righteous because of Jesus' blood, you will see the effects of wearing His robe of righteousness. You will see miracles happening before your very eyes. You become a blessing magnet, a favor or grace magnet. It is not your own righteousness, but the righteousness of Jesus which you have put on, that is attracting all these blessings of God into your life.

My friend, have the consciousness of being clothed with Jesus' robe of righteousness. Every day, come to God and say, "Father, I thank You that Jesus is my burnt offering. He covers me from head to toe with His righteousness. What He is to You, I am. As He is now, so am I. I am in Him." And you will see the manifestations of the blessings of health, wholeness, protection and prosperity that the robe attracts!

Thought for the Day
It is not your own righteousness, but the righteousness of Jesus which you have put on, that attracts the blessings of God into your life.

He Is the God of Your Valleys Too

1 Kings 20:23
²³ Then the servants of the king of Syria said to him, "Their gods are gods of the hills. Therefore they were stronger than we; but if we fight against them in the plain, surely we will be stronger than they.

In 1 Kings 20, we find the Syrians being defeated by the Israelites. Then, some of the Syrian king's advisers gave the king what they thought was the reason for their defeat. They said that they had fought on the hills and lost because Israel's God is the God of the hills. So if they were to fight the Israelites on the plains or in the valleys, they would win.

What stupid advice! They thought that the God of Israel only helped His people up in the hills and mountains, and not down in the valleys.

Now, mountains refer to our good times, and valleys, our bad times. Some people have this idea that God is the God of our good times, but He is not there when we are going through bad times. They think that He leaves us helpless in the valleys, especially when the troubles are of our own making.

My friend, I want you to know that our God is the God of the mountains, but He is also the God of the valleys!

God the Son laid aside His crown of glory, His royal majesty and came down for us, stepping into a human body as a baby. He came down to where we were for the sole purpose of dying on the cross for our sins, so that He could bring us up to what God the Father has for us at His right hand. Jesus came down to crown us with glory and honor, to clothe us with robes of righteousness and make us His bride, sharing everything that He has with us. That is the grace of God. He came down to our valley.

So whatever you are going through right now, know that God is right there in your valley with you. He is holding you in His arms and carrying you through the valley. Victory is already yours. Just as the Israelites were also victorious in the valley (vv. 28–29), so will you be because the God of the valleys is right there with you!

Thought for the Day
God is right there in your valley with you, holding you in
His arms and carrying you through the valley.

How Tender Is God's Heart Toward You

Ephesians 2:7
⁷That in the ages to come He might show the exceeding riches of
His grace in His kindness toward us in Christ Jesus.

Have you ever blown things out of proportion and gotten angry with God when you were going through a trying time? This happened to Jesus' disciples when a storm hit them hard. In their fear of drowning, they cried out to Jesus, who was getting some much-needed sleep in the boat, "Teacher, do You not care that we are perishing?" (Mark 4:38).

For accusing Him of not caring, you would think that they received a rebuke from Jesus. But it was the wind which received His rebuke, and a great calm followed. (v. 39.) Because of His tenderness toward His own, Jesus did not waste time taking offence. Instead, He wasted no time taking care of the problem that had caused His disciples so much anxiety and fear.

This also happened to two sisters, Martha and Mary, who did not hesitate to let Jesus know how they felt when He finally showed up days after their brother Lazarus had died. Both sisters made the same remark to Him: "Lord, if You had been here, my brother would not have died" (John 11:21, 32).

Both sisters had seen Jesus' miracles of mercy and love. Now, in their grief, they focused on how He could have prevented their brother's death, but did not. They did not know His heart — how tender it was toward them and how His help would never fail them, but would even extend to raising their dead brother. (vv. 41–44.)

Beloved, your heavenly Father sees you trying to stay afloat when you are in the midst of a storm. He sees you trying to provide for yourself and your family, and thinking, *If I don't take care of these things, no one else will!* And He wants you to know how tender His heart is toward you, how He is not offended by all the bad things you have ever said of or to Him. He wants you to know how much He wants to and will help and bless you. So let go and experience afresh the exceeding riches of His grace in His kindness toward you!

Thought for the Day
In the midst of your storm, Jesus wants you to know that
He wants to and will help and bless you.

Righteousness and Not Sin
Imputed to You

Romans 4:8
8"Blessed is the man to whom the LORD shall not impute sin."

Y ou are blessed today because all your sins are forgiven in Christ. God does not count your sins against you. Instead, He counts you righteous in Christ. That is why you are the blessed man to whom the Lord **does not** and **will not** impute sin!

What happens to such a person? Let's look at the story of Jacob to find out.

The Bible records how Jacob had deceived his father and cheated his elder brother, Esau, of his firstborn blessing. (Genesis 27:1–41.) Yet, in spite of his sin of deception, God chose to speak to Jacob. And no, God did not say to this cheat, "You terrible sinner! How can you deceive your own father? You are cursed!"

No, to deceitful Jacob, God said, "I am the LORD God of Abraham your father and the God of Isaac; the land on which you lie I will give to you and your descendants… Behold, I am with you and will keep you wherever you go, and will bring you back to this land; for I will not leave you until I have done what I have spoken to you" (Genesis 28:13–15). Here was a man to whom God did not impute sin!

God did not rebuke Jacob at all. Instead, we hear Him telling Jacob, "I will give to you… I am with you… I will keep you… I will bring you back… I will not leave you…" Jacob certainly did not deserve these blessings. This is one man who walked in the truth of Romans 4:8 — "Blessed is the man to whom the LORD shall not impute sin"! Now, I am not encouraging you to sin, but I want you to see the love and grace of God toward us.

If Jacob was so blessed, how much more you and I today, who are under the new covenant of grace established by the blood of Jesus. How much more is our blessedness because Jesus has removed all our sins at the cross!

Beloved, because of Jesus' finished work, God does not impute sin to you. What He does impute to you is **righteousness** apart from works. (v. 6) And because you are righteous, get ready for His blessings! (Proverbs 10:6.)

Thought for the Day
Because of Jesus' finished work, God does not impute sin to you,
but righteousness apart from works.

When God Ran

Luke 15:22
²²"But the father said to his servants, 'Bring out the best robe and put it on him, and put a ring on his hand and sandals on his feet."

If you are a believer, you are probably familiar with the touching story of the prodigal son that Jesus shared. Who do you think the father in the story represents? Jesus' Father in heaven, of course. Jesus was giving us a picture of His Father, who is also our Father.

In the story, the father was seen running toward his son, who was returning home. (v. 20.) Do you realize that God is never described as being in a hurry in the Bible? He is always cool and composed. The only time He is portrayed as being in a hurry is in this story. Though improper in Jewish culture, the father held up his robe and ran. Where was he running to? Why was he in such a hurry?

The father was in a hurry because he had seen his son, who was still a long way from home. He was running toward his son as he could not wait to embrace and kiss his child again.

The father was in a hurry to clothe his son with the best robe. My friend, our Father has put the best robe — the robe of righteousness — on us. In doing so, He has reinstated us as sons of the Most High God, a position that we had lost when Adam fell.

The father was in a hurry to put a ring on his son's hand. Like the authority that is invested in the signet ring of a rich man's son, our Father is eager to put back into our hands the authority to invoke His name, so that we can walk in dominion every day.

The father was in a hurry to put sandals on his son's feet to assure him that he was still his son — only servants went about barefoot. Our Father never wants us to feel like hired servants or outcasts. We are always His sons.

Beloved, if the Father appears to be in a hurry, it is only because He is in a hurry to assure you of your position as His precious child!

Thought for the Day
If the Father appears to be in a hurry, it is only because He is in a hurry to assure you of your position as His precious child!

'Help Me Pray, Holy Spirit'

Jude 1:20
²⁰But you, beloved, building yourselves up on your
most holy faith, praying in the Holy Spirit.

When my daughter Jessica was little, she woke up one night crying. She was not sick, but would not stop crying even though her mother and I tried to pacify her. I did not know what to do. I went to the restroom, sat on the floor and cried out, "Holy Spirit, You know what is wrong with my child. You know what she needs better than I do, so I yield her to You now." I started praying in tongues and she stopped crying immediately!

Now, I wish that such instantaneous results are the norm, but they are not. On another occasion, I experienced severe pain from the back of my neck to my shoulders. I prayed for healing, but the pain persisted for quite some time and I was quite concerned.

One night, in my room, I knelt down and prayed, "Holy Spirit, You know this condition. I don't know what it is, but I am asking You to make perfect prayer against this condition." I started praying in tongues. I don't know how long I prayed, maybe an hour or so, until I felt the burden lift. I finally fell asleep, still in pain. But when I woke up, all the pain was gone!

When you are faced with a crisis, you can tell the Holy Spirit, "I don't know how to pray about this problem. I have done everything I know, but I don't seem to be getting my breakthrough. Help me pray, Holy Spirit."

And as you pray in the Spirit, you will feel like there is a prayer going on within you. Flow with it until you feel a release. You will feel peace, the burden lifting and a note of victory inside you. The Holy Spirit will assure you that everything is going to be all right or He will prompt you to do something. Then, you will find that what has been hindering you from receiving your breakthrough is removed, and in its place is the answer you need!

Thought for the Day
When you don't know what else to do and don't seem to be getting the
breakthrough you need, ask the Holy Spirit to help you pray.

Jesus' Blood Is on the Mercy Seat

Leviticus 16:14
¹⁴He shall take some of the blood of the bull and sprinkle it with his finger on the mercy seat on the east side; and before the mercy seat he shall sprinkle some of the blood with his finger seven times.

If you have watched the movie, *Raiders of the Lost Ark*, you would remember that when the lid of the ark was lifted, strange-looking creatures floated out and destroyed the people around it. Interesting as it may be, this is biblically inaccurate — the ark of the Bible did not contain strange-looking creatures. What were the things inside it then?

There were three items in the ark: the golden pot of manna, Aaron's rod and two stone tablets on which God had written the Ten Commandments. (Hebrews 9:4.) These items are actually symbols of man's rebellion. The golden pot of manna represents man's rejection of God's provision. The rod of Aaron represents man's rejection of God's leadership and the two stone tablets of God's commandments represent man's rejection of His standard of holiness.

But because God delights in mercy, He had these items put away in the ark and covered with the mercy seat, which had two cherubim on it. (Hebrews 9:5.) And once a year, the high priest would enter the holy of holies where the ark was and sprinkle the blood of the animal sacrifice on the mercy seat. This means that God's eyes, represented by the eyes of the cherubim, did not see the symbols of man's rebellion. As long as the blood was there on the mercy seat, He saw only the blood and accepted the people.

Today, Jesus is our High Priest and He Himself has sprinkled His own blood on the true mercy seat in heaven — the throne of grace. (vv. 23–26.) Interestingly, the number of times that the Old Testament high priest had to sprinkle the blood on the mercy seat — seven — speaks of Jesus' **perfect** sacrifice. And because His sacrifice is perfect and He is perfect, we who are in Christ have perfect standing forever before God!

My friend, as you come to God today, don't worry about falling short of His standard of holiness. He does not see your sins. (Hebrews 8:12, 10:17.) He sees His Son's blood on the mercy seat. You have perfect standing before Him forever!

Thought for the Day
God does not see your sins. He sees only His Son's blood on the mercy seat.

Sin Cannot Stop God's Grace!

Romans 5:20
²⁰Moreover the law entered that the offense might abound.
But where sin abounded, grace abounded much more.

When a top executive is charged for corruption or a church minister is caught in the very act of adultery, you will probably hear the phrase "fallen from grace" being used of them. We have come to believe that when someone falls into sin, he falls from grace.

But God wants us to know that when someone falls into sin, he does not fall from grace — he actually falls **into** grace! Thank God His grace is there to put the person back on his feet.

The Bible tells of prostitutes and corrupt tax collectors — sinners — who fell into God's grace and got back on their feet. If the sin in their lives could stop God's grace, they would never have been able to receive His grace of healing, help and power to live right.

Now, it is important you understand that God hates sin because it destroys our lives, relationships and bodies. Sin is evil! But sin is not overcome by us talking about it and relying on our willpower to overcome it. It takes God's grace to destroy sin. In fact, it is when you are under His grace that sin has no dominion over you. (Romans 6:14.) It is when you see His grace in providing His Son to put away your sins and make you eternally righteous that sin will not dominate you.

The devil will say to you, "You think that you can still expect God's blessings after what you did this morning?" That is when you must remind yourself that Christ alone is your perfection and righteousness. All of us have faults. None of us deserve God's blessings. That is why we plead the grace of God, which is His unearned, unmerited and undeserved favor toward us.

Sin does not and cannot stop God's grace. If His grace can be cut off by sin, Jesus would never have come to save us because we were all terrible sinners. But praise God, "where sin abounded, grace abounded much more"!

My friend, God's grace is bigger, deeper, wider and more powerful than all the world's sins put together. Receive His grace right now to walk in total victory over that weakness or evil habit in your life!

Thought for the Day
God's grace is bigger, deeper, wider and more powerful than
all the world's sins put together.

Know and Believe God's Love for You

1 John 4:16
16And we have known and believed the love that God has for us....

You may know that God cares for you and loves you, and that He demonstrated His love for you by dying on the cross for you, but do you believe it? It is one thing to **know** about the love that God has for you, but another thing to actually **believe** it in your heart.

It is one thing to know that the sun shines on us during the day. But it is another thing to believe that the sun is still shining even though we don't feel its warmth and all we see are dark clouds. Sometimes we are slow in believing God's love for us when we are going through a tough time. But God wants you to know and believe that He loves you in the midst of the deal falling through, when that job is slow in coming, when the boss is fault-finding or when your child still refuses to come home.

In the midst of the pain, He wants you to know and believe that He is wholly on your side defending and taking care of you. And if God, the most powerful being in the universe, is for you, can anyone or anything come against you successfully?

Perhaps you feel like you have messed up big time. God wants you to know and believe that though others may be angry with you, He will never be angry with you. Neither will He condemn you. The sum total of His anger against your sins fell upon Jesus at the cross. So He wants you to know and believe that He will never punish you because Jesus was punished in your place.

When you feel unworthy because you have just blown it for the umpteenth time, know and believe that your heavenly Father still offers you the gift of no condemnation. So come boldly to His throne of grace to obtain mercy and find grace. (Hebrews 4:16.)

My friend, know and believe that since He loved you and died for you while you were still a sinner (Romans 5:8) at your worst and ugliest, how much more is His love for you now that you are His beloved child and the righteousness of God in Christ! (2 Corinthians 5:21.)

Thought for the Day
**If God, the most powerful being in the universe, is for you,
can anyone or anything come against you successfully?**

Expect Good Things to Happen to You

Ephesians 6:17
¹⁷And take the helmet of salvation...

When the phone rings at odd times, most people think, *Oh dear, it must be bad news.* They don't think, *I wonder what the good news is that it cannot wait till morning!*

When we hear, "The boss wants to see you," instinctively, we think, *Oh dear, this is not good.* But how do we know that it is not going to be about a promotion?

Our minds are inclined toward the negative. So to guard our minds against negative thoughts, we are to put on "the helmet of salvation," which is "the hope of salvation" (1 Thessalonians 5:8).

If you are going through a trial right now, putting on as a helmet the hope of salvation means that you have a confident expectation of good coming your way. It means that you choose to believe that this trial that you are going through is only temporary because God will see you through it. It means that you believe that this difficult period will end with your salvation — your preservation, wholeness, wellness, health and prosperity!

You may not know what is going to happen this week. But one thing you can do is to put on the helmet of the hope of salvation and tell yourself that you are going to have a fantastic week!

"Well, you know, Pastor Prince, you never know what to expect. We hear so much bad news these days — another flu outbreak, another company retrenching its workers... I really hope that I will not be retrenched next. But I cannot be sure. I am keeping my fingers crossed."

No, my friend, biblical hope is not "I hope so" but "I know so"! You can have a confident expectation of good happening to you because you are not like the people of the world. You are a child of the living God. You have a Savior watching over you. There are more angels given charge over you than there are demons against you. And greater is He that is in you than he that is in the world. (1 John 4:4.) There is every reason for you to have a confident expectation of good happening to you!

Thought for the Day
As a child of the living God, you can have a confident
expectation of good happening to you.

The Lord With You Equals Success

Genesis 39:2
²The LORD was with Joseph, and he was a successful man...

Y ou may have no qualification, position or wealth — nothing in the natural. But when the Lord is with you, you will end up with everything because He will cause you to be successful.

Joseph had nothing when his Egyptian master Potiphar bought him from the slave market. Yet, even then, it was said of him, "The Lord was with Joseph, and he was a successful man..."

Joseph the slave a successful man? He was a nobody with nothing, not even a shirt on his back, not a dime to his name, no family members with him and no friends to turn to. All he had was the presence of the Lord. But it was precisely because of this that he was successful wherever he was. He eventually became the most powerful man in Egypt, second only to Pharaoh, who set him over all the land of Egypt. Joseph was given power, authority and riches (Genesis 41:40–44), all because the Lord was with him.

A junior college student worshiping in our church experienced good success in his examination results for the same reason. The first to admit that he was just an average student, he obtained his first ever straight As for all his subjects when he sat for the Singapore-Cambridge General Certificate of Education (Advanced Level) Examination simply believing that he would be successful because the Lord was with him!

Another church member, who was a fresh university graduate, believed that because the Lord was with her, she would be successful in the workforce. Even though she had no work experience and was faced with a gloomy job market, she succeeded in getting her first job in a short period of time and which gave her a salary beyond her expectations. Then, in spite of a directive from the parent company to freeze the wages of all employees, she received a pay increment as well as a company scholarship for further education!

Beloved, it does not matter if you are a nobody with nothing in the natural. When the Lord is with you, you will end up with everything because He will empower you to succeed, prosper and live the abundant life. Indeed, you will end up enjoying His favor, goodness and grace!

Thought for the Day
When the Lord is with you, you will end up with everything because He will empower you to succeed, prosper and live the abundant life.

Forgiveness Is for the Undeserving

Matthew 18:21
²¹Then Peter came to Him and said, "Lord, how often shall my brother sin against me, and I forgive him? Up to seven times?"

Peter asked the Lord how often he should forgive his brother. The Lord's answer to him was simple: up to 70 times seven times. (v. 22.) In other words, all the time!

"Well, Pastor Prince, he does not deserve my forgiveness."

Neither did you deserve God's forgiveness.

There is not a single person alive or dead who did not break all ten of God's commandments. There is no such thing as a "partial sinner" or "great sinner." All of us were great sinners when Jesus saved us. And when we realize that we are forgiven much, we will love much. (Luke 7:47.)

"Pastor Prince, how can you say that I have broken all of God's commandments? I have never committed adultery."

My friend, Jesus said, "If you lust after a woman in your heart, you have already committed adultery with her." (Matthew 5:28.) That is God's standard. Man looks outward, but God looks inward at the heart. Moreover, if you break one law, you are guilty of all. (James 2:10.) So everyone has broken all of God's commandments. Everyone is a great sinner.

Now, you are no longer a sinner if you have received Christ as your Savior. You are a new creation. But you were a great sinner and God forgave you your huge debt through the death of His Son.

So if someone has wronged you, tell yourself this: "I did not deserve God's forgiveness, but He forgave me through Christ. So I forgive this person also." If you say something like, "He does not deserve it," it makes no sense. Forgiveness is not for people who deserve it. If they deserve anything, it is punishment. But forgiveness means that you extend grace — undeserved favor — like how God extends undeserved favor to you.

Beloved, if you choose to hold on to bitterness, no one suffers but you. You lose your peace, then possibly your health. It is just not worth it. God says to you, "Let go. Forgive them their debts, just as I have forgiven you yours."

Thought for the Day
When we realize that we are forgiven much, we will love much.

Good Success Is in Your Mouth

Joshua 1:8
⁸This Book of the Law shall not depart from your mouth, but you shall
meditate in it day and night… For then you will make your way
prosperous, and then you will have good success.

I had always wondered why the Torah (the first five books of Moses) is read out loud by the Jews. Then, a Jewish Christian told me that for generations, they read God's Word out loud because of Joshua 1:8 — "This Book of the Law shall not depart from your mouth, but you shall **meditate** in it day and night…"

The word "meditate" in English means to ponder. But in Hebrew, it is the word *hagah*, which means to utter or mutter under your breath. In other words, when you meditate on God's Word, you speak forth or confess His Word instead of just giving it mental assent.

My friend, *hagah* God's Word by confessing verses in the areas that you are believing God for breakthroughs. When I was working in sales, I confessed verses like, "Honor the LORD with your possessions, and with the firstfruits of all your increase; so your barns will be filled with plenty…" (Proverbs 3:9–10). In the first year, I became the top salesman in my company! My way was made prosperous and I enjoyed good success.

"Pastor Prince, I am waiting for God to make my way prosperous."

No, the Bible says that you will make your way prosperous when you *hagah* God's Word. So speak forth verses in the areas which you want to see breakthroughs and you will have good success.

Some people have success that destroys them — you don't see them in church anymore and their family members don't get to see them either. That is **bad** success. But when you *hagah* God's Word, you will have **good** success that does not destroy you.

Now, confessing God's Word does not move God to do things for you. It is not a formula. God had already moved when He gave up Jesus to die for you. However, when you confess His Word, it moves you from a position of doubt to faith. It moves your heart from a position of "Is it true?" to "I believe it!" When that happens, "you will make your way prosperous, and then you will have good success"!

Thought for the Day
When you meditate on God's Word, you speak forth or confess
His Word instead of just giving it mental assent.

You Will Have Whatever You Say

Mark 11:23
*²³For assuredly, I say to you, whoever says to this mountain, 'Be removed and
be cast into the sea,' and does not doubt in his heart, but believes that
those things he says will be done, he will have whatever he says.*

God says that we will have whatever we say. So whatever we want to have,
we can say it and have it. Unfortunately, we often say what we **don't**
want to have.

For example, we say, "I don't know why I go through my money so fast
every month. Even when my boss gives me an increment, there never seems to
be enough money." And true enough, we see a lack of money at the end of every
month.

You see, you will have whatever you say, good or bad. So why not change what
you have been saying to, "From now on, I will have more than enough because
Jesus became poor at the cross, so that I might become rich — 2 Corinthians 8:9.
So poverty, be gone in Jesus' name!"

Whatever mountain of difficulty you have, be it a mountain of debt or serious
health condition, Jesus says, "For assuredly, I say to you, whoever **says** to this mountain, 'Be removed and be cast into the sea,' and does not doubt in his heart, but
believes that those things he **says** will be done, he will have whatever he **says**."

Jesus highlights the importance of saying by mentioning the word "say" three
times, but the word "believe" only once. Our problem today is that there is more
preaching on believing than saying. So the reason people find it hard to walk in
faith is that they are not saying enough of the Word.

But if we would focus more on saying God's Word, faith will come. That
is how God quickened Abraham's faith. He changed what Abraham was saying when He changed his name from Abram to Abraham, which means "father
of many nations" (Genesis 17:5). From then on, whenever Abraham introduced
himself, he would say, "Hi, my name is Father of Many Nations."

Beloved, declare your abundance, saying, "The Lord is my shepherd, I shall
not want." (Psalm 23:1.) Speak forth your healing, saying, "By Jesus' stripes I am
healed!" (Isaiah 53:5.) And you will have whatever you say!

Thought for the Day
Whatever we want to have, we can say it and have it.

God Daily Loads You With Benefits

Deuteronomy 28:6
⁶Blessed shall you be when you come in,
and blessed shall you be when you go out.

In the Jewish community, the promise, "Blessed shall you be when you come in, and blessed shall you be when you go out," refers to being blessed in the affairs of one's daily life, whether in or outside one's home.

So here, God is saying that you are blessed in your everyday life. Do you believe it? Do you believe that every day, your family and work life are blessed? Or do you think that you are blessed only during Christmas when you receive your gifts and year-end bonus, or when you get that promotion you have been wanting? Perhaps you think that the blessed life only begins when you meet the man or woman of your dreams!

No, my friend, you are blessed every day and you have God's Word for it. Psalm 68:19 says, "Blessed be the Lord, who **daily loads us with benefits**, the God of our salvation!" And because God's Word says so, believe that every day of your life is loaded with benefits. Every morning, when you get up, believe that it is a day that the Lord has made, and rejoice and be glad in it. (Psalm 118:24.) Start the day expecting it to be loaded with the benefits that God has prepared just for you.

At night, when it is time to sleep, know that you will be blessed when you get up in the morning because there will be another load of benefits from your heavenly Father, who so loves you unconditionally, waiting for you!

You can't make your blessings happen. But if you will just believe what God has said in His Word and act like it is so, the blessings will manifest in your life. In fact, God wants to bless you more than you want to be blessed! His Word declares it: "Blessed shall you be when you come in, and blessed shall you be when you go out… Blessed be the Lord, who daily loads us with benefits, the God of our salvation!"

Beloved, believe God's Word. Believe Him for the blessings and you will find yourself loaded with His daily benefits!

Thought for the Day
Start the day expecting it to be loaded with the
benefits that God has prepared for you.

Claim Your Restoration!

Acts 3:20–21
²⁰... that He may send Jesus Christ, who was preached to you before,
²¹whom heaven must receive until the times of restoration of all things....

As a believer, you have a right to expect restoration of the things that the devil has stolen from you. It may be your health, marriage or finances, but payback time is definitely coming!

Acts 3:20–21 tells us that before Jesus comes back for His church, we will experience "the times of restoration of all things." What a hope that gives us, knowing that God will restore to us all things before Jesus returns!

My friend, if the devil is attacking you in any area, tell God, "Father, I will not allow the devil to rob me of my health, marriage, children or finances. These blessings are blood-bought and paid for by Your Son!" Claim your restoration in Christ and heaven will hear you.

There will be such times of restoration of all things to the body of Christ that His people will only get better, stronger, healthier, and more prosperous and glorious! When God restored, even under the old covenant, His people always received much more than what they had originally lost, in terms of quality and/or quantity. How much more will our restoration be under the new covenant because of the shed blood of the Lamb of God!

A divorcee with a teenage son came to our church and accepted the Lord in May 2003. She began to pray for the restoration of her marriage and the reunion of her family. She knew that the chances of this happening were close to zero since she had not met nor spoken with her ex-husband since their divorce 10 years earlier. She did not even know if he had remarried. But God caused their paths to cross at a wedding at the end of 2003. Today, their relationship is healed, and together with their son, they worship as a family in church.

Even though what happened for that sister may not happen for every divorced person (God can give you a better spouse and marriage), I believe that God wants you to know that your times of restoration are here. Heaven is waiting to hear you stake your claim for restoration!

Thought for the Day
You have a right to expect restoration of the
things that the devil has stolen from you.

God Is Raining Blessings on You

Deuteronomy 28:12
¹²The LORD will open to you His good treasure, the heavens, to give the rain to
your land in its season, and to bless all the work of your hand.
You shall lend to many nations, but you shall not borrow.

In the Bible, rain usually speaks of blessings. Even today, Israelis thank God when it rains because they know that when He gives them rain, their blessings will be plentiful. Their cattle will feed in large green pastures and eat cured, winnowed fodder. And when they see rivers and streams of water flowing from their mountains and hills (Isaiah 30:23–25), they know that times of refreshing have come.

Likewise, you can expect God to rain His blessings on you and bless the work of your hands. Then, you will come to a place where you will "lend to many nations, but you shall not borrow." In fact, Jesus wants you to know that this is a blessing which He died to give you because when He died, He did not even have a tomb of His own. He was laid in a **borrowed** tomb, so that you can have the power to **lend**.

Indeed, our church bears testimony to this blessing. When I first joined the church full-time, it was very small — about 100-odd members. The Lord has, however, rained His blessings on us and blessed the work of our hands. Today, we have a congregation of more than 16,000 members and we are still growing. In fact, our church is lending its support to many ministries, both locally and overseas. We continue to see God pouring His blessings of prosperity and increase on us, and we thank Him for all the good things that are happening to us.

My friend, there is nothing you can do about the rain but to let it fall. So just expect God to rain His blessings on you! Let them fall! And you will be blessed with more than enough, so that with your needs and your family's needs more than met, you can be a blessing to others too!

Thought for the Day
When God rains His blessings on you, you will be blessed with
more than enough so that you can be a blessing to others.

Called From Your Mother's Womb

Galatians 1:15
15... God, who separated me from my mother's womb and
called me through His grace.

Beloved, you are not an accident with no destiny. God has called you from your mother's womb. You have a special calling and a destiny in Christ, and it is all by His grace!

There are Christians who are called by God to be doctors. But I believe that among them are those separated from their mothers' wombs for the healing ministry. They are passionate about seeking cures to alleviate the sufferings of humanity.

Likewise, I think that there are Christians who are called by God to be teachers in secular schools. But among them are those separated from their mothers' wombs to be Bible teachers. What gives them tremendous fulfillment is seeing lives saved and transformed under their teaching.

What about those famous magicians you see performing tricks on television? They have a love for the mystical and supernatural. If they were to become Christians, they might just become prophets with ministries marked by the miraculous!

The apostle Paul knew that he was called from his mother's womb. He had a misguided passion for God though, as he was persecuting the church, until he had his encounter with Jesus. (Acts 8:3, 9:1–6.)

If Paul, a terrorist to the early church, could be touched by Christ to become an apostle of grace, what about today's terrorists who blow up people in the name of their god? For all you know, if they receive Christ, they might just become trailblazers in the kingdom of God!

Now, don't think that your calling has to do with your qualifications, abilities, achievements or even your walk with God. You were called from your mother's womb by His grace. As a fetus in your mother's womb, there was not much you could do — good or bad. That is why your calling is all by His grace. And since He has given you a calling, ask the Holy Spirit to help you discern the desires that He has placed in your heart, the passions that drive you in life, and fulfill your calling and destiny in Christ!

Thought for the Day
By the grace of God, you have a special calling and destiny in Christ!

Your Standing Is Wrapped Up in Jesus

Hebrews 2:17
¹⁷Therefore, in all things He had to be made like His brethren,
that He might be a merciful and faithful High Priest in things
pertaining to God, to make propitiation for the sins of the people.

In the Old Testament, the Israelites' standing as a nation before God was wrapped up in the standing of their high priest. What the high priest was before God, so was the entire nation before God.

If the high priest sinned, he brought guilt on his nation, and God would reject the entire nation no matter how law-abiding the people were or how faithful they were in bringing their sacrifices.

Conversely, if their high priest was without fault and acceptable to God, God would accept the whole nation even if the people were sinful.

Unfortunately, the high priests of Israel often failed because like any human being, they were imperfect.

Thank God that today, you and I have Jesus as our High Priest, who is 100 percent Man and 100 percent God. As our High Priest, His standing before God is always right. Jesus is always acceptable and pleasing to the Father. Therefore, we can never lose our acceptance with God because as our High Priest, Jesus only brings righteousness on His people.

In heaven right now, Jesus our High Priest is seated at the right hand of God the Father. (Romans 8:34.) This means that God does not look at you. He looks at Jesus. If Jesus is good, you are good. If Jesus is accepted, you are accepted. If God sees Jesus perfect, then He sees you perfect. If Jesus is righteous, then you are righteous. And we know that Jesus our High Priest is good, accepted, perfect and righteous, which means that that is how God sees us!

My friend, you cannot lose your right standing because Jesus Christ **is** your High Priest. To lose your standing, Jesus has to lose His standing first. But we know that we have in Jesus a High Priest who is perfect and who cannot fail. So you need never be afraid or conscious of your faults when you come before God. Because your standing is completely wrapped up in Jesus your High Priest, you can come to God boldly and receive all that you need from Him!

Thought for the Day
God sees us the way He sees Jesus our High Priest —
good, accepted, perfect and righteous.

Christ Is the Treasure in You

2 Corinthians 4:7
[7]But we have this treasure in earthen vessels, that the
excellence of the power may be of God and not of us.

The verse tells us that we have "this treasure" in earthen vessels. Who is the treasure? Christ! Who are the earthen vessels here? You and I! Thank God the treasure is in the earthen vessels.

My friend, Christ the treasure is in you, so don't get frustrated when you see your "earthiness." You will always be "earthen" as long as you are in your mortal body, but remember that Christ the treasure is in you.

Should you lose your cool with your spouse or children, remember that Christ in you is your patience. When I feel impatient, I don't pray, "Lord Jesus, give me patience... now!" No, I look to Jesus and I say, "Lord Jesus, I thank You that You are my patience."

In my younger days and even when I first got married, I had a bad temper. I tried all sorts of anger management techniques, but I never got very far until I told God, "God, I am so frustrated trying to overcome my anger. I give up! I cannot. You can. I rest and depend on You." Not too long after that, my wife commented, "You know, you have improved in the area of your temper."

I thought about what she had said and realized that I was not even conscious of the change in me. When family members can see the patience of Christ manifesting through a naturally impatient person, God gets the glory.

Perhaps you are frustrated with your smoking and drinking habits. Or maybe you are discouraged by your feelings of jealousy, distrust, bitterness, depression and defeat. Don't condemn yourself for being earthen. Don't try to "cast out" your earthiness. Just realize that you have Christ the treasure in you.

The more you see that treasure in you, the more Christ's brilliance shines forth in you. And in the midst of your earthiness, God gets the glory as you yourself are transformed from glory to glory! (2 Corinthians 3:18.)

Thought for the Day
The more you see Christ the treasure in you, the more
Christ's brilliance shines forth in you.

The God of More-Than-Enough

Luke 5:9
⁹For he and all who were with him were astonished at the
catch of fish which they had taken.

As a young Christian, I grew up hearing preachers say that God only supplies our needs, not our wants. Yet, in the Bible, God clearly shows us that He wants to meet not just our needs, but also our wants.

For example, the famous "shepherd psalm" begins with "The Lord is my shepherd; I **shall not want**" (Psalm 23:1). Another psalm says, "Oh, fear the LORD, you His saints! **There is no want** to those who fear Him. The young lions lack and suffer hunger; but those who seek the LORD shall not lack any good thing" (Psalm 34:9–10).

One of the names of our God is *Jehovah Jireh*, which means "the all-providing One." He provides more than enough. The God of more-than-enough came in the flesh and walked among His people. And as He walked by the Sea of Galilee, He did not give His disciples small blessings. That is why He said to Peter, "Launch out into the deep and let down your **nets** [plural] for a catch" (Luke 5:4), and not "let down your **net** [singular]." And what a catch it turned out to be — a boat-sinking, net-breaking catch! It was such a big and unexpected blessing that Peter "and all who were with him were astonished at the catch of fish which they had taken."

Beloved, see God's heart for you today. He wants to prosper you greatly. Don't settle for anything less, thinking that He only supplies your needs and not your wants. If you need a job, know that He wants you to pray not just for a job, but for a position. When you have a position, you have influence and you are able to impact lives. Maybe what you need is a pay increment. Then, pray not just for that, but also to be in a position to give increments!

You may start out poor when you follow God. But you cannot remain poor when you follow the God of more-than-enough. In fact, like Peter, you too will be astonished that God supplies more than what you need and beyond what you have asked!

Thought for the Day
The God of more-than-enough wants to meet
not just your needs, but also your wants.

Just Trust God's Goodness and Pray in the Spirit

1 Corinthians 14:14
¹⁴For if I pray in a tongue, my spirit prays, but my understanding is unfruitful.

God has given us a powerful prayer gift — praying in tongues, which is not limited by distance, time or head knowledge. When you pray in tongues, you could be praying for your future or even a loved one overseas. You won't know what you are praying unless God tells you. This is because your "understanding is unfruitful" — your mind is not involved.

"But Pastor Prince, I must know what I am praying!"

Sometimes, it is better not to know what you are praying. In 1993, I had a long season of praying in the Spirit. If I had known then everything that I was praying in tongues, I would have freaked out! For example, I would have been afraid if I had known that the Holy Spirit was saying, "Father God, in the year 2002, anoint Joseph Prince to preach six messages every week to more than 10,000 people." That has come to pass. But back in 1993, one service was enough to tire me out!

So I thank God that I don't know what I am praying when I pray in tongues. I simply trust His goodness and pray in tongues for everything that He has planned for me to come to pass in His perfect timing.

Beloved, don't stop praying in tongues just because you don't know what you are praying. You could be praying for the safety of a loved one in a life and death situation. Especially when you feel an urge to pray because you sense danger, pray! Pray until you sense a release as the burden is lifted. The Holy Spirit will know exactly what is going on, who is in danger and how to pray for deliverance. (Romans 8:27.)

You may say, "Well, I can just pray in English." You can, but your prayer will be very limited because you don't know everything. It is better to pray in tongues because the Spirit knows all things.

My friend, you don't belong to the natural, limited realm. You belong to God who is unlimited! So pray in tongues, and see great things happening for you and through you.

Thought for the Day
It is to our advantage to pray in tongues because the Spirit knows all things.

No Leaven but the Truth

Leviticus 2:11
*¹¹'No grain offering which you bring to the LORD shall be
made with leaven, for you shall burn no leaven nor
any honey in any offering to the LORD made by fire.*

When I was a young Christian, I heard of an illustration for Psalm 23 about shepherds who sometimes break the legs of sheep which habitually stray, so as to teach them not to stray. That erroneous teaching — "The Lord is my Shepherd, He breaketh my legs" — stuck with me for years, causing me needless fear of God's punishment when I felt that I had strayed from Him.

Such erroneous teachings are what God's Word refers to as "leaven." That is why Jesus cautioned His disciples, "Take heed and beware of the **leaven** of the Pharisees and the Sadducees" (Matthew 16:6). The leaven of the Pharisees was their doctrine of legalism, which judges and condemns people who fail to keep God's laws. The leaven of the Sadducees was their doctrine of humanism, which discounts the supernatural and teaches that everything can be explained away using reasoning or science.

When God told His people in Leviticus 2:11, "No grain offering which you bring to the LORD shall be made with leaven," we are reminded that how we appreciate Jesus, our grain offering, must not be mixed with wrong teachings. For example, when we talk about suffering with Christ (Romans 8:17), we must know that it is not about suffering sicknesses or lack, things which Jesus has redeemed us from, but suffering persecution, scorn and rejection for His name's sake, which we are likely to face as good Christians.

My friend, what you believe about Jesus is important because the Holy Spirit bears witness only to the truth. (John 16:13.) So ask Him to unveil the beauty of Christ and the perfection of His finished work to you when you read God's Word. Find out from the Word how Christ has redeemed you from every curse and paid for you to enjoy all of God's blessings with His sacrifice at the cross.

Beloved, get rid of any leaven in your believing. Believe and declare that you are healed, not sick; prosperous, not poor; and forever righteous in Christ. And when you start believing and confessing God's truths, the anointing of the Holy Spirit will be released for the breakthrough you need!

Thought for the Day
**What you believe about Jesus is important because the
Holy Spirit bears witness only to the truth.**

Ask in Jesus' Name and Receive

John 16:23
23 "... Most assuredly, I say to you, whatever you ask the
Father in My name He will give you."

D o you always end your prayers with "in Jesus' name"? Maybe your Sunday school teacher taught you to do this, or maybe you have heard church leaders and other believers utter it at the end of their prayers.

I used to say "in Jesus' name" very quickly as if those were magic words that would get my prayers answered. Then, one day, I heard the Lord asking me why I was doing that.

The Lord wanted me to realize that whenever I pray and say "in Jesus' name," I am putting my entire faith for my prayer to be answered not in who I am or what I have done, but in the person and name of our Lord and Savior Jesus Christ, and what He has done at the cross!

Whenever we ask God for anything in Jesus' name, Jesus says to us, "Most assuredly, I say to you, whatever you ask the Father in My name He will give you." This means that in your prayer for healing, when you say "in Jesus' name," healing comes over your sick body because it is by His stripes that you are healed. (1 Peter 2:24.) In your prayer for protection, when you say "in Jesus' name," you are kept safe because the blood of Jesus protects and delivers you from evil. (Exodus 12:13.)

Beloved, the good name of your family cannot save you. Your pastor's name cannot save you. Even the name of the latest medical breakthrough cannot save you. Only one name under heaven can save you — Jesus! And the good news is that His name in Hebrew, *Yeshua*, means salvation — healing, preservation, wholeness, wellness, provision, prosperity, safety and deliverance for you and your family!

So these days, whenever I pray, I slow down at the end of my prayer and say, "Father, I ask all this not based on what I have or have not done, but based on Jesus and His finished work at the cross. I ask all this in Jesus' name. Amen!"

Thought for the Day
Jesus assures us that whatever we ask the Father in
His name, the Father will give to us.

Use Your Double Portion of Speaking Power

1 Peter 2:9
⁹But you are a chosen generation, a royal priesthood,
a holy nation, His own special people...

God calls us "a royal priesthood." This means that we are kings as well as priests under the king-priesthood of Jesus Christ. This has never happened before in the history of God's people. In the Old Testament, kings and priests were two distinct groups of people. You were either a king or priest, but not both at the same time.

Today, because we are in Christ, we are king-priests — a royal priesthood. This means that we have a **double portion** of speaking power because as kings, "Where the word of a king is, there is power" (Ecclesiastes 8:4), and as priests, "by their word every controversy and every assault shall be settled" (Deuteronomy 21:5).

So if you are a Christian businessman, you will have an edge over worldly businessmen. What you say about your business deals will come to pass. And if you are falsely accused, know that by your very word, every controversy and every assault will be settled!

And as a king-priest parent, when you bless your children, your words have the power to set in motion supernatural events which will bring them into God's prosperous abundance and superabounding grace. And there will be such a courage and resilience about them that it will empower them to win the fights of life!

When the devil comes to you and says that you will die young because your father and grandfather died young, or that you will never be successful because you are not well-educated, you must remember that the devil is neither a king nor a priest. There is no power in his words. But there is power in yours because you are a king-priest in Christ!

So instead of agreeing with him, believe and declare, "I will not die young. With long life He will satisfy me and show me His salvation!" Say, "The Lord will make my way prosperous and give me good success!" Use your double portion of speaking power and see these blessings come to pass!

Thought for the Day
You have a double portion of speaking power because
you are a king as well as a priest in Christ Jesus.

God Wants to Set You Up for a Blessing

Ruth 2:12
12 "The LORD repay your work, and a full reward be given you by the LORD God of Israel, under whose wings you have come for refuge."

Have you ever wondered why, in some Bible stories, God asked the people to give what little they had to Him? It may appear cruel, but the truth is that God was setting them up for a blessing! God's way is to use whatever we have, and multiply it back to us once we put it in His hands.

The widow of Zarephath had only a handful of flour and a little oil to make one last meal for her son and herself before they faced starvation. But she trusted God and used a portion of the little that she had to make a cake for the prophet Elijah. And God rewarded her by making sure that her bin of flour was not used up and her jar of oil did not run dry until the drought ended. (1 Kings 17:8–16.)

Similarly, the boy who gave his little lunch of five loaves and two small fish to Jesus not only ate well, but he also saw it being used to feed more than 5,000 people with 12 baskets full of leftovers! (John 6:1–13.)

Whenever we give what little we have to God, whether it is money, time or energy, it opens up our hearts so that God can fill us up with more. And when we give our lives to God, we can trust Him to make things right for us and to be the rewarder of our faith.

When Ruth, a childless Moabite widow, left the comfort of her home to follow her mother-in-law, Naomi, and the God of Israel back to a foreign land (Ruth 1:16), she was given a full reward by the Lord. God gave Ruth protection and ensured that she was well-provided for through Boaz, a wealthy relative who took on the role of kinsman-redeemer for her and Naomi. (Ruth 2:9, 4:9–10.)

Beloved, as you trust God with what you have today, know that He loves you and is setting you up for more blessings. So expect to see even more of His provision and abundance in the days to come!

Thought for the Day
***Whenever we give what little we have to God, it opens up
our hearts to receive more from Him.***

Blessed Are Your Baskets, Kneading Bowls and Nets!

Deuteronomy 28:5
⁵"Blessed shall be your basket and your kneading bowl."

In Bible times, reapers carried baskets on their backs to collect the harvest from the fields. They had to ensure that their baskets were strong and sturdy, so that what they collected would not fall out. The women of that day used kneading bowls to knead dough for making bread. If they used poor-quality bowls, which broke easily, they would not be able to make bread.

So baskets and kneading bowls in those days represented the means by which one got his tangible blessings. Beloved, your Father in heaven does not want you to worry about the means by which you get your blessings. Because of the sacrifice of Christ, He says to you, "Blessed shall be your basket and your kneading bowl."

This means that if you are a cab driver, your cab will not break down on your rounds because God says to you, "Blessed shall be your cab." If you are a businessman, your capital investment will not fail you because God says to you, "Blessed shall be your capital investment." And if you are a salesman, your products will be looked upon favorably because God says to you, "Blessed shall be your products."

These blessings are yours because Jesus paid for them with His death and He enforced them with His resurrection.

On one occasion, Jesus told Peter to throw his nets into the water. When Peter threw one net down, he caught so much fish that the net "**was breaking.**" To save the bumper haul, the other disciples quickly filled their boats with the fish, lest the net gave way completely. (Luke 5:4–7.)

After Jesus rose from the dead, a similar incident took place. Once again, Jesus asked His disciples to cast their net out. They caught a multitude of fish. But "although there were so many, the net **was not broken**" (John 21:11). Notice that in the first case, the net was breaking. In the second case, it was not! Something supernatural happened to their nets after Jesus rose from the dead!

Beloved, because of the death and resurrection of Jesus Christ, not only are you blessed (Ephesians 1:3), but your nets, baskets and kneading bowls — the means by which you obtain your blessings — are also blessed!

Thought for the Day
Because of the death and resurrection of Jesus Christ, you as well as the means by which you obtain your blessings are blessed!

Launch Out Into the Deep

Luke 5:4
⁴When He had stopped speaking, He said to Simon, "Launch out into the deep and let down your nets for a catch."

God wants to bless you — big-time! It was for this reason that He said to Simon, "Launch out into the deep and let down your nets for a catch." The deep is where you will find a whole lot of fish. You won't find them near the shore in shallow waters. But to launch out into the deep is to move away from the comfort of the shoreline.

My friend, God wants you to break away from your comfort zone and step out in faith to do what He has put in your heart. It may be something simple, but which you have never done before or only dreamt of, like attending a care group. A church member did just that and found love. Today, she is happily married.

Now, our Lord Jesus who said, "Launch out into the deep..." also said, "... let down your **nets** for a catch." Notice that He used the plural "nets" and not the singular "net." Beloved, God wants to give you more than what you need. His dream for you is bigger than anything you can ever dream of. Dream big and God will exceed your dream because He delights in giving you exceedingly abundantly above all that you ask or think. (Ephesians 3:20.)

Another church member who was formerly working for someone else had wanted to start his own company. When praying with him, I received a word from the Lord for him to launch out on his own. When he did that, he made a handsome profit at the end of the first month alone! Today, he has more than one company and his businesses are flourishing. God is blessing him beyond his wildest dreams!

Beloved, God wants to bless you beyond your wildest dreams. He did it for Simon who was astonished at the size of the catch of fish. (Luke 5:9.) But it was not until Simon launched out into the deep that he ended up with the net-breaking, boat-sinking load of fish. (vv. 6–7.) You, too, will be astonished at your catch when you step out of your comfort zone and launch out into the deep with the Lord!

Thought for the Day
**Break away from your comfort zone and step out in faith
to do what God has put in your heart.**

Thanksgiving Can Raise the Dead!

John 11:41–42
41... And Jesus lifted up His eyes and said, "Father, I thank You that You have heard Me. 42And I know that You always hear Me...."

After Jesus had said these words, He cried with a loud voice, "Lazarus, come forth!" And the man who had been dead for four days came out of his tomb! (vv. 43-44.)

This is one of the greatest miracles that Jesus performed. Lazarus had been dead for four days when Jesus raised him to life. Wouldn't you agree that death is indeed an extreme problem? Having no money in the bank, being sick and losing your job, bad as they are, are not as bad as being dead!

But what I want you to see is this: If Jesus, in the most extreme of problems, shows us that the solution is still, "Father, I **thank** You," then how much more should we thank God in the midst of the less serious problems we face. If thanksgiving can raise the dead, then let us give thanks in spite of the negative circumstances and we will see victory.

Unfortunately, we tend to do the opposite — murmur and complain. But murmuring and complaining only magnify the problem. Thanksgiving, on the other hand, is the language of faith which pleases God. I am not saying that we give thanks for the problems we have. No, we thank God that He is our answer and that He has already given every blessing to us. (Ephesians 1:3.)

"But Pastor Prince, what I have is so little."

My friend, thank God for the little you have and it will multiply. Jesus thanked His Father for the five barley loaves and two small fish, a little boy's lunch, and they were multiplied to feed more than 5,000 people with 12 baskets full of leftovers! (John 6:8–13.) And notice that when the Holy Spirit talked about this event again, He specifically mentioned the Lord giving thanks — "the place where they ate bread after the Lord had **given thanks**" (John 6:23). The Holy Spirit seemed to be more pleased with the act of giving thanks than the miracle of multiplication or the 12 baskets full of leftovers.

Beloved, the more you thank God, the more you please Him. What little you have will be multiplied and whatever is dead in your life will be raised to life!

Thought for the Day
Thanksgiving is the language of faith which pleases God and causes miracles to manifest in your life.

Thank Your Way to Peace

Philippians 4:6
⁶Be anxious for nothing, but in everything by prayer and supplication,
with thanksgiving, let your requests be made known to God.

You probably have read this verse before, but would you like to know how to apply it in your everyday life? Let me give you an illustration to help you.

Let's say that you are one of those in your company eligible for a promotion and you will know tomorrow whether you get it. You want the promotion badly because it means more income for your family. So you lie in bed at night tossing and turning. You pray, "Father, please take away all my worries about this promotion. Give me faith." One hour later, you are more anxious than ever. It seems like God is not answering your prayer!

How come? Because you are not doing it God's way.

Pray like this instead: "Father, I cast all my worries about the promotion into Your loving hands because You care for me and love me." The Bible tells us to cast all our cares upon the Lord for He cares for us. (1 Peter 5:7.) Then, say, "Father, I would like to have the promotion." It is okay to ask Him for that. Now, here comes the most powerful part — thanksgiving. Finish off with thanksgiving. Thank God for His faithfulness.

Say something like, "Father, whether I get the promotion or not, I thank You that You will always provide for my family with more than enough. You who feed the birds of the air and clothe the lilies of the field will take care of us. So I am not going to worry about this promotion. You are the source of all my blessings." (Matthew 6:30; Philippians 4:19.)

When you pray like this, all of a sudden, you are no longer held hostage by the promotion. I call this the "thank You" therapy. The more you know God's Word, the more you can thank Him. The more you thank Him, the more His peace reigns in your heart. And many a time, before you know it, it is morning! You don't even remember falling asleep. The peace of God reigns like that.

My friend, whatever your concern is, bring it to your Father in prayer and thank your way to peace!

Thought for the Day
The more you know God's Word, the more you can thank Him.
The more you thank Him, the more His peace reigns in your heart.

Creation Can't but Redemption Can!

John 9:7
⁷And He said to him, "Go, wash in the pool of Siloam" (which is translated, Sent).
So he went and washed, and came back seeing.

When Adam sinned and fell, everything about creation fell. Yet, people today are still putting their trust in creation. For example, they try to become healthy by eating what is called the "Eden diet"—vegetables and no meat. They are acting as if creation did not fall. They also forget that there are people who eat well and exercise regularly, and still drop dead in the prime of their lives!

Thank God that what creation cannot do, **redemption** can and did. Jesus demonstrated this when He spat on the ground, made clay with the saliva and put it on a blind man's eyes. (John 9:6–7.) Now, it is certainly unusual to put clay on a blind man's eyes because he would become doubly blind!

So why did Jesus do that?

He was demonstrating to us that all our body parts come from the ground and that because creation is fallen, the work of creation cannot open a blind man's eyes. But the work of redemption can! That is why He sent the blind man to the pool of Siloam. The word "Siloam" means "Sent," referring to the sent One, Jesus. When the blind man washed his eyes in the pool of the sent One, he received supernatural healing for his eyes.

Beloved, when we go to Jesus, the sent One who came to redeem us with the price of His blood, and we rest in His finished work, we will receive the miracle we need. If we believe that by His stripes we are healed (Isaiah 53:5), we will have greater health than those who trust in creation.

Jesus was sent to redeem us from every curse that came upon creation with the fall of Adam. (Galatians 3:13.) He has redeemed us from sickness, pain, sorrow, depression, poverty and even death. The world may know Him as the Creator. But today, we know Him as our Redeemer. Where the work of creation cannot save us, His work of redemption can and has!

Thought for the Day
Where the work of creation cannot save us,
Jesus' work of redemption can and has!

Jesus Is Your Restorer and Nourisher

Ruth 4:15
¹⁵And may he be to you a restorer of life and a nourisher of your old age...

Famine impoverished the life of Naomi, an Israelite. But it was the deaths of her husband and two sons that left her completely destitute. (Ruth 1:1–5.) Or so she thought, until Boaz, who was a wealthy and close relative, entered her life.

As her kinsman-redeemer, Boaz married Ruth, Naomi's widowed daughter-in-law. And through that union, Naomi had a grandson. The birth of her grandson gave her a new lease on life, causing the womenfolk in her village to declare that the restorer of life and the nourisher of her old age had come into her life. (Ruth 4:14–16.)

Boaz is a picture of Jesus, our kinsman-redeemer. Jesus became our kinsman when He was born into this world as one like us. And He became our Redeemer when He paid with His life and blood at the cross to redeem us.

Jesus gave Himself to us as our restorer of life and nourisher of our old age. When the restorer of life is in our lives, what we have lost can be restored. (Joel 2:25–26.) And with the nourisher of our old age in us, our bodies can be gloriously renewed even though we advance in our years.

That is why when Moses died at the age of 120, his eyes were not dim and his natural vigor was not diminished. (Deuteronomy 34:7.) Caleb, at 85 years old, could still drive out the giants from the land. God had literally nourished his body and made it strong for war. (Joshua 14:11.) Sarah was certainly rejuvenated in her old age by God for she was still desirable to a king at the age of 90. (Genesis 20:1–2.) God even renewed her womb. She received strength to conceive seed (Hebrews 11:11), giving birth to Isaac in her old age.

Beloved, God is outside of time and your faith in Him brings you into this timeless zone. There, what the years have stolen will be restored. And even as your years increase, you will not grow weak and weary because the restorer of life and nourisher of your old age is in you!

Thought for the Day
With Jesus the nourisher of our old age in us, our bodies can be gloriously renewed even though we advance in our years.

Blessed With the Excellent and the Plenty

Deuteronomy 28:4
⁴"Blessed shall be the fruit of your body, the produce of
your ground and the increase of your herds, the increase of
your cattle and the offspring of your flocks."

Would you want to buy a chair that Jesus made? I would, even if it cost $1,000 because it would be of superb quality. Whatever Jesus did, He did it with perfect excellence.

And because Christ is in you, the things which you produce will be of exceptional quality too. That includes your children, who will be champions. Deuteronomy 28:4 says, "Blessed shall be the fruit of your body, the produce of your ground and the increase of your herds, the increase of your cattle and the offspring of your flocks."

God was using terms that the Israelites understood since they were farmers and shepherds. Today, "your ground" is the place of your work. This means that "the produce" of your work shall be of excellent quality.

That is not all. God promises that quantity will always follow quality because Deuteronomy 28:11 says that "the LORD will grant you plenty of goods, in the fruit of your body," which means that you will have plenty of children, and also "in the increase of your livestock, and in the produce of your ground," which means that your business will flourish and you will be a leading producer in the area of your specialty.

My friend, your excellence and plenty do not come by your efforts. They come by the grace of our Lord Jesus Christ, who paid for your prosperity — "though He was rich, yet for your sakes He became poor, that you through His poverty might become rich" (2 Corinthians 8:9).

Jesus was made destitute of all material things at the cross. He had nothing! As He hung on the cross, He watched the Roman soldiers gamble for His robe. His last possession on earth was gambled away. He became poor, so that you could be blessed with the excellent and the plenty!

Thought for the Day
Jesus was made destitute of all material things at the cross,
so that you could be blessed with the excellent and the plenty!

God Hears Your Prayers

Romans 4:7–8
[7]"Blessed are those whose lawless deeds are forgiven, and whose sins are covered; [8]blessed is the man to whom the LORD shall not impute sin."

Some people think that if they were more "right" with God, then He would hear their prayers. For example, they sometimes believe that if they had not quarreled with their wives or had those bad thoughts earlier in the day, then God would answer their prayers.

God is not like that. He wants you to know beyond any doubt that you can always come to His throne of grace with boldness and have every confidence that you **will** receive His mercy and grace. (Hebrews 4:16.) You see, because of Jesus' finished work on the cross, you are already right with God. You don't need to do anything to make yourself more right with God.

In fact, by faith in Jesus, you have received the righteousness of God Himself! (2 Corinthians 5:21.) And no matter how many mistakes you make, you will never lose that righteousness because in the first place, God gave it to you **apart** from your works. (Romans 4:5–6.) In other words, God did not impute righteousness to you because you were good, but because you believed in Jesus.

Because of what Jesus has done for you at the cross, all your sins — past, present and future — are forgiven. God will by no means ever remember your sins or count them against you! (Hebrews 8:12, 10:17.)

My friend, because Jesus has been punished for your sins, today, God is not counting your sins against you. This means that your sins won't stop Him from hearing and responding to your prayers. So you can always run into His presence knowing that you can boldly stand in and enjoy His presence and His love.

When you know this truth, it is going to set you free in your relationship with God. You can talk to Him without fear or any sense of condemnation. You can practice His presence and trust that He always hears you. Should something happen at home or at work, you don't always have to call for your church leaders — you pray and God hears you!

Beloved, you are righteous in Christ and God hears your prayers — all because of Jesus!

Thought for the Day
Because of Jesus' finished work on the cross, you are already right with God. So when you pray, God hears you!

God Knows You Intimately

Matthew 10:30
30But the very hairs of your head are all numbered.

A s much as I love my wife and daughter, I have never bothered to count the number of hairs on their heads. I don't have the time to do so and I doubt I will ever want to.

Every day, your hair drops. Yet, God knows how many hairs are left on your head. And He also knows how many are growing back! He knows because He bothers to count them again. When it comes to you, He always has time for every little thing about you.

So when Jesus said, "But the very hairs of your head are all numbered," He was not exaggerating. He never exaggerates. He means what He says and He says what He means. So for the Lord to say that the very hairs of your head are all numbered means that He wants you to know that He is very interested in you and has intimate knowledge about you — your body, family, finances, relationships… everything in your life!

He knows the pain you have been having in your body. He is aware of the financial worry which you have been keeping from your family. He sees how your nasty boss is treating you. He understands the hurts you have been keeping in your heart. He hears your heart's cry for a miracle baby.

Your heavenly Father wants you to know that as long as something concerns you, He does not overlook it, even if it is about your pet, as a church member found out. She panicked when she first discovered that her pet terrapin had gone blind. Then, remembering my messages on confessing healing for our bodies, she did the same for her pet! Three months later, the terrapin's eyes were wide open and able to see!

God knows you intimately. He knows every small problem you are worried about and every single burden you have. And when you approach Him for help, He has all the time for you as if no one else exists. That is how valuable you are to Him and how absorbed He is in you!

Thought for the Day
**God knows every single care you have and He has
all the time for you as if no one else exists.**

How Much More Will God Take Care of You!

Matthew 6:26
²⁶Look at the birds of the air, for they neither sow nor reap nor gather into barns; yet your heavenly Father feeds them. Are you not of more value than they?

Perched on a tree branch, two birds were observing passers-by rushing from one place to another. Looking at their faces, one bird asked the other, "Why is man so full of worries and cares?" The other bird answered, "Maybe they don't have a heavenly Father like we do."

I believe that the Lord made birds to tell us that we are of more value than many birds put together. In Matthew 10:29, Jesus said, "Are not two sparrows sold for a copper coin?" Then, in Luke 12:6, He said, "Are not five sparrows sold for two copper coins?" If you do the math, you will realize that these sparrows are so cheap that you can buy four of them for two copper coins, and you get one thrown in for free!

Sparrows are common creatures in Israel. Yet, not even one of these cheap birds falls to the ground without the Father's knowledge. (Matthew 10:29.) Not one of them is forgotten before Him. (Luke 12:6.) So will He forget you who are of more value than all these birds put together?

Jesus said, "Look at the birds of the air, for they neither sow nor reap nor gather into barns; yet your heavenly Father feeds them." And if your heavenly Father feeds the birds of the air, how much more will He feed you, His precious, beloved child!

"Why don't I see the supply then?" you may ask.

The answer is worry. That is why Jesus also said, "Therefore do not worry, saying, 'What shall we eat?' or 'What shall we drink?' or 'What shall we wear?'… For your heavenly Father knows that you need all these things" (Matthew 6:31–32).

Beloved, if your heavenly Father cares for cheap, common birds, and feeds them every day, how much more will He care for you, His dear, precious child! Let your heart be at rest as you hear Him say to you, "Do not fear therefore; you are of more value than many sparrows" (Matthew 10:31).

Thought for the Day
***If your heavenly Father cares for common birds and feeds them every day,
how much more will He care for you, His dear, precious child!***

Your Sins Will Not be Screened in Heaven

Hebrews 10:17
¹⁷ Then He adds, "Their sins and their lawless deeds I will remember no more."

When I was a young Christian growing up in Singapore, I read a little tract entitled *This Was Your Life*. In that tract, it said that when you get to heaven, God will replay your entire life, including all your sins, on a huge video screen for all the angels and other saints to watch!

The idea that God was making such a video of my life with the intention of screening it for everyone to watch used to make me feel awful and condemned before God. How could I ever stand boldly in His presence? And how was I going to face my loved ones and Christian friends in heaven?

I was a nervous wreck, thinking about all my sins that God was recording down, until I read this in the Bible: "Blessed is the man to whom the LORD **shall not** impute sin" (Romans 4:8). Hallelujah! I jumped for joy when I found out that God was not counting my sins against me, and that He has given me something called "non-imputation of sins"!

My friend, the reason that God does not impute any of our sins to us is that He has already imputed all of them to the body of His Son Jesus when He hung on the cross 2,000 years ago. Not only that, when God punished His Son for our sins, He caused the curse of the law to fall stroke by stroke upon Jesus' entire body until every curse had been fully satisfied. That is why we have been redeemed from the curse of the law. (Galatians 3:13.) That is why, instead of imputing sin to us, God imputes righteousness!

God wants us to know that our sins and lawless deeds He will remember **no more**. The words "no more" in the original Greek text carry a strong double-negative meaning. In other words, God is saying, "No way, by no means, will I ever remember your sins again!"

Beloved, since God says that He will remember your sins no more, why do you still remember them? Or for that matter, your spouse's or neighbor's sins? God does not want you to be conscious of sins because He is not. So rejoice! Come to Him boldly and expect Him to show you mercy and grace because He remembers your sins no more!

Thought for the Day
Since God remembers your sins no more, why do you still remember them?

God Abundantly Supplies All Your Needs

Philippians 4:19
*¹⁹And my God shall supply all your need according to
His riches in glory by Christ Jesus.*

According to this verse, you **are** rich. You are not **trying** to be rich. It does not matter how much you are earning or how much you have in your bank account. You are rich because as your need arises, God's supply will be there for you.

This was the case for a church member who worked as a consultant. For months, he could not secure any major deals. But while attending one of our church camps held in Kuala Lumpur, Malaysia, he received a word on financial prosperity. After the camp, he extended his stay in Kuala Lumpur and bumped into an old friend who gave him a big project that paid a huge sum! He needed a major breakthrough and God abundantly supplied his need.

In the Bible, there is an account of a couple who had a big need on their wedding day. They had run out of wine. Now, you would expect wedding couples to know how many guests to expect on their big day and to plan accordingly. But perhaps this couple did not have the money to buy enough wine. Whatever the reason was, Jesus saved them from embarrassment and shame. He saved the day when He supplied their need by miraculously turning six pots of water into top-quality wine. (John 2:1–10.) Our Lord Jesus abundantly supplied the need of that couple.

Beloved, whatever needs you have, God wants you to know that His supply will be there for you. You have His Word for it. He promises that He will supply **all** your needs, not just some. And He will supply all your needs **according to** and not out of His riches. This means that He lines up from A to Z all His riches for your supply! All His riches are yours!

My friend, rejoice that you are rich "according to His riches in glory by Christ Jesus." This is far greater and more dependable than the temporal riches that you might have from any earthly source!

Thought for the Day
God lines up all His riches for your supply! All His riches are yours!

God Makes All Things Work Together for Good

Romans 8:28
²⁸And we know that all things work together for good to those who love God, to those who are the called according to His purpose.

In this verse, "all things" is literally all things — the good, the bad and the ugly! Now, it does not mean that all things are from God. Some things, such as accidents, sicknesses, broken relationships and divorces are not from Him. They are from the devil or just part of the fallen world that we live in. But what this verse does tell us is that "**all** things work together for **good** to those who love God, to those who are the called according to His purpose." That is our inheritance as God's beloved children.

Do the people of the world have this inheritance? No. When bad things happen to them, they are what they are — bad things. But when bad things happen to the children of God, it does not end there. God can make those bad things work together for good. In other words, the devil may throw lemons at you, but God can take those lemons and make refreshing lemonade for you!

For example, if you have been retrenched, believe that God, who makes all things work together for good, has a better job for you. Indeed, we have received testimonies from church members who have ended up with better jobs and higher salaries after they were retrenched.

It is important you remember that God is not behind anything bad or ugly. But when those things happen, know that He can make all things work together for good. And don't let anyone tell you that all things will work together for good only if you love God and are called according to His purpose. These two things are not conditions but descriptions of believers. Believers are those who love God because they know that God first loved them. (1 John 4:19.) And they are called according to His purpose for they have been born again and belong to Him.

My friend, because you have been born again, all things in your life will work together for good. This is your inheritance as a beloved child of God!

Thought for the Day
God is not behind anything bad or ugly. When those things happen,
know that He can make all things work together for good.

A Way of Escape

Psalm 23:5
⁵You prepare a table before me in the presence of my enemies;
You anoint my head with oil; my cup runs over.

The table is set. The bread and wine are there, and Jesus says to you, "Come, My child, partake." But you tell Him, "Lord, I am unworthy!" You are afraid to come to the Lord's table perhaps because you have been taught that if you partake in your "unworthy" state, you will come under God's fiery judgment.

My friend, Jesus has washed you whiter than snow and qualified you with His own blood, so you are as worthy as worthy can be! The most humble thing you can do now is to acknowledge His perfect sacrifice and accept His invitation with gladness.

In 1 Corinthians 11, Paul tells the church how to partake of the Lord's Supper so that they will not drink judgment to themselves. The word "judgment" in verses 29 and 34 is *krima* in the original Greek text. It refers to a divine sentence. And in the context of this passage, the divine sentence refers to sickness.

But when was this divine sentence of sickness passed? It was passed when Adam sinned. (Genesis 3:19.) When he sinned, death entered the world (Genesis 2:17), and man would grow old and weak, fall sick and die.

So it is not that God is passing sentences of sickness on people today. How can that be when Jesus said, "For God did not send His Son into the world to condemn the world, but that the world through Him might be saved" (John 3:17). God is not in the business of condemning but saving. And the Greek word for "saved," *sozo*, also means to preserve, heal and make whole.

God does not want you to suffer the divine sentence of sickness that is already in the world, so He has given you a way of escape, paid for by the blood of His Son. He wants you to be healthy and whole, without the diseases of the world, and He has made this possible for you through the Holy Communion.

So don't be robbed of this tremendous blessing any longer because of erroneous teachings that have put fear in your heart. Come boldly to the Lord's table today and receive afresh His health, strength, wholeness and life!

Thought for the Day
God wants you to be healthy and whole, without the diseases of the world,
and He has made this possible for you through the Holy Communion.

Feed on God's Word Daily

Matthew 4:4
⁴But He answered and said, "It is written, 'Man shall not live by bread alone,
but by every word that proceeds from the mouth of God.'"

The Bible tells us that God breathed into man and he became a living being. (Genesis 2:7.) It also tells us that "all Scripture is God-breathed" (2 Timothy 3:16, NIV). This means that when you read the Bible or listen to God's Word preached, you are imbibing the very breath of God, which gives you life.

That is why there may have been times you walked into church feeling tired at first, but left at the end of the service feeling refreshed and energized. God's Word had breathed life into your body! I have also seen many of our church members becoming healthier, stronger and even younger-looking because they spend time in God's Word.

It is no wonder that Proverbs 4:22 tells us that God's words "are **life** to those who find them, and **health to all their flesh.**" So if you are under the weather or if symptoms are attacking your body, double up on God's medicine. Simply feed more on God's Word, and you will find life and health flowing through your body again.

Jesus said that "man shall not live by bread alone, but by every word that proceeds from the mouth of God." If it is important to eat our meals every day, how much more feeding on God's Word? Jesus wants us to know that we need God's Word even more than our daily meals. He made us, so He knows best what our bodies need daily.

So whatever you do, remember to get your daily feeding of God's Word. Read your Bible in the comfort of your home or in the office during your lunch break. Play sermon CDs while driving to work or doing household chores. If you prefer something more visual, watch DVDs on the preaching of His Word. Choose whichever form you prefer and get His Word into you!

Beloved, you cannot live when you stop breathing. In the same way, you cannot live without the Word because it is the very breath of God, which gives you life and health!

Thought for the Day
If it is important to eat our meals every day,
how much more our feeding on God's Word?

Call It the Way God Calls It!

Romans 4:17
¹⁷... God, who gives life to the dead and calls those
things which do not exist as though they did.

Many a time, when we look at ourselves, we don't see what we can become. But when God looks at us, He sees what we can become by His grace.

When Jesus first saw Simon, whose name in Greek means "reed," He changed his name to "Peter," which means "rock." But did Peter instantly become someone with the characteristics of a rock — solid, stable and unshakable? No, for a long time, he continued to act like a reed that bends every which way the wind blows.

Once, when Peter saw Jesus walking on water, he took a bold step of faith and said, "Lord, if it is You, command me to come to You on the water." Then, as he was walking on the water, he saw the boisterous wind, got scared and when he began to sink, cried out, "Lord, save me!" (Matthew 14:28–30). Another time, he said, "Lord, I am ready to go with You, both to prison and to death" (Luke 22:33). Then, a few hours later, he denied knowing Jesus not once, but three times. (vv. 54–62.)

Yet, throughout his reed-like behavior, Jesus kept calling him "rock" until one day, how Jesus saw him began to take root in him. That day, on the Day of Pentecost, Peter stood up to preach and 3,000 people were saved! (Acts 2:41.) Peter had indeed become a rock, a pillar in the early church.

That was how Jesus transformed Peter. And that is how God wants us to change the people and situations in our lives.

"Pastor Prince, are you telling me to call my wife 'a fruitful vine' as in Psalm 128:3? You should see my wife. She looks more like a dried-up sour prune!"

My friend, God did not tell us to call those things which exist as they exist. What is the point of stating the obvious? It is not going to change anything. No, God tells us to call those things which do not exist as though they did, and they will!

Thought for the Day
God tells us to call things which do not exist as though they did, and they will!

Divinely Arranged, Beautifully Timed

Ecclesiastes 3:11
11He has made everything beautiful in its time....

Nothing happens to you by accident when you have God in your life. Even a "chance" meeting with someone is part of His plan to set in motion His blessings in your life.

Such was the divinely arranged meeting of the Shunammite woman and Prophet Elisha. It led to the prophet pronouncing over her the blessing of a miracle child even though she was barren and her husband was old. (2 Kings 4:8–17.) A few years later, it was this friendship with the man of God, that saw her through a crisis when her son fell seriously ill and died — Elisha raised her son back to life. (vv. 18–37.)

When God is the one orchestrating the events in your life, neither lack nor danger nor destruction can affect you. When famine hit the land, the Shunammite woman's family did not suffer because through Elisha, God had told them to leave the land. They went to the land of the Philistines and dwelt there throughout the seven years of famine. (2 Kings 8:1–2.)

God can place you at the right place at the right time, even through your daily decision-making. The Shunammite woman returned to Shunem after the famine had ended. She then decided to appeal to the king of Israel for help to regain her house and land, which had been illegally acquired by others during her absence. This decision brought her before the king on the same day that Elisha's servant, Gehazi, was in audience with the king.

The king wanted to hear all about the miracles performed by Elisha. This gave the Shunammite woman the opportunity to share firsthand with the king how Elisha had raised her son from the dead. The thrilled king then ordered the restoration of her house and land, including all the proceeds of the field from the day that she had left until then. (vv. 3–6.) The Lord had timed and set up everything beautifully for her!

Beloved, God can also make all things beautiful in its time for you. As you involve Him in your daily life and trust His love for you, you too will see Him lead and place you at the right place at the right time to enjoy His blessings.

Thought for the Day
Involve God in your daily life and trust His love for you,
and He will make all things beautiful in its time.

Jesus' Blood Speaks Better Things

Hebrews 12:24
²⁴To Jesus the Mediator of the new covenant, and to the blood of sprinkling that speaks better things than that of Abel.

Today, forensic science tells us that blood has a voice. DNA can be extracted from just one small drop of the murderer's blood and the results used in court as evidence.

So blood in a sense can speak. And when it is the blood of Jesus, it "speaks better things" than that of Abel. Abel's blood cried out, "Vengeance! Vengeance!" after his brother Cain murdered him. (Genesis 4:8–11.) But Jesus' blood cries out forgiveness for our sins, healing for our bodies, and peace and soundness for our minds. It cries out protection for our coming and going, prosperity for the works of our hands, the righteousness of Christ as our acceptance before God and much more!

In the Bible, Jesus' blood speaking of "better things" is found in the context of the last days when things are being shaken, so that the things which cannot be shaken will remain. (Hebrews 12:27.) God wants you to know that you will not be shaken when you put your faith in Jesus' blood, which speaks better things for you. That is why God wants you to see Jesus' blood shed for you in every area that causes your heart to tremble and your confidence to be shaken.

For example, if you are afraid of losing your job, speak the blood of Jesus over your job. His blood cries out, "Favor with his boss!" And in these days when you are shaken by fears that terrorism may strike anyone, anywhere, anytime, plead the blood of Jesus, which cries out, "Protection and deliverance!" When fear rises in your heart as the doctor gives you his prognosis, plead the blood of Jesus over your body. His blood cries out, "Healing and wholeness!"

The eternal blood of Jesus, which speaks better things, will never lose its power. Beloved, see that you do not refuse Him who speaks. (Hebrews 12:25.) See that you keep hearing the voice of grace, which speaks salvation, righteousness, protection, deliverance, prosperity and healing over your life!

Thought for the Day
You will not be shaken when you put your faith in Jesus' blood, which speaks better things for you.

Jesus' Authority Has Been Given to Us

Matthew 28:18–19
¹⁸And Jesus came and spoke to them, saying, "All authority has been given to Me in heaven and on earth. ¹⁹Go therefore...."

When God created man, He gave man authority to have dominion over everything on earth. (Genesis 1:26.) But when man sinned, he gave this authority to Satan. And when man's authority was transferred to Satan, Satan brought in diseases, poverty, strife, bitterness, pain, loss and death. He messed up everything on earth for man.

"Pastor Prince, why didn't God just grab the devil by the neck and throw him out of the garden?"

God did not do that because He is a judicial God. It was a man who gave away his authority to Satan. So it had to be a man who would legally take it back. And God has done this through a Man. His name is Jesus!

By His death on the cross, Jesus righteously restored all that man had lost. That is why, just before He went back to heaven, He said, "All authority has been given to Me in heaven and on earth. Go therefore..." Those words tell us that He has transferred His authority to us. The same authority that He had over the storm, evil spirits, sicknesses, diseases and even death is now ours to use.

So when there are reports of a flu epidemic and of young children falling sick in the media, know that you have dominion over the epidemic. Declare, "By the authority given to me in the name of the Lord Jesus Christ, this flu virus will not come near my children. I plead the blood of Jesus over them."

If you have been told that your family has a history of heart disease, take dominion and declare, "By the authority given to me in the name of the Lord Jesus Christ, I destroy every form, manifestation and hereditary cause of this disease. By His blood, my family has been redeemed from this and every other curse."

My friend, the authority which has been restored to us is not just the authority on earth that man had before the fall, but Jesus' unquestionable and complete authority in heaven and on earth!

Thought for the Day
The same authority that Jesus had over the storm, evil spirits, sicknesses, diseases and even death is now ours to use.

Pray Up Your Immune System!

1 Corinthians 14:4
⁴He who speaks in a tongue edifies himself....

Many Charismatics believe that when you speak in tongues, you edify or build up your spirit man. Well, that is only one-third true. The Bible does not say that the speaker edifies his spirit. No, it says that the speaker "edifies **himself.**" This means his entire self — spirit, soul and body. So he who speaks in tongues builds up his spirit, soul and body.

Does this include building up your immune system? Yes, it does! Brain specialists at City of Faith hospital, built by Oral Roberts in the 1980s in Tulsa, Oklahoma, found out through research and testing that when a person prays in tongues, his brain releases two chemicals that are directed to his immune system, giving it a 35- to 40- percent boost. Interestingly, these secretions are triggered by a part of our brain that has no other apparent activity and which is activated only when we pray in tongues.

Now, your immune system is your first line of defense against diseases. During the SARS outbreak in Singapore in 2003, not everyone who had the disease died. Only those whose immune systems were weak succumbed to the disease and died. Therefore, many people resorted to vitamins and herbs to boost their immune systems.

A 74-year-old church member decided to build up his immune system against more heart problems. Two of his arteries were 70 percent blocked and five smaller vessels were 80 per cent blocked. So during a church service, when I asked those who wanted to be healed of heart problems to stand up, he stood up, placed his hand over his heart and prayed in tongues.

He shared that at that moment, he believed that the Holy Spirit touched him and he became a different person. When he went for his medical check-up, his surgeon found that all the blockages in his blood vessels were gone! Even a scheduled heart-related operation was cancelled as there was no longer any necessity for it. Indeed, he was a different person. He literally had a change of heart, a new heart from God!

Beloved, you may not have a heart condition, but you can still pray in tongues and pray up your immune system!

Thought for the Day
Praying in tongues, help boost your body's immune system!

You Have a Strong Kinsman-Redeemer!

Jeremiah 50:34
³⁴Their Redeemer is strong; the LORD of hosts is His name.
He will thoroughly plead their case....

R uth, a young, poor and childless widow in the Old Testament, lay at the feet of Boaz, her potential kinsman-redeemer. (Ruth 3:7.) As a rich and close relative of her in-laws, Boaz had the power to redeem her from her plight.

Ruth was simply obeying Naomi, her mother-in-law, who had told her to go and lie down at Boaz's feet. In the Jewish custom of those days, this was a posture which said, "Please redeem me for you are a close relative." Notice Boaz's response to Ruth: "And now, my daughter, do not fear. I will do for you all that you request..." (v. 11).

Beloved, Boaz is a picture of Jesus who is our kinsman-redeemer. He is our kinsman, having been born into this world as one like us. And He is our Redeemer because He redeemed us at a great price when He shed His blood for us on the cross.

As your Redeemer, not only is Jesus willing, but He also has the power to restore to you all that you have lost. That is why you can go to Him and say, "I blew it and now my family is suffering. My finances are dwindling fast. But I come to You, my kinsman-redeemer..." And you will find that He will redeem you because your Redeemer is strong. The Lord of hosts is His name. He will thoroughly plead your case, causing only blessings of wisdom, deliverance, restoration, prosperity and liberty to come out of your situation!

Just as Ruth lay at Boaz's feet, the feet of Jesus is the place of redemption and blessings. Both Jairus, the synagogue ruler (Mark 5:22), and the Syro-Phoenician woman fell at Jesus' feet. (Mark 7:25–26.) And there at His feet they received healing for their daughters.

When you take your place at Jesus' feet, looking to Him for help, expect to receive His blessings. There is nothing to fear knowing that as Boaz did for Ruth, Jesus, your heavenly Boaz, will do for you all that you have requested!

Thought for the Day
As your Redeemer, not only is Jesus willing, but He also has the
power to restore to you all that you have lost.

Practicing God's Presence

Matthew 1:23
²³ *"... and they shall call His name Immanuel," which is translated, "God with us."*

God has promised you His constant presence (Hebrews 13:5), but are you conscious of His presence every day? When you are conscious of His presence every day, you will experience a peace that gives you rest, joy inexpressible in your spirit and a power that nothing in this world can offer. In fact, you will begin to be peaceful and powerful like Jesus. You will speak and behave like Him. This is because you cannot be in God's presence without His beauty, love, peace, power and glory rubbing off on you.

But how do you practice being conscious of God's presence?

Start by seeing God with you in whatever you do and wherever you are. For example, at your board meeting, while deliberating on issues, see the Lord there in the boardroom with you, guiding you in your thinking. And you can be sure that His presence will bring clarity of thought and wisdom to you. You will find yourself flowing with great and sound ideas.

If you are going for an interview, see the Lord there in the interview room with you, putting answers in your mouth. Your nervousness will melt away as you see His favor on you bringing on smiles and approving nods from the interviewers.

Perhaps you are going for surgery. Well, see the Lord in the operating theatre with you, guiding the hands of the surgeons. Your worries will dissipate because nothing can go wrong in the Lord's presence.

If you are in the middle of an argument, see the Lord standing within earshot. Your words will change and your body language will become more reconciliatory as you see Him right there with you extending His grace to you. There will be a restraint which is not borne of willpower, but which comes supernaturally when you know that the One who loves you and watches over you is with you.

Beloved, when you become conscious of God's presence in your life, worries and fears will have no foothold in your mind. You will see Him maximizing your joy and fun, and prospering you in what you say and do!

Thought for the Day
You practice God's presence when you see Him with you in
whatever you do and wherever you are.

Never Alone, Always Cared for

1 Peter 5:7
⁷Casting all your care upon Him, for He cares for you.

It does not matter how tightly knit our families are or how many close friends we have. When we go through a difficult time or trial, many a time, we still feel all alone and that no one really cares or understands.

Martha knew that feeling. She had on one occasion cried out to Jesus, "Lord, do You not care that my sister has left me to serve alone?" (Luke 10:40). Jesus' disciples also knew what it was like to feel small, alone and in trouble. They cried out, "Teacher, do You not care that we are perishing?" when they were swept up in a terrifying storm. (Mark 4:38.)

Today, maybe the cry of your heart is also, "Lord, do You not care that I am left all alone... that I am going under... that I am perishing?"

My friend, the Lord does care for you. He loves you so much that He wants you to cast all your cares upon Him — not just some but **all** your cares. He wants both your big and small cares. There is nothing too small or big for Him. If it is a care in your heart, He wants you to cast it upon Him.

When the apostle Peter wrote "casting all your care upon Him," he was talking about the continuous act of casting all your cares upon the Lord. As a care comes, God wants you to cast it to Him. That is the lifestyle He wants you to adopt. Why? The verse gives us the reason — "for He cares for you." You are casting all your cares upon the One who loves you, and who left all of heaven to come and die for you. That is who you are casting your cares to. It is not just any person, but it is the One who gave His life for you!

When you are going through a difficult time, God wants you to believe that you are never alone because He Himself has said that He will never leave you nor forsake you. (Hebrews 13:5.) As the object of His care, He will take care of you for the rest of your life. You are never alone and always cared for!

Thought for the Day
You are never alone because God Himself has said that
He will never leave you nor forsake you.

Do You Know the Jesus of the Bible?

John 14:7
*⁷"If you had known Me, you would have known My Father also;
and from now on you know Him and have seen Him."*

Someone once told me that just because you ask God for something, it does not mean that He will give it to you. Quoting 1 John 5:14–15, he said that we first have to ask according to His will before He hears and gives us what we ask of Him.

Of course, we do not ask for things that are against God's will or Word. But what is normally implied in the earlier statement is that we don't always know what God's will for us is — "what will be, will be." But didn't Jesus say, "He who has seen Me has seen the Father" (John 14:9)? This means that if you want to know what the Father's will, mind, heart or attitude toward you and your family is, just look at Jesus in the Gospel stories.

So if your child is sick, is it God's will to heal him? Well, look at Jesus and see how He ministered to children who were sick — the Syro-Phoenician's daughter who was demon-possessed (Mark 7:24–30), Jairus' daughter who was dead (Mark 5:22–24, 35–43), and the widow of Nain's only son who had died and was about to be buried. (Luke 7:12–15.) Jesus cast out the demon. He raised the dead. He healed them all!

Beloved, don't say, "We can never know God's will. Sometimes He heals, sometimes He doesn't. He may prosper us, but He may also take away our prosperity." The Jesus of the Bible never made anyone sick. He never made anyone poor. He made the little become much with 12 baskets full of leftovers. (Matthew 14:20.) He gave a net-breaking, boat-sinking load of fish to fishermen. (Luke 5:6–7.)

My friend, the Jesus of the Bible loves to heal, deliver, prosper and save people. This Jesus is the same yesterday, today, and forever. (Hebrews 13:8.) And He says to you today, "If you had known Me, you would have known My Father also; and from now on you know Him and have seen Him." So you can know God's will for you. You can see what He will do for you when you know the Jesus of the Bible and what He did.

Thought for the Day
**To know what the Father's will, mind and heart toward you and
your family are, just look at Jesus in the Gospel stories.**

See Your Situation Through God's Eyes

Psalm 1:3
³He shall be like a tree planted by the rivers of water, that brings forth
its fruit in its season, whose leaf also shall not wither;
and whatever he does shall prosper.

When darkness covered the face of the earth, God said, "Let there be light," and there was light. (Genesis 1:3.) When a certain man paralyzed for 38 years lay helpless at the pool of Bethesda, Jesus said, "Rise, take up your bed and walk," and immediately, the man was healed, took up his bed and walked. (John 5:8–9.)

You don't say such words unless you see something others don't. God does not see the way man sees. Man, however, must see the way God sees. We must see the vision of the Almighty.

The prophet Balaam saw the vision of the Almighty when the Spirit of God fell on him. As he looked down from a mountain at the camp of the Israelites, he found himself saying, "How lovely are your tents, O Jacob! Your dwellings, O Israel! Like valleys that stretch out, like gardens by the riverside, like aloes planted by the LORD, like cedars beside the waters" (Numbers 24:5–6).

Balaam would not have said this unless he saw Israel not in the natural, but as God saw it. At that time, the Israelites were a discontented lot, always murmuring and complaining in the wilderness. But when God looked at them, He saw them like flourishing gardens planted by the rivers — fruitful and prosperous.

Beloved, God wants you to see yourself the way He sees you — "like a tree planted by the rivers of water, that brings forth its fruit in its season, whose leaf also shall not wither; and whatever he does shall prosper." So see yourself like a tree planted by the rivers of water, bringing forth fruit in your season. See yourself as one who will not wither, whose health will not fail. See whatever you do prospering!

See the vision of the Almighty. That vision is always a good vision. Whenever you see your situation through God's eyes, you will find that your situation will change because when you see as He sees, you allow Him to work as the Almighty in your life!

Thought for the Day
See your negative situations through God's eyes and
those situations will change.

You Are Next!

Psalm 50:10
¹⁰For every beast of the forest is Mine, and the cattle on a thousand hills.

Suppose you have just heard of someone whose financial debts have been miraculously cleared. Or your elated friend has just told you that despite being an average student in school, he scored straight As in all his subjects. Perhaps on Sunday, you heard a couple share about how they had become proud owners of a condominium which was the grand prize in a supermarket lucky draw, or how a once-childless couple is now expecting their miracle child.

When you see or hear of others being blessed, do you ever wonder when it will be your turn? Or do you even find yourself saying, "Oh, he got blessed with the very thing that I have been praying for. There goes my blessing."

Now, just because man's economy operates on the principle of shortage, it does not mean that God operates in the same manner. So the next time somebody gets blessed, tell yourself, "I won't be disheartened. I won't be jealous. I am the next one to be blessed!"

Always remember that God does not have to bless anyone at your expense. Nor does He have to bless you at anyone's expense. We don't have to be jealous of each other. There is a portion that God gives to you which no man can touch because it has your name on it — "A man can receive nothing unless it has been given to him from heaven" (John 3:27).

Our God is a rich God. He owns the whole universe. He has contacts and blessings you do not know of and which are reserved just for you! There is more than enough for everybody with plenty of leftovers. In fact, you will not be able to take it all because when the blessings start coming in, they will come in a net-breaking, boat-sinking style. You will have to call for your friends in the other boats to come and help you! (Luke 5:1–7.) That is the kind of blessings that our God gives. So get ready for your blessings and overflowing abundance!

Thought for the Day
God has contacts and blessings you do not know of and
which are reserved just for you!

Your Next Stop Is a Place of Abundance!

Psalm 66:12
12... we went through fire and through water;
but You brought us out to rich fulfillment.

Are you in a situation where people are stepping all over you and they seem to have the upper hand? You feel as if the challenge you are facing is so big that you are going through fire. And you are so overwhelmed by everything that is happening around you that you feel as if you are drowning.

My friend, I want you to know that your heavenly Father hears your cry for help and He **will** rescue you. The psalmist says that "we went through fire and through water; but You brought us out to rich fulfillment." If you have been through the fire and water, then your next stop is a place of rich fulfillment or abundance!

This place of abundance was indeed the next stop for a church member who had suddenly found himself facing allegations involving some money laundering activities within the bank where he was one of the top executives. Investigations later exonerated him, but because of the bad vibes caused by the incident, he was asked to resign.

He was then aged 52. Friends told him to retire and relax, but retirement was far from his mind. This brother believed that if God had allowed this to happen, it must be that He was leading him to a better place, one of rich fulfillment. And indeed, soon after this difficult experience, one of the top banks offered him a handsome salary to join them in one of their top positions.

A few years later, at age 56, he was headhunted by one of the biggest public-listed companies to start a new division. He accepted the offer and was paid double what he had been earning.

Beloved, your heavenly Father does not lie when He tells you that He will bring you out to rich fulfillment if you are going through a difficult time. Trust Him and you will find yourself stepping into your place of abundance!

Thought for the Day
If you have been through the fire and water, your next stop is a
place of rich fulfillment or abundance!

Fix Your Eyes on God's Unshakable Word

Philippians 4:19
19And my God shall supply all your need according to His riches in glory by Christ Jesus.

People of the world feel helpless as the systems of the world go up and down. They turn on the television and they hear, "This war will plunge the world into a recession." They open the newspapers and they read that "Unemployment is at an all-time high."

Beloved, God does not want you to feel helpless because you are not of the world. (John 17:16.) You are of God and therefore need not be subject to the world's systems. Whatever the world's situation is, fear not because "God shall supply all your need according to His riches in glory by Christ Jesus."

Notice that Philippians 4:19 says that "God **shall** supply **all** your need." It does not say that God **may** supply **some** of your needs. It also says that God will do it "**according to** His riches." It is not **out of** His riches. If a millionaire gives you a hundred dollars, it is out of his riches. But if he gives to you according to his riches, it means that he is lining up his millions for you!

Lastly, the verse says that God does it "according to **His riches** in glory." It is not according to the riches of your company or how well the economy is doing. No, it is according to God's riches in glory!

So how do you stop yourself from feeling helpless in uncertain times? The same way I stopped myself from getting seasick when I was on board a navy ship for the first time during my National Service stint. A senior naval officer had advised me, "Don't look at the waves around you. Look at the horizon far away. Look at that stable, stationary line and you will feel better." When I fixed my eyes on that unshakable, unwavering line, even though the ship bobbed up and down in the rough sea, I did not feel so seasick anymore.

My friend, don't look at your circumstances or the bad things that are happening in the world because you will get "earth-sick." Instead, look at the unshakable, eternal Word of God. Your heart will become stable and you will see your God supply all your needs according to His riches in glory by Christ Jesus!

Thought for the Day
Fix your eyes on the unshakable Word of God. Your heart will become stable and you will see God supply all your needs!

Rich Through Jesus' Poverty

2 Corinthians 8:9
⁹For you know the grace of our Lord Jesus Christ,
that though He was rich, yet for your sakes He became poor,
that you through His poverty might become rich.

When we think of God, we think of the most powerful and richest being in the whole universe. But do you know that our Lord Jesus was actually born into a poor family? We know this from the offering His mother, Mary, brought to the temple after Jesus was born, according to the Law for purification. (Luke 2:22–24.) She brought a pair of turtledoves or young pigeons, which was the only type of offering the poor could afford. (Leviticus 12:2, 8.)

But with Jesus in their lives, Mary and her husband, Joseph, didn't remain poor. Wise men came to Jesus with treasures — "And when they had come into the house, they saw the young Child with Mary His mother, and fell down and worshiped Him. And when they had opened their treasures, they presented gifts to Him: gold, frankincense, and myrrh" (Matthew 2:11).

Jesus' presence brought gold, frankincense and myrrh — two of the most expensive spices — to His family. The wise men must have come with quite an entourage for the Bible records how all Jerusalem was fearful when the wise men came to the city. (v. 3.) Can you imagine the amount of gold, frankincense and myrrh which accompanied that entourage, and which was given to Jesus' parents?

My friend, the moment you are born again, you have Jesus in your life. And when you have Him in your life, get ready to prosper for gold will come to you! But don't look for the gold, look to Jesus — He is the power to get wealth. (Deuteronomy 8:18) The presence of the Son of the living God in your life attracts prosperity. Because of His grace toward us, Jesus, though He was rich, was made poor at the cross for your sake so that "you through His poverty might become rich."

Beloved, when you have Jesus in your life and when you know that He has paid the price for your prosperity, you can boldly declare, "Jesus was made poor at the cross for my sake so that through His poverty, I am made rich in all things!"

Thought for the Day
The presence of the Son of the living God in your life brings prosperity.

God's Glory Has Been Restored to You

John 17:22
²²And the glory which You gave Me I have given them,
that they may be one just as We are one.

When God made man, the Bible says that God crowned him with glory and honor. (Psalm 8:5.) The word "crowned" here means to encompass or to surround like a glorious circle. The glory of God was therefore man's clothing. In other words, Adam's whole being was gloriously radiant.

When man sinned against God, he forfeited the glory of God. (Romans 3:23.) But when Jesus Christ was born, the glory of God came down. (Luke 2:9.) And many years later, Jesus, before He died, said to His Father, "The glory which You gave Me I have given them, that they may be one just as We are one."

So the glory of God, which man forfeited, has now been restored to him because Jesus has come. When Jesus died on the cross, He took our shame, gave us His righteousness and restored the glory of God to us.

But what exactly is the glory of God? *Doxa*, the Greek word for "glory" here, means having a good opinion concerning one that results in praise, honor and glory. This means that in restoring to us His glory, God wants us to have the sense that we are praiseworthy, honorable and glorious because of His constant good opinion of us!

Beloved, because God's glory is on you, there is a weightiness about you. People don't know why, but their spirits are lifted when they are in your presence. There is something about you that impacts them even if they have only been with you for a short while. When you talk, they listen because there is substance in what you say.

Also, because God's glory is on you, you can expect it to touch every aspect of your life — your finances, relationships, work and health. Your body, for example, will glow with divine health.

So my friend, because Jesus has come and restored the glory of God to you, be conscious of God's constant good opinion of you. Know that there is a weightiness about you and arise, shine!

Thought for the Day
When Jesus died on the cross, He took our shame, gave us
His righteousness and restored the glory of God to us.

Fear Not, Your Savior Is Here!

Luke 2:10–11

¹⁰Then the angel said to them, "Do not be afraid, for behold, I bring you good tidings of great joy which will be to all people. ¹¹For there is born to you this day in the city of David a Savior, who is Christ the Lord.

My friend, if all is silent and dark in your life now, and you feel like you have been left out in the cold, just know that Jesus came to be your Savior at such a time as this.

He was not born in the comfort of a warm, cozy room, but in a cold manger. There was no room for Him in the inn (v. 7), so that there will always be room at the cross for your healing, deliverance, wholeness and prosperity, and a mansion in heaven waiting for you!

Jesus was born very quietly, so quietly that the Bible says that only a group of shepherds came to Him, while the rest of Bethlehem slept. (vv. 8–9.) Like manna falling quietly from heaven in the Old Testament, the true bread from heaven came quietly. It was a silent night, but that was not all.

Jesus was also born during the darkest time in Israel's history. Israel was under the tyrannical rule of the Romans. It was during this time, when everything was so dark, that Jesus was born. Beloved, He will come to you in the darkest period of your life.

On that cold and silent night, the shepherds were afraid when the angel of the Lord stood before them. But the angel said, "Do not be afraid, for behold, I bring you good tidings of great joy which will be to all people. For there is born to you this day in the city of David a **Savior**, who is Christ the Lord."

Beloved, it was not a judge or lawgiver who was born. It was a mighty Savior. He came to save His people. He came to save you and me. So even if you are in a cold, dark period of your life, don't be afraid — the Savior has come and He will save you to the uttermost!

Thought for the Day
If you are in a cold, dark period of your life, don't be afraid —
the Savior has come and He will save you to the uttermost!

Born to Die So That You Might Live

Luke 2:12
12 "And this will be the sign to you: You will find a Babe
wrapped in swaddling cloths, lying in a manger."

Y ou are probably familiar with the story of Jesus' birth in Bethlehem. The Bible says that when the time had come, Mary "brought forth her first-born Son, and wrapped Him in swaddling cloths, and laid Him in a manger" (vv. 6–7). But have you ever wondered why the angel told the shepherds that the Babe wrapped in swaddling cloths and lying in a manger was a "sign"?

A manger is actually a feeding trough for livestock. Do you know what a feeding trough in those days looks like? I have seen a similar one at Solomon's stables in Meggido, Israel. It is basically a big rectangular block of stone with the trough hewn out of it. So baby Jesus, who was wrapped in swaddling cloths, was placed in such a stone trough.

But why was that a sign? Because if you have seen the empty tomb of Jesus at a place called The Garden Tomb in Jerusalem, you would have noticed that the place where His body was laid, inside a tomb hewn out of rock, resembles a stone trough. The Bible says that after Jesus' crucifixion and death, Joseph of Arimathea took Jesus' body, wrapped it in linen and laid it in a tomb hewn out of a rock. (Mark 15:43–46.)

Can you see the similarities? Wrapped in swaddling cloths and laid in a manger, baby Jesus would one day be wrapped in linen and laid in a tomb. That was the sign the angel was referring to. It pointed to Jesus' death.

Jesus was the only child in all of humanity born to die. Once you realize that, you will realize how much God loves you. You will realize that He gave up His Son for that one purpose, and that His Son willingly came for that one purpose — to die for your sins and mine.

Beloved, can you imagine living your life knowing that you are just qualifying yourself to die on the cross to save the world? That was the life that Jesus lived. He lived to die, so that we might live and enjoy life abundantly today!

Thought for the Day
Jesus was born to die and He lived to die, so that we might
live and enjoy life abundantly today!

Don't Sweat It, Rest!

Ruth 3:18
*¹⁸Then she said, "Sit still, my daughter, until you know how the
matter will turn out; for the man will not rest until
he has concluded the matter this day."*

God does not want you to "sweat." Sweat here does not refer to your body's perspiration, but your self-reliance or self-effort. God does not want you to believe that if you don't do anything, nothing will happen. That may be true for someone without God in his life, but it is not true for you because you have God. And when He is in the picture, the God-factor changes everything!

When you are resting in God, He works for you. In fact, when He works, you end up with more. He is the One who is giving to you. It is not about you trying to give to yourself.

This was what happened to Ruth in the Old Testament. After laboring in the barley fields from morning to evening, she was able to glean one ephah of barley (Ruth 2:17), which was equivalent to a 10-day supply of barley. Certainly, this amount was a blessing to her.

But when she **rested** at the feet of Boaz, her kinsman-redeemer, and did not labor, she received six ephahs of barley (Ruth 3:15), which was equivalent to a 60-day supply! When Ruth sought her own blessing, she obtained only one ephah. But when she sought the blesser, she received much more.

Ruth's blessings did not stop there. While Ruth **rested** and **sat still** as her mother-in-law, Naomi, had instructed; Boaz, who was the owner of the barley field, went to work, initiating actions, executing them and speaking on Ruth's behalf. Right through it all, Ruth **sat still** and **rested**. Eventually, Boaz, the barley man himself, married Ruth. (Ruth 4.) That meant no more measured wealth of six ephahs, but the yield of the whole barley field in total!

Boaz is a picture of Jesus, our heavenly kinsman-redeemer. When we rest in the Lord, He will not rest. He will work on our behalf. What do we do then? We just trust in and enjoy His love for us.

Beloved, stop striving and be at rest. If salvation, the greatest work, comes to us by resting in Jesus' finished work, how much more will all the other blessings?

Thought for the Day
***If salvation, the greatest work, comes into our lives just by us resting in
Jesus' finished work, how much more will all the other blessings?***

God Sees Glorious Things in You!

1 Samuel 16:7
⁷"... For the LORD does not see as man sees; for man looks at the
outward appearance, but the LORD looks at the heart."

Picture David when he was a shepherd boy. Many who knew him in his pre-Goliath days would very likely have seen just an ordinary youth — one who lived at home with his parents and siblings, enjoyed the outdoors and loved music. But where others saw a typical teenager, God saw a king in young David. He saw David's name being uttered in honor forever, for even the Lord Jesus is called the Son of David!

Picture Moses after he had settled down comfortably in the desert with a beautiful wife, lovely children and good in-laws. He might have seen himself happily retiring in the near future. But God had bigger plans for him. God had big dreams for him. God saw the Red Sea opening up before him and an entire Egyptian army being wiped out in his presence. God saw in Moses the deliverer of His people.

Now, step back a little less far in time with me. See a little boy standing alone during playtime. Nobody wants him on their team because he is scrawny and seen as a weakling. As he grows into his teens, he suffers from an inferiority complex. He stammers and stutters so much that all his classmates laugh at him.

But today, he is the senior pastor of New Creation Church in Singapore. Several times each week, he stands in front of a crowd of more than 16,000 people to preach. And he receives invitations to speak in churches and pastors' conferences worldwide. In those early years, there was no way I could have ever conceived in my mind what God saw in me and the dreams that He had for me.

Beloved, God does not see as man sees. God saw in fearful Gideon a mighty man of valor and called him so, even when he was hiding from his enemies in fear. (Judges 6:12.) God saw in young David a king and anointed him as one. (1 Samuel 16:10–13.) God saw in meek Moses a deliverer and drew him out from obscurity. (Exodus 3.)

Today, God looks beyond what man sees and says about you, and He has dreams for you that are bigger than you can imagine!

Thought for the Day
God looks beyond what man sees and says about you, and He has
dreams for you that are bigger than you can imagine!

Your Problem Must Bow to Jesus' Name

Philippians 2:10

¹⁰... at the name of Jesus every knee should bow, of those in heaven, and of those on earth, and of those under the earth.

Whatever is troubling you, if it has a name, it must bow to the name of Jesus! Cancer must bow to the name of Jesus. Poverty must bow. Shame must bow. The Bible tells us that God has highly exalted Jesus and given Him the name which is **above** every name, that at the name of Jesus **every** knee must bow!

That is exactly what happened when a severely demon-possessed man saw Jesus. The demons in him — called Legion for there were many of them — not only begged Jesus not to torment them, but they also fled when Jesus commanded them to go. The man was left whole, healed and in his right mind. (Luke 8:26–35.)

My late father was similarly delivered from his drinking addiction of many years. I remember how he was in a drunken stupor one day. I prayed over him in Jesus' name for him to be loosed from his addiction to alcohol. He threw up violently soon after that and from that moment on, he never touched the bottle again!

Beloved, if your child is sick, lay hands on him and say, "In Jesus' name, cough, stop. Fever, go in Jesus' name. Health flows in your body in Jesus' name!" If there is strife and confusion at home, deal with it the same way. I have used the name of Jesus as I prayed for a couple who were quarrelling in a food center. It was amazing. All the strife between them seemed to melt away and they started to talk calmly after that.

That is the power of the name of Jesus because that is the name of the One who died for you, who rose again and today is at the right hand of God, for you! That is the name which is above every name, and at which every knee must and will bow!

Thought for the Day
Whatever is troubling you, if it has a name, it must bow to the name of Jesus!

Born Again to Have Dominion

Genesis 1:26
²⁶Then God said, "Let Us make man in Our image, according to
Our likeness; let them have dominion over the fish of the sea,
over the birds of the air, and over the cattle, over all the earth
and over every creeping thing that creeps on the earth."

When God made man, He gave man dominion over everything on earth. To have an idea of the kind of dominion that man would have had had he not sinned, let's look at the perfect Man, Jesus Christ.

When Jesus wanted to pay the temple tax, He only needed to command a fish to bring the money to Him. (Matthew 17:24–27.) When He wanted to feed a multitude, He only needed to multiply five loaves and two fish in His hands. (Mark 6:34–44.) When a storm threatened the lives of His disciples, He only had to speak to the storm and there was perfect calm. (Mark 4:35–41.) And every sick person who was brought to Him went away healed. He even brought the dead back to life because He had dominion over death!

Today, you have the same dominion that Jesus exercised because Christ is in you. (Colossians 1:27.)

"Pastor Prince, forget about having dominion over the sea, air or earth. I want dominion over my backache which has robbed me of my time with my children. I want dominion over my financial situation."

My friend, because God's purpose for you is to have dominion on earth, He will keep you healthy. After all, it is hard to rule the earth when you are sick and lying on your bed. And God will prosper you because it is hard to want to do things when you are poor.

We need to understand that since God's greater purpose is for man to have dominion on earth, it would include the lesser blessings such as health and prosperity. Then, we will see ourselves as God sees us, walking in dominion, and we will walk in victory over our negative circumstances in the natural realm.

Beloved, you have been born again of the Spirit, born to rule and have dominion over everything on earth!

Thought for the Day
Since God's greater purpose is for man to have dominion on earth,
it includes you walking in health and prosperity.

Take the Snake by Its Tail

Exodus 4:2–3
²So the Lord said to him, "What is that in your hand?" He said, "A rod."
³And He said, "Cast it on the ground." So he cast it on the ground,
and it became a serpent; and Moses fled from it.

God wants to take the natural things in your life and make them supernaturally blessed. He does this by asking you to give Him what you already have in the natural, and He will do the supernatural.

That is why the Lord told Moses to cast his rod on the ground. And when Moses cast his rod on the ground, which represents him giving the rod to the Lord, that same rod became the rod of God. With that rod, the Red Sea was opened. (Exodus 14:16,21–23.) And when that rod was used to hit a rock, water flowed out of the rock. (Exodus 17:5–6.) It was no longer a natural rod, but the supernatural rod of God!

But why did the rod become a serpent when Moses cast it to the ground?

Moses never realized that there was a "snake" in his rod. You see, because of the fall of man, there is a touch of the curse — a snake — in every natural thing, including your career, natural strength, talents and ministry.

So how do you deal with the "snake" that is in all the natural things in your life?

First, cast it to the Lord. Then, do what the Lord told Moses next: "Reach out your hand and take it by the tail" (Exodus 4:4).

Now, it could be fatal to take a snake by its tail because it can easily turn its head around and bite you. So why did God say that?

When you take it by the tail, God will take the head! He wants you to let Him handle the head, and not grab it or hold on to it tightly in fear or self-effort. That is how you see your career, strength, talents and ministry supernaturally blessed.

Beloved, there is a snake, a touch of the curse, in everything in the natural. But give what is natural to the Lord and see the touch of the curse replaced with the supernatural touch of God!

Thought for the Day
Give what is natural to the Lord and He will make it supernaturally blessed.

It Is Finished!

John 19:30
³⁰ So when Jesus had received the sour wine, He said, "It is finished!"
And bowing His head, He gave up His spirit.

Imagine looking at Leonardo da Vinci's famous Mona Lisa painting in the Louvre museum. Would you think of adding more brush strokes to it? Of course not! It was done by a master, so what could you possibly add to the painting to improve it?

In the same way, that is how we are to look at Jesus' work on the cross. He cried out, "It is finished!" You cannot complete a completed work. You cannot finish a finished work. Our salvation is won. Our sins are all forgiven. We are made forever righteous by His blood. Christ paid completely and perfectly for our total forgiveness, righteousness and every blessing!

In fact, these three words, "It is finished," come from one Greek word *teleo*. In the days of Jesus, a servant would use it when reporting to his master: "I have completed the work assigned to me." (John 17:4.) The word means, "It is finished, it stands finished and it will always be finished!" Perhaps the most significant meaning of *teleo* is how it is used by merchants: "The debt is paid in full!" When Jesus gave Himself on the cross, He met fully the righteous demands of the law. He paid our debts in full!

Today, it is not our works that will bring us the blessings. It is Christ's finished work. Christian living is not about **doing**, but **believing** in His finished work. Under the law, we must **do**. Under grace, it is **done**!

Maybe you are faced with overwhelming odds today. Jesus promises, "It is finished!" You are not going to be delivered because you have already been delivered. You are not going to be healed because you are already the healed! God healed you 2,000 years ago! Isaiah 53:5 declares, "By His stripes you **are** healed!" You are already pregnant with healing. Keep resting in His finished work and it will manifest!

My friend, the work is finished. The victory is won. Our enemies have been made Jesus' footstool. Our blessings have been bought by His blood! Live life knowing that there is nothing for you to do — only **believe**! It is finished!

Thought for the Day
It is believing in Christ's finished work that will bring us the blessings.

Salvation Prayer

If you would like to receive all that Jesus has done for you and make Him your Lord and Savior, please pray this prayer:

> *Lord Jesus, thank You for loving me and dying for me on the cross. Your precious blood washes me clean of every sin. You are my Lord and my Savior, now and forever. I believe that You rose from the dead and that You are alive today. Because of Your finished work, I am now a beloved child of God and heaven is my home. Thank You for giving me eternal life, and filling my heart with Your peace and joy. Amen.*

We Would Like to Hear From You

If you have prayed the salvation prayer, or if you have a testimony to share after reading this book, please send us an email at info@destined2reign.com.

Topic Index

- July 5
- July 23
- August 9
- August 20
- October 3
- October 17
- October 22
- December 3
- December 16
- December 26

4. Forgiveness of Sins
- January 3
- January 4
- January 18
- January 31
- March 25
- April 9
- April 19
- May 2
- May 13
- May 21
- June 1
- June 9
- July 4
- July 22
- August 2
- August 5
- September 4
- September 20
- October 9
- November 4
- December 4

5. No Condemnation
- January 20
- February 4
- February 20
- March 5
- May 10
- June 15
- July 2
- October 4

6. The New Covenant of Grace
- January 9
- January 10
- January 22
- February 6
- February 7

- February 24
- March 9
- March 10
- March 29
- April 5
- April 11
- May 11
- May 22
- June 17
- July 6
- August 3
- August 19
- August 29
- September 5
- October 5
- October 11
- November 5

7. Faith
- January 11
- January 12
- January 24
- February 9
- February 10
- February 25
- February 26
- February 27
- March 11
- March 12
- March 17
- March 30
- April 1
- April 12
- April 13
- April 23
- May 15
- May 18
- May 24
- June 24
- June 26
- July 8
- July 18
- August 4
- August 8
- August 11
- August 12
- August 15
- August 22
- September 21
- October 6

- October 23
- October 24
- October 25
- November 7
- November 20
- November 21
- November 25
- November 26
- December 6
- December 18
- December 31

8. Favor
- January 15
- January 25
- January 28
- January 29
- February 18
- March 1
- March 18
- May 30
- June 29
- July 10
- August 14
- September 7
- October 7
- October 28
- November 8
- December 10
- December 11

9. Healing
- January 14
- January 27
- February 12
- February 13
- February 28
- February 29
- March 14
- March 15
- April 3
- April 17
- May 3
- May 5
- May 16
- May 25
- June 2
- June 5
- June 20
- June 28

- July 25
- July 27
- August 13
- August 26
- September 6
- September 8
- October 8
- October 26
- November 9
- November 29
- December 7
- December 28

10. Power of God's Word
- January 13
- January 26
- February 11
- March 31
- April 2
- April 14
- April 15
- April 16
- April 24
- May 6
- May 17
- May 27
- June 21
- July 7
- July 9
- July 28
- August 23
- September 9
- September 10
- September 22
- October 10
- November 10
- November 11
- December 8

11. Protection and Deliverance
- January 16
- February 16
- March 2
- March 16
- March 19
- April 4
- April 6
- April 8
- April 20
- April 28

- May 7
- May 28
- June 6
- June 11
- June 13
- July 11
- July 13
- July 30
- August 18
- August 24
- September 11
- September 12
- September 25
- October 13
- December 12

- June 19
- June 22
- July 16
- August 7
- August 25
- September 3
- September 19
- October 16
- November 3
- November 19
- November 27
- December 1
- December 13

12. Prosperity
- January 17
- February 2
- April 25
- June 7
- June 12
- June 23
- July 14
- July 26
- August 6
- September 13
- September 23
- October 14
- November 24
- November 30
- December 5
- December 19
- December 20

13. Wisdom
- January 30
- February 17
- March 3
- April 29
- May 19
- July 15
- September 14
- September 26
- October 15
- November 15

14. Prayer
- May 8
- June 8

Destined to Reign
The Secret to Effortless Success, Wholeness, and Victorious Living

Join the revolution of Grace! Find everything you need to know about the Gospel of Grace in one definitive book.

Believers everywhere are discovering why success in the covenant of grace is truly effortless! Now you can begin reigning over every adversity, lack, and every destructive habit that is limiting you from the victory you were destined to enjoy!

Start reigning over sickness, financial lack, broken relationships, and destructive habits today!

Destined to Reign
978-1-57794-943-5

Available in stores everywhere or from
www.harrisonhouse.com.

Fast. Easy. Convenient.

For the latest Harrison House product information and author news, look no further than your computer. All the details on our powerful, life-changing products are just a click away. New releases, E-mail subscriptions, Podcasts, testimonies, monthly specials—find it all in one place. Visit harrisonhouse.com today!

harrisonhouse

The Harrison House Vision

Proclaiming the truth and the power

Of the Gospel of Jesus Christ

With excellence;

Challenging Christians to

Live victoriously,

Grow spiritually,

Know God intimately.

Become a receptical + receive what is being offered (the Word!) - "receive your healing - not "get" your healing!
In christ,
I'm free "from" things + free "to" things!

Joseph Sermon # 203 but must be DVD
Huntley St. Prayer Line
1 - 866 - 273 - 4444